Love Is . . .

The doorbell rang

Dear Sally ~

It's been fun getting to know you. Thanks for all your chat & cheerfulness!

Love & God bless you always.

Daphne xx

ISBN No. 978 0 9564 269 0 1

Published by John and Daphne Hope, Chalcedony, La Route des Genets, St Brelade,

Jersey, Channel Islands JE3 8LF

Printed by Hobbs The Printers, Totton, Southampton.

Also writing as **Daphne Mills:**

The Road To Emmaus: a comprehensive Bible Study

ISBN 0 906309 11 5

Come Walk With Jesus: Introductory Bible Study

ISBN 0 906309 12 3

Writing as **Daphne Mills Hope**:

365 Genesis to Revelation (e Book on GOOGLE: www.spectatus.com/365/

ACKNOWLEDGEMENTS

Biblical quotations from the New International Version

Quotation from TheTransforming friendship by Leslie Weatherhead

Excerpt from the song: The Dancing Lesson by Ferrari/Teschemacher

Excerpt from the song: The Book by Gotwald, Roberts, recorded by David Whitfield

Excerpt from the song: The Stranger of Galilee by C H Morris

To: My children: Tessa, Nigel, Abigail

And my grandchildren: Jenna, Luke, Benjamin, Robert, Joseph ,

Gavin, Jasmin, Matthew, Jasper

And my great-grandchildren: Cherish, Max, Emma, et al.

Love and thanks to my sister Valerie and my brother Roger for some great memories!

Grateful thanks to John for all the proof reading, help, encouragement, hot drinks, brilliantly cooked meals – and for putting up with my silence as I pounded away on my laptop! I love you!

For support in reading through various stages of the manuscript, and advising and encouraging me, I would like to express my gratitude to Tessa Reid, Jean Charles, Sir Tom Lees, Jo Mulliner, Chrissie Pollard, Pam Humphries, and Rev Cliff Bembridge. Grateful thanks to Stewart Reid for all his help and advice at the printing stage and design of the cover.

Front cover photo: by Jenna Mears, taken on the beach at St Brelades, Jersey

FOREWORD BY SIR THOMAS LEES, Bart.

Post Green House in Dorset, my wife Faith's and my family home for over 40 years, was in 1968 the centre of a remarkable scene of spiritual renewal. Every day we felt our lives were being led by the Holy Spirit into a series of adventures. We saw God working in people's lives, with conversions, healing, deliverance from fears of all sorts, and miracles that glorified God and pointed people to Jesus. We had families coming to camp in the paddock outside our house, regular times of prayer and worship, and for many, many people a new vision of what it might mean to have a living relationship with God and Jesus Christ.

As the work grew, people came needing help and reassurance, others came offering help. David and Daphne Mills were among those willing to share who they were and what they had to support the ongoing ministry coming from Post Green. Since those earlier days in 1968 and all through the years following, they were part of the group from which the whole ethos of Post Green came to be formed.

Much of the early Post Green story has been told in Faith Lees' book "Love Is Our Home".

" ***Love Is . . "*.** is a sequel to this, though it stands as a very moving and fascinating account of Daphne's life in its own right. I commend it to you.

Tom Lees

Preface

A year ago I started to write this book for my children, my grandchildren, and an increasing number of great grandchildren. At the request of many friends and acquaintances I have decided to invite a larger audience into the journey I have made and have now committed to writing.

You are welcome to read this book and I hope you will find laughter and joy and an increase in your faith in God, in amongst the inevitable trials that befall us all at some point in our journey through life.

If any mistakes have survived all the proofing please put it down to my irresistible urge to tweak the manuscript until the last possible second!

I have decided to give the profits for the sale of "***Love Is . . .***" to the wonderful charitable work of Avenue St Andrews United Reformed Church in Southampton: a church that enriched my teenage years above and beyond my deepest dreams. When I walk into that church today I am filled with gratitude that God inspired someone to cycle through the wind, the rain, the darkness to ring our door bell one evening; and from that point on my life changed!

You will read how that episode led me on a journey that brought me to Post Green Community in 1968, where I saw and experienced the miracles of God just like the early church encountered in the first century when the Holy Spirit fell on the first disciples of Jesus at Pentecost.

Devastated by the break-up of my marriage, and later laid low by Glandular Fever and Myalgic Encepholomitis, God helped me to re-build my life, and touched me with an amazing miracle of healing at the church where it all began.

This is my story – this is my song!

Daphne Mills Hope

LOVE IS . . . .

The doorbell rang mid evening. It was dark and windy. Torrential rain was falling. Voices floated up the stairs, and then the sound muffled as the lounge door shut. But ten minutes later footsteps ascended the stairs. I slid down further under the bedcovers and waited. Yes! A knock on the door! "Daphne! You have a visitor!"

I thought, "What good is a visitor if I can't speak?" I was well in the throes of my usual annual bout of laryngitis. But I slithered back up the bed again, leaned against the pillows and waited. "Daphne, this is Mr Nicholson, you remember? The Choir master from the Avenue Church!" A very damp mackintosh emerged into the room, dripping hair, and amazingly penetrating eyes. (I later discovered Mr Nicholson was a customs officer in his spare time!) "Ah, good evening, Daphne. So sorry to call when you aren't well. I meant to call last week but ran out of time. I was impressed with you and your sister joining in the enlarged choir for the BBC broadcast recently. We need some new young voices and I wondered if you would like to join the church choir."

I looked at my father still hovering in the doorway, smiling, watching me. Mr Nicholson proceeded to explain what this would involve. "We have choir practice every Friday evening, 7.15pm until around 9pm. We expect all choir members to be there unless they have a very good reason to be away. The choir, as you know, sing an introit and an anthem and lead the worship every Sunday morning and evening! If you enjoy singing you will enjoy the choir."

I then discovered what had been going on downstairs before this conversation. Mr Nicholson had already approached my older sister, Valerie; and she had turned down the idea, saying she couldn't manage it and her homework too. I was amazed that I would be allowed to do anything like this on my own. The choice was mine! This was a first for me, and I immediately thought of two things! Freedom for once in my life to do something that was separate from my sister and parents. And also I passionately loved singing and music, and had no chance at all to do it –except play my recorder in the bedroom. My answer came quickly, and I croaked, “Yes, please!”

Mr Nicholson moved from hovering at the bottom of the bed, and came forward and shook my hand. I was very embarrassed and blushed bright pink! For a fourteen year old, well chaperoned and sheltered in a tight family unit, this was a big occasion for me! And I think Mr Nicholson considered that it was well worth a cycle ride in pouring rain, to get a new young recruit for the choir.

So on looking back later, I had no idea that decision would change my life forever!

The following Friday evening, in February 1953, with my voice back to normal, I cycled from our house, using the same route my sister and I had taken to school earlier in the day, stopping just before the Southampton Common, a mile away from home. I wasn’t sure where to park my bicycle, or where to go! I soon discovered the front doors of the church were locked, so cycled around to the side of the church where I found other people and other bikes.

Mr Nicholson saw me walk in the door by the choir stalls, and hesitate. He stopped assembling his music-stand and walked over to me. “As you don’t have much experience reading music I will seat you next to some strong singers.” He proceeded to usher me into the front row of the choir stalls, and introduce me to the sopranos on either side of me. I felt very self-conscious, sitting there, in my dark green school uniform, feeling bewildered and totally outside of my usual environment (of either school or home!).

As luck would have it, I was thrown severely into the deep end! The choir were practising Handel’s Messiah – with high notes and complicated runs. I hardly made a squeak, I was so frightened. I was seated about two metres from the choir master, who peered constantly over his half moon glasses, and was, so it seemed, checking up on me all the time. We also practised about four anthems, two for next Sunday’s services and two for the following Sunday. We sang solidly for just over two hours. During little pauses in the singing when the tenors and basses had to practice their music, I glanced around me. The choir was seated in two rows in a semi circle, with the organ dividing the choir pews in half. I realised that the tenors and some sopranos were in the row behind me, and basses and contraltos (called altos) were in the choir pews opposite.

We finished off the evening with a very good rendition of the Hallelujah Chorus, I just pretended to sing, especially as I had a vague idea there was a dramatic silence written into the music somewhere, and I did not want to be caught out singing when everyone else had paused! Quickly, after the last notes died away, people handed their music in, donned their coats, put on cycle clips on their trousers or pulled out their car keys; everyone was making a fast exit after a very crammed full practice. Mr Nicholson called me over, and said I needed to get kitted out with my choir gown. Mrs Fuller, the wardrobe mistress, was instructed to take me up to the choir loft and sort it out. I felt very excited. I was "in" – "accepted" – a new world was opening up for me!

I was given a long, royal blue gown, with white cotton collar and a pair of white sleeves! To complete the outfit I was handed a black velvet mortar board type hat. "The collar and sleeves you might want to wash and starch before Sunday." Mrs Fuller said. "Don't forget to bring them back. Your gown is on peg number 27, just behind the middle sliding door of the wardrobe!" I thanked her, and she reminded me to be up in the choir vestry half an hour before the service started on Sunday morning, and that I would need to be there at 6pm as well, half an hour before the evening service.

I found my way out through the darkened church corridor onto the street where I had propped my bicycle against the fence.

Thus began an amazing journey into choral music of a very high standard. I began to love it! Up until then I had found pop music more to my taste. But learning to sing so many church anthems week after week, many of them set to Bible verses, poetic, majestic, powerful, comforting, with the organ at times thundering out the most amazing sounds just feet from where I was sitting, my whole life began to change.

Just before I joined Avenue Congregational Church choir, I had auditioned for our school choir – I had to sing a verse of a hymn. Miss Ferguson, the Atherley School music teacher, turned me down. But a year later, well trained by now in the church choir, I auditioned in the same week for the school music festival and the school choir. The Music Festival audition came first, and I remember I sang a song, "How beautiful they are, the lordly ones, who dwell in the hills . . ." for which I got highly commended. So with that result I was a bit more hopeful for the school choir audition. I sang a hymn as requested by Miss Ferguson. A week later the results were put up on the music room notice board. I was in!

Now I am writing this story 55 years later, since when I have done many auditions and hundreds of solos! But I don't think any of it would have happened if Mr Nicholson had not taken it into his head to pursue Valerie and me for his choir.

Because I joined the Avenue Congregational Church Choir, I became drawn into the church drama club, and took a key role in playing the part of the Virgin Mary in a three act play called "Daybreak over Bethlehem" around Christmas time one year. I was 16, and fortunately Mary didn't have many lines to say, as I was hopeless at learning things by heart, and I still am. But I adored the rehearsals, the excitement and challenge.

Following on from that I did several more plays with the Avenue Players, auditioning for parts, and never expecting to be given one! I often did get a part but eventually I became the prompter, feeling more relaxed holding the book of words and prompting those who forgot what they were meant to be saying. We had one or two actors who did not learn their words thoroughly and would ad lib around the stage, making things up – a nightmare for me on stage, while waiting my cue – a key word I had learnt off by heart so I could say my next lines, and a nightmare for me later as prompter!

It wasn't long before I also discovered two of the young women in the choir talked a lot about "last night at operatic" – or "We won't be here next Sunday, Mr Nicholson, as we have the dress rehearsal for operatic!" I got curious, and asked one of them what it was "Oh, we belong to Southampton Operatic! You know, Gilbert and Sullivan, mostly. Why don't you think about joining?" June and Barbara seemed wholeheartedly committed to the operatic. I had adored it for years, and our parents used to take Valerie and myself each year to their annual production at the large Guildhall, in Southampton.

Wow! But after further investigation I discovered getting a place in the Operatic was nearly impossible, and certainly not possible without having singing lessons. I was still at school but asked my father if I could have singing lessons. He ridiculed the idea. "What makes you think you can do music when you can't even do maths properly? I pay a lot of money for you to be educated; you've been thrown out of the maths class – you can't do half your lessons properly. You need to concentrate on working hard at school, not trying to learn something else. What good is learning music?" I was very sad. I knew I had no hope of getting into the opera company without having some training.

I had settled into the choir so happily. I was the youngest member for the next two years, and I felt cared for and respected by most of the choir – they felt like a family to me. I very rarely missed any choir practice or Sunday service. I refused to go out with my parents and sister on a Sunday afternoon unless Dad would guarantee he could get me back for choir and evening service. He seemed very puzzled by my commitment to the choir above all else. I was given two solos in the second year! I sang the opening solo, then the whole choir came in with the main anthem – it was terrifying and thrilling. My parents came to church to listen, which scared me even more.

There were some older teenagers and early twenty year olds in the choir, and we would meet up with others on Sunday afternoons. We held a service in the Little Chapel, a beautiful and smallish room along a corridor behind the organ and en route to the large Avenue Hall. The Youth Group, as it was called, took services at little Congregational churches and chapels in the New Forest during the summer months. We would usually cycle on our bikes out into the forest, take the service and stay for tea afterwards. Then rush back in time for choir in the evening. I began to do a few solos in the chapel. Barbara Vick used to play the piano for me. For my very first solo she encouraged me to stand at the back of the chapel, beside the piano, and sing from there. It worked brilliantly, as no one was looking at me and I could concentrate on my song. Gradually I learnt to calm my nerves just a bit and then sang from the front.

I greatly admired Barbara. She had the most wonderful, rich soprano voice. She also was friendly and helpful towards me. I tried to sit next to her as often as I could in choir. She was fun to be with and never minded when I asked her something about the music – or in fact any question I had about anything. She became a role model for me – and a true heroine in my eyes. I either copied my sister Valerie or my friend Barbara, and I didn't seem to have an abundance of initiative in some areas of my life without help. I discovered that Barbara lived in the same area as me – and we would often walk or cycle to and from church together. As we walked through Portswood High Street we would often put two pennies in a slot machine outside one of the shops and check our weight. Barbara was usually 8 stone something, and I always seemed to be 9 stone 3 pounds, with coats on!

During this idyllic time for me, one evening after Valerie and I had finished our homework, Dad called us into the dining room at our house in Abbots Way, in Southampton. "Your Mother and I have some news for you, can you guess what it is?" Valerie immediately said, "Yes, you're having a baby!" "Well," said Dad, "how on earth did you guess that?" Valerie looked a bit embarrassed but said she thought Mum had got rather fat recently! I was totally amazed at this news. We were sworn to secrecy. "Don't tell anyone! Don't tell your friends, it's a secret for the time being!"

Valerie and I were given the news in June. School finished in July – and we kept the secret and told no one. Mum was over forty years old, and had been told not to have more children since she had been terribly ill during World War 2, and had a kidney removed. I remembered how awful that time was. We lived in a huge house called The White House in Curdridge, on the outskirts of Southampton. Dad had bought the house during the war. At first Valerie and I, and our nursemaid Jean, a lovely seventeen year old girl, spent the early part of the war in a farm cottage near Wimborne in Dorset. Dad thought we would be safer there, away from the bombing.

We were there in the cottage with Jean Monday till Friday each week. On Friday evenings Mum and Dad would drive down from Southampton, through the New Forest, to our cottage in Wimborne. Then Jean would get on her bike and cycle back through the New Forest, to her home, the far side of Southampton. It was blackout time – no lights could be shown anywhere. All windows were blacked out with black fabric, then curtains drawn as well – not a chink of light could be shown. You would be heavily fined if any light shone through. Jean would cycle in the pitch black on Friday nights, and return the same way on Sunday night. Early Monday morning our parents would drive back to Southampton, where Dad ran a road transport company. After about 18 months Dad bought The White House. It was sufficiently far enough away from Southampton and the Docks to be safe, so Dad thought! I was three years old, and Valerie was four by this time. Even at the age of three I remember the drama that unfolded when we got home to The White House that afternoon.

While Dad had been fetching us from Wimborne, with Jean, and all the luggage of eighteen months away from home, things had been happening in the field at the bottom of The White House garden. A huge searchlight, which I can still see to this day sitting strongly in my memory, stood bold and proud just over the fence; and not only a searchlight but also a large gun alongside it: a sitting target for any German plane flying low overhead. The searchlight was often busy after the air raid sirens went off. Mum would come rushing into our bedroom on many a night, "Quick, get out of bed, the Germans are coming. Hide under the stairs!" Valerie and I would scramble out of bed, run down stairs, and sit in the alcove under the stairs. Then someone would turn the dining table on its side and roll it across the entrance to protect us from the Germans, bombs, flying glass and whatever else was meant to be getting us. We would remain hidden under the stairs until the last droning of the airplanes had died away. It was a truly frightening childhood. We would sit or lie down, listening to the drone of the airplanes; we got used to the "German sound" and the "English sound" of planes, and could soon tell the difference.

But next morning, as soon as Valerie and I finished breakfast, we would put on our coats and search the grounds for shrapnel and bits of silver paper. These were our perks after the fear of the previous night!

I went back years later to The White House, and the house is now a home for elderly residents. The alcove where we sheltered under the stairs is now the cocktail bar for the residents!

I digress, sorry. Well poor Mum was so ill during the war, with very little medicine available, and she was away in hospital for quite a long length of time. Jean Griffin, our beloved nursemaid, had joined the A.T.S. and was away from home. We had a cook, a butler, a gardener, and I think someone else, running the house and keeping an eye on us at various times. Our toys were kept in a drawer in the kitchen, near the old black kitchen range, where it was nice and warm. The trouble was it seemed the people who were meant to be keeping an eye on us were not keen for us to be in the kitchen, so we couldn't always get to our toys.

Jean Griffen came back after the war to look after us for a while, before training as a nurse and eventually emigrating to Australia. She had a prestigious career nursling in Melbourne, and later after becoming a Christian at a Billy Graham Crusade, she became a nurse in the Flying Doctor Service with huge responsibilities. At the point when most of us would be thinking about retiring, Jean joined the Leprosy Mission and worked in India and Bangledesh for many years. Her sheer grit and determination has been a great example to me over the years.

Anyway, years later, Valerie and I absorbed the news of a coming baby with interest, but basically got on with our own lives. Our family hobby was going to Speedway racing – that is 600cc motorcycle racing, no brakes and no gears, on a cinder track (as it was in those days).

Dad would sometimes phone the Atherley School and ask for his two daughters to be allowed out of school early afternoon, as he had an important meeting in London and needed to pick us up before the final school bell rang at 3.50pm. Valerie and I would get a message delivered to us in our form rooms. "Be ready outside the school gate at 3pm. Your father is fetching you early!"

Valerie and I would meet up with each other by the gate. "Where do you think Dad's taking us tonight? There's a good speedway match at Wembley tonight!"... "Or Wimbledon!"

Dad would draw up in his car about three o'clock, and we would both jump in the car, pull off our school hats as soon as we were out of sight of the school, and dump our satchels on the floor.

"I hope you haven't much homework tonight! We're off to Wembley! We won't be back till one in the morning. You can do some of your homework on the way up in the car," Dad would say!

One evening in September we all trooped off to watch speedway at the Southampton Stadium. By this time we had moved to Highfield, Southampton; so the stadium was only about two miles away. Mum decided at the last minute not to come with us. She didn't tell us the baby had already started to come! She stayed crossed legged all evening, hoping we would be back before things really got going. Valerie and I went straight to bed when we arrived home, as we had school the next day. We woke to find that our baby brother Roger had been born during the night at a nursing home nearby. We would be allowed to see him after school at 4pm that day.

It shows how well I kept The Secret – none of my school friends knew my mother was expecting a baby. And when I got to school that day, I did try and tell my best friend but she called me a liar. I was really upset. Shortly after school assembly we had a needlework lesson. The teacher went round the class asking us what we would like to make that term. I said very firmly when it came to my turn, "I want to make a romper suit for my baby brother." After the lesson none of the other girls spoke to me. I had been "sent to Coventry". This lasted until someone challenged my sister as she was walking along the school corridor. Her friends were with her. They said of course it was true! So I was then believed. What a price to keep a secret!

Along with Speedway, we often went to watch the Hampshire Cricket Team play at the County Ground in Northlands Road. And we all went to watch the Southampton Football Club matches. Valerie and I would meet up with her friends and stand by one of the corner posts at The Dell to watch the Saints most Saturdays. Dad and Mum had season tickets for a seat in the stands, but it was much more fun where we stood. Around this time Dad became a Director of the Saints and then he and Mum went into the Director's Box to watch the matches.

When Roger was a few months old, I was asked to be part of the Avenue Choir to sing at a wedding on a Saturday afternoon. Of course, I said "Yes!" – singing at a wedding would be something different, and I didn't mind missing football once in a while. I told my parents when I got home from Friday choir practice that I would be singing at the wedding tomorrow. My father put his foot down firmly. "No you are not! If football isn't that important to you, from now on you can look after your baby brother each Saturday afternoon, and let your mother go to football now Roger is old enough." My father would not budge from his decision. I felt terrible letting the choir down, and hugely disappointed. The next day instead of singing at the wedding, I wheeled Roger in his pram up to Avenue Church and watched the bridal party and the choir pour out of church at the end of the service. For years from then on during the football season, I would look after Roger, pushing the pram or pushchair for miles, visiting friends if they were free to go for a walk.

The first time I took baby Roger in his pram to watch a school lacrosse match, the head mistress, Miss Laidlaw, came striding across to speak to me. She peered into the pram, admired the baby, and said, "Is it yours?" I was a bit shy and confused, as she never usually spoke to me at all unless I was in trouble. I replied in astonishment, "No! It's my mother's!" She also looked surprised and smiled politely and walked away. I was 15 years old, had no idea about the facts of life and what made babies, and in those days no one under the age of 18 had babies, and no one had babies before they were married. I thought Miss Laidlaw very strange. A few days later my parents were at the Atherley School Dance, and happened to be on the top table, and heard Miss Laidlaw telling a joke about a conversation she had had with one of her pupils about her new baby brother. When my parents, knowing I was the subject of the joke, reported the joke back to me the next morning at breakfast, I finally cottoned on to the fact that Miss Laidlaw was only asking if the baby was from our family, or was I taking a neighbour's baby out for a walk!

I had already had an adventure with my new baby brother. The very first time I had been allowed to take Roger out in his pram was when he was a few weeks old. Mum put him in his pram, with yellow jacket and bonnet, and yellow blanket, and put him gently into the pram, carefully doing up the waterproof apron, and putting the pram hood up. Roger was safely sheltered both from the weather and people's germs. I was sent off to get some shopping, which included a loaf of bread and some stamps. I was as pleased as punch! I pushed the pram (nearly as big as me) along the pavement in Abbots Way, round into Highfield Lane, and turned right into Portswood Road. Here everyone was shopping; it was a Saturday morning. I did all the shopping, finishing up at the Post Office. I parked the pram carefully outside the Post Office, a big long building, and nipped in for the stamps. In those days it was very safe to leave babies in prams, and children in pushchairs outside shops. When I came out of the Post Office with the stamps safely stowed in my handbag, I went straight to the pram, kicked off the brake and walked home. I was just about to turn into our driveway when I glanced at Roger, who was still asleep, and noticed he was no longer in his yellow outfit, but was now dressed in blue. I was totally mystified! I lifted up the pram apron to check on the bread and other bits of shopping, and saw nothing there at all. Horrors! Not only had Roger's outfit changed colour but my shopping had disappeared. Then it dawned on me: wrong pram, wrong baby. Luckily I hadn't turned the corner into the driveway. I turned the pram round, and ran as fast as I could all the way back to the Post Office. Parked the pram, and proceeded to peer into all the other prams, and at last I found the bread under a pram apron. Yes, yellow pram set, yellow baby outfit. Roger, still fast asleep. I ran home with the pram bouncing over all the bumps and kerbs, just anxious to get back before my parents said, "You were a long time, what kept you?" No one ever found out, and I wasn't about to tell anyone.

CHAPTER TWO

I still hadn't given up my quest to join the Operatic, but without singing lessons it wasn't possible. A year or more went by, and I was really struggling with my school work. We were preparing for 'O' level exams (now GCSE), and I was taking 11 subjects, which meant a lot of work. Valerie had left school the year before, before taking her exams, because she was going to work in the family business. Dad had said she could leave before the exams and work in his office. Valerie worked for Victory Transport Limited, but at a different depot to where my father was. Dad was Managing Director, and my mother and a man called Mr Wise, were co-directors. So Valerie worked in the shop distribution depot in Parsonage Road, Northam, Southampton. She would cycle to work, from Highfield, about 15 minutes ride, and cycle back for lunch. I found it very stressful trying to do my homework in the evenings, with a baby crying, our new television on in the other room, and Valerie and I quite often babysitting, particularly Friday evenings, when our parents always seems to have a Ball or Dance to go to.

The teachers at school were all getting uptight with us, threatening us that unless we worked harder we would never pass our exams. I thought, what is the point of all this hard work if we are going to fail anyway? So I pestered my father to let me leave school before the exams. He agreed in the end on condition I worked in his office. As I was fairly certain I would be made to work in his office anyway I agreed. So my parents wrote a letter to the school and gave notice that I would be leaving at the end of the term, a day before my 16th birthday. The headmistress protested and refused to accept the notice. On the last day of the spring term in 1954, at school assembly, all school leavers names were read out – but not mine: so no one said goodbye to me!

I shed a few tears as I walked my bicycle down the school drive for the last time, but was glad to be free of the pressure of school examinations. The next day I celebrated my 16th birthday, and a month after that I commenced at Miss Wright's Secretarial College for Girls. This was rather a posh college, and only girls whose fathers were "someone" were allowed to go. As far as I know my father was interviewed over the phone, his credentials checked, and I was allowed in. I had a crash course in shorthand and typing. I was known as Miss Barber, and was told that any job I got, I would be known as Miss Barber – one didn't use Christian names in those days to address work colleagues.

Mum knew Pitman's shorthand and had given me a few brief lessons that stood me in good stead when I began to learn this new "language" – I found it fun. And we learned to type to music. We were left to our own devices quite a bit, once having been given some work to be done. The music, for the typing exercises came from old 78 vinyl records that had a good regular beat. When the record ran out, one of us would get up and put it back on again, or choose another one from the pile of Pitman typing records. One day I discovered, in the record pile, some Gilbert and Sullivan Opera records. So I put on the overture to the Pirates of Penzance, and we happily typed away to the somewhat irregular and erratic beat of the Pirates. Oh joy, this is more like it: I'm really happy now! But about half an hour later Miss

Wright (known behind her back as Bella) stormed in and shrieked about how we dare put on her personal records and type to them. So bang when the Pirates and we were back to Pitman music again.

I had only just started at Miss Wright's when my parents decided it would be good for me to stay in France for a few weeks with a French family that we had connections with. So early one morning, during May 1954, we all drove up to some small airport near London, and I flew to Paris. I wandered around Paris on my own all day – walking along the banks of the river Seine, and exploring the famous city, and keeping an eye on my watch. I had to catch a train from La Gare de Lyon at 6pm. I arrived in Lyon in the pitch darkness, met by my friend Isabelle du Jonchay and all her family. We drove at breakneck speed through the cobbled narrow streets of Lyon and out into the countryside. Apart from Isabelle, no one else spoke anything but French to me. I realised that schoolgirl French isn't the same language as real French people speak! I soon learnt the correct pronunciation, and some swear words that stood me in good stead during the following weeks.

A week after arriving in Lyon the teenagers of the family packed their bags, and we caught a train down to a chateau in Cantal for their summer holiday. It was the gathering of the clans down there, and there were a huge number of male teenagers, who played crazy jokes on Isabelle and me. One night I tried to put on my pink nightdress, only to discover it had been machined up and was impossible to get into – so I climbed into bed with my underclothes on – uh oh! Apple pie bed – I couldn't get into that either! Isabelle and I spent a rather restless night, there seemed a lot of odd noises in the bedroom – it was a huge room in a large creepy castle, with a curtained alcove with bidet, basin and loo. Just as it was getting light an alarm clock went off and a great clucking noise started up. Isabelle shrieked in her best French all known swear words (some I recognised) and started opening and shutting cupboards and drawers. Suddenly as she opened a drawer in the dressing table, a huge chicken flew out, went berserk, and poohed all over the room. Isabelle made it worse by chasing it – as I watched in horror from my bed. Eventually the chicken settled down behind a curtain, and Isabelle went over to the drawer, and drew out the alarm clock which had rung itself into silence. It had a picture of hens pecking in time with the ticking of the clock. The boys all got into trouble and spent the morning cleaning the room! Isabelle and I spent the morning playing tennis with a French priest – who had no sense of humour. I did one of my super serves that hit him square in the middle of his head as he bent on our side of the net.

While I was in France I pondered on whether to try and join the Southampton Operatic that summer. Just before I had left for France I discovered that one of my sister's friends, Mitsi, who worked in the office with Valerie, was having singing lessons with Madam Myra Dudley. I decided to pursue this contact as soon as I returned to England.

"I don't take just anyone who wants singing lessons, dear. Bring along a song and I will decide if I can take you on. Come next Wednesday evening, 6pm, to Lumsden Avenue." As I wanted to be a pop singer I took along a song called: "The Book". I had heard it on the radio many times, sung by David Whitfield, and I had a copy of the music from the local store in Portswood. I rang the doorbell and waited. An elderly man answered the door and invited me to come in and wait. I heard a singing lesson in progress. Wow, some voice! I will never be as good as that. My nerves were clicking in and I began to shake! All too soon I heard farewells being said, and the front door slam. "Go on in, dear," said the elderly gentleman," It's the first door on the right." I knocked on the door and walked in. There at the piano was the grandest elderly lady I had ever seen. Flawless complexion, and pure white hair, Piled neatly on top of her head. She smiled, and said, "And what have you brought to sing?" holding out her hand for my sheet of music. She glanced at it, and said, "Well, I haven't heard of this song before, but we will see how we go." She played the opening bars. I loved the song, and began to sing, "There's a Book that my mother gave me, that I read when the long day is through, and the stories of old, in leaves edged with gold, guide me whatever I do. And I know in those worn old pages I shall find peace of mind when I look, and the wisdom of all the ages, is there in my mother's Book!"

"Well, dear, I can teach you at 6pm every Wednesday – the first term will be just breathing lessons and we won't get on to singing songs until next term. I charge two pounds and ten shillings per term of 10 lessons." Madam Myra handed me back the music and smiled. "But I want to audition for the Operatic this summer." I said. "How old are you?" "Sixteen." "Well, I think you need to wait a year. You are too young. All my pupils who have auditioned have got in, but there are a large number of people trying for a very few vacancies."

I left determined to find out the dates of the auditions, and apply! I wrote off for the information, and had a letter back saying I was welcome to audition but the minimum age was 17years. So I decided to wait a year, and work hard at my singing. The following year I was invited to audition, in the music rooms at the Southampton University. I was exceedingly nervous, and my friends who had already auditioned warned me the acoustics were very echo-y. Which they were! I had a letter back within a week, dated July 1955, saying I did not "quite qualify this year." I felt devastated, and sad that I had broken my singing teacher's record of never having a pupil fail the audition! I didn't have long to grieve. A letter came in the post from the music director of the Operatic, asking me to consider doing the solos in The Wayfarers Dramatic Society performances of The Tinder Box. So although I hadn't past the audition, I was considered good enough for the Wayfarers, the biggest and best drama company in Southampton! Yippee! It was all a bit scary, and I had to sing off stage, but obviously loud enough for the audience to hear! I enjoyed the rehearsals and the performances immensely. Show business is definitely for me!

I was still singing a lot of choral work with the Avenue church choir, including many oratorios, which I learnt to love. I so enjoyed doing drama with The Avenue Players, the church drama group, and remembered the first audition when I was given the main role of Mary in a three act play to run over the Christmas period of 1954. The note delivered to me read: "Daphne Barber – Please play "Mary". Study the WHOLE play carefully. First rehearsal of Scene 1 on Thursday 14th at 7pm in the Church Parlour. Signed Guy Pursey."

My social life was full almost every evening; singing lessons, piano lessons, choir, solos, drama, and helping take services at small churches in the New Forest. I cycled everywhere.

Saturday afternoons were frequently taken up with finding interesting things to do to occupy Roger while the others went to football. One Saturday I opted to travel with Mum and Dad to Southend where Saints were playing – and I would take Roger along the front and the pier while the match was on. Roger wanted an ice cream, and kept pestering me to buy him one. I could just see it dripping down his smart prep school uniform, in which he was dressed. He was now four years old. I kept saying "No!" and Roger started to cry. I felt really mean – but didn't want either of us to get into trouble for having ice cream stains all over his clothes. As we walked along the pavement we came across a man holding a baby monkey, for one shilling (the price of a really nice ice cream!) Roger could have the monkey sit on his shoulder. I opted for that treat instead. Roger stopped crying and the monkey quietly sat on Roger's shoulders. A photo was duly taken, which I have in my possession till this day. It never entered my mind that the monkey could have pooped all over Roger and made more of a stain than an ice cream would have done!

Dad warned Valerie and me that life was about to change in a big way. I had escaped school, done two terms with Miss Wright, and had a hurly swirly social life, all to my liking. My secretarial course was cut short by my father needing a new secretary, where he worked at the Old Mill Quay in Northam. Even though I hated the work, my evenings were my own, and with my bicycle nothing was going to stop my evening outings. But then my father announced that he had bought Rownhams House, on the outskirts of the north west of Southampton, and he was moving us, the family, and all the business under one roof. Oh NO!

Valerie and I were both upset! There was a huge amount of building work and repairs, and rewiring to happen at Rownhams House, so we worked out we wouldn't be moving anytime soon. And large warehouses had to be built in the grounds. But all too soon the work was done, and the move took place over Christmas. After we moved I used to cycle over one hundred miles a week, in the evenings and on Sundays, never dropping one activity in Southampton.

After about a year a friend of mine came to visit me from the New Forest, on her new little motor bike. Sheila was one of my class from Miss Wright's Secretarial College. She said it was easy to learn to ride! So I saved up my money and bought myself one, passing my test on streets laden with snow. My emergency stop was a dramatic skid, but I didn't fall off.

Now I had far more freedom, I could cover my one hundred miles a week in a quarter of the time! The only problem was that if I went too fast for too long the plugs got oiled up and the engine would konk out. But it was quite an easy job to swop my oiled up plugs over for the spare set in my saddle bag, and move off again.

Sheila phoned me one day and suggested we went on holiday together, not far – just down to Swanage. It was so exciting. I packed my pyjamas, toothbrush and spare knickers into a bag on my bike, met up with Sheila en route, and we took turns in being in the lead as we rode through the New Forest, across Bournemouth and onto the Purbeck Hills.

We were ready for a lunch break by the time we got to Corfe Castle. After a brief snack we left our motor bikes parked in a lay-by and decided to climb up the huge mound that Corfe Castle is built on. We climbed up the steep side, of course! We were about three or four metres apart when we reached the top, and we both stretched out our hands at the same time to grab the railings around the castle. We both found ourselves hurtling and somersaulting down to the bottom of the hill, at full speed. I lost my glasses half way down and had to climb up again and find them. We were both shaken by the experience.

I now know a ghost is known to haunt the castle, and I think he didn't like us trespassing on his patch and pushed us! It did feel like we were pushed. Up till then I was like a mountain goat, climbing every wall around the beaches in the Channel Islands on our summer holidays. But since that occasion I am truly terrified of heights, even tiny little ones.

Sheila and I had a great holiday, and I thought the Corfe Castle fall was a thing of the past. But I never got over it!

Back home I passed my Operatic audition second time around and was still the youngest member of the cast. Madam Myra told me she was so pleased, especially as there were one hundred applicants for only five vacancies. My first opera was Gilbert and Sullivan's Iolanthe – and I loved every moment of it. The following year we performed "Princess Ida" – one of the least known operas, and one of my favourites. We rehearsed on Wednesday evenings, so I used to spend the hour between my singing lesson, and operatic, by visiting my grandmother, my mother's mother who lived in Norfolk Road, just around the corner from Lumsden Avenue. Grandma Lomax usually gave me fish and chips, and it was lovely getting to know her. She gave me some money to buy myself a piano, which I really appreciated.

I bought my piano and kept it in the "music room" next door to our kitchen in Rownhams House. My father rarely came into that room, but after I had had a record made of my singing two songs: "St Nicholas Day in the Morning" and "Bless This House", he would occasionally bring in a friend to listen to the record. When Dad brought in his business partner Mr Wise, they listened to the record and then Mr Wise said, "I never did like sopranos! I much prefer contraltos!" I never knew what my father made of that remark!

We were well into rehearsals for Princess Ida, and had been measured up for our garments, when we were warned that the first scene's gowns would be crinoline hooped dresses. This would mean five girls would be cut out of the scene as the dresses wouldn't fit on the stage! I had a letter the following week saying that I was one of the ones "the axe had fallen on." I was very upset and disappointed. I told my father what happened and he said, "Daphne, it is not the disappointments in life that count but the way you react to them." So I held my head up high, went to all the rehearsals, and made the most of the rest of the opera!

Wednesday evenings were my favourite times each week: singing lesson, then Operatic. I had an hour in between to visit Grandma Lomax in Norfolk Road, Southampton. One Wednesday my Blood Donor appointment clashed with my usual arrangements. So I had my singing lesson, skipped supper with Grandma, and rode on my motor bike and gave away my blood. I was told to lie down for a certain length of time, and then have a drink and biscuit before going home. When the nurse wasn't watching I skipped off out of a side door and got on my bike. I rode at full speed to Operatic, walking in late as they were all singing the first chorus. I quickly slipped my jacket off in the cloakroom and squeezed into my place in the soprano line.

I hadn't been singing for long when I felt weird. I remember starting to fall forward. I woke up later, laid out on the floor of the cloakroom. I had fainted for the first time in my life! When I felt better I went and sat on the edge of the stage, listening to the music but not singing, just in case I made another exhibition of myself. At the end of the evening the women were told they could go home, but the men were needed for one more song. As I was leaving, I walked over to the conductor, Dr Cecil Williams, and apologised for fainting. Before I had a chance to explain about being a blood donor, he said, very loudly so all the men could hear: "The trouble with you women, you will wear things that are too tight for you!" I was very embarrassed and presumed he thought I was wearing "corsets" like in Victoria times!

In the meantime the Avenue Church Choir was carrying off the winner's shield for choral performance at every Music Festival in Southampton, and it felt good to be part of an excellently trained choir. I was asked to do the occasional solo at church, which my parents sometimes came to listen, but mostly I was on my own, and my family did different things. I still looked after my baby brother Roger most Saturdays, and found various things to do so I wouldn't be bored.

What about my love life? I wrote in my journal on Wednesday 25th February 1953: "I am still crazy over Spencer. I think this is the first time I've been in love." On

Tuesday 17 February, the journal says: "I danced with Spencer so that he could help me, Mrs Morris said." Once or twice a week Valerie and I went to ballroom dancing lessons in the pavilion opposite our house. Frequently Mrs Morris would send someone across to fetch us, even if it wasn't our night for a lesson. She often had too many boys, and needed us to help swell the female numbers. Spencer was the best dancer, very handsome, in a Gregory Peck sort of way. And he never saw me. I used to cycle slowly to school, once I discovered he went to St Mary's College, and was to be seen cycling in the opposite direction to us. In his brown and gold school uniform and his sports racing bike, he blended in with the crowd of boys all cycling down Westwood Road, Highfield, on route to school. I would note in my diary, "Saw Spencer today. He didn't see me." "Saw Spencer today. His bike has a very high saddle, and drop handle bars." "Saw Spencer today as he cycled past. I don't think he saw me." And on it went. I soon found out he was going out with Berry, the best female dancer at Mrs Morris's; and I gradually gave up and decided there was safety in numbers (emotional safety, I mean!). So I had lots of "boyfriends" and no one in particular – about 9 in total – and none of them were very special! In those days kissing and a bit of cuddling was as far as most couples went. I suppose one might say that life before "The Pill" was very different to what happened once the pill had been invented. I learnt a song at Madam Myra's that summed up my love of Spencer and the way things were:

"I'm just seventeen, I've never been to any stately ball.

A shy young maid, I'm half afraid to raise my eyes at all.

But I must learn to twist and turn, to set my feet aright.

So come, Pierrot, and strive to show me how to dance tonight.

Dance on, Pierrot, I soon shall learn, (How soft the music flows!)

Your arm is lying round my waist, That's usual, I suppose!

My hand in yours is tightly clasped, how well you guide my feet,

O dear Pierrot, I did not know that dancing was so sweet.

It is the rule for maids at school to dance with one another.

To choose a "he" might dangerous be, unless he were your brother.

But now I know it is not so, as here I dance with you.

Tonight it seems that all my dreams, dear Pierrot, have come true.

Dance on, Pierrot, the night is young, The stars gleam fair above,

How tenderly your eyes look down, How sweet your words of love!

The world is fading far away, And all things sad and false.

O dear Pierrot, I love you so, Tonight we'll dance love's waltz!"

(Herbert Oliver wrote the music and Telechmar the words)

Southampton used to boast of having an ice rink. This was in a huge old aircraft hangar which Mr Charlie Knott had found in an old disused airfield somewhere after the war. He was determined that the inhabitants of Southampton should have a chance to enjoy themselves again after all the bombing. He set up the hangar, filled it with water, froze it, and invited all who wanted to have a go to come and skate. He lent ice skates out for a fee. My special friend Shirley Bass and I used to go in the school holidays. Shirley had much more confidence than me and would skate off into the middle of the rink in amongst the crowd of skaters, but I spent a lot of time skating near the barrier as I made my way round the rink, and never got up any speed. Sometimes Shirley and I would hold hands and then I could skate around with more speed into the centre of the ice. I loved the music, mostly Mantovani and his orchestra, or the latest pop songs. The atmosphere was magical and exciting!

For a while at school Shirley and I were nicknamed the Terrible Twins: though we didn't do anything terrible at all, but we seemed to spark each other with our sense of humour and enjoyed doing lots of things together: a few things against school rules, that were actually rather harmless. We certainly did not do anything as awful as one girl did at the Atherley School. The whole school assembled as usual in the school hall for assembly one morning. The first hymn was announced and we hurried to flick through the pages of our own individual hymn books, and then looked up expectantly for the opening bars to break forth from the piano. Silence! We all stared at the pianist. She thumped the opening bars again – silence! She tried one more time – no sound came forth. We were not in any way trained to sing unaccompanied, and there was an embarrassing hush and quiet fidgeting in the school hall. Then the headmistress strode over to the piano at the same time as Miss Ferguson, the music teacher, also hastened up onto the platform. They lifted the lid at the back of the piano – and found it stuffed with cotton wool.

The guilty person was commanded to wait outside the headmistresses study immediately after assembly, and we proceeded with a Bible reading and short prayer from the Book of Common Prayer. We listened to the school notices. Then instead of marching out to the music of Trumpet Voluntary we filed back to our classrooms in silence. As soon as our form room door was closed we all chattered excitedly, wondering who on earth would have the nerve and courage to play such an ingenious trick.

CHAPTER THREE

Valerie and I soon settled down at Rownhams House. And we had our own bedrooms at long last. Rownhams House had sixty rooms, alcoves and corridors. The 60th room being outside our bedrooms in the corridor, under the carpet! On rolling back the carpet there were two trap doors with little brass pull rings. On lifting these up, there was a stair case leading down to a tiny lobby and a small room. When we first discovered it, there was a padded "treasure chest". Newspapers inside were of the Leicestershire Times, I think, and a very gory detailed account both of a hanging that went wrong, twice, but on the third attempt the criminal died. And of a nasty lift accident and details of the deaths of those involved. We were told there was a passageway from the house down to the sea, which was an escape route in olden days, but we never found it. The house has an amazing history, which my brother Roger Barber has written about in a separate book, entitled "The Lords of Rownhams". (See www.rownhamshouse.com).

Our life at Rownhams House was very different from living in attractive suburbs in Southampton. When we left The White House in Curdridge, we had rented a house beside The Dell, home of the Southampton Football Club. Each Saturday, Valerie and I sat on the gate, asking everyone as they came out of the football match, "What's the score?" and while the match was in progress we would wander up the road honking as many motorcycle horns as would work without the engines being switched on. In those days there were far more motorbikes, and sidecars, than motor cars!

While we were renting 77 Northlands Road (now pulled down and replaced by a block of flats), Mum and Dad were trying to find a suitable house that would take most of our furniture from the White House. England had still not recovered from the war by 1950 and it was still difficult to get new furniture, and other household goods. Our furniture from the White House was rather on the large side.

We eventually moved to 19 Abbotts Way, Highfield, and soon afterwards we moved to 15 Abbotts Way, using two of Dad's orange lorries and about six of his employees to do the move, just two houses up the road!

Both were fairly large houses, but very small compared with The White House and Rownhams House.

The house at No.15 Abbotts Way had a gate at the bottom of the garden, this led straight into beautiful woodland. There were an assortment of large trees and small bushes. It was quite dark in the woods, and you couldn't see the sun or the sky! A pathway led through the woods eventually coming out into some allotments. Our parents decided to keep chickens! So our allotment was turned into a large fenced-in chicken run; also in the run as well as about fifteen chickens, were two chicken houses. Every evening at dusk, usually Valerie and I were sent to close up the chicken houses to protect them from foxes. We would walk along the pathway through the woods as fast as we could, pretending to one another that we weren't scared. In the gathering dusk we would peer into the chicken run and check that the hens had put themselves to bed. Then we would shut the little doors, and put the wooden pegs in place to keep them closed. And run home as fast as we could.

We had marvellous freedom, comparatively speaking, at Rownhams House. We were meant to be in at 11pm, latest. But the plan was to sneak in through a side door, nip up the back staircase, get into our night clothes, nip back downstairs, and saunter into the lounge as though we had been in the house for ages!

Rownhams House, at the time we were living there also housed other people. Entering by the side door at the front of the house, turning right and then immediately left, is a staircase. Up the stairs were two or three flats. These accommodated essential staff at different times. The Walker family lived in one. Mr Leonard Walker was transport manager for Victory Transport.

Leonard and his wife Vera had known my father since he left the sea at the age of twenty three, after having qualified for his Masters' Certificate at sea. My father lived with the Walkers for a time, before he met and married my mother. My father joined Victory Transport Limited, straight from leaving the sea. He lived on the premises with the Walker family, having quickly bought out the other two partners in the business, and began to run it on his own. The premises were at 428 Bitterne Road, Southampton, and had space behind for the horses, carts and lorries needed to run the business, which included delivering coal. Years later the Walkers used to babysit Valerie and myself at The White House, Curdridge, together with their daughter Pamela. We used to play hide and seek in the dark, with Mr Walker looking for us – I remember the shrieks of glee and excitement and fear as we crept around the house in the pitch black darkness!

Graham Rodaway, chief accountant, and his family lived in Rownhams House for a while, as did John Baker and his wife. John was the company secretary for Victory Transport. We also had Mr Hayball, together with his wife, living there. Mr Hayball, who had only two front teeth, except for very special occasions, when he seemed to have a mouth full of teeth and looked very smart, was the chief fitter for the company. He had several people working with him and was in charge of all vehicle maintenance of about one hundred vehicles. One of my many jobs for Victory Transport was working out all the petrol/diesel consumption of each vehicle, and giving the figures to Bert Hayball. When the vehicle was gobbling up the fuel it was time to have it in the workshop. He also maintained my Lambretta scooter for me – it was nearly always "the plugs" that needed attention as I used to go too fast and oil up the plugs!

In the Coach House adjoining Rownhams House, lived Mr Bill Barnaby, who was one of Dad's original employees. They seemed to have lived in great poverty near Old Mill Quay in Northam, Southampton, and we often gave them our old toys, clothes and shoes for their children. When they moved to Rownhams House, the idyllic setting with grass, trees, lake, peacocks on their roof, they must have wondered if they had moved to paradise. On the other hand, they may have missed all their neighbours, living in terraced houses, and sitting on their doorsteps hour after hour in the evenings chatting to each other. Millbank Street, where Old Mill Quay was situated, was the road where many seamen lived who went down with the "Titanic" ship. I think that road never recovered from such a sad loss of so many sons, husbands and fathers.

I did not always enjoy my life working for my father – he was often very strict, and prone to get annoyed over the most unexpected thing. I had to sit in on lots of meetings and take the Minutes. One day there was a meeting between Dad and the Transport Managers of his company, Victory Transport. Dad was yelling at the elderly "Morrie" for allowing one of the long distance drivers to drive too many hours. "What would have happened if he had fallen asleep, and knocked some child of his bike and killed him?" Morrie Wakeford sat silently, and Mr Walker looked on, going scarlet in the face in the stress of the meeting. I burst into tears, and fled the office! I produced no Minutes for that meeting!

Dad was a very popular boss with the staff and had great compassion on those who fell on hard times. One employee who went to prison for a serious crime of passion (one might call it!) was promised by my father that he would have his job back as soon as he had served his prison sentence. There were many great kindnesses offered to other staff at various times. He was a greatly respected employer and I never heard anyone grumble about him. He was just very strict at times with his own family!

On Thursdays Dad did the Chairman's Remarks for the Southampton Football Club programmes for the Saturday matches. I would type these up, then jump on my Lambretta, and whiz down to The Dell (five miles away) and deliver the notes. That was one of the perks of the job, for me, to have a little outing on my bike in the middle of the office day.

On Fridays, once all the wages were calculated and the bank's cheques written out, I would be handed several empty cotton Lloyds Bank cash bags and would ride on my Lambretta into Shirley. I would park my scooter in Shirley High Street, walk into Lloyds Bank, collect several hundred pounds in loose cash, put them into the bank bags, stuff these into my shopping bag, and then walk nonchalantly out of the bank. When I reached the Lambretta, I would balance the money bags by my feet, and race back to Rownhams House. There the cash was handed over to the accountants and I got on with work at my desk.

One day Dad was late going to Rotary Club on the Friday lunchtime, and went looking for me to give me a letter to type. When he couldn't find me he started asking around, "Where's Daphne?" "Oh, she's gone to the Bank to fetch the wages!" I heard later the balloon went up! How dare they send a young girl, his daughter at that, to get so much money out of the bank. She could be kidnapped, beaten up, left for dead, the wages stolen!

The following Friday everything changed. Mr Baker, company secretary, and Mr Rodaway, company accountant, were sent into Shirley, with a new heavy duty black brief case, with a chain to one wrist, and told to drive a different route to Lloyds bank, and at different times, each Friday. They used a different car each week for security purposes.

The highlights for me, working at Rownhams House and living there, were probably many. But the best was going out on the lake in our little rowing boat at lunch times on sunny days. But on Wednesdays I did my singing practice, listened to by all the staff, but at the time I didn't realise they could hear me from our part of the house.

The Saints players came out from The Dell, quite often during the week to play on our football pitch in the grounds of Rownhams House, and this kept the grass smooth, nice and green for the Saturday matches at The Dell. We had floodlights around the pitch for dark days and evening practice matches. In the woodland beside our house were the dressing rooms. The Saints players would arrive during a weekday morning, climb out of the coach, go for a run, then come back to the coach to change from their running shoes into football boots and commence to play football. I conjured up a plan for their next visit. The coach duly arrived one weekday morning. I checked that my father was engrossed in some work in his office. Then watched the Saints football players emerge from the coach and go off for their run. About half an hour later they returned, sat down on the grass and changed out of their running shoes and into their football boots. Once they had left all their running shoes neatly in pairs on the grass outside my office window, they jogged off down to the football pitch to commence their game. I slipped out of the office, and ran across the gravel drive at the front of Rownhams House, and proceeded to mix up the twenty-two pairs of running shoes, leaving them neatly wrongly paired up. About an hour later the Saints came jogging and walking back from our football pitch, and sat down on the lawn to put on their shoes. The girls in the upstairs offices had seen what I had done, and they were already leaning out of the windows laughing at the scene on the grass. The footballers reacted perfectly – and the scene was chaotic! I sat at my desk, observing the scene of chaos, with great amusement. The girls upstairs got the blame, and no one ever betrayed me! One of the girls in my office was married to one of the football players, but she never let on that it was me that had muddled up their shoes.

Southampton was being rebuilt after the blitz, and each time we went down the town there were less and less big bombed gaps. Houses and shops were going up everywhere, and the lovely trams disappeared, replaced by boring buses. Instead of two pence a ride it was more like two shillings! My father was busy with many charities in the town. Fairly soon after the war he started an old people's club, initially meeting twice a week at the Central Hall Methodist Church – giving many old people a cup of tea and a buttered bun, and some form of concert or entertainment. Valerie and I would go quite often and help Mum butter the buns, and get the cups and saucers out. We were always embarrassed to walk in to the hall with Dad as everyone would applaud him. Later he started an old people's all day club, which was open every day and gave light cooked lunches. This was supported by the Southampton Rotary Club and we would help raise funds by driving round Southampton on the back of a lorry at Christmas time, singing carols and rattling the buckets to collect the cash.

While I was secretary to my father, who was Managing Director of his company Victory Transport Limited, Dad was also chairman of many charitable organisations including the Southern Area of the British Sailors' Society. This charity ran Jellicoe House as a hostel for seamen who docked in Southampton, and had a full time chaplain and other staff. I went there once a month with my father to take the minutes of the meetings, and learnt to appreciate the benevolent side of my father. One Christmas Day, at Rownhams House, we were interrupted by a phone call. "Please could Mr Barber come down to Jellicoe House immediately. A fight has broken out and Mr Devereux can't handle it by himself." Dad left his Christmas lunch, half eaten, and raced down to the docks in his car. He returned two hours later and all was under control again.

Valerie, in the mean time, did a different kind of socialising to me, and made some good friends amongst the Young Conservatives. I was occasionally invited to join some social gathering. But I always felt a bit like a fish out of water! I would rather socialise through activities, singing, dancing, drama, rather than standing chatting over a drink. One day Valerie said she and three others were going to go down to Bournemouth for the day. Around 6pm the phone went, and Valerie said she would be back later in the evening as they had decided to go and listen to the oratorio by Mendelssohn called "Elijah". As Valerie was far more into pop music than I was, I was quite amazed that she would go and listen to an oratorio! It turned out later that one of the young men in the group she was with was called Basil, and he fancied the music. This was the first I had heard of Basil. I waited up for Valerie to come home, and sat on her bed at Rownhams House while she recounted the day's events. Basil sounded very nice, and Valerie sounded quite keen on him. About three months later, as Christmas drew near, Valerie appeared with a largish box, which she carefully unwrapped. Inside was a beautifully painted and decorated box with a green door. The pop song of that time was, "What's behind the Green Door?" We were about to find out! Valerie cautiously opened the green door, and there wrapped up in lots of cotton wool, shone some very lovely sparkly jewellery. I was very impressed! I thought, I wonder if anyone will ever love me enough to give me such a lovely present so beautifully wrapped!

Valerie's romance blossomed, and we all liked Basil.

Life at Rownhams House flourished. The family transport business grew larger, and Dad built more huge warehouses. For a while they were the biggest open plan warehouses in England. My father's bright orange lorries could be seen on almost any journey we ever took. It was such fun looking out for the conspicuous vehicles looming over the horizon, or emerging from some town street. Years later when I was newly married and lived in Newcastle under Lyme in Staffordshire I would often see one of the Victory Transport lorries waiting at the traffic lights in the high street. I would long to catch a lift back home to Rownhams House. But home wasn't the same anyway – my bedroom decorated in ivy clad wall paper was gone – my young six year old brother Roger had claimed my bedroom for his own. His two sisters were married and gone – and he was the only child left at home! I had loved my bedroom: one window overlooked the stables and the fourteenth century coach house, and the other window looked out onto woodland, lawns and the lake. The peacocks resided on the roof of the coach house, squawking and howling as the clock struck every hour day and night. Later George and Mary, our two swans, would come to reside on the lake.

Roger had his own adventures in and around the house and grounds. There was a great fuss one day when Roger, aged about three, had followed Jack, the maintenance man, up the ladder and onto the roof of the Coach House. Having discovered him sitting astride the apex of the roof, the next problem was to encourage him down without either panicking him, or sounding cross so that he climbed further away from safety. This took quite a while, but eventually he slid down the roof and climbed backwards down the ladder.

Another time, on an icy, snowy, Saturday afternoon, I was left in charge of Roger, while the rest of the family went off to watch the Saints play football at The Dell. I invited my friend Judith to come out to Rownhams House and keep me company. She arrived about 2pm, just after the family had left. I said, "Don't take your boots and coat off, Judith. Let's wander down to the lake and see what the ducks are doing." I called Roger over to me, and slipped on his brown, woollen tweed coat, and his smart cap. Then slid his little feet into his wellington boots, and told him we were going to walk down to the lake. I grabbed my coat and scarf, and we all left from the side door, walking along the path and then across the lawn down towards the pond. Judith and I were in deep discussion about old school days, and how life had been since we had both left the Atherley School. I looked up from the snowy grass to check that Roger was safely with us, only to discover he was nowhere in sight. After scanning the grounds from where we stood, it didn't take long for Judith and me to spy my toddling brother. He was standing on the ice in the middle of the lake – where it was about 12 feet deep if the ice broke. Judith giggled nervously, and I stood totally shocked. I knew well that if I shouted at Roger he would run further into the centre, where there was a small island, which could be extremely dangerous. I was not sure how strong the ice was, but I dare not put it to the test and try walking across to fetch him. "Roger! Roger!" I called gently. "Come on, we're going off to the football pitch now. Are you coming with us? You don't want to be left all on your own do you?" Judith and I turned away from the lake, not daring to make a fuss. On glancing back I saw Roger slowly toddling towards the edge of the lake. "Come on, Roger!" I called again, pretending a calm that I did not feel. As he got near the edge of the lake, we turned back and I grabbed him. I then raised my voice and yelled at him. "Don't you ever, ever, walk on the lake again, you silly, silly boy. You could have disappeared through the ice and we would never have seen you again." Roger, a very sensitive young child, started to cry, and I picked him up and hugged him, wiping away his tears. We wandered up to the football pitch, on safer and higher ground – not even a frozen puddle in sight. After a while I stopped shaking, and Judith and I held Roger's small gloved hands firmly in ours. By the time Mum, Dad, and Valerie returned from football, Judith had left to go home, and Roger had hopefully forgotten his near scrape. Fortunately as he wasn't yet talking no one ever found out the near tragedy that had occurred that sunny, snowy afternoon.

Roger was very popular with all the Victory Transport staff, both the office staff, and the warehouse staff. One rather elderly and very difficult member of the office staff adored Roger, and frequently pulled up an extra chair to her desk and let Roger play with pencils, pens, paper, paperclips, bulldog clips, rubber bands and other oddments lying around. Roger would play for hours, talking his own version of gobble-de-goop. When boredom set in, he would hop down from the chair, and make his way down to the warehouses, where he would (pretend?) to load the lorries with shop delivery stuff, and be given a few pennies for his trouble.

In the long summer holidays my father would not allow any of the Saints footballers to wander around the town unoccupied. Oh no, not at all! Bad for morale! So they were all offered jobs in the warehouses, loading lorries, or hosing down the vehicles as they drove back onto the premises. I think most of the footballers hastily found other jobs, but about five of them would take up Dad's offer and earn a few extra pounds from May till August.

CHAPTER FOUR

Before we moved to Rownhams House and were still living in Abbotts Way, Highfield, in Southampton, Valerie and I were invited to something called Crusaders on a Sunday afternoon. Because the two girls who invited us came from respectable, known families, Dad thought it would be a good idea if we went to something like that! So at 2.45pm every Sunday Valerie and I would walk about three quarters of a mile, up Abbotts Way, along Brookvale Road, and into Blenheim Avenue. We would get to the house, front door wide open, and lots of young girls assembling for the afternoon. When we first went we sat on an odd assortment of chairs, cushions, and the floor. But after a year or so some very state of the art tubular chairs arrived. We all soon discovered that they rocked. So most of the afternoon, while we were being entertained with talks about the Bible, missionaries, Africa, and sang songs and hymns, we rocked backwards and forwards in an erratic rhythm. No one ever reprimanded us. In fact Mrs Judson, who ran the class, and Mrs Lockhart, who helped her, were so amazingly loving and caring of all of us, that I discovered that Crusaders had a unique atmosphere that I had never experienced before.

We had frequent talks about Jesus, the good Shepherd, who laid down his life for his sheep. And if we wanted to follow Jesus, we should give our lives to him. Valerie and I went to Crusaders for several years, and we went to a camp one spring holiday, held in a boarding school at Burnham on Sea, Somerset. It was all a good experience; and later I went to several more Girl Crusader camps in different parts of England and made some good friends.

We were only about 11 and 12 years of age when we first started going to Crusaders. One afternoon we walked home together, and Dad was standing on the doorstep fuming. "Where have you girls been?" Valerie was always the spokesman of the two of us, and replied, "To Crusaders, of course." "You're lying! You didn't go to Crusaders! Where've you been?" An indignant argument took place. I backed Valerie up, and said that of course we had been to Crusaders. The argument continued indoors. Then Valerie said, "Well ring them up at Crusaders then." So Dad got out the phone directory, looking up Dr Lockhart's number in Blenheim Avenue. He dialled the number while Valerie and I watched, nervous and self-righteous. "John Barber here! Could you tell me if my two daughters have been to Crusaders at your house today? Yes, I'll wait..... Oh, yes, well thank you. Sorry to have bothered you! Goodbye."

"Well, it does seem that you did go to Crusaders. If I ever catch you pretending to go and you go elsewhere, there will be trouble. Do you understand?" and Dad walked off into the dining room and left Valerie and I to glance silently at each other in the hallway – not daring to pull a face in case he walked back out again and caught us. We slowly climbed the stairs, and whispered in the bedroom. "What was all that about?"

About two years later the Crusaders cancelled their usual Sunday afternoon meeting, and said we would all meet down at the Central Hall Methodist Church, where there was a special choir and a speaker called Tom Rees. I have no idea how we got down there, may be by bus. All I know is that I genuinely heard the call of Jesus on my life, and decided to "give my life to him." I took a "Decision Card" that was being handed out as we left the Hall, as discreetly as I could, and slipped it into my pocket. The next day at school, my friend Thelma bounced up to my desk just before Assembly. "I saw you take a Decision card yesterday. Does that mean you've given your life to Jesus? Have you filled the card in?" I was embarrassed. I wanted to be a secret disciple! I would serve the Lord, but in my own way, and privately! Thelma was about to say more when the bell rang. We filed in line, with our Bibles and prayer books, and marched down the corridor, class by class and into the main hall. Thelma was still standing next to me. She whispered, "Now that you are a Christian you can't mess about in prayers anymore, and you must close your eyes." Horrors! Things were going to have to change. I had had various forms of entertainment to be used during prayers – my favourite being to pull an over-perfumed handkerchief out of my gymslip pocket and waft it in the air as we knelt on the hard floor to pray. The perfume was so strong that the girls around me could never resist looking up to see where the scent came from.

But a new day was dawning. I genuinely wanted to give back to the Lord something of my life, for what it was worth. So I knelt and closed my eyes during the collect, school prayer and intercessions. I felt very conspicuous, as though the whole school noticed that Daphne Barber had shut her eyes, and she was a changed person!

Thelma didn't let up. She pestered me to fill in the Decision Card and post it off to the Tom Rees organisation. I didn't even need to put a stamp on it! I re-read the card again. It said, "For God so loved the world that he gave his only Son, that whoever believes in him should not perish but have eternal life." (St John's gospel chapter 3 v 16)

The thought of eternal life definitely attracted me!

There were a few more scriptures on the card: "Truly, truly, I say to you, he who hears my word and believes him who sent me, has eternal life; he does not come into judgement, but has passed from death to life." (John chapter 5 v 24,25).

The words from the Bible spoke powerfully to me. I fished out my school Bible from my satchel and found the verses, and underlined them rather clumsily in ink. I found myself reading the rest of John chapter 3 and also chapter 5. It did seem that a response was required! One had to make a definite decision to follow Jesus. So I re-made the decision, just to make quite sure. Then after school that day I put our two Scottish Terriers, Dinah and Bruce on their leads, and walked down to the post box with the decision card filled in.

It was posted off and I forgot about it. I did try and tell Valerie, but I explained it so badly that it upset her. I realised that before I tried to tell someone else I would need to get my words and facts better organised and understood. But I did change, and I changed for the better! I could no longer misbehave and be cheeky, as I had for the last three terms at school. I realised that it wasn't just Crusaders that had influenced me for good but two sixth form prefects who were in the choir. They were well known Baptist church members, and when the whole school turned to face the East for the saying of the Apostles Creed every Friday, Doreen and Hilary refused to turn. I became curious, and asked them why they didn't turn and face the East. "We believe God is everywhere – not just in the East!" they replied to my enquiry. It set me thinking. These two particularly lovely and popular senior girls genuinely believed in a living God. I began to watch them at every possible opportunity. Yes, there was something different about them and their faces shone with peace and happiness. It was at that point that I began my quest to seek after a living God, and an experience that would make me more like Doreen and Hilary.

The postman usually came about 7.30 in the morning, and there was a second post at lunch time every day except Sunday. My father handed me a letter as I came down to breakfast. "What's this?" he asked. I looked at the envelope. "Tom Rees, Hildenborough Hall" was the return address printed in bold letters on the front of the envelope. "Ah!" I stuttered. "Um, I sent off for some information - to do with Crusaders," I hastily added. My father eyed me, and deciding I wasn't lying, turned back to his own post.

I felt I had always done my best at school – and I know Valerie worked diligently as well. But neither of us was good at passing exams and we were by no means anywhere near the top of our class at school. But the year following my "conversion" experience I came second from top both in Old Testament Studies, and New Testament Studies (both different subjects with different teachers). I think this was because the Bible had suddenly become a living book to me and I just couldn't stop reading it. I also got honours in Art for the first time. We used to break up from the Atherley School at midday at the end of every term, and each of us was given a brown manila envelope to put in our school satchels. These were meant to be carried home safely and handed, unopened, to our parents. Valerie and I were no exception – except the envelopes had to sit on the dining room table and were usually opened in front of us by Dad as we all sat down for the evening meal. Almost every report caused Dad to get very upset. He was paying a lot of money to get us educated. Why was he wasting money on his two daughters who weren't prepared to work hard? Why can't you come top of the class like I used to be? Dad fumed.

Consequently Valerie and I changed our modus operandi. As soon as we got home from school with our reports we went into the kitchen and filled up the kettle and waited for it to boil. Valerie was the skilled one, so she steamed open her report and mine. We then quickly scanned our own report and carefully re-sealed them. If they weren't too bad we would sit down for the meal altogether in the evening and put up with Dad's scathing remarks. But if one or both reports were particularly bad (which was normal) then Valerie and I would leave Mum to face the music. Valerie and I locked ourselves in the large, warm, comfy airing cupboard. We could hear Dad's raised voice, muffled because of all the laundry around us. Mum would come up about 7pm and say, "You can come out now, your father's gone out to a meeting."

But on the occasion of my "good report" – having steamed open the brown manila envelope and seeing three lots of honours – all written in bright red ink – I boldly sat down for the evening meal and waited for Dad to finish some of the meal before slitting open the (re-sealed) envelopes. I waited expectantly for some relief and praise from my father. "What's this?" he shouted, looking at me. "Two useless subjects you get honours for! Why couldn't it have been Maths or English?" I think Dad was much more upset than usual, and I felt as though neither Valerie nor I would ever be able to please him with any school work.

We had a school rule, not kept by everyone. On the first Sunday of every new term at the Atherley, we were all meant to go to our own church and ask God's blessing on the term ahead. Every first Monday morning of the new term the form mistress asked us to put up our hands if we had been to church the day before to ask His blessing on the term. I would look around the class and about half or more of the girls had their hands up.

I decided that next time this happened I would have been to church and could put my hands up with the rest of them. So with this in mind, I told my father I was going to church next Sunday because it was a school rule. I said I would go with Mrs Legge, who came and stayed every weekend to look after us, while my parents went out. She went to Highfield Church on a Sunday evening, and I occasionally went with her.

Dad thought for a minute, his strong blue eyes fixed on me. "No," he said. "We are Congregationalists. My father was a Congregational minister, and my mother is still ministering in their church in Worpleston, Guildford. We will go to The Avenue Congregational Church, just up the road. We will all go as a family. It's time we started going to church again."

All this happened as he said. We all dutifully got in the car and drove up to the church the following Sunday morning. We were ushered into the right hand side aisle pews – and there we were to be found most Sundays from then on, until I joined the choir! The church had a new minister, the Rev Vine Russell; an attractive man who filled up the church and better still filled up a large portion with young people, all of whom became my friends for many years.

I was upstairs doing my homework, when I heard the doorbell ring. After about five minutes my father called up the stairs. "Daphne, can you come downstairs for a minute?" I closed my homework book with a thump, sighed, and thought, "Now what?" I walked down the stairs, and realised there were voices coming from the dining room. I opened the door and walked in. There stood my father, my mother and Rev Vine Russell.

Vine Russell immediately turned to me and said, "I've had a letter from someone called Tom Rees. He says you recently attended one of his meetings and ... um .... decided to receive Christ! Is this true?" I was horrified at such an exposure of my "secret discipleship". "Er... yes..." I said. Vine Russell smiled and congratulated me on my decision. "I see you in church most Sundays with the family, so I will write to Tom Rees and say you are in good hands."

The next time Vine Russell visited us was more traumatic for me. It was about a year later.

We had continued going to the Avenue Congregational Church regularly.

A few months after Roger was born, the door bell rang – and Rev Vine Russell was ushered in again. He was a most attractive man with a big personality, and conversation flowed easily. After polite chit chat our minister then turned to my father and said he had been wondering if our family would all like to become church members. A short discussion took place, and Dad went and fetched his diary, and a date was set for this ceremony to take place at the end of a morning service.

Then my father said to Vine Russell, "Alma and I were wondering about having young Roger baptised. He's already six months old. Perhaps you could arrange for that to be done as well?"

I held my breath, horrified, tightening my lips together to seal them closed. I imagined Vine Russell to say, "Oh, well, no hurry, we will sort Roger out at a later date!" But, no! Diaries out again, "I could manage one of these two Sundays during the morning service if you like?"

But Dad replied, "Well, Alma and I wondered if we could have a private service on a Sunday afternoon, and invite some of our friends." "Sure, that can be arranged easily," replied the minister. More dates were tossed around and a date finally agreed. I slipped out of the room, my lips still tightly closed, and my heart pounding!

The trouble was that as a new and very sincere disciple of Jesus I had already decided weeks ago that my parents would never bother to get Roger baptised, christened, or whatever, so I had taken this tiny baby into my arms, and with some fresh tap water from the upstairs bathroom I had baptised him myself. "In the name of the Father, and of the Son, and of the Holy Spirit, I baptise you Roger John Barber. May the Lord always look after you and keep you safe." Then I had kissed his brow, on top of where I had signed the cross on his forehead, and popped him back into his carrycot. This was all done one Saturday afternoon while the rest of the family had gone off to football, leaving Roger, my baby brother, in my tender care.

I didn't dare consult anyone, about whether or not it was dangerous to baptise someone twice. I was beginning to get to know about the love of God, the love of Jesus, and I thought He could be totally trusted to answer my baptismal prayers for Roger, and if the Church wanted to repeat the ceremony then Roger would get a double blessing. With my mind nearly at rest, I got on with my homework.

Everything took place as planned at the Avenue Church; we all became church members, and Roger had his formal baptism or christening. The Barber family used to slip into the same pew every Sunday, and Dad always remarked on the two nice young men who handed out hymn books and ushered us to our pew on the south aisle. Little did he know that I would end up marrying one of them in spite of some opposition from my father and huge opposition from my future mother-in-law, who was an awesome and somewhat fearsome member of the church choir.

Vine Russell had some kind of a job with the British Broadcasting Corporation, as well as being a retired naval chaplain. The Avenue Church was quite often asked to do a broadcast on the radio, and later on television. When the church was asked to do a Sunday Half Hour broadcast, it was at this point that Valerie and I were drawn in to help swell the choir, and raise the standard of the singing! When Mr Nicholson, the choir master, asked us if we were soprano or alto, we had no idea what he was asking us. So he sat us with the sopranos, vowing to do his best to make us permanent members of his robed choir on a Sunday!

By the time we moved out to Rownhams House, I was well entrenched in the choir and the church social life. And the rest of my family came to church just occasionally, usually only when I was singing a solo or taking part in a drama. I loved my own independent social life and gradually learnt to fight my own battles in life instead of sheltering behind my one-year-older-than-me sister. I began to read women's magazines like Woman, and Woman's Own, and to unravel the mysteries of growing up. I learned about Max Factor Cream Puff, Yardley lipstick and Eau de Paris perfume from the older girls in the choir – and I also learned that some men in or outside the church, married or single, were not all to be trusted!

CHAPTER FIVE

Valerie's romance with Basil continued. He was studying to be an architect, working during the day and studying in the evenings. In the meantime I was getting interested in one of the young sides-men from church. He was also in the church choir although was missing for weeks at a time. I gradually worked out that he was away at University. It turned out that he was studying for a science degree at Exeter. I happened to be at the same table as his mother one day at some church social, and she said, very proudly, "My David has decided to go into the ministry!" I wasn't interested enough to ask, "What ministry?" as I didn't think it would ever involve me anyway. Being the daughter of a business man and town councillor, I presumed David's mother meant some ministry in parliament, agriculture or something.

But then a few Sundays later it was announced in church with great excitement that one of the young people had felt the call to go into full time ministry in the Congregational Church. It was made into rather a big thing, and David was invited to preach in the church quite often when he was home from university. I later discovered he had "failed" his degree in science, having lost interest and having decided to pursue theology instead. When I next saw David Mills, and when he had stopped joking and fooling around, which he always seem to be doing, I asked him what had happened about his change of career choice. He said that some of the university students who attended a church in Southern Hay, Exeter, were asked to take an evening service. They drew straws to decide who should preach, and David had drawn the short straw.

He shared a room with a young Baptist student who realised that although David went to church he didn't really know the Lord at all. The young student had decided to get some friends to pray that David find God for himself. David said, "I didn't know people were praying for me. And in the mean time I had a sermon to prepare. I found myself drawn to a verse in the Bible over and over again."

I was hovering in the doorway between the choir stalls and the minister's vestry, and people were squeezing past us to go home after choir. I held my gloves and my scarf in my hands, and David was still holding my crash helmet. He liked to tease me, and others, and on this occasion had run off with my crash helmet. This had drawn us into conversation, and I was wasting no time trying to find out why David was suddenly a ministerial student rather than a budding scientist.

It was a warm summer's evening, still daylight at 9.30. We continued our conversation as I walked out towards my Lambretta. I stuffed my gloves and scarf in my bag and held out my hand for my crash helmet. David said, "I'll push your bike and walk you home! Then I can tell you the rest of what happened."

I was a bit shy and embarrassed, and would have preferred to finish the conversation and start my bike up and roar away up the Avenue. "Well, we've moved out to Rownhams," I said. "That's a long way to walk!" David laughed and said, "Oh well, we will walk up the Avenue, as far as the cut, then I will make my way home to Leigh Road, and you can ride the rest of the way home to Rownhams."

So we crossed over the Avenue and walked slowly up the road, and David continued to tell me what happened next in Exeter. "The Bible verse that kept going over and over in my mind was:"Who do men say that I am?" It's in one of the gospels, and Jesus was asking his disciples what people were saying about him." David smiled at me and continued to push the Lambretta along the Avenue. I said, "Yes, I know that verse. Peter answered and said to Jesus, "Thou art the Christ, the Son of the living God!"

"Well done! Daphne! You know your Bible! But as I was thinking about this question, "Who do men say that I am?" I realised that actually I didn't know the answer for myself. And as I prepared the sermon for the following Sunday evening, I had to face some facts. How could I preach about Christ if I didn't know who He was or what I was talking about." David said, as he continued to push my Lambretta, northwards up the Avenue.

I was deep in thought, gazing across the Southampton Common, grass, shrubs, bushes, little pathways. I knew the common well. Valerie and I had cycled across it to school for years. I glanced up at David, who was slowing up. The Lambretta was heavy, and we were nearly at the cut where he needed to turn off to the right for home. We stopped and looked at each other. David continued: "I found myself asking Jesus to tell me who He was, and as I continued to try and prepare my sermon, it was as though He revealed himself to me. He truly is the Christ, the Son of the living God! I suddenly knew the truth for myself. You might say I was the very first convert of my very first sermon ever preached!"

I laughed, impressed. "Well, good luck with your new chosen career!" I said. "Thanks for telling me your story! I wondered what had happened, and now I know!"

David explained that he would be starting at Northern Theological College, attached to Manchester University the following Autumn. I thought how much I would hate to start studying again and was glad I was free and earning my own living!

I kick started the Lambretta, which I called "Bambi". "Bambi" and I were great friends and Bambi took me everywhere. Without Bambi my social life would fall apart! I waved to David as he crossed the road, and switching my headlights on, roared on up the Avenue towards Rownhams House. It would be another two years before David and I had any further conversation of any depth.

Meanwhile I continued singing and doing drama, and going for lovely long rides on Bambi. One weekend I visited my half cousins who lived in Kent. I set off from Rownhams early in the morning, with a small overnight bag strapped to the pillion seat, and a map in my pocket. Dressed in my warm grey corduroy jacket, fully flared, flowery patterned skirt, red high heels, and white crash helmet, I set off. When I eventually drew near to Seven Oaks, Kent, I found a phone box and phoned home. Mum answered the phone. "Where are you, have you arrived?"

"No, I haven't yet! I'm a bit saddle sore! I'm taking a break for a few minutes. I only have a few more miles to go and I'm so stiff at present. I will look like an idiot trying to walk up their drive!" My mother heard the pips go in the phone box."Don't put any more money in, ring us when you arrive." And the phone went dead. I walked back to Bambi slowly, glancing at the town high street, but deciding not to get distracted! "Uncle David and Aunty Margaret will be waiting for me. I'd better get a move on!" With no mishaps, and a couple of stops to read my instructions on how to find their house, I arrived at their gate. Penny and Susan were sitting on top of the gate. "Where've you been? We've been waiting hours for you!" I laughed and reminded them I had ridden a very long way.

Looking back I am so glad that my parents allowed me to be adventurous and be optimistic, that what I set out to do I could achieve. Dad told us he used to set off from Ashburton, Devon and cycle to his school, Caterham in Surrey, when he was in his teens. May be that was why Valerie and I were encouraged to go off on our bikes. When we lived in Highfield, Valerie and I, and a friend or two, would cycle miles to Farley Mount or Crab Wood, taking a picnic with us, for the day.

About two years after David Mills had told me his conversion story I went to a New Year's Eve party at the church. It was just for the young people. I had a new outfit from the C & A shop - a white blouse and a full black skirt, belted at the waist! It was perfect for dancing in, and I danced every dance I could, including the Paul Jones, where you never knew which partner you would land up with. We had a Ladies Invitation dance, where the girls had to choose one of the men to dance with. As Spencer wasn't there I had no particular person I wanted to dance with, so I chose John Addis, the brother of a friend from school. He wasn't very good looking but he was gentle and friendly. We swirled away and danced together for another couple of dances. Then the evening finished with a very slow waltz, where couples who were couples got very close and affectionate. As the music drew to a close, the band struck up "Auld Lang Syne". We all held hands in a huge circle, looking at one another, smiling, and wondering what the New Year ahead would bring.

The band packed up their instruments and all the young people piled into the front pews of the Avenue church having walked through the passageways at the back of the church or taking a short cut across the church car park. It was a half hour service finishing just after midnight. David Mills was the preacher and he preached a challenging and encouraging word that I found hugely helpful. After greeting my closest friends with "Happy New Year!", I slipped off into the darkness. My Lambretta was waiting forlornly in an almost deserted church car park. I slipped on my helmet, kicked the bike into action and rode away, deep in thought.

I wrote in my journal that night all the details of my fun night out, who I danced with, and what my New Year's resolutions would be. I also wrote a note to David Mills to thank him for his excellent talk. At the weekend there was no sign of

David in church – maybe he had gone back to Manchester University? So I handed the envelope to Mrs Mills, who was taking off her choir robes and hanging them in the wardrobe in the choir vestry. "Please would you give this to David for me?" I asked. She looked at me, silently, and then looked at the envelope. She nodded, and said."You haven't been to our house for a singing practice recently. Is there something wrong with us or have you found someone else to play for you?" I slipped off my own choir gown, folding the cuffs neatly and tucked them into the bag hanging on my coat hanger. "Well, I don't like to keep pestering you to teach me my songs. But if it really is no bother maybe I could come next week?" I said.

"Well, it would be nice to see more of you. David won't be there of course. He's gone back to Manchester. But Ian will probably be in." We arranged a date, and I walked away a bit cross with myself. I always needed help learning my songs, even though I had a piano I was not much good at sight reading, and certainly I couldn't play some of the more difficult music I was now doing. But I felt that Mrs Mills seem to think I was after one of her boys, which I wasn't. Nobody could compare to Spencer!

I had a very nice brief letter back from David Mills in Manchester, and he suggested that I might like to come along and hear him preach at Hythe Congregational Church, in the New Forest, in April. He had been made student pastor there, and would be taking the services on the Sundays during the Spring vacation. I thought no more about it. I heard Mrs Mills speaking loudly and clearly in the choir vestry about David's engagement to marry a girl called Grace as soon as he had finished his degree. Later when he was home for the holidays he brought Grace with him; she seemed sweet and quiet, and not the kind of girl I thought would attract David Mills!

Just before the last weekend of the Easter holiday Mrs Mills approached me and said, "Would you like to come and hear David preach at Hythe on Sunday evening?" My first thought was what excuse could I give Mr Nicholson for missing choir on Sunday evening? But I said, "Yes, that would be lovely. What time and where shall I meet you?" Mrs Mills explained they were taking their caravan out to Hythe and parking it in a field near the church for the weekend. "We will be here for the morning service, so why don't you come with us, back to the caravan for lunch and we will bring you back home after the evening service. "

I walked into our lounge at Rownhams House on my return from choir practice. Dad was sitting in the arm chair reading the newspaper. Mum was sitting in the other chair doing some needlework. Roger had gone to bed, and Valerie was out with Basil.

“Um.... Mrs Mills has asked me if I’d like to go with them to Hythe Congregational Church on Sunday evening. I’ve said yes.” My father lowered his newspaper, and looked at me. “Why do you want to go to Hythe for the evening service. You never want to miss going to Avenue to sing in the choir. Haven’t they got a service on Sunday evening?”

“Um... well, it’s not that... but Mrs Mills thought I might like to hear her son preach at Hythe.”

Dad regarded me silently. “Is that the one who is training to be a minister? What’s his name, David, is it?” “Um.... er ... yes. That’s right, David Mills. You remember, he and Ian Mills used to give out the hymn books on the side aisle when we first started going to Avenue Church.”

I could tell my father was getting angry. I stood on one foot, then the other, hovering, and wishing I could just say, “Well, goodnight!” smile and walk out. But I had to wait, to make sure I did have permission to go to Hythe with the Mills family on Sunday evening.

“Well, I suppose so, Daphne. But I will tell you one thing, Daphne. I would rather you married a farm hand than a Congregational Minister!” my father glared at me, and resumed reading his paper. I then muttered, “I’m not going to marry him. I’m only going to listen to him at his mother’s invitation.” I left the room, amazed that my father would ever think I’d marry David Mills. He was five years older than me, and engaged to someone else for heaven’s sake. I climbed up the stairs, wishing Valerie was in and we could have a good pow-wow!

I lay in bed listening for her return. At long last I heard Valerie walk past my room and go into her own room. Her wardrobe door opened and closed. I hopped out of bed, cautiously opening my bedroom door, which faced the long corridor leading to the staircase and my parent’s bedroom. No one around! I quickly turned left out of my room, and whispered at Valerie’s door, “Can I come in?”

“Here I am, come in!” she called. Valerie had started getting ready for bed. “Have you seen Mum and Dad?” I asked. “Well, only to say goodnight. I didn’t stop and chat. Why, what’s the matter?”

I explained the dilemma about going to Hythe Church on Sunday to hear David with the Mills family and Dad's comments. Valerie listened and said, "Dad has said yes, you can go, so don't worry about it! But I don't like David Mills very much." I looked at Valerie, surprised. "When we went on that weekend to the Isle of Wight with all the young people from the church, he ran the games, remember?" I nodded. "He got me to speak for one minute on "A cabbage" or something stupid. I felt a total fool. " I remembered the game. I had had to talk for one minute on "Jazz" without repeating myself. I shrugged my shoulders and asked Val if she had had a nice evening. We chatted for a while and said goodnight.

I quite enjoyed my trip to Hythe and the Mills' caravan, but it all seemed a bigger deal than it should have been and I was glad to get home. My father seemed reconciled to the fact that I was going to marry David Mills, and remained silent, asking no questions. Mum told me later he was very upset about the whole situation. I found out later that Dad felt his father had had a tough time in the church – especially caused by his deacons and he didn't want me to get hurt in the same way.

David and I exchanged one or two letters that following term while he was at University, mostly discussing theological issues that interested me, and trying to find out what kind of subjects he was studying as part of his degree. Just before the end of the summer term Mrs Mills phoned me up at home one evening and said that David's engagement with Grace was off, and he was very upset. Would I consider going on holiday with the Mills family to Wales in their caravan and awning as a companion to try and cheer David up? She needed to know quickly or she would try and find someone else to go with them to make up a foursome.

My parents were in the dining room, sat at the "Duke of Wellington's banqueting table", which we used for all our meals. I told Mrs Mills I'd check to see if I could get two weeks off work and ring her back. I confronted my parents with the invitation. Dad said he would talk it over with Mum and tell me later in the evening. The next hour went very slowly! Mum came to find me, washing up in the kitchen with Valerie. "Your father says it's all right for you to go with the Mills to Wales. You'd better find out what you have to take in the way of bedding and things." I couldn't believe it! I rang Mrs Mills back. George Mills answered, and said that Molly was out but he would give her the message.

I found out what I needed to take on holiday and one of Mum's friends made me a new skirt and a pair of shorts. I bought some warm trousers and a new blouse, and a warm anorak. And I made myself a sleeping bag using blankets and large safety pins! Time flew by, and Mrs Mills was much more friendly towards me in choir. Things were looking up!

We had an excellent two week tour of Wales. I had never been there before and thought the scenery was spectacular. I loved every minute of it. Mrs Mills swung between organising David and me to go off on walks together, and trying to make sure we didn't spend too much time alone together. I felt I was walking a bit of a tight rope! I loved the empty beaches and the majestic hills and mountains in Snowdonia. By the time the two weeks were up I decided that I really rather liked David Mills, though the family dynamics were unpredictable and complicated at times.

David unexpectedly came home from Manchester University for half term and we went for a drive to Farley Mount. David talked about finances and marriage in general as we walked through the woodland and along a farm track.

We went back to his parents' house for tea, and David dropped me back home in his mother's little Fiat around 10.45pm, just before my deadline. "When are you going to let me know the answer to my question?" David asked as he walked up to the side door at Rownhams House. "What question?" I asked. "The one I asked you at Farley Mount!" David said, looking at me significantly. I was genuinely mystified, searching my memory for a question asked and not responded to. I looked at David, staring at him in the darkness. I put the key in the door and switched on the passageway light. "What question?" I said again. David looked at me as though I was crazy or something. "Well you had better repeat the question as I don't remember one!"

"I asked you if you would marry me!" David said. I was totally amazed. I could only think that the question was an unasked question wrapped up in the conversation we had had at Farley Mount on marriage in general and family finances in general. I said I'd let him know. He turned away and walked back to the little Fiat. I walked in through the side door and closed and locked it behind me. I walked along the passageway, through the offices and up the main staircase, thinking, "Oh my goodness me!" What worried me most was the obscure way David had popped the question and was this going to be a pattern of miscommunication in future? That really concerned me. I phoned David the next morning from the office. "Yes, I think so! Yes! But whatever is your mother going to say?" David was silent for a while."She will be pleased. I am too! I go back to university tomorrow, my parents are driving me. I will tell them on the way up to Manchester." "Well, when shall I tell my parents?" David said, "Wait till I've told mine, and I will let you know!" "But you've got to come and see my father and ask for my hand in marriage! That's the proper way to do it!"

There was another long silence on the phone. "Are you still there, David?" "Yes, sorry. Look, I think we better keep it quiet till Christmas. Then I can come over and see your father and tell my parents at the same time. What do you think?" "I think that's a better idea. We will get engaged at Christmas, and be together when we tell the parents. And we can get a ring for each other as well." I replied.

We wrote to each other nearly every day, and I longed for my daily letter, often taking it out in the rowing boat on the Rownhams House lake at lunchtime to read and re-read it. I began to type David's sermons and to feel a part of his ministry. He was preaching every Sunday in different churches around Manchester, and by Tuesday of each week I would usually have had a report on what happened at the weekend, and whether there had been a baptism, holy communion (extra ten shillings for that!) and what the hospitality had been like.

Christmas holidays arrived, and David and I had already actually bought our rings in Southampton (mine) and Manchester (his) and got them made to size. On the 13th December David came out to Rownhams House and had a formal chat with my father in the lounge. Then I was called in from the dining room where I had been hovering. Dad said he was giving us his blessing to get married. Then he turned to David and said, "Daphne has a heart of gold; a big, loving heart. Don't you ever, ever hurt her."

I was amazed. And may be for the first time I realised that my father loved me and wanted to protect me. But I was in love and that's all that mattered at that moment. We then climbed into the little Fiat 500, Mrs Mills' car, and drove the five miles to Leigh Road in Highfield, Southampton. I was wearing my new engagement ring, and David left me in the hallway while he went to tell his mother the "Good news of our engagement".

Molly Mills was in the kitchen putting the finishing touches to the Saturday lunch. I could hear David talking quietly to his mother and then became aware of pots and pans being banged around and my future mother-in-law's voice rising several decibels. George Mills put his head round the kitchen door, then hastily called out, "Lunch is ready!"

Ian emerged from his small bedroom off the hallway, next to David's room. He was quick to sense an atmosphere. "What's up?" he said looking at his father George and me, standing by the dining room table. I held up my hand with the engagement ring on it. His eyes widened considerably. The noise in the kitchen was increasing. I could still hear raised voices. David walked into the dining-room, carrying a vegetable bowl. He placed it slowly and methodically in the centre of the table, saying nothing. He returned to the kitchen. George was cracking jokes that neither Ian nor I were listening to. David returned with another bowl of vegetables and sat down. He whispered to me, "She's upset because we already have our rings!" I was very embarrassed and uncomfortable. Ian started to grin – he seemed to enjoy the constant emotional eruptions that frequently emanated from the kitchen at meal times. "Father, Daphne and I have just got engaged!" "Ah, I thought that might have happened. Your mother upset is she?" said George Mills.

At this point Molly Mills emerged from the kitchen, very flushed, carrying the rest of the meal. She sat down and we all regarded her silently. Ian made light hearted banter, which infuriated Molly, but he was trying to defuse the charged atmosphere. And I was sitting bolt upright on my chair thinking "Is this the way it's going to be for the rest of my life?" David was trying to appease his mother, and the meal dragged uncomfortably on. The empty plates were swept away and there was more banging of dishes and pans out in the kitchen. Ian went out and brought in a pot of cream, and George padded back in with a bowl of fruit salad. Ian said, "I adore cream!" and shook it vigorously. He hadn't realised that his mother had already undone the lid, and the cream shot up onto the ceiling and dripped back down onto the table cloth. I giggled nervously. And even Ian had frightened himself. "Quick, David! Go out into the kitchen and distract Mother for at least five minutes and I will clear up the mess and serve up." David hurried out of the room and I could hear him engage his mother in conversation. I heard afterwards she was raging on about the engagement, the rings, the wedding, and so on. In the mean time, Ian had climbed up onto the table, wiped the ceiling with a tea towel that had been left on one of the chairs, and mopped up the table, moving mats to hide damp patches. Then he quickly served up the fruit salad, dropping small spoonfuls of cream on each dish. He called out, "We've started our puddings. Hurry up!"

David and my new future mother-in-law walked back into the dining room, and we were silently eating our pudding. Molly reached out for the pot of cream. She sensed an atmosphere not of her own making. She looked at all our faces, and we continued eating our pudding. "What's been going on?" "Nothing, Mother. Get on with your pudding." Ian said. She picked up the pot of cream to add some more to the meagre amount in her bowl. "Where's all the cream gone? This was a full pot! Ian, it was you, wasn't it? You always take most of the cream." "Sorry, Mother, I couldn't resist it!" Ian smiled. "Anyway, excuse me now. I'm off to football." And with that Ian walked out of the room.

My mind is a blank on the rest of that day. Memorable and not all a bed of roses, and sadly it was a foretaste of sagas to come.

The following day was Sunday. I was a little late going to church as I had forgotten to put on my engagement ring. It was a bit loose when my hands were cold and I had stowed it back in its box for the night. I ran upstairs into the choir vestry and quickly slipped on my royal blue gown, and white starched collar and frilled cuffs. I walked over to the mirror to put on the velvet choir hat, and lined up with the rest of the choir ready to go back downstairs and into the church. Eleanor was standing next to me. We were very good friends. She was going out with Ian Mills. Her twin sister Susan came occasionally to the choir, and I really liked them both; they were good friends of mine. We filed into the choir pews, sang our introit, and the service began. I was very conscious of my sparkling triple diamond engagement ring and felt that everyone was looking at it. In fact nobody noticed it, until half way through the service, when Eleanor poked me, and pointed to the ring. "WHO?" she asked in a loud whisper. "Guess!" I whispered back. Eleanor glanced up to make sure Mr Nicholson hadn't noticed us whispering. He was busy perusing the music for the anthem we were about to stand and sing. I shrugged and grinned at her. "WHO?" she poked me again. I glanced at Eleanor, and pointed over towards the tenors sat near the organ. Most of them were elderly and married. "Not David Mills!" I nodded.

"The choir will now sing the anthem: "How lovely are thy dwellings fair"." We quickly stood up, and waited for Mr Nicholson to commence conducting. The organ played the entry and we were in. Sopranos leading the way. We finished the anthem and sat down, and the sermon commenced. I knew Eleanor was bursting with questions. She whispered: "I heard there was a huge upset at lunch yesterday. Ian came straight up to our house after football and wasn't keen to go home till he thought his mother had gone to bed!" I nodded my head and whispered, "We can talk later. I will phone you."

Mrs Mills decided that the engagement should remain secret from the church for a while. I couldn't see why. The following Sunday, after morning service, I filed away all the choir music in the cupboard under the organ loft, which was my normal choir duty. Then, also, as part of my job, I climbed up into the pulpit and marked all the pages in the minister's hymn book ready for the evening service. I had almost completed the job when I noticed the church caretaker standing by the choir door, observing me. I looked up and smiled. "You'll never make a minister's wife. Can't see you as a minister's wife. Nah! Never! I wouldn't even try if I were you!"

"Who said I was going to be a minister's wife, anyway?" I asked him from the pulpit. "Never you mind! I hear what's being said. Not much passes me by! There's talk about you, you know."

I ignored his last remarks and found the final hymn for the evening service and marked it, my hands shaking. I slowly put the hymn book on the pulpit ledge, checked that the Bible was handy, and the glass of water still topped up. I turned and walked down the steps, and when I looked up at the door I realised that the caretaker had gone.

I really couldn't understand why the engagement was meant to be a secret from the church! And it wasn't a secret for long as my father announced our engagement in the local Southampton Evening Echo! By this time David, probably at his mother's suggestion, had arranged for me to help run the Cubs, which was part of the Boy Scout movement at the church. This was a bit of a nightmare. I had to learn strange songs, and tying knots, and running team games, and quite a few other things that I was not the least interested in. One lad, aged about 10, with big ears, arrived every week with a new story of the way his dad had terrorised and beaten him. In those days no one took any notice; it seemed that parents could do what they liked to discipline their children. Altogether it was a very un-enjoyable task.

Time flew by and David was frantically looking for a church that would call him as their minister. If he didn't have a church by September he would be called up, into the army, to do his National Service. The race was on.

On top of this, two problems occurred. One was that David had either contracted a virus or was having some sort of a breakdown. He couldn't stop shaking, and had a fever. The matron of the theological college recommended he should be sent home for complete rest. David was on the phone to me, as was matron. David wanted me to come up with his parents to Manchester to fetch him home. His mother was not very pleased but eventually I was allowed to travel with them. I slept in Matron's flat and the Mills' slept in a guest house somewhere. We travelled back the next day and I could tell David was far from well.

The next day was Sunday, and Mrs Mills was due to sing a solo at church. I decided to skip church and visit David at his house in Leigh Road. I rang the doorbell at 11am, knowing the church service would have started. I was completely astonished when Mrs Mills opened the front door. She said, "I knew you would come, so I cancelled my solo. You can't see David. He must be left alone, in peace." I tried to persuade her to change her mind but she was adamant and said he was asleep. At this point George came to the front door, and ushered me back down the drive to the gate, where my Lambretta was parked. "Sorry!" George apologised. "Molly won't change her mind." I felt in my pocket, and handed Mr Mills some money to go toward the petrol for my trip to and from Manchester the previous day. "Don't be silly!" he said. But I smiled, and said that I was taught always to pay my way and contribute to expenses. He shook his head and I turned away, returning home and worrying a great deal about David.

I later discovered from Matron, and then from David, that Mrs Mills had been writing rather upsetting letters to David about me, and our engagement, and telling him in no way could or should he marry me. She also said in one of her many letters that she had written to the Principal of the college forbidding him to take the marriage ceremony. I later learned she had forbidden and threatened our own minister at Avenue, Vine Russell, and two other local ministers.

Finally David recovered sufficiently to return to take his university finals. He failed his Greek and Hebrew and passed everything else. This was a blessing in disguise as it meant he had to continue going to Manchester University for another year, to complete his degree, and consequently must find a church in the north of England. I thought it probably wiser to start our married life away from parents. A large and lovely church in Newcastle under Lyme showed great interest in David, and asked if I would go with him for a second visit. This I agreed to do, travelling on an overnight bus, and we spent the weekend being entertained by the church. They said they would like to call David as their minister, but would prefer that he either marry before being ordained, or else wait a year. They did not want a distraction of a minister planning a wedding at the start of his ministry.

David and I rode back to Manchester on the bus, discussing what we should do. On reaching the theological college, Matron immediately invited us in for tea, and asked us our plans. We told her our dilemma. She said, "How's David going to look after himself, and the church as well. Better to get married, and then you, Daphne, can look after the manse and the meals and so on while David gets on with the job." It sounded so sensible and reasonable.

She asked us about the manse, the minister's house, and how many bedrooms it had, how big it was. We said we had no furniture at all, except David's college stuff. She said she had a friend who ran a furniture warehouse, and another friend who sold carpets, cheaply. I phoned up my father and asked if I could have three more days off work! He said yes, be back for Wednesday evening, in time to type up the Saints programme on Thursday. With Matron's ideas, and contacts, and my savings, and a bit of money David had, we bought all the furniture and carpets we needed, and set a date for our wedding – July 18th, 1959. I was 21 and David was almost 26. David saw me back to the train station in Manchester, and waved me off from the platform. We had a plan. The train would pull into Southampton station at 7.15pm. And I would immediately tell my father we wanted to be married, no, we were going to be married on July 18th. At 7.15pm precisely, David would phone his parents and tell them our wedding date. It was now July 3rd and would mean we would need to be married by Special Licence.

I now have to digress a bit!

A few weeks before my trip up to Newcastle under Lyme and Manchester, Valerie, my sister, had announced her engagement and forthcoming marriage to my parents. We all liked Basil, and it was a foregone conclusion that they would eventually get married. But here my father put his foot down. There were yet more upsets. Valerie was forbidden to marry Basil until he had passed all his architects exams. As he was doing this in his spare time and not as a full time college course, this would be a few more years down the road.

The row would not abate, and as Valerie said she was definitely going to marry Basil this summer she was told to leave the house. Basil had already got a job in Guildford, and it was getting more and more difficult for Valerie and Basil to meet up each weekend. Mum, Dad and Roger went off on holiday to Italy, and Valerie was told to be gone from Rownhams House before they came back.

Valerie and I were deeply upset, and I really felt for her. I couldn't believe what was happening. I loved her dearly and I could feel her pain. It seemed she had to choose between home and Basil. She chose Basil. She packed her bags and left, moving into a small cottage up near Guildford, and set a date for her wedding in an Anglican church in Guildford. We kept in touch by phone.

While my parents and Roger were still away on holiday in Italy, Valerie let me know she and Basil were getting married the following Saturday and invited me up to their wedding.

I caught a bus up to Guildford, staying overnight, and drove with Valerie in a taxi to the huge church she and Basil had chosen. The wedding was lovely and a small group of friends were gathered to wish Valerie and Basil every happiness in their future.

Then I returned to Rownhams House and my parents and Roger returned from holiday. I told Mum that Valerie was married and that I had gone to the service. She was very quiet and I think she was really upset about it all.

So when I arrived back off the train from Manchester, after visiting David at his Theological College, approximately two weeks after Valerie's wedding, and told my father my wedding date, I fully expected the same treatment as Valerie had had, especially as David had failed his degree! But Dad had already lost one daughter and was being cautious about losing another. There were only fifteen days to go till our wedding day – a near impossibility! Dad had not said yes or no by the time we got home. But as we walked in the front door of Rownhams House, the phone was ringing. I walked over to the switchboard, and switched the phone through to my father's office, and he immediately headed in that direction. I hovered nearby, guessing it was my future mother-in-law. She was in floods of tears, demanding that my father stop the wedding, and trying to pull every trick she could to forbid the wedding. At this point my father got indignant. What was so very wrong about his daughter marrying Molly's son? Of course it's short notice, but the wedding will go ahead. Dad put down the phone and said, "I can't stand women in tears, trying to get their own way!"

The wedding went ahead on the 18th July, and Mrs Mills sat in the deacons' vestry, refusing to come into the service, saying she wasn't well, following a fairly recent operation in the local hospital. My father refused to allow my sister to come to the wedding, which cast a cloud over the day for me and quite a few of the guests.

When we arrived at the Manse in Newcastle, Staffordshire, the following day after our wedding, we found the church people had been in. They had filled the house with flowers, and the larder with food, and had laid out the carpets and arranged the furniture in some semblance of order. David and I had been up the previous week in a hired van, fetched the furniture and carpets from Manchester, and delivered them, plus my belongings from Southampton, and left it piled up untidily in the house. We had to rush back with the van before paying another day's hiring fee.

CHAPTER SIX

Four days after our wedding the day of David's Ordination and Induction service as a minister of Newcastle under Lyme's Congregational Church took place, attended by his parents, and a huge number of church people and local key people. David looked very reverent and handsome in his gown and clergy collar. We then settled down to "the ministry".

David commenced his twice weekly visits to Manchester University to continue his studies in Greek and Hebrew, borrowing my Lambretta, Bambi, which my father had shipped up to us on one of his lorries. I quite often rode pillion and spent the afternoon with Matron at the college. By the time he got his degree a year later I was expecting our first child, and we had changed my beloved old faithful Lambretta for a little three wheeled bubble car, a bright red two-seater Messerschmitt. We sat one behind the other, David usually driving. It had no reverse gear, so we had to get out of the car and swing it around by hand. We drove to Southampton in it after taking the Christmas morning service. Snow was forecast and the roads were icy as we drove through the Cotswolds. On several hills I had to get out and push the bubble car. I thought, "I think my unborn baby would have been safer on the Lambretta!"

The first year at the church was joyous and difficult! I discovered to my horror that as the minister's wife I was automatically President of the Women's Meeting (elderly ladies) and Chairman of The Young Wives Group (young women, not all married!). I was also automatically treasurer of the Women's Day of Prayer for Newcastle under Lyme. The trouble was as well as being ill-equipped for these jobs, I had also lost my voice. The previous March before I got married I had had a bad bout of laryngitis, but had not been allowed to take time off work, and also the Operatic were doing their final rehearsals for Gilbert and Sullivan's Yeoman of the Guard. I pushed and strained my voice, and mouthed my way through some of the performances. By the end of the week not much sound was coming out. Seven months later my father was becoming seriously worried, and arranged for me to travel from the Potteries, back to Southampton, to see a specialist.

Back at the church the women's meetings were getting on very nicely with other leaders doing my jobs, and I could sit happily in the back row and observe, without having to make speeches. So in some ways I didn't have much incentive to get my voice back – except I missed singing! But I travelled back to Southampton, praying on the way. I did a deal with God. "You give me back my voice, without any trouble and no operations, and I will only ever sing for You!"

My father came with me to see the throat specialist. If there had been anything wrong it wasn't found. The specialist concluded that I had just lost the ability to use my voice, and if given some help and tuition I would start using my vocal chords again properly! Dad was very pleased, and I was pleased, but mystified. Almost immediately my voice was back to full strength, with no outside help, but I told the Young Wives and the Women's Meeting that I was happy for others to lead them.

As I was only 21 years old my heart was really with the young people of the church. There were a large number of teenagers, boys and girls, and these became my friends. They thought it was wonderful to have a young minister and his wife, rather than the very elderly couple who came before us. They seemed a bit wild, and not very interested in the spiritual side of the church. We had become friends with the Baptist minister and his wife, and we had the bright idea to invite the Baptist young people to the Congregational church to have a combined youth evening. The young Baptists, all committed Christians, duly piled into our church hall, and played games and generally chatted with our youngsters. While we were washing up at the end of the evening, Pam Biggin, one of the more outspoken of our youth fellowship said, "You don't want us to be like them, do you?" I knew she was referring to the Baptists. I stopped washing up, and turned to face Pam who was wiping a cup vigorously with a damp tea towel. "Well, actually, yes, Pam, we do!"

With a lot of hard work and prayer, and some imaginative devotional epilogues at the end of games evenings, the young people began to change. They were always encouraged to come up to the Manse, and it soon became a habit for them all to pile into our house after church on a Sunday evening (as long as they had genuinely been to church first!). I soon realised young people were not good at wiping their feet before tramping in on our new carpets. They were also rather clumsy with our new wedding china. When my beloved best tea pot got dropped on the stone tiled kitchen floor I opened my mouth to yell. No sound came out – I found myself smiling at the guilty teenage lad, and said, “Don’t worry, it’s not important!” In a flash Jesus had shown me these young people were far more precious than a smart Denby teapot.

From then on the young people became my family, our family. And almost fifty years later I am still in touch with many of them and we are still very good friends. Some of them are now deacons, elders, junior church teachers, youth leaders, and even in full time ministry in other churches.

But I am jumping on too fast! Initially the parents of the young people were very glad that David Mills and I were helping the young people, and the group was enlarging and became a force to be reckoned with within the church. The young people always reported what people were saying about us; they were our faithful friends! One lad, aged about 16, confided in David some problem he had. The father got wind of the fact that his son had shared some secret and insisted that David tell him what it was about. David refused to betray the confidence, and the father remained distant from us for the rest of our ministry there.

The young people occasionally took an evening service and their love of the Lord was plain to see. Many of the church members told us how wonderful it was to see the church filling up with such keen mature youngsters.

Once a year David was invited back to preach at the Avenue Church in Southampton. They paid so well that it covered our travelling expenses of the four hundred miles involved, and gave us some pocket money. So we got into the habit of spending August at Rownhams House, and a few days at the Mills’ house in Leigh Road also.

David, in view of the pending extension to our family had sold the Messerschmitt, and replaced it with a Goggomobile. This was a four seater car with four wheels. It was half the size of a Mini, but we would be able to put a baby’s carrycot on the back seat! Our first baby was due to be born in the August, thirteen months after our wedding. My father organised for the Southampton football doctor to keep an eye on me, and he arranged a midwife to stand by who lived locally. The baby would be born at Rownhams House. In those days it was normal to have a home birth, and you were only allowed to have the baby born in hospital if complications were foreseen.

The midwife popped in to see me on the due date bringing a two ounce bottle of castor oil. "Take this with a cup of orange juice and the baby will be on its way in no time, dear." I duly did as I was told, though the taste was so terrible my whole body screamed in rejection of it as it travelled down my throat. But it did the trick and the baby was on its way! I spent the day wandering around the grounds of Rownhams House, probably in full view of the office staff, doubling up with contractions every fifteen minutes of so. In the evening David, Roger, Mum and I played football on the lawn. I was determined to score a goal and kicked the ball a bit too hard. I don't know where it went, as I was only conscious of a terrible pain in my pelvis.

The pain increased considerably and the baby was on its way! Finally our lovely baby daughter arrived at 4.45am, helped by the doctor and the local midwife. "It will be easier the next time, Mrs Mills," said the midwife. "You think I'm going to go through that again? Never!" was my response.

Tessa was born in Valerie's old bedroom. It had two large windows. One was facing the lake, and the other window looked out on what used to be the tennis courts. They were long since overgrown and the land was now a mini forest. The bedroom was a very long walk along the upstairs corridor, down the long wide winding staircase, along another corridor to the kitchens. There David was constantly being sent for more boiling water, or something, so that by the time the baby appeared he was totally exhausted. We called her Tessa Ruth – she was born with a full head of brown curly hair and a smart blonde streak to one side.

About 8.30 am my father knocked at the door and came in. He gazed at the new born baby, smiled proudly and said, "Another little Daph!" He wandered over to the window and stared out towards the lake. "You can phone your sister and invite her to come and see the baby if you like," said my father gruffly, and after admiring his first grandchild again he walked out of the bedroom.

My mother, who had been hugely helpful while the baby was being born, found Valerie and Basil's phone number for us, and sent David down into the hall to phone them. They came two days later, and the terrible rift in the family began to be healed. I greatly admired Valerie's forgiving capacity, though I could tell she was still hurting. When Dad was dying of cancer three years later she was the one that spent the most time at Rownhams helping Mum during those difficult days, even though by then she was expecting her own first baby, Ian.

Pam and Gwen Biggin from the youth fellowship were at the Manse when we travelled back to Newcastle under Lyme eight days later. Soon many of the young people wanted to be first to take the baby for a walk in her new pram. But at that point I said "no"! I was so looking forward to putting Tessa in her pram and taking her for a walk. Once I had done the maiden voyage, then the young people could take it in turns as long as they were very careful!

When Tessa was old enough to sit up in her cot, I draped the cot with lots of pretty plastic beads. The beads were called poppits, and they all locked together to make as long a necklace as you wanted, in many different colours. My mother in law had given me so many of these poppit necklaces that, when joined together, they could be draped all around the top of the cot. It never entered my head that Tessa would eat them! But I went to pick her up out of her cot one day after her morning nap, only to discover the poppit chain was broken and rather a lot were missing. There were no ill effects.

The church continued to expand, and Sunday morning services were almost full, and the Sunday evening services were well attended, and particularly by the young people and Keele University students. David wore his Manchester University gown with its blue and white fur lined hood every Sunday, and we both used to stand at the door at the end of every service and chat and shake hands with each person as they left. As often as I could I would go visiting the parishioners with David, and generally get to know the people. We lived in a coal mining area, with other heavy, dirty industrial factories around. There was a lot of poverty, as well as a lot of wealth in our church. The church considered we were wealthy because we both had parents who drove up to visit us in their smart cars. The Mills would bring their Rover car towing the caravan behind them and park in a nearby farm. My parents would drive up in their Jaguar to watch the Saints play either Stoke City or Port Vale. They would stay at the best hotel in the town – and the church people thought we were rich! Consequently we were kept on minimum stipend, and never had enough money to last until the end of the month. So by about the 25th day of each month we did more visiting of parishioners around meal times with the hope of being fed and saving a few pennies.

As I mentioned some students from Keele University were attending the evening services. The university was about four miles away from the church. David later became the Free Church Chaplain to Keele University. Princess Margaret was the Chancellor of the University, so I managed to see this incredibly beautiful and petite princess at close quarters. I much admired her, but the tragedy of her broken romance with Peter Townsend changed her considerably.

Two years after Tessa was born we were expecting baby number two. As the baby was due in August we followed through the same plan as before: a holiday at Rownhams House, same doctor, same midwife, and a remunerative preaching engagement for David, plus a wedding on the Saturday. Technology being a bit basic in those days, we had no idea if it was a boy or a girl; and there was some disagreement as to whether it was one or two babies, and "Are you sure you have your dates right, Mrs Mills?" One midwife said, during the month of June, while we were holidaying in Jersey, Channel Islands, "your baby looks like it is due now, within a week!" Help! Let's at least get back to the mainland before anything happens, I thought.

We returned home to the manse at Newcastle, Staffordshire, but June came to an end, July came to an end, August arrived – and no baby had appeared! For the whole month of August we stayed at Rownhams House. Dr Ramsey, the Saints football doctor, visited me regularly, having long chats with my father about football, then checking me over. Dr Ramsey kept saying, "The baby will come when it's ready. All is well!"

But it was the nearing the end of August. I then panicked. We were due back at the church in Newcastle on September 3rd, and we were already in the last days of August. "If I have the baby now," I said to David, "I will be stuck down here in Southampton for a couple of weeks, you will be working back home, and have to come back and get me – and you won't be here to help with the baby. Mum will never manage all those trips up and down the stairs for the midwife!"

"Well, what do you suggest?" said David, continuing to concentrate on his sermon preparation for Sunday at Avenue. "I think you should take me back home tomorrow, Friday, and then come straight back here. Perhaps stay with your parents? Then you can take the wedding and do the church services, and drive back

Monday morning!" David looked up from his books. "Do you think you can manage on your own? What if the baby comes in the middle of the night and you are all alone in the manse?"

"Well, why can't a couple of the youth fellowship stay with me till you get back? They'd love that!" I said.

"What about Tessa? I don't think you can manage her on your own – that's too risky! Shall I keep her down here and my mother can look after her. Mother will adore that! Leave a bag of clothes and toys here and I will bring her back Monday morning. I'll phone Mother now and see what she says."

David walked out to the hall telephone and was back very soon. "Mother would be delighted. In fact she said she will keep Tessa until after the baby is born and she and Father will bring her back and come and see the new baby at the same time."

I was very dubious. I didn't mind Tessa staying with my in-laws for a weekend, but much longer – no, that didn't seem a good idea. But I thought I would deal with that problem later. "Okay, I think we'd better start packing and organising. We will have to leave by about 7am tomorrow so you can get back by tomorrow night, ready for the wedding on Saturday."

Arrangements were hastily made, and we drove back to Newcastle under Lyme next day, leaving Tessa, aged two, with my mother-in-law. David had a quick snack lunch at the Manse and commenced the drive back to Southampton, two hundred miles – making four hundred in the day.

We had brought the budgie back in her cage, and she was chirping happily in the sunlight in the lounge. I suppose I had better telephone the surgery and let the doctor know I am back here and am his responsibility again, I thought to myself. I dialled the number and was put through to a new young doctor – Dr Kirkland, who obviously had my notes in front of him. "Hello, Mrs Mills. Well what did you have, boy or girl?"

"Well, it didn't come – I mean it wasn't born in Southampton, so I thought I had better let you know I am back here in Newcastle under Lyme."

"You mean, you haven't had the baby YET?" Dr Kirkland raised his voice in shock and annoyance.

"No – but any day now," I answered breezily.

"Right! I'll be with you in five minutes!" and the phone went dead.

I looked at my watch, desperately wanting to speak to David. He would be driving towards Stafford, heading south, oblivious to any drama back home.

The doorbell rang. I opened the door. I'm not sure what I saw first. Dr Kirkland, or the ambulance – blue light flashing. "This is disgraceful and dangerous. I'm not even going to examine you. Your life is in danger. Your baby's life is in danger. You are going straight to hospital. You shouldn't even have travelled back here. Get your bag and I will see you into the ambulance." I was totally shocked at this turn of events. I grabbed my unpacked bag and some knitting and my purse. I was nearly five stone heavier than nine months ago, so I would say I waddled towards the ambulance and clambered in. I remember gazing out of the darkened windows – they seemed like pure clear glass and I thought all the people walking along the pavements could look in and see me. The hospital, called The Limes, was about two miles away.

The ambulance drove up to the door and I was promptly put into a side room just inside the front door, and told to lie on the bench bed. Three hours went by, and I was still there, waiting, and unattended. Eventually someone came in and asked if I had had supper. When I shook my head, the nurse or orderly said in an annoyed voice, "Well supper's over now. You should have said. I will see if I can find something for you." And ten minutes later she came back with a plate of cool chips. "What's happening? I've been here since just after 2 o'clock – I haven't seen a doctor or anyone. I'd rather be back home."

The woman looked at me, shrugged and walked out of the little ante room. But within ten minutes someone came in and ushered me into the main ward, and gave me a bed half way down on the left hand side. "We've had to turn a mother out of her bed to make room for you! Here's your bed, here's your locker. Unpack, and I will put your bag in the store room. " - Oh, a great welcome indeed!

I quickly did as I was told, and changed into my night clothes and got into bed, hating the place. I looked around the ward. Three pregnant women were lying down, with a drip in their arms. Some mothers were heavily pregnant but sitting up in bed chatting to each other. On either side of me were young mothers feeding their new born babies. And a woman opposite me was sobbing on and off – I found out later she had just lost her baby.

The evening visiting was just commencing, and I suddenly realised that I had left the budgie chirping away in the lounge. And the back door of the manse was unlocked! I asked one of the young mum's if there was a phone box anywhere, and she directed me to one in the corridor on route to the bathroom. I slipped out of bed and rang one of the deacons of the church, whose daughter was part of our youth fellowship. I hastily explained that I was in the Limes, and the budgie needed to be looked after. "Don't worry about a thing, Mrs Mills. One of us will pop in and visit you and fetch your front door key. Is there anything you want?" I said there wasn't. I was so miserable, for two pins I would leave when Mrs Bradley appeared to get my key!

Half an hour later, Mrs Bradley and their daughter Elaine walked on to the ward, smiling. They sat and chatted, and asked how our holiday in Southampton had gone. They filled me in with a little bit of church news, then got up to leave. "Harold will go up to the manse and collect the budgie for you, and lock the back door – check all is well. Don't you worry about anything. Just hurry up and have your baby."

"Do you think you could just phone my mother at Rownhams House, and tell her I'm in the Limes, please? Then she can get a message to the Mills family and David will find out where I am when he gets back to Southampton." They wrote down the phone number, and left.

All the other visitors on the ward had already left. The Matron walked in, and stopped by the end of my bed. "You're for the high jump tomorrow!" she said to me. I was so shocked that I couldn't reply. "High jump? What the hell does she mean?" I thought, and began to shake. Matron had moved onto the next bed. "How's your baby, Mrs Jones?"

The new young mother, holding her precious bundle in her arms said, "He won't feed from me." Matron took the baby from her, held him up high above her face and shook him, (fairly gently). His little mouth turned down and he started to cry. Matron handed him back to Mrs Jones. "You just have to persevere." She said and walked on to cause further havoc down the ward.

By this time it was dark outside, and the windows were wide open. It was a hot, balmy night. I suddenly became aware that some of the mothers, and mothers-to-be, were getting out of bed and stamping on the floor and laughing. I watched more carefully, and realised that some "May bugs" were flying into the ward, and meeting a grisly death on the floor.

Matron re-appeared and came up to my bed again. "Your mother's just phoned. I said you were in good hands." And she walked away. I was furious and helpless! Why couldn't she have fetched me and let me talk to her? I didn't have enough coins for a long distance call from the phone box.

If I have my baby in this place I will be totally miserable, and I will hate the baby for making me be here, I thought. I waited till Matron left the room, and the ward quietened down. Time ticked by. I sat up in my hospital bed pretending to knit. I looked at my watch – 11pm – over an hour since any staff had been in to look at us. I am shaking as I tell this part of my story! The memory will never go away.

I secretly reached my handbag out of my locker and put my purse into my toilet bag. I slipped on my floral quilted dressing gown, and said to anyone who was interested, "I'm just off to the bathroom!"

I walked out of the ward, noticing Matron's door slightly open, and low voices emerging. I turned right, walking the opposite way. I nipped into the bathroom, and noticed some trestle tables propped up against the wall. I locked myself in, and thought for a moment. No one seemed to be about. I unlocked the door and peeped out. Not a soul around! I turned right, and continued down a long corridor. It was all in darkness. I came across some double doors, sort of French windows in style, and pushed them. Luckily, they swung open and I found myself in a quadrangle.

It was pitch black but there I could see lights coming from a pub across the road. By this time I was really nervous, but equally determined. I would not have my baby born in that horrid hospital! I ran across the quadrangle, with my best fourteen stone waddle, only to realise there were rusty iron railings all around and seemingly no way out! I was terrified someone from the hospital would see me. I hastily walked along the fence seeking a way out. Luckily I found a gap where some railings were broken. I climbed over a small wall, through the gap, and out into the street. I fled across the road and into a phone box outside the pub. I had two pennies, enough for a local call. There was a list of taxi cab numbers above the coin collector. I rang the first number and asked for a taxi to come as quickly as possible to the pub opposite the Limes hospital.

I hid behind some parked cars and within about five minutes a taxi drew up, and I climbed in, much relieved to be out of sight of any hospital staff.

Phew! I was free!

"Where do you want to go, Madam?" the taxi driver asked – obviously having noted that I was in my night clothes!

"4 Norman Grove, Basford, please." He turned the taxi around in the road and drove back in the direction he had come from. We were about a mile from the Manse when I suddenly remembered I didn't have my front door key! Oh no!

"Um . . I've change my mind. Could you drop me at 72 King Street, and then come back and fetch me in about half an hour?" I asked.

The taxi driver glanced in the mirror at me and sighed heavily. It was going to be one of those nights, was it? He dropped me at the Bradleys house. I rang the door bell, and heard someone coming to open the door. The taxi had driven off. By now it was about 11.30pm. Mr Bradley, one of the church deacons, opened the door. "Mrs Mills! I thought you were in hospital. Whatever...?" Mrs Bradley came running into the passageway. I started to say that I wanted my front door key, but burst into tears instead. "Whatever's happened? What's the matter? Are you all right?" Mrs Bradley put her arm around me and drew me into their sitting room. "Harold, make Mrs Mills a cup of tea."

I stopped crying and started to giggle. I wiped away my tears and looked at Mrs Bradley's anxious face. By this time Elaine, aged about 17, had walked in. "Mrs Mills has had a shock!" said Sybil. "Dad's making her a cup of tea." Stuart, one of the other young people from church, was also around.

"I ran away. I hated it. I was on my way home, but I haven't got my front door key!" I said. I felt safe with the Bradleys, they were a special family in the church and totally loyal to us.

The taxi will be back in a minute, I thought. I told the Bradleys the whole story. I sipped my tea, feeling calmer. Midnight came and the taxi hadn't arrived. We waited another half hour and still it didn't return. So Mr Bradley donned his jacket and cap and walked up to the phone box half a mile away and called another taxi. Elaine organised for Stuart's sister Gwen to stay the night with her and me at the Manse. The taxi arrived, and we climbed in.

When we got back to the Manse the phone was ringing! "Police here! Is that Mrs Mills?"

"Yes." I started to shake again."Are you all right? We had a call from the Matron of the Limes hospital to say that you were missing. We've been out looking for you for the past hour!"

"Sorry. I'm fine. I didn't want to stay there!" I replied. The policeman chipped in, "That's all we need to know. As long as you are all right! Good night!" and the phone went dead.

I showed the two young teenagers where they could sleep and we hastily settled down to what was left of the night. Around nine in the morning the phone went again. It was my mother! "What's going on? I've just phoned the hospital to find out if you had had a boy or a girl and they said you had left!"

"Well, they weren't going to do anything last night to bring the baby on, so I left and came home!" I said, crossing my fingers. We talked briefly about this and that and then Mum said, "Did you run away?" I admitted I had. "Please don't tell Dad, he will be furious and think I'm an awful coward." I pleaded with my mother. She promised to keep my secret and asked what I was going to do next. " Well, two of the youth fellowship are coming to stay with me tonight, and as soon as it's dark we are going for a run round the marsh. That'll shake the wretched baby out." I told her. "Oh Daphne, please be careful. Don't do anything silly. Shouldn't you ring the doctor?"

"No way. He will only send me back to that horrid place!"

The doorbell rang, and I hastily said goodbye to my mother, and peered out through the window. It was Dr Kirkland. I decided not to open the door. Then he started thumping the glass front door! Then he gave up and started kicking and thumping the side gate and the garage doors. I could tell he was determined to get in so I opened the front door. He was exceedingly angry and said Matron had been on to him, and I must go back right away. I had brought disgrace on the hospital and don't expect nice treatment when I went back.

I started to bargain with him. Eventually he agreed that if the baby hadn't come by tomorrow I must go back, and I agreed. I was determined the run around the marsh would do the trick. The doctor left, and the midwife arrived! She was a beautiful plump, young blonde lady, and had always been very sweet to me.

She bustled in, put her bag on the settee, sat down and burst into tears. She hid her head in her hands, as I watched her. "You must go back to the Limes right away. Your baby's life is in danger. And don't you care about your own life? Your baby is well over due. Please go back."

It was Saturday morning, the first of September 1962.

"Look, I feel fine. And I promised Dr Kirkland I would go back to the Limes tomorrow, Sunday. I've got friends here to stay with me overnight. I've got your phone number and I promise I will call you if I go into labour."

The midwife stood up reluctantly, picked up her bag and left the house.

During that Saturday I had plenty of visitors: Mrs Bradley walked up the hill to see me. Later Mrs Biggin came. She was the mother of seven children and had expert knowledge on when babies choose to arrive – she was bright and cheerful and very reassuring to me. One of her four sons, Stuart, also a member of our youth fellowship called in to see me. He had cycled up the hill, and offered to do any shopping for me.

At 9pm that evening when it was fairly dark, Elaine and Stuart arrived to supervise my evening exercise! and I ran, yes, ran round the marsh, probably a couple of miles. They never let me slow up or walk. "Come on, Mrs Mills, you said you wanted to run the whole way. Keep going. We will make you a nice cup of tea when you get back – and don't forget you've got that bottle of castor oil to take!"

We got back to the Manse. Elaine put the kettle on, and found the bottle of castor oil. "I've already taken some a few days ago." "Well, it didn't work, did it? Try it tonight!" I swallowed the bottle full, mixed up with orange juice, desperately trying not to vomit it straight back up again. My aim was to have the baby TONIGHT, and never to enter the door of the Limes again.

Stuart cycled off home, and his sister Gwen arrived to stay the night at the manse with Elaine and me.

The girls went off to bed, and I followed shortly afterwards. At 2am I woke with terrible tummy pains. Was it the castor oil or was it the baby? I lay there waiting in the darkness. I realised the pains were very strong and at regular intervals. Praise God! Thank you, God, so much. I can't believe it! I waited for another two hours, then crept downstairs and phoned the midwife. "So sorry to wake you. It's Mrs Mills. The baby is coming."

"Marvellous. Wonderful! Well done, Daphne. I'll be right over. Have you got anyone with you? Good! Would you put the kettle on – perhaps two kettles if you've got two – or a saucepan of water! See you in about ten minutes."

By this time Gwen and Elaine had realised something was going on. They got up and we all had a cup of tea. They watched in horror as I doubled up with pain every few minutes. They were only 17!

Elaine said, "I think I'd better go and fetch my mum!" She ran as fast as her high heels would carry her. She had a mile to run in the pitch darkness. She thought the baby would be born at any moment, so, she told me later, as she was running she said to God, "If I put my feet down will you pick them up for me?" The prayer did the trick, and in no time at all Elaine was back at the manse with Sybil, her mother.

The midwife arrived, smiling and cheerful. She told me to go back to bed. Sybil sat on a chair next to my bed and held my hand for the next few hours, quietly tolerating my squeezing her hand very tightly at times.

Gwen and Elaine sat on the stairs listening to any sounds that came out of the bedroom for the rest of the night! Nigel was born at 9.15am. I desperately wanted the baby to appear before David left for the morning church service at Avenue, so I could tell him the news. The midwife checked the baby all over and then allowed Sybil to make the all important phone call. The timing was perfect. David was just about to leave his parents' house to walk to church to take the morning service. David told the congregation from the pulpit that his son had just been born. Then he announced the first hymn. All was well!

Over the next three days I had forty-seven visitors, mostly the youth fellowship. They helped run the manse, answer the phone, get the meals, cups of tea and do the washing up. They boiled water and washed nappies. – I was 23 years old, and very happy. Three days later I had a message from the Limes. Please collect my belongings that I had left in my locker. Stuart, offered to go on his bike. He was a very handsome young man of about sixteen years of age. He reached the Limes and was ushered into the Matron's office. He was then reprimanded for not keeping control of his wife, and eventually was handed my personal belongings. He cycled back to the Manse, and handed me my bag. His face was scarlet, and he looked uncomfortable. "Was it all right? No problems getting my stuff?" I asked.

Then Stuart admitted that Matron thought he was Mr Mills and he had got into trouble for not keeping his wife under control! The young people and their parents who were involved in Nigel's birth kept my escapade and escape from the Limes secret from the rest of the church, and my reputation remained intact!

Not long afterwards the Limes hospital closed down.

I always tease Nigel, my son, that he had the police out looking for him even before he was born!

David returned home to the Manse and his new born son around midnight on the day of his birth. He had taken the evening service at Avenue Church and then driven from Southampton back to the Midlands to be with us. Tessa returned back home to us a few days later with my in-laws, and wouldn't speak to me for a week. She was very upset and seemed to be very dependent on my mother-in-law who insisted on staying in the area to keep an eye on us for the next fortnight. I was very upset too. I adored Tessa and we had had such a good relationship up to this point. After a short while Tessa settled down again. She loved her new baby brother and was immensely helpful in fetching and carrying baby creams, nappies and so on. She was also good at amusing him.

I had used a washing up bowl to bath Tessa when she was small and thought I could do the same with Nigel, but before he was a month old he was too big to fit into the bowl and we went out and bought a proper baby bath.

Tessa loved playing "Mummy". One day I strapped Nigel into his pushchair, ready for us to go for a walk. Nigel was sucking his bottle (made of pyrex glass in those days). I opened the front door, and reached for my handbag. Tessa anticipated the next step. Push the push chair out of the front door, and down the step. But the push chair was heavier than she thought, and tipped over. Baby Nigel fell face down onto the concrete pathway, and his bottle smashed. I grabbed the pushchair, and unstrapped my screaming baby. He was covered in so much blood from the broken bottle, I just ran up the road to a neighbour's house. Fortunately she was in.

I held Nigel while she bathed his face with warm water and disinfectant. The cuts were minor, though I suspect he still has a scar or two!

CHAPTER SEVEN

When I moved into the Manse in Newcastle under Lyme I brought with me a box of twenty or thirty pairs of assorted shoes. David said there was no room for them in the house and why would anyone want more than two or three pairs of shoes anyway? So the box was left in the garage. The shoes went mouldy and had to be thrown out. I also brought with me fifty pairs of clip-on earrings. There were gold gypsy earrings, my favourites, clusters of flowers of all colours, assorted bead earrings, a pair of black cats with green eyes, plain silver balls, gun metal grey clip on ones, and you name it, I had a pair of earrings for every possible outfit and occasion. Mysteriously, one by one, many gradually disappeared. Some snatched off by toddlers' sticky fingers, some seemed to roll off the dressing table, never to be seen again. When I sorted the remaining pairs and odd earrings I realised something mysterious was happening to my precious jewels.

Around this time, in the middle of one particular night, there was a huge crash and bang. I shot deep under the bed clothes, to protect myself from I knew not what. David moved in the opposite direction and was sat bolt upright in bed. I said nothing. My heart was thumping!

After a minute of silence, I felt David get out of bed. I remained deep under the covers. I heard him switch on the light, and waited expectantly for him to say, "Oh goodness me!" or something. I thought by this time that maybe the mirror had fallen off the dressing table. Nothing was said. I heard David go into the other two bedrooms, switching lights on and off: then the bathroom. Down on to the half landing where the toilet was: still nothing was said. I heard him walk down to the bottom of the stairs, more lights switched on and off. French windows opened. I heard David outside in the garden, beneath our bedroom window. Still nothing! By this time I had slid back up the bed, and was waiting for David's return, to tell me what he had found – probably the chimney had fallen off the roof and was lying on the lawn.

Lights were switched off and David walked back into the bedroom. He said nothing. "Well?" I asked impatiently. I didn't really worry about outside damage; the church had to pay for all repairs to do with the building!

"Nothing! I found nothing." This was scary! We both heard a huge crash; it couldn't possibly be nothing!

We eventually got back to sleep. Next morning I ran round to our elderly neighbours whose house was attached to ours. I asked them if they had heard a noise during the night?

"There's always noises in these houses!" the old man replied. He was really old – he had fought in the Boer War, he had told me proudly.

"Well, what is it?" I asked. "Well, you know we live over a coal mine. They blast day and night! It was probably a rock fall last night."

I was amazed, and wondered how far down the tunnels were under our house. I remembered baby-sitting, all alone in the house, and my hairbrush had slid off the mantelpiece. And another time when I was all alone in the house except for the children in bed a pencil had rolled off the dining room table when no one was near it. Mystery solved! Mr Hughes, our elderly neighbour, continued. "I expect you have noticed your floor boards – cracks widening? And the skirting boards are pulling away from the edges?"

I nipped back home, telling David I now knew where all my earrings were – they had fallen through the cracks in the floor boards! Later the Coal Board came round and sealed up some large cracks on the outside of the house, but refused to sort out the sinking floorboards inside.

When Nigel was born he was three pounds heavier than the average baby of those days at just under ten pounds – and always hungry. Whether he was allergic to milk I don't know, but he seemed to wail and scream a lot and no one had much sleep. Two of the church youth fellowship, Cynthia and Elaine, offered to sleep at our house for a few nights and look after the baby for us! So they came, and spent hours rocking the carrycot between them. They still laugh about it to this day. A young mother at the church who heard of our dilemma with Nigel, offered to take him for a few days and get him into a feeding routine. She had twin boys aged about five. We said, "Yes, please!" and Betty took Nigel off our hands while we had a few nights blissful uninterrupted sleep. Betty soon knocked our young son into shape and he returned home with a new feeding chart and an assortment of pots and tins of food!

We took a trip back to Southampton, and my father was very distressed to see his two little grandchildren squashed in the back of a very tiny midget of a car. He proceeded to negotiate with one of the transport managers to buy his blue Ford Anglia off of him! And then gave it to us. Then my father got annoyed with David for not being grateful enough for this wonderful gift. I was a bit irritated and embarrassed as well, with David! I felt he should have been prolific in his thanks! But David said later to me, “It’s all very well having a large car, but how are we going to afford to run it? It will cost more in insurance and petrol, and I’m not sure we’ve got the money. Besides the church people will really moan and criticize us for being too wealthy for them!”

There was no way we could give the gift back to my father and we sold the little orange Goggomobile locally and drove back to the Potteries in style.

Now we had a decent car we decided to take a regular day off each week and we often drove either into Wales or over towards the Peak district if it wasn’t raining.

Around this time David and I were asked if we would consider being counsellors at the Manchester Billy Graham Crusade. If we said “yes”, then we would have to go up to (I think) Liverpool for several once a week sessions of training. Our dear friend Sybil Bradley was volunteered by daughter Elaine to babysit for us! It was so kind of Sybil to come up to the manse and stay with Tessa and Nigel while we drove north for our training. The teaching was meticulous and thorough in every way, and I learnt to admire the Billy Graham organisation. Billy Graham first came to England when I was a young teenager, causing a huge furore in the national papers: both good and bad publicity.

Billy Graham toned down his Americanisms, in speech, dress and behaviour, and became a totally acceptable evangelist in Britain. Over the years I went to several of his campaigns, usually held in football stadiums, and often relayed by television screens to extra churches and halls for overflow meetings. At one point I was in the choir, directed by Cliff Barrows. Billy Graham did not come on stage until at least halfway through the proceedings, but when he did come on you could feel the dynamism and power of the Holy Spirit emanating from him. I would say he changed the face of England and brought many hundreds of people to meet Jesus Christ for themselves.

One of Billy Graham's team was Joe Blinco, formerly the Methodist minister at the Central Hall Church in Southampton. He knew my father well because it was his church hall my father borrowed for the old people's concerts and teas. Joe invited David and me to have a meal with him at their hotel in Manchester before the start of one of the evenings. As we got up to leave the table after dinner Joe said to me, "Tell your father I covet him for the Lord!" I gave Dad his message.

To attend a Billy Graham Crusade, was an awesome experience. To see the power of God at work, and to watch hundreds of people get up out of their seats and make their way towards the front of the arena, often some considerable distance from the back of the stands in the stadium, was a thrilling moment. As counsellors we would then get up out of our seats and stand alongside someone who had gone forward. After Billy Graham had spoken to them about how to commit their life to the Lord, then the counsellors would speak to each person on a one to one basis. We would take their name and address and the Billy Graham organisation would put them in touch with their nearest sympathetic church to follow them up.

One evening during the crusade in Manchester, I went forward myself, taking off my counsellor's badge, as I felt God calling me to rededicate myself to Him on the next stage of my work for Him. I had a wonderful wise counsellor, a minister, who gave me a scripture that still means a lot to me: "Faithful is He who calls you, who also will do it." Or another translation reads, "He who calls you is faithful, and He will do it." (1 Thessalonians chapter 5 verse 24).

It was the perfect word for me! If God calls me to do something, and I say yes I will, then He will actually do the job for me! And I have proved that true all my life while serving Him. The minister kept in touch with me for a year or so, just odd letters of encouragement, as I also kept in touch with those I had counselled on previous evenings.

We would get home about midnight, and David or I would give Sybil Bradley a lift home in the car. Sometimes Harold Bradley had walked up and joined Sybil for the evening. It was around this time that we had our first, black and white, television, and hopefully this was a bit of entertainment for the Bradleys on the rather long evenings, as we used to leave around 5pm to drive up to the Manchester Crusade.

One summer, we had a little girl of four to stay with us. Julie's mother had T.B. and was a long term patient in a sanatorium. She had five children, all parcelled out to various families in the church. Three children were hard work, but they enjoyed playing together in the garden and Julie made some friends just around the corner from the Manse. She had just returned home and we had the house to ourselves again when the door bell rang around eight o'clock one morning.

I ran downstairs to answer it! There stood a smart lady friend of ours, suitcase in hand. She was in some distress. She had had a row with her sister and brother-in-law with whom she lived. She had been asked to leave. They were strict Plymouth Brethren. I never found out what the row was about but I think our friend had found a boyfriend they didn't approve of. She lived with us for many months.

Around the same time Gladys Aylward, the London parlour maid turned Chinese Missionary, was brought over to England from Taiwan, Formosa, for a "This is Your Life" broadcast by English television. In one of our recent days off we had driven into Snowdonia, and driven past a film set. It looked like a Chinese village on fire. Next day in the newspaper we saw a report of a film being made of the story of the famous English missionary Gladys Aylward! The part of Gladys was played by Ingrid Bergman. David and I watched the broadcast of "This is your Life" and were very impressed with the tiny missionary and her small orphaned adopted son Gordon. Shortly after this we were told that Gladys was being inundated with invitations to preach and speak all over the British Isles, carrying with her two large suitcases of unopened letters. We were asked if we could help her.

Our contacts at the University came to the rescue and we set up an office in our dining room, and a team of people gave all their spare time to slitting open the letters, booking and banking the cheques and cash that had been sent in aid of her orphanage. Gladys and Gordon took over one of our bedrooms and we all squeezed up. Our friendly Brethren lady was still with us as well. For a three bed-roomed manse we were full to overflowing. Gladys made herself at home and was a pleasure to have around. Gordon, the little Chinese baby was younger than Tessa and older than Nigel. We used to bath them all together and they had great fun together, splashing each other and throwing sponges and flannels at each other.

I typed a lot of her personal correspondence. Gladys often stayed up after we had all gone to bed – and she would fill up two or three hours of tapes, dictating letters to her family in Taiwan, and friends in the British Isles. I would then spend hours typing these letters ready for Gladys to sign and send off. She was very homesick for her children, her rescued orphans. She was still looking after about a hundred children – her third family, as she called them!

Gladys was not only the star of the film “The Inn of the Sixth Happiness”, but also the heroine of the best selling paper back by Alan Burgess called “The Small Woman”. Although neither portrayed the story of Gladys’ exploits totally accurately, to her distress, the gist of the story is true. I became Gladys’ assistant secretary for a while, and organised her South coast tour of speaking engagements, and also drove her to various engagements in the north of England.

For a lady who had lived rough on the mountains of China, rescuing over a hundred children from the invading Japanese army, she was amazingly particular about her appearance. I once ironed her Chinese pantaloons, putting the crease in the wrong place. She snatched the offending garment off me, and re-ironed the creases correctly, reprimanding me for not doing the job properly!

Gladys loved any speaking engagements to the disadvantaged in prison, and was not so enthusiastic being asked to talk to my Crusader class that I helped to run locally. She regarded Crusaders as a money-privileged group of young ladies! One day she came back from Nottingham Jail with a very large and heavy stuffed toy dog. I think it was made of five or six coshes. Gladys gave it to Nigel. It was too heavy for Gordon to have and take back to Taiwan!

Gladys agreed to speak at an evening service in our Church in Newcastle just before returning back home to the orphanage she ran in Taiwan. So we booked her for the evening service, checking it out with our deacons first. Some of them didn’t know who Gladys Aylward was, but by all means let her preach if she wanted to. Some of those deacons walked in five minutes before the evening service to sit in their usual pew only to discover the church was packed, and it was standing room only, or maybe a seat tucked away at the back of the balcony. Wherever Gladys went she filled huge auditoriums. She was an amazing orator and had a great gift for winning souls for Christ, and volunteers for the mission field. Gladys was just under five feet high and we had to find a box for her to stand on so she could be seen over the top of the pulpit. We all felt very privileged to hear her speak. She not only spoke her Christianity, she lived it too!

Then when Gladys left to go back to Taiwan, our house became her head office.

CHAPTER EIGHT

The longer I was in the ministry, the more I became involved deeply in people's lives. I hold many secrets that can never be told! But I feel very glad to have been allowed by God, yes and trusted to share the hopes, fears, joys and failings of many people. I have sat beside people when they were dying, tried to comfort those grieving, and mopped the tears of teenagers in the grip of some trauma. I can't help thinking how many experiences I have had since the day I took a decision card at the Central Hall in Southampton and had decided to follow Jesus! I remember at a joint Crusader meeting with the boys and girls classes that we had a talk given by a missionary. At the end we were asked to put up our hands if we felt called to the mission field. I presumed this would mean Africa! I put up my hand – I was just sixteen years of age!

The winter that David and I had got engaged to marry was a very busy time at the Dell for the Southampton Football Club. My father asked David if he would like to earn some extra money, and instead of helping out at the post office as he usually did, perhaps he could help at the Dell. David agreed and became assistant secretary for the next few weeks. He did so well at the job that my father offered him a full time position. He was given twenty four hours to think it over! A choice – either be a minister and serve Christ, or be a secretary for a football club!

I also had twenty four hours to think about it. At first it seemed an attractive proposition. I could live in Southampton, my own home town, and we would be comfortably off financially. But I knew if David turned down his ministry and went the football route I would break off our engagement and hand back my ring. I didn't realise how very strongly I felt about God's call on my life till Dad dangled the carrot in front of David. But I knew if David was tempted to give up the ministry then I couldn't marry him. David was not tempted at all, I found out later when we had a chance to speak together, and he flatly turned my father's offer down. Dad again tried to tempt David, but the answer was a firm "no thanks".

In spite of the hectic way of life we led at the Manse I decided not to give up my singing now that I had my voice back. Someone in the church told me of a singing teacher who lived in the town who might help me learn more songs and keep my voice in good condition. I went to see her one Monday morning about a year after we had arrived in Newcastle under Lyme. I liked her immediately. Her name was Beryl Wood. She sang and played the harp and had several times sung on BBC Radio Three, and she had also sung in St Paul's Cathedral in London. She was crippled from polio which she and her brother and sister had contracted when they were children. Her mother would push the three children in a large pram two or three times a week up to the hospital, some miles away, for physiotherapy. At the point when I started my singing lessons with Beryl she was just getting over the death of her sister Alma, who had suffered health problems all her life since the polio epidemic.

One day David came back from the church choir practice and dropped a bombshell. The choir were due to sing "Olivet to Calvary" a cantata by Maunder, in just over a week's time. The trouble was there were two or three solos written into the music, which the choir director thought the whole choir could sing. But it wasn't sounding good. So would Daphne be an angel and do the solos. I managed to get hold of a copy of the music the next day, and phoned Beryl. She fitted me in for three lessons (this was before tape recorders, so I had no other way to learn the music!) Then I had a rehearsal with the orchestra. The conductor was brilliant and I enjoyed the practice. I remember I was expecting Nigel at the time, and had great difficulty finding a maternity outfit to suit the occasion.

Good Friday 1962 was the date of the performance; it was a wonderful occasion and I loved the music. I loved singing with an orchestra and it was immensely reassuring to have a conductor to bring me in at the right point! it was a great start to Easter time.

When Tessa was four and Nigel was two years old, we took all the youth fellowship on holiday to Devon. We booked three large mobile homes – one for the boys, one for the girls, and one for our family. I found it rather hard work, but the young people adored their holiday and still talk about it forty five years later!

But we had already found out from the Moderator of our area, who lived near Stratford on Avon, that there was a group of twelve adults in the church who were asking for our removal . The Moderator listened to what they had to say but told them it was not his responsibility to ask us to leave. David and I were totally shocked that the leader of the group, a local doctor's wife, was the key person. She and her husband were friends of ours and we had been to their house several times for a meal, and they seemed very affable. We were amazed at some of the other names of the twelve, and not surprised at others.

David and I felt it was probably time to consider moving on. Not just because of the twelve, but I had been going down with laryngitis and bronchitis with gathering frequency and the last time it had happened our doctor said I would never recover while I was living in the Potteries. The air was sooty and filled with too many chemicals.

In the meantime back at Rownhams House my father was extremely ill with cancer. The symptoms had been masked for sometime because he had put himself on a slimming diet. But he suddenly ran a high temperature and had some pain, so Dr Ramsey sent him into hospital for tests. While Dad was in the hospital he apparently said to my mother: "I wish I had Daph's courage. If I did I would walk out of here!"

When my mother told me this later, I was truly amazed – both that he had worked out for himself that I had run away from the Limes Hospital, and that he thought I was courageous and not a coward!

Dad perked up considerably and we thought the crisis was over, and no diagnosis had been made. The Southampton Football Club were doing exceedingly well in the F.A. Cup and had got as far as the semi-cup final. Each of the Saints players was given a batch of tickets for their own personal use. But Dad thought they were selling them on the black market for considerable profit. It was difficult to get a ticket for the semi-final. If I remember rightly Saints drew! And we had to play again away from home at White Hart City. Again Dad was worrying about the players selling tickets on the black market as he felt it was morally wrong. The tickets were for the footballers' families and close friends. Dad got very stressed not just with that problem but the allocation of tickets for all the supporters. He desperately wanted the real supporters to get tickets and not those who would only go to a special football match.

I travelled to Birmingham to watch the match with my father in the Directors Box at White Hart City. Dad was very thin and very pale, ashen in fact. I was shocked and concerned. Saints lost the match and we were not in the F.A. Cup Final. It was a relief, as I didn't think Dad could cope with any more ticket allocations. But as the weeks went by and he didn't get any better it was finally diagnosed as cancer. He lived about six months after the semi cup final. I came down as often as I could from Newcastle under Lyme, leaving Tessa with one family and Nigel with another family in the church. Valerie alternated with me, to help Mum and give her support. The last time I saw my father up and about, he was rushing off to a board meeting at the Southampton Football Club, which was still at the Dell. He was thin and frail, but determined to be there for the Saints.

It seemed that the whole of Southampton turned out for his funeral at the Avenue Congregational Church – well certainly all the Saints players, first and second teams, junior team, directors, and the mayor and mayoress, and Dad's fellow Justices of the Peace, many of the Victory Transport staff, fellow Rotarians, people from the British Sailors' Society, the Old People's All Day Club, and representatives from many other local organisations. I noticed in the newspaper cutting that the chairman of the Portsmouth City Football club was there too. Dad was very friendly with the chairman of Pompey even though the two clubs are meant to be sworn enemies!

My father's death around the time of David looking for a new church meant that we felt we should try and move nearer to my mother to support her and my young brother Roger.

CHAPTER NINE

Our hearts were heavy as we considered the move. Yes, looking for pastures new was scary and fun. But we dearly loved the people of Newcastle. The young people by this time were strong Christians, who knew how to pray and study their Bibles, and lead their friends to find Jesus for themselves. We couldn't stay there forever. In the last weeks before we left, but before we announced our plans, we invited all the adults of the church up to the manse, in groups of twelve, every Sunday tea time for high tea. Almost everyone accepted our invitation, and the whole idea proved to be a great success. Even our "enemies" came, and were nice to us, as we were to them. It seemed a time of forgiving and reconciliation – a time of loving, caring and getting to know each other in a deeper way.

The Moderator found a possible church for us at Tilehurst in Reading. He said it was a strange situation because they had already called a new minister, then changed their minds and cancelled the call to him.

I was dying of curiosity, and before a date was set for our visit, I left David babysitting the children and drove all the way down from Staffordshire to Reading in Berkshire one afternoon to see what kind of a district the church and the manse were in. It was okay. Tilehurst seemed to be a bit like an old village, surrounded by a couple of modern housing estates. The church buildings looked friendly enough! Mission accomplished!

I started driving home, and by the time I was on the big dual carriageway heading towards the Midlands, I realised I was very low on petrol. It was nearly 11pm and I drove more slowly, frantically looking for the up-coming lights of a petrol station. Every time I saw lights up ahead, it turned out to be a pub or some other useless building! I finally ground to a halt – no fuel left in the car. I had glided off the road and onto the grass verge. There was no choice but to get out and start walking, hoping to find petrol, somewhere. I had walked about a mile, stumbling in the pitch dark, half on the grass verge and half on the road – in my high heels which I always wore in those days. I heard a heavy lorry puffing up the hill towards me, and made sure I was on the grass. It overtook me very slowly and stopped. I went hot with fright! The driver lowered down the passenger window, and shouted, "Is that your car back there?" "Yes." I replied. "What's the matter? Run out of petrol?" he persisted. "Yes." I said, torn between asking him for help and hoping he would drive away and leave me safely to continue walking.

"Hop in. I'll give you a lift. There's a garage about two miles away."

I hesitated. "Look," he said. "I've got a daughter about your age. I wouldn't want her walking around here on her own. You're safe with me, I assure you. Come on, hop in!"

He opened the door of the cab, and with difficulty I climbed up, and sat on the passenger seat.

He revved up his engine and pulled away, making small talk for the next two miles. He seemed a really nice middle aged chap. I began to relax.

We finally saw the lights of the garage ahead. It was still open, just this side of midnight! The lorry driver helped me fill a can up with petrol, enough to get me back to this garage to do a proper fill up. Then he turned his huge lorry around and we drove back to our car, an Austin Cambridge, sitting forlornly by the road side. The driver hopped out and organised the re-fuelling. The engine wouldn't start, and

I had no idea what to do. “Ah, no problem. You just have to jiggle this to get the fuel through. There’s probably an air lock.” He jiggled something and the engine started!

“Off you go! Don’t forget to stop at the garage and fill your car up properly!” he called out to me. I thanked him profusely. And thanked God just as much.

It was well after midnight when I crept up stairs at the manse. David and the children were all fast asleep. David half woke up. “What took you so long?” he asked.

“I’ll tell you in the morning!”

“What’s Tilehurst like? Was it worth the trip?”

“I’ll tell you in the morning!” I whispered, and promptly fell fast asleep.

We visited Tilehurst Congregational Church twice “on view”. This means we viewed them and they viewed us. We had to stay with one of the deacons. We were very quickly told about our predecessors.

The previous minister and his wife, with whom we had contact years later – a lovely couple, had a small son and another baby on the way. The baby on the way turned out to be twins, born in the manse. There were no scans in those days, and the second baby was a huge surprise when it popped out just minutes after the first baby had arrived. There was only one carrycot for one baby, so they quickly emptied a drawer and popped the second baby in that, lining it with a pillow. Such was the excitement in the manse upstairs that the small son downstairs felt a bit neglected. To amuse himself he threw his books and toys into the fire in the lounge.

When smoke and flames began to fill the house the fire engines were called. The fire was quickly put out, and the manse returned to its usual calm. But about a week later, the young lad, feeling bored and neglected, remembered the fun of the previous week: the fire engines, the excitement, and the friendly firemen. So with the remainder of his toys and books to hand, he began to fuel the fire in the grate again. I think the second fire was bigger than the first.

The deacons, nervous by now for the future safety of the manse, talked to the young minister and his wife, and suggested that maybe it was time to move on to pastures new.

David and I were told the story and the deacons said that the reason I was invited down on view with our two children was because they wanted to make sure I could discipline and keep control of any children living in the manse! I think Tessa, four, and Nigel, two, must have wondered what had come over me that first weekend. I was very strict with them - loving, but absolutely firm and no room for messing me about. When we were invited back for a second weekend (which meant the church was quite serious about us) I warned the children the discipline would be strict again. "Mummy loves you very much – but you must do what I say immediately. And if I say you mustn't touch something or do something, you must take notice of me right away. We will be staying in someone else's house and you have to be very good. Do you understand?"

They were perfect angels and we got the job.

We had to give three months notice to Newcastle under Lyme church. This was a time of grieving, loving, and building the church for a future ministry. Everyone made the most of the last three months.

We moved down to Tilehurst, Reading, Berkshire, in September 1964. Tessa was four and Nigel was two years old. When the furniture van turned up at the manse in Norman Grove, Basford, Newcastle, to load our furniture and belongings to deliver to Tilehurst, I realised we had a bit of a problem with two small children, and all the doors wide open; and men carrying heavy stuff out of the front door. I borrowed two tea chests from the lorry and placed them on the front lawn. I put Tessa in one of them, and Nigel in the other. They could safely watch all the activities from a safe place. They giggled and laughed and jumped up and down, and thoroughly enjoyed the morning's entertainment! I kept an eye on them, but was also able to keep an eye on the emptying of the manse after five years of habitation!

A bus load of people from Newcastle came down and joined us for the Induction Service at Tilehurst Congregational Church in Reading.

Gwen and John, two members of the youth fellowship, stayed with us. John took part in the Induction Service and was ordained, himself, a few years later. John and Gwen married and went on to full time ministry both in England and in Africa.

Our lovely special friends the Bradleys promised to come and visit us as often as they could – but first they had to buy a car and Harold had to learn to drive. Within a year they were able to visit us regularly which was wonderful. I still acknowledge that if it hadn't been for Sybil's love, care, friendship and hospitality to me and the children, I am not sure I could have survived my time at Newcastle under Lyme. Elaine was the first to link me up with her mother Sybil. When David and I were asked if we would be counsellors at the Billy Graham Crusade to be held in Manchester in the early 1960s, Elaine heard about the invitation, and immediately volunteered for her mother to babysit! I knew Sybil could be totally trusted. She helped me with Tessa and Nigel the whole time I was in Newcastle, and of course held my hand while Nigel was being born.

Reading is a commuter town for London, and we soon found that evening meetings had to start later as people were still travelling home on the train at the time meetings normally started in Staffordshire. Again we spent a large part of our time working with the young people; and we also worked with the many young mothers who mostly lived on a new housing estate nearby.

There were some very kind people in the church who offered to babysit, so that occasionally I could go to the evening service on a Sunday, or some midweek meeting. I was soon asked by a lovely lady called Mrs Gray, if I would be prepared to have a monthly prayer meeting for the Overseas Missionary Fellowship, which used to be called the China Inland Mission. I had read quite a few books about brave missionaries from the C.I.M., particularly the story of Hudson Taylor and his wife Maria, and another amazing missionary called Isobel Kuhn. So I said yes, I'd love to have a group come up to the manse once a month and by all means we would pray for the missionaries abroad.

It was always an enjoyable evening – except for one thing: the door bell rang!

I would put Tessa and Nigel to bed around 7 o'clock. They should have been asleep by half past seven. But the door bell would ring, and the children would be up, out of bed, hanging over the banisters and giggling. Even when I left the door on the latch and told people to creep in quietly, the two monsters upstairs would start their antics. I'm glad none of our deacons ever came to the meetings – they would not have been impressed with my disciplining skills. David was always out at a meeting or visiting people in their homes, or in hospital, so it was up to me to keep things under control, and I felt I failed miserably.

I will jump ahead at this stage and say that when my third child was born the O.M.F. missionary group gave me a lovely prayer plant – and found somewhere else to meet! The plant is still going strong, and after I looked after it for more than thirty five years I presented it to my third child, daughter Abigail, as it was a gift to me to celebrate her arrival!

The young people at Tilehurst were very different from our young people in Newcastle. They seemed more sophisticated, had more to occupy them mid week, and yet they longed to know more of God.

Most of our work with them went fairly smoothly, and they gradually found faith in the Lord and wanted to come around to the manse any chance we invited them: either to play with the children and just "be", or to spend time asking questions about Christianity and the Bible, or even life in general. Either way, they were always welcome, and I don't recollect any opposition from any parent.

One evening, while David was taking the evening service around the corner at the church, the phone rang. "Hello! Mrs Mills? It's Jack here! Could you do something for me? I'm in a phone box near Theale. The thing is, could you run round to the church before the evening service finishes – I've left a letter for the youth group on the church notice board. Please could you take it down before anyone finds it?"

"Well, of course, I will! We've got a little while before they all come out of church, I'll grab the children, put them in the car and nip round and get your note."

"Oh thanks so much. You see, I've changed my mind....." Jack said. (Not his real name).

I could tell he was fighting back tears. "Where are you? Do you want me to pick you up after I've been round to the church?" My mind was already buzzing with the dynamics of getting the children, already in their night clothes, putting them in the car with blankets, and rushing around to the church with minutes to spare.

Jack said, quickly, "Oh yes please. Look I will wait just here by the phone box; it's on the corner before you get to the pub on the way to Theale."

I knew roughly where he was, and hoped he would jump out and wave when I got near. It was already dark.

Luckily Tessa and Nigel had only just gone to bed. I said we were going out for a fun night drive, and please hurry up. Dressing gowns on! Slippers on! And I grabbed a large blanket for them. In minutes, we were in the car and racing down Crescent Road, round the corner into Victoria Avenue, and across the next road and into the church car park. I could hear a hymn being sung in church. I checked my watch. The sermon couldn't possibly have finished early. That meant they were running late and David still had to do his sermon. Great! That gave us a bit of extra time. I crept into the church lobby – and there in the centre of the notice board was a letter, written in pencil on lined notepaper addressed in large hand writing "To The Youth Group". Yes, definitely that needed to be moved promptly before anyone saw it. It was an emotional farewell letter – life wasn't worth living any more – sorry to let you, my friends, down but I can't take any more of this life.....

I snatched the letter off the board, stuck the drawing pin back, and put the letter in my pocket. (I still have it somewhere – Jack didn't want to see it again! And I didn't have the heart to throw away such a cry for help.)

I got back to the car in the church car park. Tessa and Nigel were giggling away and enjoying the excitement of a night trip out in the car. I turned the car round and sped out of Tilehurst, turning right into Bath Road, the A4, and drove along towards Theale. I soon saw Jack hovering by a lit up phone box. I stopped the car, and opened the passenger door. He was obviously upset, but in a jaunty sort of way. The children had dozed off to sleep. I turned the car around and we started driving back towards Tilehurst.

"Do you want to talk about it?" I asked gently.

"I had a row with my father. We are in disagreement about my career. I'm working hard at school but he wants me to study different subjects and go into his business. I know I can't do that." He sounded desperate and miserable.

I changed gear and drove more slowly. I wasn't sure where he wanted me to take him. But I also felt he needed to talk a bit more. He went silent. So I said, "Would it help if my husband popped in to chat with your father? He doesn't need to know anything about this evening. They could just have a general chat and my husband could mention your name and ask how you are doing at school, and just see if the subject comes up naturally."

"That would be brilliant. My dad likes you both. I'm sure he'd listen to you. Just promise you won't mention about tonight, please?" he eyed me in the darkness. "Your secret is safe with us!" I replied.

"Do you want me to drop you home, or do you want to come back to the Manse?" I asked Jack.

"I'd love a cup of tea, and the youth fellowship will be round your house tonight as well, won't they?"

We swung into the drive. Jack helped me carry the children up to their beds .We put the kettle on.

The door bell rang. Jack opened the door for me and all the young teenagers rushed in, laughing and talking. One of the young people said, "Mr Mills says he's got to talk to someone after the service so he'll be a bit late, Mrs Mills. He said just get on without him!"

"Right!" I replied. "Let's have a cup of tea and get started, shall we?"

CHAPTER TEN

To move on to the next part of my story we have to wade deeper into spiritual matters. Around 1963, while we were still living in Newcastle under Lyme, we began to hear about "a new move of the Holy Spirit" in some churches. I remember being asked to sing at Stoke on Trent's Youth for Christ. While we were waiting for all the youth to arrive David and I were standing chatting to a small group of ministers. One of the ministers was saying, "Well, I also have difficulties in my church too. I've got some church members who are "speaking in tongues". How about that for a problem!"

I always enjoyed listening to the chat between clergy. They all seemed to have an immense sense of humour when they were together. In spite of the load of people's cares that they carried on their shoulders, when they got together there was genuine laughter and a lovely depth of sharing.

I thought to myself: "Speaking in tongues? In other words speaking different languages! It's mentioned in the second chapter of the Acts of the Apostles in the New Testament!"

I said aloud to the minister who was complaining, "At least you have a spiritual problem! Count your blessings!"

The young people gathered over the next half hour in the huge church we were in and the evening proceedings were under way. I sang my two songs, and forgot about the local minister's complaint about his excessively spiritual church members!

But the rumours increased, about this "speaking in tongues". It sounded a bit excessive, but I kept reading anything I could find on the subject – little snippets in Christian magazines, and occasional comments from the local ministers' fraternal. The correct translation in modern day English is "speaking in other languages". It seemed the experience almost always was received after the laying on of hands and prayer. In other words a person who had already received the gift of the Holy Spirit could then pray and lay their hands on the other person's head so they could receive the Holy Spirit as well.

David came home one day from the monthly Stoke on Trent Ministers' Fraternal, as it was so grandly called. "You'll never guess what! You know Philip Smith, vicar at St John's? Well, he's received this baptism in the Holy Spirit we've been hearing about – and I heard him speak in tongues, you know, in a foreign language! You should see the change in old Philip – he's a different person; he used to be a bit morose and serious, but now he can't stop smiling!"

I stared at David, shocked! If Phillip Smith could change like that it was a miracle. "Oh, and by the way, I said the next Minister's Fraternal could be here at the manse. You don't mind making them cups of tea, do you? It's the first Monday next month, 9.30am."

That month seemed to go faster than any other! The day dawned for the ministers to visit the manse for their meeting.

The door bell rang.

David was upstairs, still making notes of people he needed to visit that week following information given to him at church yesterday.

I could see one solitary man standing the other side of the glass front door. I opened the door. It was the Rev Philip Smith – or was it? Gone was the rather dour, depressed looking clergyman with his loose dog collar. In his place was a very smiley, relaxed, face-shining man. The only thing I recognised was the loose dog collar, still not fitting his neck properly. I greeted him, but didn't shake his hand. Instead I stepped backwards, giving him a wide berth. I was really scared that this Holy Spirit thing was catching. I never doubted that it was of God. But there was a depth of spirituality that wasn't for me. And in my heart of hearts if anyone had questioned me at that point I would have said, "It's too costly! I'm happy to be a disciple of Jesus, but this Holy Spirit stuff is deeper than I feel I can go."

David came running down the stairs and greeted Philip warmly, making up for the fact that I hadn't even shaken his hand. Philip enquired after my welfare, and that of our two children, and then he and David walked into our lounge together and I went into the kitchen to start making tea for about ten ministers. The door bell continued to ring and the laughter emanating from the lounge increased. I carried in the tray of tea and biscuits, and left the men to get on with their meeting. The laughter continued for about another ten minutes, then it all quietened down, and I could hear nothing more. At midday the laughter and chatter signalled the end of the ministers' meeting and I heard the front door opening and closing. I thought everyone had gone so I went into the lounge to collect up the cups and saucers. To my surprise David was sat chatting to Philip Smith. Before I had gathered all the china on to the tray, Philip Smith had stood up, shook my hand, smiling with face shining, and left.

David carried the tray into the kitchen and we started to wash up.

"Are you allowed to tell me what you talked about this morning?" I asked David tentatively.

"Well, after we did a short Bible study and had a time of prayer, someone asked Philip if he would tell us what had happened to him. Most of the ministers had heard something on the ministerial grape vine. Philip was only too glad to fill us in." David replied as he continued washing up.

I heard Philip Smith's story. I was impressed. But nothing changed my mind. Those spiritual waters were too deep for me. The weeks went by and we gradually heard of a few more ministers who were having this experience of "the baptism of the Holy Spirit", and we even had a group of three women in our own church in Newcastle who had had the experience and were encouraging David to consider praying and asking God for "It"!

Every Friday afternoon David, and sometimes myself, went to visit Victoria House, a home for retired teachers. David was the chaplain, and over the four years we had been in Newcastle we had made friends with quite a few of these lovely learned people.

"I'm off to Victoria House now," called David up the stairs to me. "Do you want to come?"

I'd forgotten it was Friday and I had other things planned for the afternoon. "Oh, sorry, I promised the children we would go down the town, and then call on Sybil Bradley on the way back up the hill for a cup of tea." I called down the stairs.

"That's okay. See you around 5 o'clock then." And the front door closed. I heard the car engine start up, and David reverse out of the driveway. I finished what I was doing, put the children's coats on, popped Nigel in the pushchair, and we start to walk down into the centre of Newcastle under Lyme. The afternoon was fairly uneventful. We wandered around the shops. Then we stopped at one of the two larger stores. I left the pushchair outside the shop, and Tessa, Nigel and I wandered around the counters. I held tightly onto Nigel's hand and Tessa hovered near us. I found something I wanted to purchase, queued at the cash desk, and searched inside my handbag for my purse. Having completed the transaction, I looked down either side of me – horrors! No sign of Tessa or Nigel.

Things were much safer in those days, but I anxiously searched the shop floor for some minutes, and could see no sign of them. I walked out of the shop and looked up and down the road, but couldn't see them. I walked back into the shop and was about to ask a shop assistant for help, when an elderly lady came up to me and said, "Are you looking for two small children?" She could obviously see the anxiety on my face and the way I was looking around.

"Yes! Have you seen them?" I asked her.

“Well, there’s two children going up and down in the lift, having a marvellous time!” the old lady said, pointing to the lift area. I thanked her profusely and ran over to the lift. The red light said it was on floor one and going upwards. It seemed to take forever, stopping at every floor, and eventually continuing on up. Then the red light showed it was coming back down again. It was stopping on every floor for the duration of expelling shoppers and receiving new inmates. Eventually it arrived on the ground floor, and the lift doors slowly opened. There were Tessa and Nigel, right in the front of the crowd of passengers, eyes travelling from the opening doors to the red light above. I ran forward and grabbed my four year old daughter and my two year old son.

“I hope you had fun! Come on, let’s go and see Sybil and have a drink!” I said to them as I held their hands firmly and strapped both of them in the single-seater push chair, and we proceeded up the steep hill to the Bradley’s house and safety!

By the time I had sat and chatted to Sybil and told her about our afternoon’s adventure, I heard Harold Bradley arrive back from work. We stayed for a few minutes while he played and chatted with the children, then we said our goodbyes and I continued to push the children on up the steep hill that led to our house. I just had time to start preparing the tea when I heard our car arrive in the drive.

I went to open the front door. David stood on the door mat.

When we usually returned from Victoria House we were always a bit tired, having sat with many elderly people, concentrating on what they had to say, and being fed rather unappetising cakes and biscuits.

So I was expecting a rather weary husband to be standing on the door step. But what I found was a smile going from ear to ear!

Shock! The words fell out of my mouth. “I know where you’ve been! You’ve been to see Philip Smith! You didn’t go to Victoria House at all, did you?”

David walked into the house, shrugging off his jacket, and I stood staring at him, a bit frightened of the grin I saw on his face!

“What happened? You said you were going to visit the old dears at Victoria House!” I said, anxiously.

"Well, I did set off for Victoria House when I left here. But when I got to the end of the road, I felt compelled to turn left towards Stoke, rather than right towards Victoria House! Then I knew where God was telling me to go. I drove to Philip Smith's house in Burslem. I didn't even know if he would be in. But he was, and he invited me in to his study. We spent the afternoon talking about the Holy Spirit, then he offered to pray for me to receive the power of the Holy Spirit for myself, so I said yes please! So he laid his hands on my head and prayed for me."

"Well, then what happened?" I asked both nervously and cautiously.

"We ran out of time. Philip had to rush off to some appointment, and we shook hands and we both left the vicarage at the same time."

"Well," I said and looked again at David. "You've got the same smile and shining face as Philip, so something must have happened! I could see you hadn't been to Victoria House. You seem a different person! What about this speaking in tongues thing? The two experiences seem to go hand in hand from what I've heard. "

David nodded and said, "The "tongues", as it's translated in the New Testament, is actually the same word as "languages"; and yes, I found as I was driving home that I could speak in a different language. I don't know what it is but it just flowed, and I felt as though I was praising God at a depth I have never known before."

At this point, Tessa and Nigel came running downstairs. "Is tea ready yet?"

Reality kicked in, and I went into the kitchen, laid the table and got on with feeding everyone, but remained deep in thought.

We went two days later "on view" to Tilehurst for our first visit. It happened to be Pentecost Sunday.

Pentecost is the time in the church calendar each year when the giving of the Holy Spirit to the apostles and other disciples of Jesus is celebrated. David had already chosen the hymns and sent them down two weeks beforehand for the choir and organist to practice. The first hymn he had chosen for the morning service at Tilehurst was, "O for a Thousand Tongues to sing, our great Redeemer's name!"

As we launched into this rousing first hymn I thought, "So that's what it means! A thousand tongues, means a thousand different languages: a thousand different languages from every tribe and race that has ever existed on earth - all praising our great Redeemer, Jesus." My heart was uplifted and I think I felt closer to God than I had in a long time.

We drove home to Newcastle after our weekend in Tilehurst, Reading; and I plucked up courage to ask David to pray for me and lay hands on my hand to receive the gift of tongues, languages. I certainly couldn't have asked Philip Smith to pray for me – that was stepping in too deep for me. David prayed for me. I thought we had prayed for about ten minutes, but when we looked at the clock it was four o'clock in the morning! We had prayed for hours and in the presence of God the time had flown by supernaturally. Sadly nothing much changed in me. It took another two years before my prayers were answered, and then only because I realised one key thing. I'd been asking for the gift of a special language for myself - I hadn't been asking for the Holy Spirit! I wanted The Experience, not really a deeper walk with God. In the mean time I jokingly called Philip Smith and others like him, the Hallelujah People.

We had been living in Reading for two years when David was asked to help lead a mission at the University of Reading. Together with some well known ministers of that era, including Rev David Watson from York, the mission got under way. We had two missioners staying with us. One of these was Rev Michael Christian Edwards. Unknown to me the guests in the house, realising that I had not had the same experience of the Holy Spirit that they had, agreed together, privately, to pray for me. I knew nothing of this until a week later, by which time God had answered their prayers!

That week was hard work; lots of cooking and clearing away and washing up; and the three of them, David, Michael and someone called Violet, were in and out all the time. A lot of the time they were up at the University, and sometimes they were back at the manse studying, praying or relaxing. On the Friday night of the mission, with two more evenings to go, I arranged to go along to the University, and listen to Rev David Watson speaking to the University students.

Mrs Cleever, from our church, arrived in plenty of time to babysit, and I drove myself over to the University – the other three having left the house an hour beforehand. Having had a bit of a rush getting the three missioners off to the University, and getting Tessa and Nigel bathed and dressed in their pyjamas, I was a bit exhausted when I eventually entered the main hall and sat down with about six hundred students.

The evening was excellent and totally geared for students. David Watson was the main speaker and he made sure he cracked a joke or told some anecdote every few minutes to make sure his audience wasn't bored. At the end of his talk he invited any students who wanted to receive the Lord Jesus Christ into their lives to stay behind for a further few minutes of instruction and prayer. Almost no student left the hall. I looked at my watch and realised it was time for me to leave so that Mrs Cleaver could be relieved of her baby sitting duties and get home.

I slipped out of my seat in the middle of the row of students, and slowly walked back to our car in the darkened university car park.

I unlocked the car and sat in the driver's seat, putting my head on the steering wheel for a moment. I felt weary, lonely and depressed. I said to myself, "Whatever has happened to my Christianity, if I can witness over five hundred students wanting to hear how to receive Jesus into their lives, and I walk out of an evening like that feeling depressed?"

I switched on the ignition and drove out of the University campus. Driving along the Bath Road, I was deep in thought. I was angry with myself and felt a failure – a spiritual failure – empty and bereft. The car gathered pace and I turned right off the Bath Road and cut up through Cockney Hill. I said a prayer out aloud. "Lord, sorry, but unless you baptise me in the Holy Spirit before the end of Cockney Hill, I'm chucking up Christianity. I can't carry on working for you when I feel so powerless and empty. You said your disciples had to wait in Jerusalem to receive power before they started their ministry. And the power came and their lives were changed. They evangelised the world with that power! " I knew only too well those passages in the book of the Acts of the Apostles, chapters one and two. I had been researching them for two years!

I continued to drive slowly along Cockney Hill to give God a chance to answer my prayer. By the time I neared the last twenty yards of Cockney Hill I was driving about four miles an hour! I waited expectantly. Nothing happened. "Okay, Lord. I will give you one last chance! Before I get to the end of St Michael's Road you must fill me with the Holy Spirit or I mean what I say! Please Lord, sorry Lord!"

I drove even more slowly along St Michael's Road! By the time I got to the end of that road I felt my spirit was full of peace and quiet joy. I just knew that God was present with me in the car and was changing me. Turning right again, and then sharp left, I was nearly home. Pulling into the manse driveway, I got out of the car and knocked softly on the front door. Mrs Cleever opened the door, already putting on her coat. “Did the children behave themselves for you?” I asked.

I’m sure she said “yes” but I never even listened. All I knew was that my voice had sounded different, more soft-sounding and more gentle. I bundled Mrs Cleever out of the house, without engaging in chit chat. Thanking her so much for babysitting, I waved at her as she walked down the drive. I closed the front door and walked into the lounge and fell on my knees by our sofa, grabbing my Bible on the way.

“Lord, I think you have filled me with your Holy Spirit. But how can I know for sure? I don’t want to wake up tomorrow and find it was just an emotional experience! Please could you give me the gift of speaking in tongues as well - just as proof?”

I didn’t know quite what to do! But I thought that as a step of faith I should praise and thank God any way. So I opened my Bible, and it fell open at the book of Psalms. I started reading out aloud the first few verses of Psalm 103.

“Bless the Lord, O my soul; and all that is within me, bless his holy name! Bless the Lord, O my soul, and forget not all his benefits, who forgives all your iniquity, who heals all your diseases, who redeems your life from the pit, who crowns you with good as long as you live so that your youth is renewed like the eagle’s.”

I read these verses aloud several times, my heart lifting in happiness and joy at the truth of the words and the holiness of this moment on my knees by the sofa.

I felt some strange words going around my head, and then I spoke them out aloud, to mingle with the praises in the Psalm I had just read. The new words increased and I knew the Lord had given me a new language as proof to me of his presence in the Holy Spirit. So I said, “If I can speak in tongues, could you also help me sing in tongues? “And immediately an ancient sounding melody began to ring in my head – I opened my mouth and sang the tune and the foreign words came at the same time.

This holy hour was very precious to me. I was so grateful to God that in my hour of need he had given me a most wonderful gift. I sat back on the sofa, and devoured again the first few chapters of the book of the Acts of the Apostles.

I quickly felt drawn to what Jesus Christ said at the very end of his life on earth. Just before he ascended into heaven he said to his close followers: “. . . . I send the promise of my Father upon you; but stay in the city (of Jerusalem), until you are clothed with power from on high." This is written in Luke's gospel chapter 24 verse 49. Then I read verse 48! ". . . it is written (in the Bible) that the Christ should suffer and on the third day rise from the dead, and that repentance and forgiveness of sins should be preached in his name to all nations, beginning from Jerusalem." These are the words of Jesus.

I thought about this: ". . . clothed with power from on high." I had to admit that a lot of what I had done had been in my own strength, and I was weary from the struggle.

In the first chapter of the book of the Acts of the Apostles, I read that the followers of Jesus, and this included his mother Mary, other women, and his brothers, all stayed in Jerusalem as he told them to. And they met daily, praying together. In verse 8 of the first chapter, it reiterates Jesus' final words, where he said, ". . . you shall receive power when the Holy Spirit has come upon you; you shall be my witnesses in Jerusalem .... and to the ends of the earth!"

Well that clarified one thing. It's not very easy being a witness for Jesus without the power he said we needed. I felt we had had some of the power, but not as much as he intended. It was as though we had been sprinkled with his power but not totally dunked in it! Because baptism in New Testament times was a complete immersion in the river Jordan, head and all! So also when Jesus promised his followers would be baptised in the Holy Spirit it meant they would be completely immersed in Him. I say "Him" not "it" because The Holy Spirit is part of the Trinity: God the Father, God the Son (Jesus) and God the Holy Spirit. And looking at the beginning of the first book in the Bible I noticed that immediately the Spirit of God is mentioned as being part of the creation of the world.

I then re-read Acts chapter two. The miracle happened! Everyone was baptised in the Holy Spirit as Jesus said they would be. There was a physical sign on this first occasion and it seemed that flames appeared over everyone's head. Then they all spoke in different languages, that they had never learnt. They burst out onto the streets of Jerusalem, and people thought they were drunk! But all the foreigners in the city of Jerusalem who heard them talking in other languages, heard their own mother tongue and were amazed that simple peasant workers and fishermen from Galilee could speak so many foreign languages.

As I skimmed through the following pages I noticed how many miracles began to happen as the followers of Jesus went around telling the story of Jesus. Mark, one of the younger followers of Jesus, also wrote down Jesus' final words before he ascended. I decided to look them up as well. In the last few verses of his book he quotes Jesus as saying: "Go into all the world and preach the gospel (good news) to the whole of creation. He who believes and is baptized (in water) will be saved; but he who does not believe will be condemned. And these signs will accompany those who believe: in my name they will cast out demons; they will speak in new tongues/languages . . . . they will lay their hands on the sick, and they will recover."

All that I read seemed to say that Jesus would give power, in the Holy Spirit, to help to do his work of preaching the gospel, healing the sick, dealing with satanic damage in people, and all that was needed for a powerful, effective ministry.

May be things will change for me and I will be more effective in serving people for God?

The door bell rang!

It was David, Michael and Violet returning from the University – almost midnight. David took one look at me and said, "I know what's happened to you! Hasn't it?" I nodded and laughed. It felt as though life was starting all over again, from this point onwards – it couldn't get any better!

Saturday the three were off to the University all day. I felt a bit strange, but amazingly peaceful. David took the Sunday morning service as usual at our church in Tilehurst, then went back up to the University. Before he left he said, "The youth group are due to come to the manse after church tonight. I've arranged for a visiting minister to take the service but he's not free to come back to the manse after to help with the young people. Do you want him to read out a notice and cancel them coming round after church?"

"No, don't worry – I'll give them cups of tea, and let them chat amongst themselves for a while. We'll just see what happens." I replied.

I had no baby sitter so didn't go to the evening service. But about eight o'clock, the door bell rang. There stood a large group of teenagers – more than usual. Help! I thought.

"Come in, come in! The kettle's on, make yourselves at home!" They all poured in. Some went into the lounge and some went into the kitchen to finish making the tea. I slid the doors back that divided the lounge and the dining room, enlarging the space, and put out more chairs. I threw some cushions on the floor, and eventually everyone found somewhere to sit. They laughed and talked and sipped their tea.

"Where's Mr Mills?" someone asked. So I explained about the mission up at the University, saying it was finishing tonight. "Did you go, Mrs Mills?" someone else asked. "Yes, just for one evening – Friday actually." I answered. "What happened?" another voice chipped in from another teenager.

I laughed. "Do you really want to know? You might get more than you bargain for!"

I have to explain here that it had been harder work encouraging the youngsters at Tilehurst to deepen their Christian faith than it had been with the young teens in Newcastle under Lyme. A few of the young people in our new church had given their lives to Jesus and had become lovely changed people. But it seemed many of the teenagers just weren't interested, though they loved meeting together and coming around to the manse.

"Go on, Mrs Mills, tell us what happened at the university." The young teens seemed all in agreement, and all eyes were fixed on me.

So I spent the next twenty minutes telling them about Friday evening and what had happened to me. I felt very bold and yet very nervous as I finished my story. In the room there was total silence.

All I can say about what happened next was that the Holy Spirit seemed to fill the room and a large group of the young people said they wanted to give their lives to Jesus. So I talked and prayed with those who wanted to give their lives to God, and I promised we would give them help and teaching over the coming months. By the time David returned home, all was quiet at the manse and I had already gone to bed – and was sitting up reading.

He was full of the final evening up at the University, and we had our two guests for one more night under our roof. "Did you manage the young people?" David asked.

I told him that for once every one of the youngsters had turned up – and recounted what had happened. It was a most amazing breakthrough in our work with the youngsters. David was due to meet with them all at their games evening on Tuesday, so he was interested to see how they were all making out. He came back after the Tuesday evening club, and told me that the five young teens who hadn't given their lives to the Lord on Sunday night, had come to him at the end of the games evening, and asked David to pray for them. He had led each of them to the Lord. From then on the atmosphere amongst the teenagers changed and they became a loving, caring co-operative group, serving in the church and helping their school friends.

As the power of God began to move more strongly in the church we discovered some very strange goings on. We became aware we were in a spiritual battle, and some things that had seemed okay turned out to be positively dangerous. On investigating further we discovered that before our arrival at the church a well known spiritualist medium and "healer" had been invited to speak. I think he came two or three times, and had been invited by one or two of the church members, who didn't realise how dangerous this was.

You cannot mix the Holy Spirit with the work of Satan or the evil one. The more people in the church who became filled with the Holy Spirit the more things we uncovered about satanic practices that were going on the periphery of the church and in our neighbourhood. David had one or two contacts in other churches who he knew were mature in the things of the Spirit. He spent some time on the telephone getting advice, and he studied the scriptures.

I don't need to go into details at this point but sufficient to say that David returned one evening from a young mothers' Bible study meeting with the most extraordinary story of what had happened that evening, and that Satan had reared his head and one of the mothers had collapsed. On further investigation it was discovered that she had inadvertently been dabbling in the occult. David and the other young mothers prayed strongly in the power of the Holy Spirit and the demonic manifestation was rebuked and cast out – just as Jesus had done in New Testament times.

Although I was shocked, scared and a bit dubious about the story it wasn't long before I was present when something similar happened with some other people who had been messing around with occult stuff. There are many things around that seem harmless but are linked with the occult. And we soon found out that these included reading stars signs, palm reading, tea leaf reading, going to a fortune teller, pendulum swinging, relying on crystals, tarot cards, and even some seemingly harmless children's games that were being sold in the shops. The star sign fortune telling, written in almost every daily paper and many magazines, is the work of a medium, consulting "the stars"; we are warned not to consult mediums – it's dangerous and very displeasing to God. Many people do it "for a joke" – oblivious that they are endangering themselves spiritually, and in other ways as well.

I looked up some scriptures in the Bible and found quite a bit in Leviticus, such as: "Do not turn to mediums or wizards; do not seek them out, to be defiled by them: I am the Lord." Leviticus chapter 19 verse 31. And in chapter 20 verse 6: "If a person turns to mediums and wizards, playing the harlot after them, I will set my face against that person, and will cut him off from among his people."

We both discovered, with the help of more experienced Spirit-filled ministers, that we had to be on our guard and "Put on the full armour of God" (see Ephesians chapter 6) to protect ourselves. At one point a couple of years later, when helping at a Clergy Conference in Yorkshire, I became overwhelmed with fear, and did not realise I had started believing satanic lies. Fortunately some lovely Christian friends prayed for me and I was set free from a most terrifying experience. I vowed then and there to try and keep close to God, and always try and be filled with the Holy Spirit, and read my Bible daily – both to protect myself from further attacks of the enemy, and to be able to help anyone who had been caught up in Satan's snare and was asking for help.

CHAPTER ELEVEN

Having moved south to be nearer to my mother after my father had died, we tried to go down to Southampton most Mondays. My sister Valerie lived near Basingstoke, about half way on our route to Rownhams. Sometimes we stopped off to visit them. I also was able to resume my singing lessons with Madam Myra Dudley, which was a great joy; I worked on learning new songs that were more useful to my life style and was often asked to sing and speak at women's meetings and church services around the Reading area.

We used to have to hurry home on Monday afternoons to be back in time to meet Tessa from school, about half a mile from the manse. She usually came home for lunch, but on Mondays I would give her a packed lunch box and remind her to stay at school during the lunch hour. On returning to Tilehurst one Monday a young mother who lived opposite met me at our gate and said, "I hope you don't mind, but I found your daughter wandering around at lunch time. She was trying to open your front door, but I could tell there was no one in, so I gave her some lunch and then I took her back to school. "

I thanked her and apologised profusely and explained there must have been some misunderstanding as Tessa had her own packed lunch that she should have eaten at school! Tessa had a mind of her own, and it wasn't always easy to get her to follow through the plan set for her as you will hear later.

Just after the Reading University mission I realised baby number three was on its way. I had one visit to the doctor to confirm the pregnancy – and he told me to come back in another month. A few weeks later I was asked to speak and sing at a women's meeting somewhere in Reading. I sang about six songs and spoke, covering about forty minutes altogether. I returned home tired. As I opened the front door our baby sitters' dog jumped up at me and her two front paws landed on my stomach. I thought no more about it, though I was initially a bit worried for my little unborn baby.

We shared a cup of tea together, and then babysitter and her dog left to go to their home around the corner.

The next afternoon I realised that something was drastically amiss. I had terrible pains in my stomach, and had started to bleed. I sat down in my rocking chair on a towel and asked Nigel, please, to run round the corner to Mrs Langdon's house for help. Nigel was aged three and a half. Fortunately it was a quiet neighbourhood, and Nigel was well known around our area. Nigel ran off, seemingly understanding the urgency of the matter. Nigel was back in no time and five minutes later Mrs Langford arrived. She worked at our local doctors' surgery. She told me to go upstairs and lie down, and she would arrange for the doctor to call, but the most important thing was to lie still.

Up to this point I hadn't been so very keen for another baby. But suddenly all my maternal instincts clicked in and I desperately wanted to fight for my baby's life. The pains increased at regular intervals and I knew I was having contractions. The doctor came and said I was to stay in bed and keep as still as possible; but he didn't hold out much hope that the baby would be saved. He said he would call in first thing in the morning.

David came back home from an afternoon's visiting around the district. And I asked him to phone the local Holy Spirit-filled Baptist minister and get him to come and pray for me and anoint me with oil. This was the instruction in the New Testament: James chapter 5 verse 14. I knew the Baptist minister was one of the lovely Spirit-filled people in the area. He arrived very late in the evening, and my regular pains were increasing in strength. I knew I was losing the baby, and I desperately wanted to keep it. Harold prayed, anointed me with oil, said some comforting words to me and left. The doctor had given me a strong sedative, and I slept soundly all night. When I woke the next morning the pains had all gone, but I had bled heavily in the night, and wasn't sure if I had lost the baby or not, but I feared I had. And yet I felt such a God-given peace that I thought God had actually had mercy on me and saved the baby.

I stayed in bed for about four weeks during which time the Christian Union at Reading University set up a rota of students who ran the manse and looked after Tessa and Nigel, thoroughly enjoying themselves in the process. I had a mirror rigged up in such a way as to be able to see who was outside the front door. If no one happened to be in the house, which didn't happen often, I could throw a front door key out if need be!

Eventually I felt safe to get up but still seemed to be bleeding, so sat in the rocking chair and prayed that all would be well. I eventually went down to the surgery for a check up. The doctor listened to what I had to say. " I'm sure I haven't lost the baby as I am getting fatter." He explained about phantom pregnancies and sent me home, convinced that there was no baby. In my heart I knew the baby was still there, and I continued to get bigger. A few weeks later I decided to go to the local pre-natal clinic and see a midwife. She checked me over, fetched a second midwife who checked me over, then someone else came in and checked me over! I lay on my back while all these experts felt my stomach, mystified at what was going on. There were no scans in those days, just feeling the size of the baby and listening for a heart-beat. "This seems to be a multiple birth, definitely more than twins," was the general consensus of the experts. I came back home on the bus, laughing my head off. What was I going to tell David? The last multiple birth at the manse had caused so much trouble they had all had to leave!

When Nigel was expected part of the drama was caused by the fact that he was larger than he should have been, so I must have my dates wrong and the baby was due earlier than the dates I had given.

I thought to myself: it's probably another big baby, and I'm not having history repeating itself. So when asked my dates for the baby's possible arrival, I firmly gave wrong dates, to give myself ten day's grace. This was very naughty I realise now. The baby was due a few days before Christmas, but I gave my date as nearer the end of December.

All was going well and I had no more problems with the pregnancy, so David and I, together with Harold, Sybil and Elaine Bradley from Newcastle, Staffordshire, caught a train to Venice, and boarded a Greek ship to the Holy Land. We had a marvellous three week holiday, exploring wonderful ancient holy sites such as Jerusalem, the Temple, the Wailing Wall, Bethlehem, Bethany, and we saw the Pool of Bethesda, and the Pool of Siloam. It made the Bible come alive in a new way! It was just before the now famous Six Day War, and because of security our tour operator had to fly us down to Egypt, right over the wilderness where the children of Israel had spent forty years wandering around. As I gazed out of the plane window and we flew over mile after mile of mountainous desert terrain, no pools of water in sight, I marvelled at the miracle God had made to happen to help the Israeli slaves escape from Egypt, all those hundreds of years beforehand. We had a wonderful time exploring the pyramids and stayed in a huge hotel on the River Nile. The bulrushes where Moses was hidden are still there!

Sybil made us laugh when she recounted to us what kept happening when she tried to switch the light off to settle down in bed in our hotel by the Nile. Within moments there would be a knock at the door and a very large African servant would be standing there asking her what she wanted. She would assure him there was nothing needed, climb back into bed and pull the cord to switch off the light again. Within moments the same or a different servant would be knocking on the door. Sybil never did remember which cord was for the light and which cord was for a servant to appear.

Please go to the Holy Land if you ever get the opportunity! It will truly bring the Bible alive for you and make you think!

It was an excellent tonic after my weeks in bed. The baby was growing by the day, and the medics were still saying it was a multiple birth, although eventually they thought I was the size for twins, but then as they could only hear one heart beat, may be there's just one baby in there! The nearer I got to the due date the more normal everything became! I was only too glad the baby I nearly lost was safe, and I was absolutely sure that without prayer and the anointing of oil I would have lost the baby the night I had had such terrible pains and loss of blood.

The week the baby was due we celebrated Christmas at Tilehurst, and Valerie and Basil and their two boys, Ian and Neil, joined us to watch the church nativity play. Once Christmas was over I began to get a bit anxious. On December 31st the midwife strongly recommended I swallow two ounces of castor oil. "It almost always does the trick, dear. I think it's the shock to the body which kick starts the baby coming!" she said. I bought a bottle of castor oil and as I opened my mouth to swallow it, the smell reached me first and I was promptly sick. I eyed the castor oil again. I mixed it up with very strong neat orange squash. I tried to swallow it – and I think about half went down before I was sick again.

It was a wasted effort and the baby didn't come. On January 5th the doctor said I must go into hospital in a day or two and have the baby induced. I didn't fancy that, remembering the Limes hospital, and told the doctor so. He laughed and said, "Well, they say a good strong curry will do the trick! Go down the town and have a nice hot curry in the new Indian restaurant."

David and I debated it! But I really wanted to go to Thursday Extra. This was a meeting for Christian business people down in the town centre of Reading. People brought their sandwiches at 1pm on a Thursday – ate and chatted together, then there was a twenty minute talk by some well known Christian business man, and then everyone packed up their lunch boxes and went back to work.

We decided to skip the curry and trust God to bring the baby that night anyway; and we went to Thursday Extra.

That night, in the early hours of the morning, the strong tummy pains started, and the baby was on its way. I had of course opted to have the baby at home. We waited a couple of hours then phoned the midwife. She said there were three babies being born and only two midwives on duty! But not to worry as one of them would be along shortly. Throughout the night they took it in turns to pop in. The whole process was long and drawn out and there appeared to be a problem. By 11.45 am the midwife said, "We've called an ambulance. You have to go to hospital. Your husband is packing a bag for you." I had had rather a lot of "gas and air" and was a bit woozy. But I heard the word hospital and promptly said, "No way!" The hospital was about ten minutes away, I reckoned.

I glanced up at the window, and saw that it was snowing. Marvellous! That would slow the ambulance up and give me a few more minutes. I started to push and push and push. The ambulance and the baby arrived at exactly midday!

A darling little girl – what a struggle. The senior midwife slipped off to attend one of the other pregnant mums and the junior midwife was left to await the arrival of the placenta. When it came she found a strange lump in it, but wrapped it all up in newspaper and told my husband to burn it on the fire downstairs! I was so relieved to have my baby safely in my arms that I didn't really acknowledge to myself that I may have been carrying more than one baby. I was so glad to have little Abigail Daphne. The midwife said the baby was well over due – look at her finger nails, and her skin! You must have got your dates wrong, dear!

Abigail was definitely going to be my last baby, I decided, so I wasn't so keen for the young people to take her out in the pram for walks. I wanted to make the most of my last chance with a little baby!

Things were settling down at the manse in Tilehurst, and I was getting used to having three children, though it was very hectic at times. A day or two after Abigail was born Tessa and Nigel went down with measles! The hard work had begun! They recovered well, and Nigel started school. Tessa got a post card from the hospital to say she was due in to have her tonsils out. She had been on the urgent list for this operation, having been very ill on several occasions with tonsillitis.

David and I discussed the timing of Tessa's operation. "You remember how upset she was when Nigel was born? She was so insecure for months! Although it's all been different this time, I feel for her to go into hospital now could be a bit disastrous for her." I said.

David turned the hospital card over in his hands. "Well, we could always postpone it; but that will put Tessa at the bottom of the list for the operation."

"We can explain that it's too near the birth of her baby sister, and the timing is bad." I persisted.

We continued to discuss it; and decided we would cancel the appointment. But we also decided to pray over Tessa, anoint her with oil, and ask God to heal her. She never had tonsillitis again, and she never had the operation. I wished over thirty years later we had done the same for Nigel, who as an adult had frequent bouts of tonsillitis and had to have his tonsils removed – a painful operation always, but far worse as an adult.

The door bell rang. It was early evening.

I went to answer the door. A small girl stood on the doorstep. I recognised her as she was one of our neighbours' children.

"Is Mr Mills in? Please say he is!" she asked.

"David!" I called. "You're needed!" David emerged from the dining room where he had been typing out Sunday's sermon.

"Please, Mr Mills, come quickly. One of my sisters is going crazy. And she's got a carving knife, and Mum's trapped in a corner and Pat (I've changed her name) won't let her move. Everyone's terrified."

David grabbed his jacket and they both ran down the road together. I got the two older children together, who had heard the conversation on the doorstep. "I think we'd better pray!" I said. We went into the lounge and held hands and we each said a prayer for the safety of the neighbours, and now for Daddy too!

A short time later the phone rang. It was David (at least he was alive and hadn't been stabbed, I was very relieved!).

"Pat's given me the knife. I think to defuse the situation we had better have her to stay at our house for a few days till the family have recovered. Is that all right with you?"

I thought about our three small children – and our carving knives in the kitchen drawer!

"Yes, as long as you think we're safe with her; by all means bring her." I replied.

"She's calmed down: quite subdued. Don't worry." David informed me.

I hid all our sharp knives. Five minutes later, the door bell rang, and Pat stood there, alone. "Mr Mills is just coming. He told me to come on and he will bring the bag Mum is packing for me later." I welcomed her in, and made her a cup of tea. She immediately started to play with the children and make herself at home.

Pat stayed for a couple of weeks and was no trouble at all. But over the next couple of years she did show signs of strange behaviour and went into hospital for a while. I've heard long since that she got married and had children and seemed totally normal again.

I felt after that visit it was time we all went down into the town centre of Reading and wandered around the shops. I totally identify with Petula Clark's song "Down Town" – When you are feeling low, just go down town! I thought I would prepare an egg salad for when we came back. I put six hard boiled eggs in a saucepan on the gas stove, and then ran upstairs to tell the children our plan. We were all excited. I expect Tessa and Nigel already had plans for how they were going to spend their pocket money, down town! Shoes on - coats on - and baby Abigail in her carrycot on the back seat of the car. One child sat next to her and the other in the front seat. We drove off, through Tilehurst , down onto Oxford Road, and found a car parking space right outside the big main store. We had great fun! It was only as we were getting back into the car I remembered our lunch! The eggs would be drastically hard boiled, still cooking on the gas stove. Oh NO!

We drove back home in double quick time. I drove into our driveway at the manse. I left the children to sort themselves out, gather their purchases, and hopefully keep an eye on Abigail. I rushed into the kitchen – smoky and smelly! The gas was still flickering on low, and the saucepan was black – and empty! I was mystified, and presumed the heat had burnt the eggs to nothing. It was about a week later when I happened to glance up at the ceiling. There were the eggs! Stuck like little mushroom type bombs on the ceiling. I cleared up as best I could but the marks were still there when we eventually left the manse!

The morning post arrived. There was a letter from the Billy Graham Crusade that had just taken place in London. A young man called Gerald had gone forward to commit his life to Christ. He was in a hospital near Tilehurst Congregational Church. Would someone from our church follow him up, and perhaps invite him along to church.

David went along to visit Gerald – and discovered he had quite a story to tell.

He had been sent to a young offenders' prison in Reading, having been arrested in possession of a knife out on the street somewhere. Gerald had come from a rather difficult home background in the Midlands, and was one of eleven children. Part way through his sentence in Reading Jail he started complaining of a pain in his leg. His complaints were ignored because no one took him seriously. The pain increased and Gerald was finding it difficult to walk. He was allowed out to go for a hospital check up and it was discovered he had cancer, in the leg, but it had spread and was inoperable. The prognosis wasn't good – so he was allowed out of prison for hospital treatment and his prison sentence was suspended.

Gerald said some of the nurses at the hospital had taken him up to the Billy Graham Crusade and were continuing to pray for him. He was now in a smaller hospital near Tilehurst. He walked around using crutches. The prognosis was so bad that we telephoned a lot of our Christian friends and asked them to pray for Gerald as well. He was just twenty years old. With a huge amount of prayer support surrounding Gerald, David and one of the young people in our church, Michael, went along to the hospital and prayed for him, both laying their hands on him and anointing him with oil, and also giving him a cloth that had been prayed over by a group of Christians who were praying for Gerald in Kent, as was done in New Testament times. If you would like to know more, read Acts chapter 19 verses 11 and 12.

The miracle happened and all the pain in Gerald's leg went. He ran up and down the ward in great excitement. The nurses were very alarmed to see Gerald putting all his weight on his leg and took away his shoes. He arrived in church the next Sunday in a pair of slippers! Soon after that the hospital put his leg in plaster to stop him putting his weight on it. But nevertheless the doctor said he no longer needed to stay in hospital, so he was released into our care.

One of the young mothers at church, an ex-police woman, with a most delightful sense of humour, offered to have him live with her family of two small boys and her husband. Arrangements were made and Gerald moved in with Iris and Les Bridges, and their two small boys Ian and James. Gerald's first task was to chip away at the leg plaster, gradually over a few days of living with Iris and family. He also was a great walker! He took off sufficient plaster to make it possible to walk from Tilehurst to the Royal Berkshire Hospital, a distance of four or five miles, to spend time chatting with all his nurse friends. He seemed to have no comprehension of meal times or any normal understanding of family life. His timetable was totally his own and he was a law unto himself. He would turn up at the Manse, and he always wanted to feed our little baby Abigail. His method of doing this was to prop her up somewhere and stick the bottle in her mouth – hold it for ten seconds then find something to prop the bottle up and then walk off and leave her. I didn't want to hurt Gerald's feelings but I had been taught that was a dangerous and unacceptable way to feed a small baby! I used to keep an eye on the situation and then gently intervene and pick Abigail up.

Gerald would be around the manse most days. He adored the children and made them a huge Wendy House that lasted many years. His yellow skin had disappeared and he looked young and healthy again. The prison didn't want him back so he got himself a job helping a greengrocer with his delivery van. In Gerald's spare time we never knew where he was, if he wasn't at the Manse or with Iris and her family. Iris was in despair at the number of meals she made for him which he never turned up to eat. He didn't see the importance of "being home for meals".

We took him from Reading to Newcastle under Lyme when David was asked to take a wedding up there. He was good company on the journey, and while we went to visit the bride and her family Gerald went off for a walk. Half way through the wedding he reappeared. I was feeling cross with him and had been wondering where on earth he had got to.

Gerald slipped into the pew and sat next to me.

"Sorry I'm late, Daphs." He whispered.

"Where've you been?" I whispered back, wondering whatever could have befallen him.

"I went into St George's Church to pray and got chatting with the vicar and told him my story. The time just flew. Sorry, Daph," he said appealingly. I smiled at him, calming myself down and concentrating on the wedding ceremony.

After the wedding and reception, we all squeezed back into the car, five of us plus Gerald. As we drove South, Gerald was reading the sign posts. "We aren't far from my home. Please can I just go and see my Mum and her new baby. I haven't met my baby sister yet. Besides, Mum said she has packed up all my things and put them in a box ready for me to collect some time."

We agreed to divert off the route and go and find Gerald's house. We drove miles through heavily built up areas, and Gerald began enthusiastically showing us the way the nearer we got to his old home. We arrived, and parked the car in the street. Gerald jumped out of the car, ran down the path and disappeared into the house. He was gone quite a while. So, anxious to be on our way, we got out of the car and went to investigate. Gerald was playing with his baby sister, and there seemed to be children everywhere.

I had never ever seen such poverty. A little girl of about three years of age clung to me. When I looked at her hands I realised her fingers were so dirty they were stuck together and she couldn't move them apart. So I found a wash basin, ran the warm water tap out of which flowed cold water. With great perseverance I got the dirt off and she started to wriggle her fingers again. She said she was hungry. We went back to the kitchen but Gerald and his mother were talking elsewhere. The little girl pointed out the larder cupboard, and got a chair and dragged it near the cupboard. I opened the door. There were three empty shelves and half a pot of jam. That was all!

David in the meantime was telling Gerald we must continue our journey – we still had a long way to go and Tessa and Nigel needed their sleep, and also Abigail would need feeding soon. Gerald said his mum had just given him some money to get chips for the kids! He ran up the path and out of the gate and we waited, hoping the fish and chip shop wasn't too far away! But he was back fairly soon with a bag of chips which he put on the kitchen table. The children emerged from all over the house and started to eat.

We said goodbye and left to get back into our car. We were just about to set off when Gerald jumped back out of the car and said he'd forgotten his box of belongings. He ran back into the house and emerged moments later with a box about one foot square. We put it in the car, and Gerald's mother holding the baby stood by the gate and waved goodbye.

Gerald chatted all the way home. He was so excited to have seen his family. I was very quiet, trying to process the shock I felt at the poverty I had seen.

The months flew by and Gerald was fit and well and walking miles, when he wasn't working with the local green grocer and his delivery van. Our local doctor had been assigned to keep an eye on him, but proclaimed him fit and mysteriously healthy. Gerald had a good colour in his cheeks and looked really well. The cancer had disappeared from his leg and elsewhere in his body. There were no scans in those days, but all the evidence was that God had healed him.

The months went by and Iris began to feel a bit overwhelmed with Gerald's unpredictability, and her two boys were beginning to copy some of Gerald's habits; Iris asked about whether there was anyone else who could take Gerald on, now that he was fit and well again. A young Christian couple, youth leaders, on the other side of Reading offered to have him. They were used to young people, and we felt it was a good next step.

Gerald kept in touch with us even from the other side of town, and all seemed to be well. We all relaxed and life seemed to go back to normal.

Gerald reached his 21st birthday, and began to show signs of a tumour on the brain. Our prayer group that met weekly at our house got down to prayer for him again. The general feeling was that Gerald was in a spiritual battle.

We were puzzled that Gerald refused to come to church and didn't want to come to the midweek prayer and Bible study group. He avoided any conversation that was about God or Christianity. We offered Gerald many times the opportunity to be prayed for again for healing. But he refused.

The more we prayed the more information came to us over the following week or two. We discovered that while Gerald had been in hospital a group of people involved in the occult had started to visit him and were having séances to help him! Once Gerald was healed he had moved out of the hospital environment and lost contact with this other group of people. But at some point recently this group involved in occult and spiritualism had befriended Gerald and somehow pulled him into their circle of influence again.

As we prayed it appeared that God was warning us He was going to take Gerald to Himself, so that he would be safe from the satanic clutches of this group of people. A few days later Gerald's symptoms all disappeared, he appeared completely well, having his old energy back and was his old smiling self again. Our doctor called in to see us, and enquired about Gerald. I told him I was sure he would die very shortly. The doctor said, "Don't say that when I am just coming to the conclusion I have witnessed a miracle!"

The last days of Gerald's life seemed perfect, but then in twenty four hours he went downhill rapidly and died. His funeral at our church was full, and we sang Gerald's favourite hymns. A couple of his family came down from the Midlands and made some lovely friends while amongst us. The group of spiritualists stood on the church steps and said to David, "We healed Gerald!"

David replied, "No you didn't! God did!"

Of course we were sad and we missed Gerald and his cheeky sense of humour. But we knew he was safe in the arms of the Lord, and could no longer be pulled into a place of satanic danger.

CHAPTER TWELVE

In the mean time David went to several ministers' meetings run by a comparatively new organisation called Fountain Trust, run by the Rev Michael Harper. As we got to know Michael a bit better he would phone us and ask if we could meet so and so off the plane at Heathrow and look after them for a day or two till the conference started at which they were due to speak.

Consequently we had several famous Christian speakers and authors to stay with us. Maybe the most famous was David du Plessis and his wife. I think they had had five children and adored being with ours. Michael set up Fountain Trust to bring good teaching about the work of the Holy Spirit to England from other continents, and to publish books and a magazine to help ministers, clergy and lay people, in the work of the Holy Spirit. It was a well known and extremely important organisation in the Church during the 60s, 70s, and 80s. And Fountain Trust and Michael Harper were known all over the world.

The door bell rang.

David was in and went to answer the door. Enthusiastic male voices were heard and it didn't seem to me as though there were any problems abroad! David walked back into the room and said, "Daphne – this is Geoffrey Gould. He's on his way down to the West Country to a Bible study and wondered if I'd like to go!" I shook hands with Geoffrey and glanced at the clock – 7pm! We were a good two hours at least from anywhere you could call the West Country! That would mean a very late Bible Study.

"What time's the meeting?" I asked curiously. Geoffrey said, "Oh, it's not tonight! It's tomorrow evening at 7.30. It's at a place called Post Green in Lytchett Minster. The Rev Jean Darnall is speaking."

I am already wondering where Geoffrey is going to sleep tonight!

David offered Geoffrey some left over dinner and a cup of tea, and I carried on putting the children to bed. When I came back downstairs the two men were deep in conversation, so I got on with the ironing in the kitchen. David came out a bit later and said, "Is it all right if Geoffrey kips down on the sofa? He's got a camper van outside but it's a bit chilly tonight."

"That's fine by me. Just warn him he may have children jumping all over him in the morning!"

I went upstairs to find some bedding, and took it into the lounge. I thought Geoffrey was a very impressive statesman like man, with lovely warm, gentle eyes. "So are you both going down to Dorset tomorrow?" I asked.

"If you can manage the children and everything up here, I'd love to go," said David.

Next afternoon Geoffrey and David set off for Poole, Dorset.

Around 9pm that evening the phone went. "Hi!" I heard my husband's voice. "I'm ringing from Post Green! I've got a favour to ask you!"

"What's up?" I asked, wondering what was up!

"Well, Jean Darnall wants to set up a youth camp in the grounds of Post Green this summer. And she's asked if I can help run it. It would mean giving up a week or ten days of our summer holiday, that's the trouble. The plan is that we would bring our caravan down, and camp with the young people, and run meetings morning and evening for about five days. There's no problem with our three children – they are all welcome!"

I thought it sounded good fun! So I said "Yes" that was fine by me.

That decision changed our lives completely in the years to come.

The weeks flew by and in no time at all we were hooking up our caravan and towing it down to Dorset. We were a bit tired after a hectic year in the church, so we gave ourselves two extra days stopover in the New Forest. By this time we had a large German Shepherd dog, Heidi, who came with us. We had a marvellous time in the New Forest, and drove on to Lytchett Minster refreshed and excited. I discovered that the place we were going to, Post Green, was a large house owned by Sir Thomas and Lady Lees. We didn't have much spare money but I had gone out and bought a couple of new things to wear to posh up for the visit.

We drove into the drive of Post Green and Faith and Tom Lees immediately came out to greet us. I soon noticed Faith's torn orange shirt, and a pocket missing from her jeans. Tom had an open neck shirt and no tie, and he too was wearing elderly jeans. I felt over-dressed! We jumped out of the car and both Tom and Faith flung their arms around me in welcome, as though I was their long lost best friend ever.

Tessa and Nigel climbed out of the car and ran to greet Tom and Faith and were welcomed with equal enthusiasm. I lifted Abigail out of her baby seat and we were shown where we could park the caravan, then were invited into the house where some other members of the team had already arrived and were chatting together. I recognised Rev Jean Darnall. We had met when we went with Michael Harper to look at a large country house where he was thinking of forming a community. He thought that David and I might join them in this venture. I remembered Jean as smart and brightly dressed American lady, with an infectious giggle.

Don Double, an evangelist from Cornwall, was there with his wife and children. He had brought a huge tent, which would be where the meetings would be held in the field opposite Post Green house. Then someone called Vic Ramsay and his wife Jan were introduced. They were working with drug addicts in Kent. We met Rev Dr Denis Ball and his wife Pinky Ball with their children; they also were planning to help at the camp. We began to get to know the team and to plan the camp. As I had three small children to look after it never entered my head that I would be on the team running the camp. But I found myself drawn into everything; the children were all being looked after and having a most marvellous time. I felt out of my depth, but realised I couldn't use the children as an excuse to opt out. Jean Darnall was most persuasive and seemed to have a God-given gift to perceive what other's abilities were.

We had a couple of days to set up the site, including painting a cow shed or horse stalls that were turned into loos for the young people. Abigail was about 20 months old, very independent and running around everywhere. Tessa and Nigel had a wonderful time in the tree house with the children of the Doubles, Ramseys, and Balls.

Just as the camp was starting a Pentecostal minister and his family were driving through Lytchett Minster towing the caravan on their way to their annual holiday. Their car broke down at the bottom of the road, and the garage said it would take several days to repair. They asked the man who ran the garage if there were any camp sites nearby and maybe he could tow them there. The garage owner towed them into Post Green! The Rev Wynne Lewis and his wife were welcomed with open arms, as we all were, and they became a part of the team for the youth camp. I don't think it was easy for Wynne though: he was a traditional Pentecostal minister – and the new move of the Holy Spirit in the more traditional church denominations seemed rather strange to him.

The young people arrived in every possible form of transportation. We had cars and drivers on standby to go to the railway stations and bus stations around Poole, Wareham, Wimborne and beyond. Cars, vans, camper vans, hikers, bikers, all poured through Post Green gates in far greater numbers than were expected. Our nice open space around our caravan on the field became covered in a mosaic of little tents and bigger tents of assorted bright colours. Heidi, our German Shepherd dog found extra food scavenging around the tents, we discovered later in the week when more and more complaints were emerging about campers sausages and other food disappearing!

The young people came from churches, schools, colleges, universities, in groups and in ones and twos. There was no charge for the camp, but I think a plate or basket was passed around on the last night. Musicians turned up to lead the singing and worship. Various speakers would be invited to take turns to share their stories and do some Bible teaching in the mornings, and Jean Darnall would be the main speaker in the evening meetings. In the afternoons the young people had optional trips off site, or sat around playing their own guitars, singing and chatting, and some played with the children.

We had a choir to help lead the singing, and I remember sitting with the choir one evening meeting when Abigail toddled in to the meeting. She had climbed out of her cot which we had fixed up in the caravan, and opened the door, climbed down on to the grass, and made her way across the field and into the big marquee where the music was coming from. She had her dinky feeder in her mouth, with a fluffy cover attached to it. Jean Darnall announced, "Oh, here comes Lamb Chop!" Everyone looked around at Abigail and laughed. A friend called Margaret Mather scooped her up and popped her back into bed for me! Abigail was nicknamed "Lamb Chop" by Jean and friends for years to come.

We hardly saw the children except at meal times; they were up in the tree house talking, sharing and even praying for one another. As Post Green was also a farm there were bits of farm equipment around – the favourite being a very large flat trolley that Tom Lees used for carrying essential supplies around the field. The children would see it coming, and if there was room on it they would all climb on for the ride. If it was full up they would run up the field following it, wait till Tom, or his son Christopher, had emptied it, then the trolley would fill up with all the children for a ride back towards the house.

I had never in all my life met such a safe, happy idyllic environment, both for the children, the young people, and the adults. I thought to myself, "This is heaven! This is the Kingdom of God! We are living in it now!"

The days flew by and it seemed that all the young people had met with God in some way or other. One evening towards the end of camp Jean Darnall invited any who wanted to be prayed for, for whatever they needed, to come forward and go into one or other of the counselling tents that had been set up before camp started. It seemed that about two hundred young people poured out of the exits to the counselling tents. There were about fifty people left seated.

Jean Darnall was still standing on the platform. As the last few campers were disappearing through the tent flaps, Jean looked across at me, sitting half way back in the marquee.

"Daphne, would you just take over the meeting for me till we come back please!"

The following five seconds seemed like a life time as I struggled with shock and excuses as to why I couldn't possibly do it. I wasn't trained, I was a mother mostly stuck at home with three small children, I wasn't prepared, I had nothing to say.....

Jean smiled and it obviously didn't enter her head that I would say "no"! I got up out of my seat and Jean immediately jumped off the platform and headed towards the exit. I climbed up on to the platform, and turned to face the fairly empty tent. The young people who were left were sprinkled in amongst rows of empty chairs. But they were precious and God loved them, and they were looking at me expectantly. I picked up the song sheet on the lectern and got them all singing. Fortunately some of the musicians were still in their seats! While they were singing I was frantically praying for inspiration! Then the Lord drew my attention to a visitor sat half way up on the right hand side. His name came flashing into my mind.

The singing finished and the campers all sat down. "It's wonderful to have you with us, Tony," I said. "I know you have a story to tell about something that happened to you recently. I wonder if you would like to come up here and tell us about it?"

I had never met Tony, but I had heard at a team meeting that he had recently come back from some mission and God had done amazing things.

Tony jumped up out of his seat and replied, "I'd love to!" and ran up the aisle between the seats, and stood next to me on the platform. He launched into his most interesting story, during which many of the young people were quietly making their way back to their seats. Tony finished his story, and as I thanked him, he climbed down from the platform and made his way back to his seat. I got the song sheet out again, and after making a few appropriate comments about Tony's story, I got the young people singing again. Half way through the second song, Jean returned and stood next to me. I handed my song sheet to her and slipped back to my seat, thinking "God is faithful! He didn't let me down!"

It was by no means the last time that Jean Darnall or Tom or Faith Lees dropped me "in the deep end" – and God always supplied the floats so that I could swim!

On the last evening of the youth camp we had the usual (fantastic) singing and worship time, and an uplifting and challenging talk by Jean Darnall. During the day we had all been sent off to find fir cones and to leave them in a pile in the centre of the camp field. As the evening meeting drew to a close Jean said, "As you leave the tent tonight you will discover a bonfire has been lit near the fir cones. If you would like to, please pick up a fir cone and stand near the bonfire. Let the fir cone represent either something you have vowed to God this camp that you will give up, or may be a decision you have made about your life, a commitment you have made. Think and pray carefully. When you are ready, throw the fir cone in the fire. This is symbolic of what God has been doing with you during the camp."

I slipped out of the exit at the back of the marquee and ran over to check how things were in the caravan. Abigail was fast asleep, safely in her cot, with her lamb chop dinky feeder lying on her pillow. We had now designed a roof for her cot, so she could stand up and look out of the window, but not climb out! Two helpers each evening kept a check on all the children, so I had no worries on that score. Tessa and Nigel were in their bunk beds, talking quietly and sleepily. "I'll be back in shortly!" I told them, grabbing my anorak and running back towards the bonfire which was now well alight. The flames were quite high, and with such a crowd of young people standing all around the fire it was hard to see what really was going on.

The sky was darkening and it seemed in no time at all I could hardly recognise any face – they all looked different in the darkness and by the glow of the fire. Very slowly fire cones were tossed into the bonfire. I picked one up off the small pile left and rolled it over in my hands. I felt deeply touched by what I had heard and seen during the past few days; and more than that, by the love that I had felt. I knew it had been in a life-changing situation.

The love and acceptance I had felt from Sir Thomas and Lady Lees – Tom and Faith – was almost overwhelming. Right from the very first moment I had met them they had made me feel different about myself! When I asked Abigail a couple of years later what she thought Jesus looked like, she replied immediately, "He looks like Aunty Faith."

Remembering our childhood, I think both Valerie and I would say that we had somehow come to the conclusion that we were failures. Suddenly I was in an environment, with comparative strangers, and I felt deeply loved, deeply trusted, and very affirmed. I felt that for those few days at Post Green I was living in heaven – or at least that heaven's gates were opened wide and we could walk in and out as we pleased. It felt like holy ground. The presence of God was everywhere – the love of Jesus seemed to be popping out of every blade of grass, and was on every face that smiled at me.

I looked down at my fir cone. I reminded myself that the fir cone was not representing "a wish" – and "Don't tell anyone what you wished or it won't come true!"

I glanced around at the hundred or more young people still standing around the fire, many still holding their fir cones, and deep in thought or prayer. I was holding my fir cone so tightly it was beginning to prickle in my hands. Come on, Daphne, I said to myself, make up your mind what this fir cone represents for you!

I threw my cone into the fire. My silent prayer was a great Thank You to the Lord for bringing me to such a wonderful place – and to vow that I would come back to Post Green and serve the Lord here if He called me to do so!

Next morning when I opened our caravan door and walked over to fill up our water carrier, I noticed four or five young people still sat on logs beside the dying embers of the bonfire. They had obviously been there all night, and I could tell by the way they sat that they were deep in prayer and doing business with God.

All too soon David and I joined with the team to wave goodbye to all the wonderful young people and then we had a final team meeting, with Tom and Faith, Pinky and Denis Ball, Vic and Jan Ramsey, Geoffrey Gould, Wyn Lewis, Don and Heather Double, and some younger people from around Dorset. Jean Darnall had already left to take some meetings elsewhere.

We gathered the children, clothes and belongings together, packed the caravan up, emptied the water containers, hooked up to the car, took Heidi for one last walk and drove out of Post Green gates, with Tom and Faith waving us off. For several miles we were all rather quiet, trying to absorb all that had happened to each one of us in the last few days. David had been very involved in all the meetings and had already been invited to do speaking engagements following on from the camp. And in any case the farewell shout from Tom and Faith were "Same time, same place next year, you Mills family!"

On returning home I wrote in my journal, "A very super, powerful, moving and God-filled experience of Love"!

CHAPTER THIRTEEN

Now I will backtrack a year: just after Abigail was born I realised that many of the young wives and mothers who had committed their lives to the Lord, were struggling with unanswered questions with regard to their new faith and the Bible. So I wrote out a six page Bible study covering the most basic questions. David had bought a little spirit duplicator, very primitive but it worked. And I typed up the six pages and gave them initially to Elsie, who was the most persistent, and then to others of the young wives and mothers in the church. A couple of weeks later the door bell rang. It was Elsie.

"I've come for the next instalment of the Bible study."

"Oh! Well, sorry, it's not ready yet. I will drop it round to you as soon as I can." Elsie was still standing on the door step. She turned down the offer of a cup of tea. She was a very busy lady.

"The study is hugely helpful and I've given my copy to someone else. So could you give me another copy for myself when you can manage it, please?" Elsie smiled her lovely radiant smile, and hastened back to the manse gate, waving to me as she closed it and hurried down the road back to her house.

"Oh, my goodness me! I thought the pages I did would have been sufficient at least to start her off."

The seven or so other women doing the Bible study sent messages via David: they were ready for the next instalment! So I had no choice but to do a proper plan, and as I started to plan the whole format and subjects to be covered just flowed as I wrote.

I based the study on the story of Jesus walking on the road to Emmaus, after his crucifixion. He caught up with a couple of people who were walking along the road from Jerusalem to Emmaus. They were discussing the appalling events of the crucifixion and the terrible end of Jesus, that wonderful man, who was a prophet from Galilee. They didn't recognise Jesus and in answer to his question about what had been going on, they told him about Jesus and his crucifixion. Jesus then opened up the story of the scriptures to these two people, commencing with the story of Moses and explaining all the prophecies that speak of the Messiah. (Read Luke chapter 24).

So I called my bible study "The Road To Emmaus". Elsie and friends were very enthusiastic about the study and were beginning to ask for extra copies for more of their friends. Every spare moment I was sat at the dining room table with my Bible and notebook writing the study. I bought myself an old cheap second hand typewriter – it was cheap because it was huge and unsellable as it had a twenty-two inch carriage, which meant you could put in huge great accounts sheets – not something the average person wanted or needed.

But the typewriter did well for me, and our little spirit duplicator was working fairly all right. Geoffrey Gould was a frequent visitor to our house and saw the Bible studies being rolled off and collated, and asked for some to take to a conference he was going to. This led to The Road To Emmaus being taken into what was the Soviet Union – behind the Iron Curtain: well not exactly taken in, but smuggled in. Eventually the study was printed in three books, and people could send in their questions on a tear-off leaf at the back of each book.

Twelve years later after many reprints it was re-published, this time by Community Publishing and made into one book and continued to sell in every continent. I had letters from all over the world, and stories of what the book had done in people's lives. Rightly or wrongly I never kept any of the letters – I felt the stories were holy and belonged to God – it was His work, not mine.

While I was occupied bringing up the three children, running the manse, looking after David (!) and writing a book, I was also running MUFFS.

MUFFS was my invention! It stood for Mothers and Under Fives Fellow-Ship. It attracted a large number of mothers around Tilehurst, mostly with some connection to our church, but some just from the locality. They would arrive at the church hall around 2pm, prams, push chairs and older toddlers. We would have lots of toys out, drinks and biscuits. Then for ten minutes the mothers would have a very short talk and prayer, and the little ones were entertained in the other room with songs and choruses, usually with actions. It was very popular and fun afternoon out. It ran for a few years, but eventually I reluctantly closed it down – too many mothers had three or four children under the age of five, and I didn't have enough adults to control the activities of the toddlers. Often the mothers would be deep in discussion and were oblivious to what their children were up to. There were some strong babies who could lift up the small chairs and swing them around their heads, endangering other little ones toddling around. In the end my nerves were completely shattered at the end of each afternoon – and when I heard that several of the mum's were expecting more babies I wilted at the knees and sadly closed it down. Besides I was expecting my third child as well! I encouraged the mums to swop addresses and visit each other in their own homes!

The piano that Grandma Lomax had helped me buy had been delivered on one of my father's lorries to the manse at Newcastle; and when we moved from there to Tilehurst, Reading, it was loaded into a furniture van and delivered to the new manse. It was regularly tuned as I dare not learn a song with some flat notes! I phoned the music shop in Reading town centre and they promised they would send out their recommended piano tuner. "He's blind. His name is John Hall, and he gets about with the help of a guide dog," the music shop spokesman told me. "I'll get him to call next Thursday around 10am."

As it was school holidays Tessa and Nigel would be home. They were very excited as they were looking forward to the big dog coming too.

The door bell rang.

I opened the door. A young exceedingly blonde man with a piano tuner's bag stood on the door step. "I'm John Hall. Are you Mrs Mills? Is this 8 Crescent Road?" He asked. He didn't look blind; he was smiling a bit apprehensively, but otherwise looked totally "normal"!

"Yes. You are at the right place, come in. But where's your Guide dog? I promised the children you were bringing a dog." I asked, as I led him into the dining room where the piano was. He put down his bag, having followed me in. He touched the piano, then he opened the lid. He turned to face me. "The dog's had to go back."

"Back where?" I asked.

John said, "Back to Exeter. I couldn't keep him. I'm not allowed a dog in the flat I'm in and I couldn't find anywhere else to live."

"That's awful! How are you managing to get around to do your job?" I said.

"It's not very easy, and everything takes twice as long. Besides I miss Mangus terribly."

Tessa and Nigel had run down stairs and were hovering around waiting to see the dog. So I explained to them that Mangus had had to go on holiday – may be next time you will see him, I said. They were very disappointed, but quickly became fascinated with what John was doing. He took the lid and the top of the piano off, then the front of the piano, so everything was exposed. Nigel loved anything mechanical so he sat down on the floor and watched John get out various tools, playing single notes, scales and chords, then eventually what sounded like a full scale concerto. The sound was marvellous and I adored hearing my piano being played so majestically.

While this was going on I ran upstairs to where David was typing up some sermon notes. I explained about John and the dog. We both were of the same mind. We would offer John a home. To separate him from his dog was totally cruel.

I ran back down stairs as John was playing the last arpeggio. I got my purse out and paid him the going rate, and he handed me a card to say I'd paid. "John," I said. "Would you consider moving in here with us. Then you can have your dog back. We'd love to have you here and we'd all welcome your dog as well." John looked in my direction with disbelief and joy written all over his face.

In less than a week John had moved in with Mangus, having gone down to Exeter to bring back his beloved Guide Dog. He lived with us for about a year, and said he had put his name down for a prefab in Tilehurst, but could he stay with us till it became available. He was the easiest of guests as was Mangus. Every now and again John Hall would phone from a coin box somewhere on the outskirts of Reading and ask me to look up an address in the phonebook for him. He only wanted one meal a day, in the evening, and he paid his way. He helped with chores around the house, and played with the children. He was excellent at lobbing a balloon around, and he was skilled at doing wooden jigsaw puzzles, though sometimes he completed them picture face down!

He was so amazing that I decided he must be partially sighted, as how else could be do the things he does. One cold morning I had lit the gas fire in the lounge. John was up early and was seated in my rocking chair by the fire. I decided to warm up my jumper and skirt before I put them on. So I ran downstairs in my underclothes, and knelt by the fire to warm them. I watched John's face very carefully. There was not a flicker of any change of expression on John's face. We engaged in conversation, and I excused myself and ran upstairs with my warm clothes to finish dressing. "He's definitely blind!" I remarked to David.

John wasn't a believer but felt he should come to church because he was living with us. We said he didn't need to if he didn't really want to. But he insisted. So he would walk to church with Tessa, Nigel, and me. Abigail was in her push chair and Mangus was on his guide dog harness. As soon as we got into church the dog harness came off, and Mangus lay down somewhere in our pew. But as the weeks went on, and John persisted on coming every Sunday, Mangus made himself more at home. He would creep out of the pew and go and stand next to David who was up at the front taking the service – and even sometimes went up into the pulpit. John would whisper, "Where's Mangus?" the reply was always, "Up the front with David!"

At some point John decided he wanted to become a Christian, and he prayed a prayer of commitment and said, he really would like to read the Bible. So we got in touch with some Blind Society, who said they would send the New Testament to John for free, written in Braille of course.

A week or so later a large post office van stopped outside our house and brought parcel after parcel after parcel to our front door. Our hall filled up. All the parcels were addressed to Mr John Hall. When John and David came back from their various appointments around tea time, it was rather difficult to get from the hall into the lounge or kitchen! John was very amused but also horrified as there was not space in his bedroom for what turned out to be the whole of the New Testament. David offered to build some shelves round at the church. The Braille books could stay there and John could take one home whenever he wanted. The deal was struck!

Life continued to be hectic at the manse, and Tessa and Nigel's birthdays were looming – a week apart. I felt I just couldn't cope with two separate celebrations and we would do something special with the children when things eased up a bit, I promised.

On the day of Tessa's seventh birthday something strange began to happen. It was a Sunday, and having been to church and shaken hands with each member of the congregation, come home and cooked lunch we were ready for a rest. We were relaxing in the lounge – and Tessa and Nigel were upstairs in their room – Abigail was lying in her pram in the sunshine.

The door bell rang. I stood up and went and answered the door. There stood one of Tessa's friends in a very pretty dress, holding what looked like a wrapped present, oh - and a swimsuit and towel. We had a large portable swimming pool in the garden and it was a warm August day. Tessa and Nigel came running down the stairs in their swim suits and they all went out into the garden. I had no sooner sat down when the door bell rang again. This time David got up to see who it was: a brother and sister, friends of Tessa's. They were carrying swimming gear also –

and seemed smartly dressed, and were carrying a bag with something in it. We sent them out into the garden where the noise and laughter was beginning to build up to a crescendo.

The door bell rang again. "I don't believe this! What's going on?" I said as I went to answer the door. This time there were three small girls on the door step, swimming gear, and what looked like nicely wrapped presents. I ushered them in and said Tessa was out in the garden, so off they ran out of the back door. I followed them out and started to count how many children were in the garden. More than I had at first thought. Kevin and Susan from next-door-but-one had also arrived, and had slipped in without ringing the door bell. They'd obviously gone straight through the side gate. Tessa and Nigel were having a marvellous time in the centre of the pool, unreachable by their mother; shrieking and splashing and playing ball in the water.

I had a horrible feeling dawning on me. I ran round to the next door-but-one neighbours. Mrs Woollen opened the door. "Oh, hello, Mrs Mills!" she said, looking a bit startled.

"Is there any special reason why Kevin and Susan are round at our house this afternoon?" I asked, although in my heart I thought I might already know the answer.

"Well it's Tessa's birthday party! Isn't it?" she said, looking puzzled, and also looking at me as though I was mad.

"Oh! Is it?" I asked helplessly.

"You didn't know?" said Mrs Woollen aghast.

"No!" I said, and tried to smile as I turned away.

"Wait! Does that mean you haven't any party food, or tea, or anything?" Mrs Woollen asked sympathetically.

"No, nothing!" I shrugged helplessly.

"Come in. As it happens I've just baked a cake and put some icing on it! You have it! Here you are!"

And I was handed a large, rather nicely iced cake. (I thought to myself, with a few candles on it could almost pass for a birthday cake!)

I thanked Mrs Woollen profusely, and carefully carried the large cake back to the manse. I explained to David that Tessa was having a birthday party, secretly arranged without our knowledge. He groaned – gone was his Sunday afternoon nap!

"Could you keep an eye on the children, please?" I asked. "Have any more turned up while I was at the Woollens house?"

"Only Mrs Hatt's little girl," replied David.

The only shop open in Tilehurst on a Sunday afternoon would be the newsagent – he only sold sweets and ice cream – no party food.

I jumped in the car and drove round the corner and bought a selection of sweets and chocolates, and a large tub of Walls' ice cream. Returning home I set out a very odd selection of "party food" on trays and carried it out into the garden. I got them all to sit down and laid the trays on the grass in front of them. Tessa caught my eye. I scowled ferociously at her to let her know I was very cross with her. She stared back at me.

"I know where you got That Cake from," piped up little Susan Woollen. I scowled at her too. "Do you really!" I replied, still glaring at Susan.

"My mummy made that this morning. I saw her ice it!" Susan insisted.

"Well, fancy that!" I answered, as I carefully cut the cake into about twelve pieces.

Later I went back round to Mrs Woollen to tell her how very grateful I was – and I felt I had got a new friend, she had been so kind.

A few months later Mrs Woollen came running around to the manse. I could tell by the way the door bell rang that it was an emergency. "Please come quick, Kevin is having a fit!"

I grabbed Abigail and ran back round to the Woollens house. Mrs Woollen was crying and saying, "I can't bear it! I can't watch it. It's happened too many times, and now it's happening more often."

I asked her if she would hold Abigail for me. Kevin was lying at the foot of the stairs. I think he was about four or five years old. He was shaking and seemed "unconscious". And I felt helpless. I had no medical knowledge and was unfamiliar with epilepsy. I could feel the tears coming in my eyes as I watched the little lad struggling, and I cautiously put my hand on his little shaking body.

"Please, Lord Jesus, heal Kevin. Please take away these epileptic fits and heal this little boy. Lord God, you love Kevin even more than his mother or father or me. You don't want him to suffer like this. Please heal him, Lord." I cried.

The Woollens weren't church goers and seemed a nice quiet respectable family. They didn't appear to need God or have any problems. But here they were asking for help in their lovely little family.

I held on to Kevin, who had stopped shaking and had opened his eyes. He looked pale, but sat up and looked at me, then across at his mother who was holding Abigail and standing a short distance away.

The love of God seemed very close in their small hallway. I just repeated to Mrs Woollen that God loved Kevin even more than they did, and He would take care of him.

It was the last of Kevin's fits, and we got to know the family well. Later when they were desperate for a holiday we towed our caravan down to Devon and put it on a site of their choice right by the sea; they had a two week holiday, and the day they left we joined them for a meal, and stayed on for another week by ourselves.

CHAPTER FOURTEEN

The longer we were in the ministry the more we found that some people, old as well as young, needed more help than we could give them just on a Sunday or a chat mid week.

We always seemed to have someone with problems staying in our house. Frequently the children were squashed up in one bedroom, and not unusually we either had someone sleeping in the lounge, or David and I were sleeping in the lounge and a couple were using our bedroom. The more we experienced the work of the Holy Spirit, and the love of God, the more we realised how much so many people needed respite and care in a loving Christian environment.

One Easter we found an elderly couple walking along the street near our house who seemed in some distress. David invited them in for a cup of tea, and it emerged that the old lady was in her 80s. The man was in his early 70s, but seemed nearly as old as his wife! Through various misadventures they had found themselves out on the street for Easter. David rang Social Services, but they couldn't consider doing anything till the Tuesday after Easter, and gave him some suggestions which turned out not to be fruitful at all. Consequently they stayed with us for the long weekend. They both seemed disorientated – and our hearts ached for them. To get to that stage in life when you should have your own home and some security, yet find yourselves homeless was terrible. They weren't the easiest couple to have in the house especially as one or both of them seemed somewhat confused – they weren't beautiful people at all – and yet we knew that God loved them and we had to love them too. I'm sorry but I can't remember where they went on to but I know we would not have let them leave us without making sure they had somewhere satisfactory to go to.

I suppose in some ways there was a pivotal incident that caused us to change direction in our ministry.

One of our lovely Holy Spirit-filled young people, Michael, was studying to be a church minister. He was away at theological college and university. He phoned us one night asking for advice. A friend of his and fellow student had a friend who was keen to go and visit a pendulum swinger (a kind of fortune teller) for information and advice. Several students at the college warned her that was a dangerous thing to do and to forget it. But she was insisting on going. Michael told David that his best friend, feeling this girl would be in danger, was insisting that he should go with her. Michael was advising him not to go – there was no way he could protect her, and he wasn't sure God would protect him if he deliberately put himself in Satan's territory.

David spoke to Michael for quite a long time on the phone, and agreed with him that Charlie (not his real name) was putting himself in a very unwise and potentially dangerous position. They finished talking on the phone, and David told me that Michael was going to do his best to warn Charlie not to go with this girl to the pendulum swinger.

At 11pm the phone went. It was Michael in some distress. Apparently Charlie had ignored Michael's warnings and gone with the girl student. On returning to college an hour or two later he had had a weird episode, a bit like an epileptic fit, and was now in an isolation ward at the local mental hospital. Michael had been forbidden to go and see him.

We prayed, and went to sleep, very concerned for Michael and Charlie.

Later the following day there were more phone calls. Charlie had more "fits" and Michael wasn't allowed to visit him. Michael kept in touch with us by phone over the coming days, and eventually Charlie was allowed out of hospital but was not well enough to return to college and university. Michael felt Charlie needed someone to pray with him as he was still pretty disturbed. The college released him into our care. So David went to fetch Charlie and he moved in with us for the rest of the term.

He was very subdued and pale, and had little to say. When the midweek prayer and Bible study group arrived on the following Wednesday evening at our house, David asked Charlie if he wanted to join in. He nodded, and went into the lounge and sat on the settee just inside the door.

The evening began with singing a few songs and hymns, and the Holy Spirit seemed to be present as the atmosphere of love and peace increased. A few prayers of praise and thanks to God were offered, and someone started singing, "When I survey the wondrous cross, on which the Prince of Glory died...", and everyone joined in. Suddenly Charlie jumped up out of his seat and ran into the kitchen and I heard a tremendous crash. Charlie had had a type of "fit" and fallen against the larder door on which I hung all the odd kitchen utensils. Several things clattered to the floor along with Charlie. Although, especially with the noise of the crash in the kitchen, the events seemed a bit scary, David and two other people hastened out to the kitchen. We finished singing the hymn, and continued to praise and worship God. And one by one we all prayed that Charlie would be set free from Satan's attack on him, stemming from his visit to the pendulum swinger with the girl from college. After about twenty minutes all four people emerged from the kitchen. Charlie looked a different chap. He was relaxed and smiling, and had colour in his cheeks. A prayer of thanks was offered to God for his great love and salvation, and we went on to follow a short Bible study. We were much more alert to God's words after the episode with Charlie. We knew we were all in a battle between good and evil, between God and Satan; and we were very relieved that God was more powerful.

Charlie stayed with us for several weeks, and did quite a lot of parish visiting, helped with the children, chatted with the teenagers, and later went on to become a minister in a church in Wales.

At around the same time as we were experiencing what it was like to "walk in the Holy Spirit", many other Christians, especially those in full time ministry, were discovering that there was a need for some people to have the opportunity to live in a loving Christian home. This was something that many had no experience of at all. And as we chatted with some of our fellow clergy we discovered they were also feeling that God was leading them to open their homes and give some people more love, care and attention than they could get in a brief chat after a Sunday service, or a short meeting during the week.

Life in the manse at Tilehurst, Reading, was really getting a bit exhausting and tricky. I was at home with three small children, often with someone or other staying who was in need of care, and David was out doing his rounds of the parish and hospitals, preparing sermons, taking weddings, funerals, baptisms, and so on. We needed space for someone mature to be helping me in the house, at the very least! It was working well up to a point, but we knew we could do so much more if we had more room.

As well as this my books, The Road to Emmaus, were constantly having to be re-typed and duplicated on our little spirit duplicator – I was so busy!

Then our friend Geoffrey Gould, who had heard us talking about our vision for the way forward, offered us his large empty house just south east of Oxford. It had about twelve bedrooms and numerous reception rooms and out-houses. We talked and prayed about it and it seemed the way forward. We had been to several conferences and meetings run by Fountain Trust and had quite a few useful contacts. Together with others we planned to run a residential training course for young people, and have space for others who needed temporary residential care. We found out later that the Holy Spirit seemed to be inspiring quite a few others with similar ideas.

When we had arrived at Tilehurst the deacons had said they wanted a youngish minister, but he was only to stay for a maximum of five years! They wanted short ministries only! With this in mind, and the fact that we had already been there four years, we seriously considered Geoffrey's offer of his huge house – which he said we could live in for free, but would be responsible for the upkeep. We had faith for that! We gave in our notice to the Tilehurst Congregational Church fairly soon after returning from Post Green youth camp, giving three months notice. It seemed a good time to move on, and do something different.

Sir Tom Lees came up from Dorset to take part in our farewell service on our last Sunday – and the church was packed. It was a wonderful farewell. We had arranged to move on the Friday following this. On Monday morning the telephone rang. David went to answer it, and I was upstairs packing up the children's toys and clothes, ready for the furniture removers to collect.

I could tell that David was having a very serious conversation, and stopped what I was doing, and hovered at the top of the stairs to try and hear what it was about. It sounded awful!

David put down the phone and started walking up the stairs. "Who was that? What was that all about?" I asked. David looked up, and said, "You'd better come down. We will chat in the lounge."

I dropped the teddy and the box of Lego I was holding, and walked slowly down the stairs, wondering what David was going to tell me.

"You remember what you thought when Geoffrey told us he couldn't be with us when we move on Friday? That he was off to Cornwall to a meeting, and he'd be gone a few days? We could pick the key up with the neighbours?" David said.

I did remember! I had been very puzzled that Geoffrey should choose to be away on the day we were moving in. The house was huge, and we would need help to find where things were. In fact I wasn't sure we could manage to move without Geoffrey being at Stanton House to direct us. But Geoffrey had already disappeared off on his travels towards the West Country and we couldn't contact him.

"Well, that was Michael Harper on the phone. He had heard of our plans, and thought he ought to warn us that there was a legal dispute about the house, between

Geoffrey and his wife, and because of a court order, no one at Geoffrey's say so can move in to it!"

"Wow!" I said. "I can't believe it! This is unbelievable! We're almost packed. We've said goodbye to the church people – and now we can't move!"

David continued, "Michael thought we might have difficulty believing what he said, and he suggests we go up to see Reg and Lucia East as soon as possible. They know the full story. Michael also said that Reg and Lucia are planning a very similar project to us, and we might consider linking up with them."

"Well, I do find this hard to believe. But when Geoffrey said he wouldn't be at Stanton House to help us move in, I had a load of doubts about the whole project." I replied.

"I know you did! And I wondered if we had heard the Lord right! It seemed a brilliant way ahead, and I really felt God was guiding us in that direction. Geoffrey's offer came just at the right time." David said. "What do you think? Shall I phone Reg and Lucia and see if we can pop up and see them?"

"I think we have no alternative. Michael said he strongly advised us to chat with them, so we had better do so. I'll go and put the kettle on while you phone them." I walked out of the lounge and into the kitchen. Half the kitchen equipment was in boxes, stowed under our bright blue kitchen table.

But the kettle was in its usual place. I filled it up with water, and switched it on. I sat down at the table and put my head in my hands. "Lord Jesus, what are you saying to us? Have we heard you wrong? We prayed and it seemed you opened the door for us to go to Stanton House. Have we made a mistake?" I began to panic! We are homeless! Surely what Michael said cannot be true? The kettle boiled and I made us each a cup of tea, and found a packet of biscuits, and carried it all into the lounge.

"Daphne, can we manage tomorrow to go and see the Easts. They can give us the whole day."

"Yes, that's fine!" I called back.

David finished the telephone call and came back into the lounge. "I spoke to Reg. You know he's the vicar of West Mersea church in Essex."

"Goodness! Well I knew he was a vicar but I didn't know they lived that far away. That's quite a trip!" I said, taking a bite at my biscuit. "So are we going to go and visit them tomorrow?" I asked.

"Yes, I've said we will. Reg said it is true that there is no way we can move in to Stanton House on Friday or at any time in the near future, and probably never!" David replied, reaching for his cup of tea. "But Reg and Lucia would love us to come and visit them. They can confirm the details, and also share their vision of what they feel God is calling them to do, and maybe we would consider teaming up with them as we seem to be going in the same direction in ministry."

We got out the map, worked out how long we thought it would take us from Reading to Mersea, which actually appeared to be an island with a road joining it to the mainland of Essex. It was a part of England I had never been to, but tomorrow would not be a day for sight-seeing. I also had a knack of falling off to sleep on long car journeys so probably would miss any sight we drove past anyway.

"We will drop Tessa and Nigel off to school and drive straight on from there. I will ask one of the other mothers to fetch them from school in case we are late back. We will have to take Abigail with us, but she's not too bad on a long journey. She's got her dinky feeder with Lamb Chop attached, that keeps her happy!"

The arrangements were made and straight after dropping the children at school we drove the long distance to the east coast of Essex. Reg and Lucia greeted us warmly. We had met them once or twice at Fountain Trust meetings but never had a conversation with them. They explained about the court order on Stanton House, which Geoffrey owned as part of his family inheritance. But his wife was apprehensive that he might give it away in his enthusiasm for his Christian faith, so had managed to get various legal restrictions put on Geoffrey.

That part of the conversation being dealt with, Reg and Lucia admitted we were in a difficult situation – three children and homeless!

We sat and relaxed in their comfortable chairs, and I began to feel I was in a safe place. They were both lovely mature Christians, and as the conversation continued they had no doubt that God had a plan for us, that He could be totally trusted to make it clear to us. The vision we had was right, and the place was wrong! They outlined their vision which was very similar to ours. It was also Michael and

Jeanne Harper's vision – so may be we could all link up together – at least consider moving in together and working together.

We drove away fairly soon after lunch. We had lots to talk about and it wasn't the time for me to sleep my way back home. We talked about other possibilities – and what we were going to say to Geoffrey!

As soon as we got home we decided to telephone Tom and Faith Lees at Post Green – their immediate response was, "Come down here, we need you! Unfortunately all our farm cottages are occupied at the moment but you could move into temporary accommodation till one is available."

So on the following day, Wednesday, we drove down to Bournemouth and had a look around for winter lets. But nothing seemed available that would suit us. And we had no income!

David phoned the church treasurer and explained we had a problem with accommodation and could we stay in the manse for a few more weeks. The treasurer phoned us back, having talked with the other church deacons, and said we could stay for another 3 weeks. Michael Harper had been asking David if he would work with him at Fountain Trust at some time in the future. So David phoned Michael and they had a discussion on the phone about the way forward. In the meantime we had found accommodation to rent in Brighton. Michael invited David to start working for Fountain Trust with him and help run conferences and do various speaking engagements on his behalf.

We telephoned Tom and Faith and let them know what our plans were. They again invited us any time we wanted to move down to Dorset and work with them. As the accommodation hadn't worked out, it didn't seem that is what we were meant to be doing for the following year or two.

We moved down to Brighton a week later, having put most of our belongings and furniture in store. We hired a thing that looked like a horsebox and filled it with our clothes and bedding, and the children's toys and set off for Brighton. On the day the furniture removers came, I got the men to put two tea chests on the front lawn. Nigel stood in one of them, and Abigail stood in the other. They watched the whole proceedings from the safety of the tea chests, laughing and jumping up and down. As I had used the same method when we left Newcastle under Lyme, for Tessa and Nigel – I would recommend the system any day!

In just over two weeks it had seemed that our world had fallen apart, and was back together again. We drove down to Brighton, heading straight for the seafront. It was a cold, sunny day. We slowed up near the dolphin sea life centre, and turned left up into Margaret Street. Our new abode was almost next door to a pub, and the road was full of terraced houses, very close together, and parking on one side of the road only.

We climbed out of the car, and using the key which had been posted to us, we walked inside the house. There had been no time to check it out earlier but the owner had sounded very pleasant and said we could have the house till March for a fairly low rent. We walked inside, straight into a small sitting room, leading into a tiny kitchen. In the sitting room was a staircase that led up to a bedroom and bathroom. The stair case then went on up another floor to two more bedrooms. The children were very happy to sleep so high up in the house. Clattering back down the stairs again, we opened another door in the sitting room - this led to another staircase leading down to a double roomed basement – which was immediately claimed as a play area. As we switched on the light and planned where the children could put their toys, we noticed legs, ankles and feet walking past. The window looked out onto the pavement, below street level. The children adored it all.

The next day we went to check out the schools. We were in a rather rough area, and having chatted with the local headmaster, felt that for the short time we were in Brighton we had better put Tessa and Nigel in a small private school we found in Hove called Windlesham. It had the same school uniform that Tessa and Nigel had been wearing in Reading, which was a definite bonus.

David was away a huge amount, travelling all over England taking conferences and speaking engagements, mostly teaching about the Holy Spirit which seemed what many churches were asking for, and was the foundation on which Fountain Trust had been formed: to teach about the work and gifts of the Holy Spirit, a subject sadly neglected in the Church for a long time.

So I was on my own a lot but the children were great company. Tessa and Nigel soon made lots of friends at their new school and began to be invited to birthday parties. These were usually somewhere in Hove. One particular Saturday Tessa and Nigel were both invited to the same party. So once they were smartly dressed, and clutching their gifts, we all piled into the car. David had gone off somewhere north on the train. Tessa, Nigel and Abigail were all sitting on the back seat, making a fair amount of noise. There were no such thing as seat belts in cars, but the children were told they must stay seated and not stand between the two front seats while I was driving. With the help of a map I found the road and the house number where the party was being held. It was in a road where no parking was allowed, so I hovered while Tessa and Nigel got out, holding their gifts. "See you later, Mum!" and they ran off, slamming the car door as they went. We drove slowly back to Margaret Street, Abigail was singing happily, alone on the back seat.

I became conscious as I drove along the sea front that the car had gone quiet. I slowed up and looked in the mirror. I couldn't see Abigail and she wasn't answering me. I glanced round, no Abigail and the car door was swinging open.

I realised Abigail had fallen out of the car – it must have been when I went round a corner; but which corner? When did I last hear Abigail singing? I jumped out and shut the back door and turned the car round and drove back the way I had come. Immediately there was a bend, and a garage. I signalled right and drove onto the garage forecourt. Getting out of the car I immediately ran to a petrol pump attendant. Before I had a chance to open my mouth he said, "Have you lost a baby?" "Yes," I said frantically. "Don't worry, she's fine. My mate is holding her in that kiosk over there." He said pointing to the far corner of the forecourt. I ran over as fast as I could. Sure enough there was Abigail, sat on this stranger's lap. In her mouth was Lamb Chop, and she looked totally unhurt and unfazed. She held up her arms to me, and I took her from the man holding her. "We saw her fall out of your car as you went round the bend. Lucky you were going slowly and there was no other traffic about!" he said.

I hugged Abigail to me, deeply shocked. She seemed oblivious to the whole episode, and I was just extremely glad she was well padded up with winter clothes and a very thick all in one snowsuit and hood. She was nearly two years old when she had this adventure.

She nearly had another adventure but it didn't quite work out. When she had a chance to sit in the front seat I would tie her baby seat to the back of the front seat and she could see very well out of the front window. There was less traffic on the road in those days, and slower speeds – and no seat belts as I mentioned before. Abigail could lean forward and fiddle with things on the shelf in front of her, which she did sometimes.

One day when I was taking the children to school I noticed a note on the windscreen under the wiper. It was a police note saying I must report to the local station with my registration disc. I looked on the windscreen and realised it had disappeared. I knew it had been there, and wasn't sure what to do. I thought I'd have a good hunt in the car later in the day. Twice more that day I had a police note left on my windscreen demanding I come down to the police station with the missing registration disc. I had searched the car and not found the tiny circle of paper. After giving the children their tea that evening I phoned the local police station.

"Look, three times today I've been told to come to the police station with the registration disc, but I can't find it. I think the baby has posted it out of the window." I said helplessly to the policeman on the phone.

"Ah, dear, Madam, we can't have that. You'd better bring your child down to the police station. We will keep her in the cells over night!" he said.

"Oh, great!" I replied quickly, "that'll be wonderful. Would you? Then I can have a peaceful night's sleep. I'll be down right away with her!"

The policeman said hastily, "No, no that's all right. Just get another disc and bring it down when you've got it!" and the phone went dead.

Time flew by, and we made quite a few friends in the area, but were conscious of the fact we had to find somewhere else to live in March. The prices of rented houses in Brighton doubled in the summer months and we realised that we would never be able to afford anywhere nearby. David was earning money with Fountain Trust but not enough for us to live in holiday accommodation alongside the beach!

Around this time some money came to us unexpectedly and we were able to consider buying a house. We looked at road and rail links that would be within easy reach of Wimbledon for the Fountain Trust offices and also within easy reach of a train station for David when I needed the car. We found a house in Esher, and moved in the spring of 1969. We stayed briefly at Michael and Jeanne Harper's house while finalising the buying of "Beulah". When we moved into the house there were no carpets on the ground floor and there were water stains up to three feet up the wall all through the downstairs rooms. The Thames had recently overflowed her banks and a lot of Esher had been under water. But we loved the house, and whether it was because it had been washed thoroughly with river water or something, but the house smelt of fresh sea air!

The local school was only about half a mile away, straight up the end of our road. When I enrolled Tessa and Nigel, I commented on the recent flood in the Esher area.

"We had a terrible day!" the headmaster said. "We had a phone call from the local police station telling us to close the school for the day and send all the children home as soon as possible. We had to phone all the parents and ask them to come quickly and fetch their children."

"What about the parents who were out, or even at work?" I asked.

The headmaster laughed. "We had no choice but to hold on to the pupils whose parents could not be contacted. By this time it was early afternoon, the river had overflowed and the water was rising. The police came in boats to take any stranded, uncollected children home."

I could just imagine the excitement for the children – going home in a rowing boat, or even one with a little motor on the back!

The headmaster continued. "One of the pupils was new to the school and had only moved house that week. He didn't know his address, and for some reason we didn't have it either. He was the last pupil to leave the school that afternoon. So I thought I had better go with him in the boat. He assured me he would recognise his bedroom curtains when we got to his house. So we cruised up and down all the roads that had now become like rivers. Eventually he excitedly pointed out his curtains. So we delivered him safely home."

The carpets were delivered back to the house a month after we moved in and the previous occupants' insurance paid for the redecorating. I got myself a little motor bike, bought a child's pillion seat, and Abigail and I rode through the heavy London-bound traffic into Wimbledon. There I found a crèche for Abigail at the Methodist Centre, and twice a week went to the Fountain Trust offices and did typing for them. The job went well, I thought, and Abigail really enjoyed herself playing with so many children. After two or three weeks in the crèche the leaders told me that Abigail was finally catching on that she wasn't in charge of the crèche, but they were!

One evening after I had been doing the job about a year Michael Harper popped in to see me. We frequently had Fountain Trust team meetings at our house, and Michael had arrived early. He very gently, politely, firmly, said he'd rather I didn't type the sales invoices any more. These were for books and cassette tapes that Fountain Trust sent out. Michael explained that I had a habit of adding the customer's discount onto their bill, rather than subtracting it. He didn't offer me another job doing anything else so sadly I stopped going to Wimbledon and Abigail missed going to the crèche.

But the timing was good! I got a rebate from the tax people, years overdue. It was enough to buy myself an old car – my first very own car. I saw a bright red Morris Traveller – four seats and double doors at the rear. Marvellous! It was a bit elderly. I could see the road through cracks in the floor but it ran perfectly and lasted me for two or three years. Almost as soon as I got my car, Faith and Tom phoned up and said they were starting twice monthly conferences at Post Green and we could come anytime we liked and stay in Post Green house. Although David was booked most weekends away from home, I was free! And so were the children! And now I had transport and no job!

So twice a month we would go down to Post Green, and the children adored the trips, and had lots of other children to play with during the weekends. I got to know Tom and Faith well, and there were excellent Bible teachers giving talks all over the weekends. I also got to know the area team who supported the work at Post Green and helped to talk to anyone who wanted help or prayer during the conferences.

It might sound as though I was full of confidence and coped with everything well. But actually I found it very difficult to enter into new situations. I hated being on my own so much, and over the years had relied on David to "cushion" me from some of life's challenges. I wasn't like it as a teenager, but having married a confident, competent, university trained minister, I gradually lost confidence and always thought David could do it better. In the end I could hardly walk into a crowded room without pushing David to go in first!

I managed to get myself and the children down to Post Green, and enjoyed the drive down to Dorset. But I was often feeling rather vulnerable, even though I hid it. One particular weekend, we arrived at Post Green for the conference and Faith had warned me they would all be out on the Friday evening, but come on down by all means. The conference started at 10 o'clock on Saturday morning. We would be in the same bedroom we had used last time. So Tessa, Nigel, Abigail and I arrived in time for supper on the Friday evening, then Tom, Faith and whoever else was in the house, all left for some meeting at Harman's Cross on the Purbeck Hills.

I was suddenly overcome with a terrible feeling of being abandoned, and desperately wanted to leave Post Green house and go back home with the children. I started to load the car, and was crying as I did so. Tessa took charge as she was worried about the way things were turning out. "I think I should ring Aunty Faith and tell her you're upset," she said.

A short conversation took place between Tessa, who was eight years old, and me. I felt as though I was falling apart. The car was loaded and we were about to leave. But I wasn't sure it was a good idea to drive such a long distance back when I was so upset. "Okay, Tessa, if you think you can, please do phone."

"I heard Aunty Faith say she was going to leave the phone number on the kitchen table in case she was needed! I will go and get it and phone her." The telephone was in the kitchen as well, and I heard Tessa say, ". . . Mummy's upset, can you come back?"

She came back into the drawing room a few minutes later, and said, "Aunty Faith's on her way. They were about to leave anyway." So we off-loaded the car again, and I had just got the two younger ones into bed when the car arrived at the front door, and I heard the two outer doors open and slam behind them. "Daphne!" I heard Faith call. Tessa ran down the stairs, and met Faith and they walked back upstairs together.

I was still tearful, but had stopped crying, feeling very embarrassed. Faith was most apologetic. "I thought you were quite happy to be on your own this evening. I'm so sorry if I misunderstood."

"No, it's not your fault, Faith. I was fine: well I thought I was fine. Then suddenly after you had gone I just felt totally abandoned. It makes no sense. And I couldn't stop crying. I thought we'd better just pack up and go home." I said.

"Look, Daphne, I think God is doing something in your life. I'm not sure what. But what I do know is that it is not at all unusual for people to come to Post Green thinking they are fine, and then to discover that they have deep hurts and needs they have never realised or acknowledged before." Faith held my hand, and Tessa's. "Shall we ask God to show you over this weekend? Then I think Tessa had better get to bed! And you can come downstairs and meet the others who are staying." Faith said. I nodded.

"Dear Lord, please help Daphne to know exactly what you are doing in her life – and where there are insecurities or hurts from the past, please heal her, Lord. You know how much we love David and Daphne, and how much we want them to join us here at Post Green, please help them to know how much they are loved and appreciated." All three of us said "Amen!"

"I will expect you downstairs in five minutes, Daphne. Good night Tessa, sleep well. You'll have lots of fun tomorrow – the Ball family and the Friend family will be here first thing in the morning – you had such a good time with Stephen, David, Martin Ball, and Lorna and Carrie Friend, at camp, didn't you?" Faith smiled and left the room.

I was feeling embarrassed still about my tears, but my spirits were lifted and I felt I could trust Faith's assessment of the situation. God had put his hand on an insecure place in me, or a past hurt that needed to be healed.

We had a marvellous time that weekend and drove back to Esher thanking God that we'd stayed for it, and not gone home early!

Tom and Faith Lees were trustees of Fountain Trust, and occasionally we had a team weekend at Post Green. Together with the teaching conferences we travelled down to Post Green quite often between 1968 and 1970.

I wrote in my journal that I was always deeply touched after a Post Green visit. Also during this time I was still extremely busy duplicating and collating copies of "The Road To Emmaus" and sold hundreds of copies at one shilling each – i.e. ten pence in today's money. I used the money to print more copies – they were selling well at Fountain Trust conferences, Post Green Conferences, and a growing number were finding their way in to Russia, Africa and Australia, Fiji, Arabia, among many other places.

David and I, together with Reg and Lucia East, were asked to run a Fountain Trust Conference at Ashburnham Place in Sussex. We met some wonderful people, who kept in touch with us for years afterwards. In the summer, together with Michael and Jeanne Harper and an enlarged team, we ran some big family camp/conferences at Ashburnham Place. Tessa and Nigel slept in dormitories with all the other children and had loads of fun. Abigail slept in our room – she was a bit young to be in a dormitory: I couldn't imagine the mischief she would get up to! The main big conferences were held in the summer, but fortunately the dates never clashed with the Post Green family camps, and the Post Green youth camps that we were invited to help at. These camps at Post Green continued annually for about thirty years, of which I attended a huge number before I took a break for a year!

CHAPTER FIFTEEN

Settling back into life at Esher, history began to repeat itself. We had people either living with us or staying with us, and the house became at times quite full. For a while we had Anne Isaacs, who had been a missionary in Persia (Iran, now). She was the perfect house mate and we all loved her and got on well with her. She was an older woman, and was happy to leave me to bring up the children without interfering ever. But she loved Tessa, Nigel and Abigail, and was always interested in everything they did.

We had a young nurse who visited us frequently, and asked to stay when she had several days off duty. We got on well together, and she adored Tessa, Nigel and Abigail. But there was a problem! She was excessively critical and judgmental – and it was like a steady drip of poison at times. I tried to deal with it, within myself and with her but the nasty comments continued. One evening when she was staying with us her visit coincided with a group of students from a local college who came each week for some singing and worship and then some Bible study. They were a lively bunch and great fun. Aileen (not her real name) surpassed herself in cryptic comments, snide remarks and destructive criticism all evening. The young people seemed to rise above it, and were still laughing and joking when they left "Beulah". But I was very distressed. It was late and I decided to sleep on it and see how I felt in the morning.

The following day, I had come to a decision. Aileen must go! I could not allow this unpleasantness to continue, especially when it was in my house! I was trying to build a loving and caring environment for these young people. And Aileen seemed to be hell bent on destroying it!

As it was school holidays the children were around all day, so I waited until after supper, and the children were in bed, to say something. I prepared my speech in my head. "Aileen," I was going to say, "Whenever you are here you are so critical and judgmental, it just destroys all the happiness and joy around. Last night you made nasty remarks about anything anyone said. I'm sorry, but I think for the time being you had better not visit us again – at least for a while...."

I walked slowly down the two staircases; the children were all happily tucked up in their beds. I walked into the dining room. Aileen was already in there, sitting on the floor by the fireplace, sipping a cup of coffee. I sat down nearby. I opened my mouth to make my prepared speech to her.

Before the first word was out of my mouth, Aileen said:

"Daphne, I want to tell you something!"

I felt she was going to say something serious appertaining to what I was about to say!

"Daphne, I want to thank you. I want to thank you very much for always welcoming me here, and for your consistent love for me."

I gazed at Aileen seriously, watchfully.

She went on: "Do you know this is the very first home I have ever consistently been welcomed and made to feel at home? After a while I always get turned out, and they don't want me to visit any more!"

I thought to myself: only God could have stopped me making my speech! What damage would have been done to Aileen if I had spoken first! She carried on talking and sharing about her past, and I began to understand her a bit better, and why she was always being turned out of other people's homes. I resolved to win this battle with Aileen through continuing to love and pray for her. We remained friends for many years after that visit! But she didn't change her ways!

Vic Ramsey, who ran the drug addict work in Kent, whom we had met at the first Post Green youth camp phoned us up one day. David answered the phone.

"I've got an ex-drug addict here. She's off the drugs, but needs to get off the cigarettes as well or she will always be vulnerable to the drug scene. Do you think you could have her living with you for a while? Her name is Mary." (I've changed her name!).

David said he would talk to me and phone Vic back. We discussed it and agreed we would try and help Mary. We understood she had been in Broadmoor and was liable to be sent back if she reoffended. We desperately wanted to help her, when we found this out.

"Thanks! I will bring her over this afternoon – failing that she can catch a bus," said Vic.

Mary caught the bus to Esher and walked up to our house.

The door bell rang.

David answered the door, and Mary walked in with a small plastic bag of belongings. We made her a cup of tea, and I showed her up to her room. We gave her the children's room, and moved Tessa and Nigel back up to the top floor where Anne had slept . Anne had moved out fairly recently into her own accommodation nearer to the Fountain Trust office at Wimbledon where she was working.

Mary adored the children and played happily with them. I have no idea how old Mary was. She looked like she had had a tough life so it was difficult to assess her age. But she was probably in her twenties. Mary had been in our house, Beulah, about two hours and had made herself at home.

The door bell rang.

I got up and went to see who it was. We rarely had unexpected visitors in Esher. We were no longer running a church, we had no youth fellowship, and no friends living close by.

I opened the front door. A slightly scruffy twenty-something young lady stood on the doorstep.

"I think you've got my mate Mary in there, haven't you?" she demanded.

"Er. . . yes!" I responded, puzzling what was going on.

"Well, where Mary goes I go. We are never separated. We've bin in prison together, we've laid in hospital beds next to each other – we are never separated." And she walked into our hall way and seemed to know in which room she would find Mary.

Actually, now as I recount this story, I am wondering for the first time if Shelley (not her real name) had travelled with Mary and hung around outside for a suitable moment to ring the door bell. I will never know!

Shelley and Mary were obviously very good friends and I could well believe they went everywhere together. They were helpful, and cleared away, washed up, and were fun to have around. They would go out for walks together two or three times a day. It never entered my head these were not just "walks" – they were hunting for cigarette ends on the pavements and in the gutters. They would piece them together and have a smoke.

We gave regular progress reports to Vic Ramsay and assured him that there was no smoking going on!

Faith and Tom phoned up one day. Could they pop in en route from London back down to Dorset? We couldn't give them accommodation, we were full up! They brought Kentucky Fried Chicken, and I had done a cheese dish, and we had a good fun meal. Faith, in her wonderful pastoral way, chatted with Mary and Shelley and made a great hit. Before they left Faith said, "You know they are smoking in the house, don't you?"

I was stunned! Having been brought up with parents who smoked, I was no good at sniffing out smokers – I was too used to the smell! I could hardly believe Faith, but she was sure that she smelt smoke in our house. We discovered she was right!

They used to go up to bed fairly early, before 11pm, which was my bedtime. I would sit on one of their beds and chat with them for a while. Then I would say a short prayer with them and say goodnight and close their bedroom door. Shelley would jeer at me, and make rude comments when I came and sat on one of their beds. One particular night I had a very bad headache and a cold starting. So I decided to go to bed early and skip my nightly routine with Shelley and Mary. I didn't feel like being jeered at that evening.

Next morning I came down to breakfast. Mary was already laying the table. I smiled at her. "Do you know Shelley cried herself to sleep last night?" she said to me.

"Why?" I said in alarm.

"Because you didn't come in and say a prayer with us!" replied Mary.

I was stunned! “But she makes remarks and laughs at me, when I come in your room.”

“She’s waits every evening for you to come in – it’s very important to her. She feels your love for her. She’s still upset.” Mary said seriously.

Shelley, Tessa and Nigel walked into the breakfast room together. I could hear Abigail slowly clumping her way down the stairs on her own. I think she was a bit bruised. Yesterday Nigel and Tessa had sat her on the top of the stairs on a tray: then slid the tray down the stairs. Half way down, Abigail had toppled off the tray and had rolled the rest of the way down the steep staircase. “It was only a game. We were going to take it in turns to go down on the tray. We thought Abigail could be first!” they said, as I had run to see what all the screaming was about.

I said, “Good morning!” to them all. “Sorry I didn’t come in last night to say good night – I wasn’t feeling very well.”

“That’s all right Daphne. We didn’t miss you anyway!” said Shelley, with bravado.

“Come on, let’s have some breakfast. Last one sitting down can do the washing up!” I said.

David continued to be away at lot, and seemed to enjoy all his speaking engagements. He met some wonderful people all over the country, and later some of those supported us with gifts of money when they felt God ask them to send us some money. It always came at a time when we needed it for a car repair, or unexpected bill.

Early one morning, just as I was about to take the children to school and then drive over and help the office staff at Fountain Trust to do some envelope stuffing, the phone rang. It was David phoning from a conference he was taking in Blackpool. He said that one of the other speakers had given him some verses from the Bible that she thought God wanted us to read. I grabbed a piece of paper and wrote down the three scriptures. We chatted for a short while then I put down the phone and told the children I’d give them a lift up to school before driving over to Wimbledon. Tessa and Nigel grabbed their school bags and hopped into the back of the car. I lifted Abigail’s baby seat (not a car seat, they had yet to be designed) and tied it to the front seat. I climbed in and switched on the engine. The car wouldn’t start. I tried again, several times – nothing worked. “Bother! We are running late. I'll walk you up to school. Quick, climb out! Don't forget your bags." I said.

I undid Abigail, and pulled the pushchair out of the back of the car. Strapping her in the buggy, we ran all the way to the school. I waved goodbye to Tessa and Nigel, and we walked slowly back to Beulah. I left Abigail sitting patiently in her pushchair beside the car, happily sucking her dinky feeder, " lamb chop", and tried the engine once more, and again. Still nothing happened.

I locked the car and wheeled Abigail in the pushchair up the path way, wondering what to do.

We entered the house and I walked back into the breakfast room. I saw the scrap of paper with the three scripture verses written down. Abigail had gone into her toy box and was pulling out a whole pile of toys. I went and fetched my Bible, sat down and looked up all three verses. They all seemed to be saying that God had a plan for us, that we would be doing a new thing, and that we should trust God. Definitely food for thought! I left my Bible open on the breakfast room table, and picked up Abigail, and went out and tried the car engine again. It started immediately.

Shortly afterwards we drove over to Wimbledon, and Abigail went to the crèche downstairs, and I helped stuff envelopes for a couple of hours. I thought to myself, "I have a feeling if I had read those Bible verses immediately I was given them, the car would have started right away. God wanted me to know that I should have realised how important it was to take notice when someone gives us scriptures like that."

From that point onwards I felt that I kept hearing from God that he was calling us to move to Post Green. But David hadn't said anything, and seemed happy and busy with Fountain Trust, so maybe I was imagining things. But nevertheless I still began to feel even more certainly that God wanted us to work with Tom and Faith, and Jean Darnall. There was another weekend teaching conference coming up at Post Green. David was free that weekend and we all went down to Post Green. Faith gave us our usual bedroom, a huge room overlooking the lawns, pond and the village church. During the conference I tried to pray more precisely about what God was saying to us. "Please, Lord, do you want us to be here? I'd absolutely love to be here. It would be like a dream come true! But I dread telling Michael

Harper and Fountain Trust that we are leaving them to come down to Dorset. That's too hard!"

As I prayed a picture came into my mind of a very high brick wall – impossible to climb over and too long to get round. Then as I looked at the brick wall, I saw the bricks in the centre being dismantled one by one till there was a big enough gap to walk through! I wondered if God is saying that the wall that seems impossible can easily be dismantled. After all it says in the Bible: "With God, nothing is impossible." (Luke chapter 1 verse 37).

When we got back after the weekend, I thought and prayed a bit more about the future. Then I said to David, "I think God is calling us to Post Green!"

He responded with a big smile. "I've been waiting months for you to say that!"

I was very surprised. I thought David would disagree and say we must stay with Fountain Trust. "Why didn't you say anything to me?" I said.

"Well, I felt we must both hear God separately. It's a very big step to make. Tom and Faith want us down at Post Green, but there won't be any salary. I will need to get a part time job, and for the rest we will trust God will give us what is needed." David was getting out his diary from his brief case as he was saying this. "Look, it's quite amazing. I'm very booked up until August, then there's nothing! We could put the house up for sale now, and pray the timing is good. We can move down to Dorset immediately after we have done the two Fountain Trust holiday conferences at Ashburnham. They run immediately after the Post Green youth camps we're helping at."

We telephoned Tom and Faith the next day – they were absolutely thrilled we were going to move down. Faith said, "I'd rather trust God for my salary than anyone else!" With that confidence ringing in our ears, we put the house up for sale and David told Michael Harper our future plans. I don't think he found it easy to accept. Jeanne Hinton and Margaret Mather had already left Fountain Trust to work at Post Green, and Reg and Lucia East were in the process of moving nearer to Post Green also. They were setting up a community about twelve miles away. We had debated working with Reg and Lucia, but they had a slightly different vision to us, and we felt it probably wouldn't work and wasn't what God was asking us to do.

Faith and Tom were certain we were called to Post Green to work with them and help with the huge numbers of people who were coming through their doors asking for help, or teaching, or prayer, or healing. Rev Jean Darnall was travelling all over the country, sometimes meeting up with David at the same conference platform somewhere, and Jean was sending many people to Post Green for residential help. Tom and Faith were desperate for more mature Christians to come and help them.

But I knew I had unresolved problems and I needed some help as well. I had sat in many meetings at Post Green, and sometimes I would feel the overwhelming need to slip out of the meeting, or even run out of the meeting. And it seemed to happen without warning. Consequently I felt I was an unreliable helper. Faith knew that I was having a battle at times to stay in the meetings. There was one particular song we used to sing that usually made my knees shake, and I would quite often slip out rapidly and go into Post Green kitchen or go for a walk!

The song was, "I'm under the blood of Jesus, I'm safe in the Shepherd's fold. I'm under the blood of Jesus, safe when the night turns cold. Safe when the nations tremble, safe when the stars grow dim. I'm under the blood of Jesus, and I am safe in Him."

Everything inside me would say, "I'm not safe! I'm not safe!" It was a mystery. Here I was a normal mother and wife, fairly mature, had lots of experience in the church and at times I felt very insecure. Faith was puzzled, but said she would pray specifically that week to try and get a clue to the whole problem; and I said I would as well. We drove back to Esher from Post Green on the Sunday evening, so the children could get to school the next day.

The door bell rang!

It was two days since we returned from Post Green. A Baptist minister and his wife from Kent were on the train en route for home, and decided to hop off the train and come and see us! We welcomed them in. We had met them at a ministers' conference run by Fountain Trust recently. We all sat down and had a meal, and enjoyed chatting together. When it was getting quite late they wanted us to drop them back to the train station. "Don't worry. We will drive you home."

We drove down to Kent. We were almost at their house when we passed a high hedge. " There's some strange school that meets there." The Baptist minister explained. I queried what kind of school it was, and discovered it was the same type of school Valerie and I had gone to during the war. I felt a bit indignant that they would call it strange! I thought no more about it.

Next day, Wednesday, I had been invited to speak to the Guildford Diocesan women about my Bible Study, The Road To Emmaus. They wanted a Bible study they could use for the whole diocese and my study had been recommended. I sat down at this huge table with the women gathered round, and a copy of my Bible study in front of each of them. Then the lady to my left said, "Do you by any chance know anything about .... schools?" She named the same educational organisation and school as our Baptist minister had named last night. "Why?" I asked cautiously.

"Well, my best friend's daughter has been teaching at one in Scotland. She's a keen Christian, but she has been sent to a London hospital unconscious. They couldn't find out what's wrong with her in Scotland and my friend insisted her daughter get transferred to a hospital in London." She said.

"Well, then what?" I asked her.

"They can't find out what's wrong with her. The doctor said, 'If this wasn't twentieth century England I would say she has been put under a curse!' My friend is trying to find out if there is anything odd about the school, you know, whether she could have been put under a curse, or something."

The lady I had been talking to turned out to be a close friend of Faith Lees, I discovered as we talked. I admitted to her that I had gone to one of those schools for a year or two when I was much younger. I knew nothing about them, but would try and find out. I took her phone number. And we got on with the meeting.

When I reached home, just as a long shot, I took out my encyclopaedia. I looked up the name and found that the schools' founder was fascinated with the occult, and was so experienced in occult matters that he had written many famous books on the subject.

I went straight to the phone and dialled Post Green's number. "Faith? You will never guess what! I was talking to your friend Ina in Guildford, and because of our conversation I have found out more about a school I went to for a year or more – the founder was into occult stuff."

Faith said, "I remember you showing me one of your old school reports – where it talked about your art and your soul life! I told you I thought you had been to a very odd school!" I remembered the conversation, and had felt indignant at the time. Now I had a feeling Faith was right. When the Holy Spirit was present in a meeting may be that was why sometimes I would have a feeling of panic and insecurity.

"Well, I've been praying for you each day since we chatted on Saturday, and I am trusting God to reveal what the key to your problem is, and I asked God to show us this week. I think you've found it may be a series of divine coincidences! Let me know if anything else happens, and we will chat and pray next time you come down. Please give my love to Ina when you phone her! Tom says 'Hi' to you all."

We finished our conversation, and I phoned Ina to give her the information I had found out. She was a very skilled praying Christian counsellor and I was sure she could safely deal with the problem with her friend's daughter.

Faith prayed with me when I was next down in Dorset, and asked God to cut off the bad influence that I may have picked up at the school. I would say I didn't experience a miraculous breakthrough but I steadily grew in confidence and felt far more secure when I saw the Holy Spirit touching people's lives. And I did feel a load had been lifted off me.

Mary and Shelley eventually moved back into Vic Ramsey's care. We continued to see them occasionally. They both came down to a Post Green camp. Mary left with Vic Ramsey and his other ex-drug addicts he had brought to camp. Shelley decided to come to the Bible College at Lytchett Minster, and eventually married one of the other students and named her first baby "Abigail".

David and I put our home in Esher up for sale, and completed our final commitment with Fountain Trust: the two large family camp/conferences at Ashburnham Place near Hastings in Sussex. We always enjoyed visiting Ashburnham Place, and particularly enjoyed our conversations with John Bickersteth who owned the property. If you ever get a chance to visit the place and absorb the atmosphere, please do!

John Bickersteth was related to King Charles the First's secretary, and consequently had some precious belongings from that era, which he showed us on more than one occasion. It was amazing to see something so historical after more than three hundred and twenty years!

The two conferences were full to capacity. We met and made friends with so many people. Tessa and Nigel enjoyed meeting up with old friends in the dormitories, and there were some marvellous children's activities during the day. I remember singing a solo on the last night of the final evening and saying goodbye to a packed auditorium.

CHAPTER SIXTEEN

As often as we could we drove down to Dorset and went on a house hunting spree. For some strange reason we could find nothing – even though we were looking in a good five mile radius of Post Green house. The end of August came, and we had to put our furniture in store again, and move into Post Green house.

This seemed exactly what God had planned. We got to know Tom and Faith and their family very well, and they got to know us. David started teaching at the secondary modern school, whose grounds adjoined Post Green. David only had to slip out of the door of our temporary home, walk down a garden path, open the farm gate and he was in school territory!

There were always other people either living in Post Green house or visiting for a few days or a few weeks – and it was a most interesting and educational time for me.

It was also educational for Tessa, Nigel and Abigail – so many new people to get to know, different ways of doing things, and a different lifestyle. Mostly they thoroughly enjoyed themselves, and were outside playing in the grounds for ages, and were often to be found in the tree house. When we first arrived at Post Green Abigail was still wearing nappies at night. When she woke up in her cot in the mornings she would usually make a reasonably pleasant noise of singing and chattering, but this would soon change to moaning and calling out for attention. Tom and Faith's bathroom was right next door to where our three children had their bedroom. On one momentous morning Tom walked into their bedroom to see why Abigail was moaning and grumbling and generally disturbing others who hadn't woken up yet. He decided her nappy was causing the trouble, so picked her up and took her into the bathroom and gave her to Faith.

"She needs a bath!" Tom said. Abigail started to scream at all this sudden unwanted attention. Tessa ran into the bathroom to try and calm things down. But Abigail was in full throttle, and continued to scream. Faith quickly took off a very wet nappy and plonked Abi in the bath. More screams. At this point I woke up, having heard the screams from the next floor up! I could hear Tom talking loudly over the screaming, and Faith talking calmly to Abi – then I heard Tessa's reassuring voice trying to calm things down. I decided to leave well alone! I could hardly walk into Sir Tom and Lady Lees' bathroom anyway at that time in the morning! They had brought up four children so they were used to early morning nappies.

Faith was a very strong determined person! But so is Abigail. One day I happened to be passing through the Post Green kitchen after Abigail, then aged about three and a half, had spilt some orange juice on the kitchen floor. "Abigail, wipe that up, please!" said Faith to her.

Abigail ignored her. Faith repeated her request. Abigail stood in the middle of the kitchen floor with her hands on her hips and eyed Faith, and didn't move. "Abigail!" said Faith firmly. Abi didn't move. I stood near the door wondering whether to wipe the mess up myself. Faith said, "Abigail spilt her orange and she has to wipe it up!" So I watched quietly not daring to rock the boat!

Abigail still did not move, but kept her eyes firmly on Faith to see what she would do next. It was an obvious power struggle between two very strong-minded people! Faith moved over to the sink and reached for a cloth, which she handed to her. Abigail took it, bent down and did a cursory sweep of the spilt juice, and held the dirty cloth very haughtily up to Faith. Faith hesitated, then took it and rinsed it in the sink. It's what you call power sharing!

By this time not only was there a very full programme of teaching conferences being run from Post Green but Rev Jean Darnall's husband, Elmer, had returned from Hong Kong and had set up an evening Bible College that was run in Lytchett Minster Secondary Modern School. The faculty of teachers included: Sir Tom Lees, Rev Rex Meakin, Rev David Mills, Rev Dr Denis Ball, Rev Jean Darnall, among many others. Even Faith Lees and Daphne Mills were invited to do some teaching there! I thoroughly enjoyed the experience!

Just before we moved down to Post Green David's mother had a stroke or heart attack and she sadly died three days later. I wept more at her funeral than any other

I have ever been to. I think it was because I was so sad that what could have been a good, happy relationship never came to fruition.

The general feeling between David and his brother Ian was that their father, George, could not be left to live on his own in their large bungalow in Surrey, not far from Esher. As we were moving down to Dorset, it was felt that we should have "Gradpa" living with us. Consequently when we were house hunting we now had to look for a larger place.

We eventually found a three bedroom bungalow up the hill from Lytchett Minster. It was built by a very good builder for himself and his family. It was high up on a hill in Lytchett Matravers, and had the most amazing panoramic views of Poole Harbour, Corfe Castle and the Purbeck Hills. It also had planning permission for two rooms to be built over the double garage – it was perfect for the Mills family! It took about three months before we could move in. The builder agreed to build the two extra rooms for "Grandpa" Mills – a bedroom and a sitting room as soon as he could find the time.

The day of the move arrived; our furniture came out of store and arrived in a huge furniture van. We were moving from a five bed house, with three living rooms, into a three bed bungalow! Grandpa Mills' furniture van arrived very shortly afterwards; he was moving from a very large bungalow into one room, shortly to be two rooms! As the furniture came off each van, we stood in the driveway saying, "Yes", "No", "Yes, and so on till Panorama was fully furnished, and all the spare furniture was sitting on the lawn in the front garden. David telephoned Tom and Faith with our predicament! They came up to look at the furniture on the front lawn. It was soon despatched to a couple of unfurnished cottages that had recently become vacant, and were awaiting Bible College students. The rest went into a large shed where spare furniture was kept on an as and when needed basis.

Grandpa had one small bedroom, the three children had another small bedroom, with newly purchased bunk beds, and we had the master bedroom that had amazing views. There was no room for visitors, and Faith felt that we should live quietly for a while. This we did until the extension was built. Grandpa and his black poodle "Soo" moved up into his two rooms over the garage. They had sloping ceilings, and Grandpa was always forgetting and hitting his head. Because he was bald, we always knew when he had forgotten to bend his head. He never remembered those injuries. But he always remembered what Abigail had done to him. She had a toy pretend iron one Christmas. It had a sucker plug to stick it to a wall, so she could pretend to iron. She decided to stick the plug on Grandpa's head. It stuck fast and securely. By the time Abigail had managed to "unplug" it, Grandpa had a big red circle on his bald head. The mark stayed for an amazingly long length of time!

Grandpa lived with us for almost fifteen years and became very much part of our family life and the life of the community around him. He brought his car with him, and went out into the surrounding towns and villages every day, driving himself until eventually he had a carer, Chris Crompton, who would drive him.

With Tessa and Nigel enrolled at the local school in Lytchett Matravers, Abigail at a local play group, I suddenly had time on my hands! But orders were coming into Post Green for The Road to Emmaus that I had written three years beforehand. By this time they had been printed in three books by Erreys, so I no longer needed to keep re-typing and duplicating them, which was a great relief. Requests were now coming into Post Green on a daily basis for The Road to Emmaus, and I would go down to Post Green office most days and send off the books, and also help send off the orders for tape recordings of Post Green conference talks.

Soon after our arrival at Post Green we had an area Team Day. The team was nearly sixty people strong, made up of various husbands, wives, and single people who lived mostly in Dorset, though some came from much further afield. Normally this would pose a problem for me– if I was to be involved who would look after the children? But this problem did not occur at Post Green – the grounds were safe and the children, of many assorted ages, all looked after each other in the early days. We took a picnic lunch, and soup and drinks were provided by Faith and other helpers in the kitchen.

We all squashed into the drawing room in Post Green house. I sat facing the windows so I could get occasional glimpses of the children and what they were up to! If they were in the tree house, that could only be seen from the kitchen windows. Abigail disgraced herself – not uncommon – by pulling her knickers down in the middle of the lawn to relieve herself – much quicker than going in the house to the loo. I hoped I was the only one looking out of the window at the time.

The sessions were quite high powered for me! Because David and I had joined, the dynamic was changing. It was agreed that there would be a nucleus, a core group, which would oversee the running of Post Green meetings, camps, conferences and other commitments. It seemed that God was beginning to do a huge work at Post Green, and everything needed to be looked at more carefully and prayed about before decisions were made. Each decision made affected everyone else; we could no longer get an idea and run with it, without consulting the others. When occasionally someone had a bright idea and did their own thing it caused unnecessary ripples in other people's lives.

We had to agree a "corporate vision". In other words, we had to be all agreed that "this is what we should be doing" – and not "that". We spent a lot of time in individual prayer and corporate prayer, asking God why he had called us all to Post Green, and what was his plan?

Hundreds of people were beginning to come to each of the conferences – many needing more in-depth counsel and prayer than we had time for in the short time available. Consequently Post Green house had several people staying for residential help and counselling in a loving, caring, safe environment.

The core team were: Sir Tom and Lady (Faith) Lees, Rev Elmer Darnall and Rev Jean Darnall, Rev Dr Denis and Pinky Ball, Rev Rex Meakin and his wife Betty, Jeanne Hinton and Diana Cooper, and Rev David Mills and myself. Jeanne had left Fountain Trust just before us and was living in Post Green house. Diana Cooper lived in a converted church in Lytchett Matravers. She was already running a prayer and intercession ministry from Post Green. If anyone telephoned for prayer (and many did) then the information would be written down on a piece of paper and given to Diana. She got several people praying right away, and on Fridays the intercessors – the people who prayed - would gather in a room in Post Green house and pray for all those on their list. Each person was prayed for, for a month – and encouraged to let the prayer team know what had happened to them as a result of prayer. There were some wonderful answers to prayer, and Diana always seemed to be radiant. Jean Darnall, who was preaching and teaching all over England, would often phone in with urgent prayer requests. Some of the most urgent needs were from people who eventually came and lived in the house for a few months or even a few years.

With five ordained clergymen on the core team there was an immense amount of experience and knowledge to be pooled and shared. This first team weekend was an attempt to make a plan for the way ahead, using the skills and ministries of all of us on the core or inner team, as well as using the love and expertise of the "outer" or "district" team.

I remember that Bryn Jones, who headed up a large independent church in Bradford came and spoke to us all. He looked round the room and said "Post Green can change the face of England". By that he meant, as he went on to explain, that there was enough Holy Spirit power among those gathered in the drawing room to re-ignite the Church. It might sound arrogant, but it was more of a prophecy of what God had planned to do through the work at Post Green over the coming years. Thousands of people passed through Post Green for many years; and later we had two, three or four teams out every weekend, preaching, teaching, leading worship – the impact was huge.

We saw miracles of healing, some immediate, some gentle and slow. We saw people delivered from satanic forces; we saw people lifted out of despair and go home with joy and hope in their hearts. Bryn Jones foresaw what would happen in the future.

He felt that Post Green was a church in its own right. Faith and Tom were emphatic: "Post Green is not a church!" – it is a facilitator – helping churches re-discover the work and power of the Holy Spirit, a gift so long neglected in many churches for sixty years or more.

We were all committed to attend our local church, wherever we lived – except for camps we never had a service or conference on a Sunday morning or evening – this left everyone free to be committed to their own church. David and I, and our family, had settled into the local Methodist church, being the nearest church to Panorama in Lytchett Matravers.

The outcome of the team day was that the core group would meet regularly once a week to pray and share our news with one another. Also to go through our diaries, agreeing dates and venues. We committed ourselves to check each speaking engagement invitation with each other before doing "our own thing". This meant we coordinated our work and ministry and we all knew what each other was doing.

During this weekend I heard God say to me that he wanted me to help Faith with all her secretarial needs in the office. It was a distinct call. I knew it was definite and nothing ever shook that call of God from me, despite outside circumstances. When I told Faith after the weekend, she smiled and thanked me, but said that Margaret was going to give up her job in Social Services and work with her! In the meantime she had a volunteer doing her typing.

As the word from God was so clear, it didn't really shake me at all. I knew the job was mine as and when God gave it to me!

I continued sorting out things at Panorama, and enjoyed the freedom of no one except Grandpa living with us, and the three children out for part of every day. I continued to go down to Post Green and send off The Road to Emmaus study books and teaching cassette tapes. The gathering point in Post Green house was always the kitchen – large and friendly. It had a table, with long benches on two sides. There was always someone sat there, drinking tea or coffee and chatting with anyone else who was there – someone preparing the next meal, or making themselves a drink.

On one occasion Margaret was at the table chatting to a couple of people. I was doodling on a piece of paper and wrote something in shorthand. Margaret saw it, and slid the paper towards her, read my shorthand and wrote back! After we had finished our drinks we walked over to the sink and washed up our mugs. Faith walked in and glanced down at the table and saw the piece of paper. She was an alert kind of person, not nosy, but she felt responsible for all the people who had gathered under her roof.

"Whose funny writing is this?" Faith asked.

I turned and looked at the piece of paper she was holding. "Oh, it's mine!"

"Does that mean you do shorthand?" Faith asked.

"Yes, of course!" I replied.

"Can you type as well?" Faith persisted.

"Yes, that too!" I nodded. I dried up the last of the coffee mugs and put them back on the shelf. The tea towel was put to dry on the rail, and I turned back to the table. Faith was still standing there. I looked at her. She was still holding the piece of paper with the shorthand written on it.

"Daphne, could you possibly do me a big favour? I need some help."

"What's the problem?" I asked, cautiously. I wasn't that good at solving problems!

"Well, the thing is that I put all my letters on a Dictaphone. Then this lady from the village comes in and types them up for me. But when I read it all back it doesn't make sense. She puts the punctuation in the wrong place, and doesn't realise when I am quoting from the Bible, so it all adds up to a confused letter. There is a pile on my desk that will have to be re-typed and I haven't the heart to ask Pam (not her real name) to do them again." Faith shrugged and pulled a despairing face.

"Can you show me what you want done then?" I asked. Faith led me down to her office at the far end of the house. There was a lovely big desk facing out into the gardens. There was a nice electric typewriter and a pile of letters with addressed envelopes lying nearby. I picked up the letters. They were all long letters, and I could see immediately that Pam didn't understand the subject matter, and there were bad spelling mistakes as well.

"I'm happy to re-type them for you, and I think I can work out where the quote marks need to go!" I responded. "I'll get on with them right away!"

Within an hour they were all ready for Faith to sign. I left them on her desk, leaving a message on the kitchen table for Faith and drove back home up the hill to Panorama.

I mention this event for two reasons. From that day on I did all Faith's secretarial work for the next five years, and then I did Tom's for several years after that. Margaret was always planning to give up her job but it was several years before she felt she could leave social services. By then she was involved in other things in the community.

The second reason for mentioning this event was that it led to big restoration of confidence in myself. It was several months before I would be anywhere around when Faith came in to sign her letters. I made sure I had gone home before she came in to sign the letters. Why? Because in my experience with working for my father – signing letters equals trouble for me! Dad could always find a mistake in one of the letters and it always seemed to lead to my getting into trouble. Consequently I was really scared of the letter signing ceremony.

But with Faith it was so different. I just couldn't believe it! She praised me, congratulated me, affirmed me, gave me a hug and said, "Well done!" so many times. In a meeting if someone ever wanted a letter or document typed Faith would often say, "Get Daphne to type it – she's fast and accurate! She will have it done in no time at all!"

We all need affirmation and praise, and we all need love. I felt that for the first time in my life I was finally living somewhere where I was in a consistent loving environment. This brought out the best in me, and I got better and better at what I was given to do.

My final test came one day when I was typing up a letter for Faith. Tom walked into Faith's office, looking for her. "I don't know where she is. She said she had a meeting." I told Tom.

"Well I was wondering if she has answered that letter we talked about this morning." Tom replied.

"Is this it? I'm just finishing typing one now. Do you want to look at it in the typewriter?" I swivelled round on the typing chair, so Tom could see the letter.

"Yes! Oh good! But do you mind re-typing it, and altering a couple of things and then adding a final sentence?" said Tom as he continued to re-read the letter.

I pulled the letter out of the typewriter, and inserted another piece of headed notepaper plus carbon copy. Tom in the meantime was writing his version of the letter, which I then copied. The first paragraph was as Faith had dictated. The second had an altered sentence. And Tom added a final sentence. All done!

I was just putting a cover on the typewriter when Faith walked in to sign her letters. "Oh good, you're still here!" said Faith.

"Yes, they're all here ready to sign. I altered one of them, and added something!" I said, watching Faith carefully for her reaction. (I knew exactly what my father would have said and done!).

"Well, I am sure if you altered anything it will be better than the original. Thanks so much Daphne!" said Faith in reply.

"Actually Tom came in and read it. He wanted something changed." I confessed on Tom's behalf!

Faith quickly glanced at each letter and signed them all, gave me a hug of thanks and walked out of her office singing.

Another happy, healing day had ended for me at Post Green!

CHAPTER SEVENTEEN

Faith Lees and Jeanne Hinton were always having meetings together! When I heard they had planned an "away" day or a "quiet" day, my heart always sank. Why? Because these always turned out to be ideas and planning days! They would come up with amazing ideas that would make a lot of work for me in the office. Out of these days came a huge number of very large events and also publications of teaching leaflets, teaching tapes, and other materials to re-educate the churches on the work of the Holy Spirit. Rev Jean Darnall was hugely helpful in both helping with the teaching materials and publicising them around the country. We also published a newsletter that went out to over four thousand people. The typing, printing, folding, stuffing into envelopes was a big job each month. Consequently the office staff enlarged from one person, me, to about twelve in a very short time.

Once the work had grown so large, we had to move the offices out of Post Green house and across the road into about three mobile homes that had been bought for the purpose! They were placed in the farmyard: idyllic surroundings for a day at the office!

In the early days of our family's life at Post Green we were all on quite a learning curve. David was busy being a teacher at the local secondary modern school, teaching subjects that weren't anything to do with theology. The children were meeting new friends both at their schools, and at Post Green conferences, camps, and team days. I was learning to run an office, and learning to work with very strong determined people! And suddenly I was no longer the little wife and mother at home, doing domestic things, but was at the forefront of a huge new work God was doing in sunny Dorset.

Being suddenly thrown into such a strong whirling current was at times overwhelming for me. I felt I had been in the shadows of life so long that I was no longer fit for purpose! As well as this I knew I needed to change, and become more loving and more out-going. With so many people around I knew I needed to come out of my shell and mix with much larger groups than I had been used to, and to do it in a loving caring way.

I felt a deep love for Tom and Faith Lees. This was only in response to a depth of love that I felt from both of them for me, and for each of my family. It seemed to me that they loved me more than anyone else! But I knew this wasn't so, because I saw Tom and Faith pouring out their love for so many other people. There in Post Green house were Jeanne, Margaret, Rudolph (a recovering alcoholic), Carol (from a children's home), Kitty (a very mentally damaged woman that Jean Darnall had helped to rescue): I think they would all say that it seemed to them that Faith and Tom loved them "the best".

As I could not conceive a love like that, I decided that Tom and Faith perhaps didn't actually love me – they couldn't love all those people equally, therefore I discounted myself. I am sure God's enemy, Satan, was laughing up his sleeve when I came to this conclusion. It caused me to doubt any show of love for me from either Tom or Faith. I began to feel unloved, and misinterpreted much that happened at Post Green, and became very insecure.

I won't go into the number of times when I "ran away". Sometimes I told someone I was going, and sometimes I just jumped in a car and went. Sometimes I was gone a few hours and sometimes it was a few days.

After one "running away" episode, I arrived back on my birthday. David said to me, "Get dressed up in your best dress. Tom and Faith have put on a party for you! They asked me what was your favourite food, and they've invited some of your friends from other households."

I couldn't believe it!

Faith had sent me out shopping for a few food items three days beforehand. I did get the food, but I didn't go back with it to Post Green. I had a "panic attack" and drove up to St Albans, and stayed with John and Sara Wheatley and their family.

Of course I phoned home and told my family where I was. We had Grandpa Mills and an au pair called Beatrice holding the fort at home, so I didn't worry about the children.

The evening of my return, we all drove down the hill from Lytchett Matravers to Post Green, past exquisitely beautiful countryside, and into the driveway. Tom and Faith quickly came to the front door, greeting me with hugs, and asked no questions. It was as though I had never left.

I put Faith's shopping, belatedly, on the kitchen table; and waited to be confronted with what I had done.

"Let's have drinks in the drawing room! Everyone else will be here in about fifteen minutes," Tom said.

"I'm just finishing off the cooking! Bring me out a drink, please, someone!" said Faith.

The Lees children emerged from various parts of the house and came into the drawing room. Christopher, Sarah, Bridget and Lizzie: all home from school for the Easter holidays. They immediately starting talking to Tessa, Nigel and Abigail, and then they all wandered off to play somewhere.

More people arrived, and the dinner gong sounded the Westminster chimes! We wandered into the dining room. The long table was set out for what seemed like a banquet!

I felt like the prodigal son (or daughter) returned.

What love! What forgiveness! What kindness! – all my favourite food, and my favourite people! The love was there, and the love was strong.

I was puzzled, mystified. I was not imagining the love, it was truly there. The whole environment around me was Love.

We had a marvellous evening; full of laughter, people's stories, children chipping in with their thoughts as well.

We drove home, slowly up the hill, in the darkness. The children were sleepy and quiet, and I was deep in thought.

Next morning I got up very early, and took my Bible into the lounge at Panorama. I pulled back the curtains, and gazed out across the balcony, onto the far distant Purbeck hills. Sheltered in a dip in the hills was the majestic remains of Corfe Castle, sitting on its own mound. I looked towards the south east, and there lay Poole Harbour. I was so glad to be home, at Panorama, and Post Green.

Why on earth had I run off? I sat down on one of Grandpa's huge, green, Parker Knoll chairs, tipping into a reclining position. As long as no one woke up early I was going to be here for a while!

I started to pray! "Please, Lord, Help me understand! Why do I doubt love? Is it your love? Or is it Tom and Faith's love? If it's your love, it's safe and it won't ever let me down. If it is just Tom and Faith's love, in their own human strength, I just can't depend on it. I feel so vulnerable. I feel like I have begun to trust love in a way I never have before. But as soon as I think it's just human love, it seems my whole world falls apart and I just feel like fleeing from it all."

As I sat in the huge comfy chair gazing out of the window onto the balcony and the hills beyond, I closed my eyes. "What's going on, Lord? What's happening in my life?" Almost immediately I saw in my mind, (or was it my soul?), a beautiful tight flower bud. It could have been a rosebud or a magnolia bud: either way it was white and pink and very tightly closed. I felt the Lord say to me, "You are like this tight flower bud, and I want the warmth of My Love to open you out into a beautiful flower. Only then will I be able to use you as I want."

In my imagination I saw the warmth of the sun shining on the tightly closed bud and gradually opening it out into full bloom with wide open, vulnerable, beautiful petals.

After praying and sitting silently for a while, a phrase from John's gospel came into my mind: "The disciple whom Jesus loved."

The apostle John wrote his own version of Jesus' life and ministry. John doesn't call himself "I" in his book. He calls himself "the disciple whom Jesus loved".

I have heard more than one sermon on "The favourite disciple". And it is never my interpretation!

I thought about the way Tom and Faith poured out their love, opened up their home, shared their wealth and their cars, and their land, and themselves. That's love in action!

I thought about the special relationship Jesus had with Peter, the fisherman: and the wonderful conversations and events recorded in the gospels about Peter and Jesus. Yes, Peter was the favourite of Jesus! Oh, and Mary Magdalene! A very special relationship: Mary was the first one to meet and talk with Jesus after the resurrection. Therefore, Mary Magdalene must be the favourite.

Then I thought about dear Thomas, another disciple of Jesus. He just couldn't believe that the Jesus he saw dying on the cross, was the same man standing before him in a locked room in Jerusalem three days later. "I can't believe!" said Thomas. Jesus allowed Thomas to look at his nail pierced hands. Jesus lifted his gown and showed Thomas the sword slash in his side. "Now do you believe, Thomas?" asked Jesus. Oh, how very special! Thomas was the first person to be allowed to see the wound in Jesus' body. No, Thomas was the most loved disciple!

There is a most wonderful story in the gospel of John, fourth chapter. How I love that story! Jesus is hot and tired and thirsty and on his own. A Samaritan woman comes at midday to get a drink from the well. Jesus watches her for a while and then asks for a drink too. The woman is amazed. Why? Because Jews don't talk to Samaritans for a start, they are sworn enemies. And neither does a man speak to a woman who is by herself.

Jesus gets into a deep meaningful conversation with the woman. He knows she is unhappy and in trouble. He tells her she has had five husbands, and the man she is now living with isn't even her husband. One couldn't be blamed for jumping to the conclusion she was an immoral woman. But we don't know how or why all the marriages ended: through divorce (her fault? His fault?); through death, so she could be a widow in deep morning four or five times! We don't know.

Jesus spent a long time talking to her, and it became a wonderful life-changing experience for her and later for her whole village. Oh, I think this nameless woman was one of Jesus' favourite people!

I thought again about the love I saw in Post Green house, poured out for some lovely people and some very needy damaged people too. The love seemed to be equal! Just as the love of Jesus seemed to be poured out equally on each person Jesus spent time with!

The love of God! That was what I was encountering at Post Green!

It was a total turning point in my life – to know without a shadow of doubt that I was in the presence of, and witnessing, the outpouring of God's love.

A day or two after my lovely peaceful quiet time that morning, I drove into Bournemouth with my friend Karen. Karen was Jean and Elmer's secretary and we had become great friends. I had met Karen and Brian at a Fountain Trust meeting, years before, at the Elephant and Castle in London, when they were talking to Jean Darnall there.

I couldn't believe it when they walked in the door one day at Post Green. Jean Darnall had told them all about the Christian Life Bible College that Elmer was running at Post Green, and they had decided to join. As the Bible College met in the evenings, all the students had day time jobs. Brian and Karen were on an extended tour of Europe before returning to their home in Canada. Brian got an accountancy job in Bournemouth, and Karen worked up at Rest Harrow, where Jean and Elmer were living. Faith sent me up to Rest Harrow one day with some papers for Jean Darnall. I walked in on a disagreement between Jean and Elmer about whose work was the most urgent, and what work Karen should be doing first. I could see Karen was upset, very upset. So I put my arm around her shoulders and invited her to come to lunch up at Panorama, and then go somewhere for a walk on the beach.

Years later I asked Karen about when we first became friends, and she reminded me of this event at Rest Harrow; which I had long since forgotten. Either way, it made me a new and very special friend. We have been great friends ever since.

Anyway, Karen and I had a wonderful walk along the beach. I was agonising about this "love" business, and asking Karen what she thought. She always had her feet firmly on the ground, and was immensely sensible. We both admitted Post Green was a special place. We both had different aspects of it we found difficult. Karen was a very private person and could be quite shy. The life at Post Green and the Bible College was rather demanding. Karen and Brian had left Canada because of a stressful event in Canada, and Karen was not keen to be put under more stress for a while. Consequently when I talked to Faith about Karen being caught between two very powerful people, both with big ministries, i.e. Jean and Elmer!, it was agreed with all concerned that Karen would continue to work for both of them, but her office would be in Post Green house.

Karen and I decided that while we were on the beach in Bournemouth we might as well pop into Keith Jones Christian bookshop. That afternoon I found the most fantastic book! It was called "Make Love Your Aim" by Eugenia Price. It was just what I needed! I so wanted to understand the love of God. Not just "Bible" love. But love as lived every day between people, and between God and people.

I looked at some of the chapter headings:

"God is still Love; What is love? Who needs love?

The freedom to love; Love is unreasonable; How do we learn to love?

Loving enough to trust; Loving enough to relinquish; Loving enough to speak the truth;

Loving the unfamiliar; Loving ourselves.

For God so loved the world."

All those chapter headings drew me with curiosity. I so wanted to love like that: to love securely and steadily – especially to be confident enough to love the unfamiliar (whatever that was!).

Karen found a book she wanted, and together we walked over to the desk, paid for our purchases and walked out into the sunshine. Karen knew only too well of my struggles with "love" and was as thrilled as I was with my find! "Please lend me the book when you've read it!" she requested.

"I think it will take me a lifetime! But you are welcome to borrow it for a short while!" I replied, as we walked back up the hill to the car park. "Woops, look at the time! We have only ten minutes to get to St Monica's to pick up Tessa! We had better get a move on."

Fortunately Tessa was playing on the grass with some friends as we drove into St Monica's and didn't seem to mind that I was late.

As I guessed, the book "Make love your Aim" was hugely helpful and I realised that up to that point when it came to "deep love" or, as it turned out, God's love, I was really rather ignorant. I knew a lot in theory, but not much in practice, I decided. I found the book immensely practical, and am just re-reading it again now, thirty-seven years later!

"We've got another team day coming up on Saturday week," Faith told me one day in the office. "Could you write round or phone the area team for me, please, Daphne? And tell them to bring sandwiches or whatever they want to eat, but we will do soup and drinks as usual. We plan to have a quiet hour, half way through the day, so everyone can go off by themselves to think and pray. Then we will all get back together again, have a cup of tea or coffee, and share what we feel God has been saying to us all."

"Okay!" I turned to look at Faith as I was removing the typewriter cover. "Do you want me to warn them of the plan for the day?"

"I think it would be a good idea! And maybe remind them to make sure they bring their Bibles! I hope it will be fine and sunny, then everyone can go out into the garden or fields or even the woodlands for their quiet time. That would be lovely. If it's wet everyone will have to spread out through the house. I will warn Mrs Prior that might happen. She can do an extra clean the day before!" Faith laughed and walked out of the office. She hated administration of any sort, and much preferred to be out and about with people and planning! I learnt not to take it personally, in the end, when she avoided the office as much as she could!

The team day dawned: warm and sunny. I looked forward to seeing all the area team. We arrived early at Post Green, and Tessa, Nigel and Abigail quickly jumped out of the car, and ran into the house looking for their friends. Cars were arriving every few minutes from all over Bournemouth and Dorset, and some from much further afield. The children of the area team all ran off together to play games in the garden, or climb up into the tree house.

The sun continued to shine all day, and we had nearly two hours in the afternoon to wander off on our own to think and pray. I found a farmyard gate somewhere remote, and sat on the top of it. It took a while for me to get comfortable, and secure, but once having achieved that I started to ask God some questions.

"What is this place? What is Post Green? What are You doing here?" I asked.

It seemed that God was saying quite clearly to me that it was an oasis.

Oasis? You will only find an oasis in the desert – in the midst of a dry and dusty, parched land. It's a place where there is water! If there is water there is vegetation – if there is vegetation, there is fruit! If there is water in abundance, then it is a place of healing. People can walk into the oasis from the desert with their wounds, and get them bathed. There will be plenty of people living in and around the oasis who will help and comfort the weary, wounded travellers who arrive.

If the oasis is large then channels can be dug across the desert to make other smaller oases.

I was really excited! So that's what Post Green is! It solved so many mysteries for me. I had heard Faith say many times that God had told her that Post Green was a place of refuge: like Ramoth Gilead, in Old Testament times. God had set up several towns as places of refuge, so that guilty people, people who had unwittingly committed a crime, or accidentally killed someone, could flee there to guaranteed safety.

Certainly Post Green was proving to be a place of refuge for a large number of people; and it was a place of forgiveness and healing. But to understand also that it was an oasis was hugely helpful to me. I now had my own vision of what God was planning to do at Post Green. And if it became very large (which it did) then channels would be made to lead to an oasis in many other parts of England and the world. The influence of Post Green would be worldwide (which it has become).

We all gathered back into the house, and the gong sounded both out of the front door and the French windows to draw back any stragglers still out in the surrounding countryside! After a most welcome drink, we assembled back into the drawing room. Faith went around the room asking people to share anything significant they felt God had said. When I had plucked up enough courage to add my vision of Post Green as an oasis, everyone got very excited, and expanded on the idea.

We drove back up the hill to Panorama, after a long happy day.

CHAPTER EIGHTEEN

It was soon time for another Youth Camp. We had so many people wanting to come to our camps that we now decided to hold two Family Camps during May and two Youth Camps in July. Later we would also hold a camp at the end of August each year.

The Youth Camps were on a less casual basis than previously. There was an official booking-in procedure and a small fee to pay. This meant there was better control over the number of young people coming, and space on the field for their tents. There were a limited number of facilities, i.e. the chemical loos in the cow shed! The fees did not cover the expenses of running the camps but a free will offering was held on the last night. The money given would cover the rest of the expenses and also a "love gift" was able to be given to each of the ministers or evangelists who helped to lead the camp.

Because there were so many camps and so many meetings the leaders were not all present at every moment in the tent. Consequently at the Youth Camp in 1971 I was tidying up the kitchen in Post Green house when I saw an expensive looking car pull up outside on the driveway. I watched curiously! A well-dressed man stepped out of the driving seat, and stood looking around. He gazed at the field covered in tents, then turned and looked at the huge marquee to the right of the field. He then turned and looked towards the house. He reminded me strongly of my father. Tall, distinguished looking, grey hair, smart dark coloured suit! He began to walk towards the front door of the house. I waited for the knock on the door, and walked into the hallway. I opened the porch door, and then the front door.

"I believe you have my daughter here!" he said.

"Oh!" I said, a bit surprised!

"Yes, some friends have brought her here to some sort of camp." The stranger continued.

My mind was racing. Was he here to complain, and take his daughter away? What's the problem?

“Well, if she is at our camp she is probably in the marquee.” I told him.

All this conversation was taking place on the doorstep. I would have invited him in but his eyes were constantly going towards the marquee. I stood silently, looking at him, feeling a bit helpless.

“I just happened to be in the area and thought I would take her out to lunch!” he added, still gazing at the marquee.

“Well, the young people have a full programme until lunch time and then there are various activities they can join in the afternoon if they want to.”

“Good, well, could you go and tell my daughter I am here?” he said firmly.

“Well, they are all in the middle of a meeting at the moment. They will be out of the marquee at coffee break at eleven.” I offered.

“No. I want to speak to my daughter now. Would you go and find her please. Her name is Patricia MacArthur. She has auburn hair.” The stranger was quite determined I should go and look for this young girl.

There was something about the whole visit that made me feel concerned. The young people had all come to the camp to be together, have fun, and learn more about God. Here was a parent that might possibly take his daughter away from all this. His manner was a trifle arrogant, and he certainly would not leave without getting what he wanted!

“Just wait here a moment, please, and I will go and see if I can find her, Mr MacArthur.” I left him standing in the doorway and walked into the field and towards the marquee. I glanced behind me and saw he had started to follow me, then had stopped and was standing by his car. I later found out that he was an important official in the police force for the Sultan of Oman. No wonder when he said “Jump!” you felt you had to jump!

I stood in the doorway of the marquee feeling somewhat overwhelmed with the task of finding an unknown auburn-haired girl in this huge crowd of people. Jean Darnall was on the platform, speaking to the audience. I hovered in the doorway and quickly scanned the rows and rows of young people, starting in the furthest corner of the tent!

It didn't take long for me to spy an auburn haired girl half way down the aisle in front of me. She had long red hair, tied back loosely with a ribbon. I crept quietly down towards her, trying not to disturb the meeting. "Is your name Patricia MacArthur?" I whispered. She nodded, looking startled.

"Your father is here!"

The girl flushed scarlet and looked deeply shocked. I could tell immediately that she was afraid, or in awe, of her father, and also excited that he had come to see her. "Here? Now?" she asked me.

"Yes, he's just outside!" Fortunately she was on the end seat, so she got up and quickly followed me outside into the sunshine. I walked with Patricia over to where her father was still standing. There was a polite greeting of each other. "What are you doing here? I thought you were in Oman?"

"I've just come back. Your Uncle Charlie told me you were here. What kind of a camp is this? Who brought you here?"

"One of our teachers at school invited us to come. She's here as well. We are having a wonderful time. I hope you haven't come to take me away?" she said nervously.

"Come on, jump in the car. I'm taking you out for lunch!" her father replied.

I could tell Patricia was both excited to spend some time with her father, but torn as well. She looked back reluctantly at the marquee. "I want to be back by mid afternoon." She said timidly.

Patricia turned and looked at me. "Is that all right? I'll be back later. Can you tell my Unit where I've gone?" I glanced at the badge on her sweater and quickly identified which unit she was on.

"Yes, of course. Have a good time, Patricia."

I watched as they drove out of the drive, praying that the young teenager would not be prevented from enjoying the rest of camp.

Around mid-afternoon Patricia walked up to me. I was standing just outside our caravan with Abigail. "I've just come to tell you I'm back. My father wanted me to leave the camp and come home with him to the Isle of Man."

"Oh!" I remarked, not surprised at all!

"But I've refused! So he is going to find a hotel nearby and come and visit me every day. It's a compromise! He's very rarely home from Oman, so I don't see him often. He came back to England unexpectedly and was really cross to find out that I was down in Dorset. Uncle Charlie told him I would only be away five days, but he came here anyway."

I looked at her, trying to work out if she was more pleased than afraid, or more afraid than pleased.

"So, he's going to come every lunch time and take me out to lunch. He says he's not sure I am eating properly at camp! I will be back each afternoon at some point. He insists that he take me back home to the Isle of Man instead of letting me travel back with my friends." Patricia shrugged her shoulders and pulled a face. "Thank you very much for coming to find me when my father turned up."

"That's fine. I'll see you around! Enjoy the rest of camp." I smiled at her, and watched her turn away and walk towards her Unit area across the field. Her hair was long and a most spectacular auburn colour. I found over the following few days that it was easy to pick her out on the field or in the marquee. She was always dressed in bright colours. After she came back from visiting with her father in the afternoons, she would often seek me out and let me know she was back. I would see her father's car parked outside the house at times and knew he was around. I walked over and spoke to him a couple of times: he was friendly enough in a detached kind of way.

I had no idea that one day I would be making a life or death call to him in Oman!

There was something about the whole situation with Patricia MacArthur that concerned me. I gently and cautiously enquired about her home life when she was chatting to me one day after the evening meeting. "Please call me Patsy! I don't like being called Patricia!" she said.

This is what she told me: her mother had severe heart problems all of Patsy's life. Her mother put off having the heart operation until Patsy was twelve years old, and old enough to look after herself, as she only had a less than fifty per cent chance of recovering from the operation. When Patsy was twelve her mother agreed to have the operation, and died. Patsy was placed in a boarding school on the Isle of Man, a few miles from her Uncle Charlie and his wife. Mr MacArthur resumed his job for the Sultan of Oman.

Patsy was heart-broken and her world had been turned upside down. Her mother was gone, her father was gone, and she was in a boarding school with no home life. Patsy also felt it was her fault that her mother had died. If her mother hadn't waited so long she might have survived the operation. On top of that she did not have a good relationship with her father. She admitted she loved him and was scared of him, which is what I had observed having seen them together. Her father was flying back to Oman very soon after camp had ended.

Almost as soon as Post Green camp finished David and I were planning to hook up our caravan, called Greensleeves II, and tour Scotland with Tessa, Nigel and Abigail. I talked to David about the possibility of taking Patsy with us. I felt she could do with some normal family life. David said, "Yes, by all means ask her if she wants to come with us."

As the last day of camp was approaching I invited her to join us for our holiday in Scotland. She consulted with her father and came back and found me later in the day. "Father says I can come with you. But he insists he takes me back to the Isle of Man and stay with him until the end of the week when he flies back to Oman. Then he says I can meet you somewhere!" Patsy reported to me.

I was very pleased she was allowed to come. I realised that we would have a problem working out where and how to meet up with her. It would mean we would have to hang around in the north of England somewhere until the following Friday week. I took down her phone number and asked her at which airports the planes landed from the Isle of Man. With this information I thought that David and I could plan a rendezvous with her.

After waving goodbye to all the youth campers, many of whom had become great friends of ours, we packed up our caravan and towed it back to Panorama. We did a quick turn around with laundry and the contents of our food cupboard. Grandpa Mills had driven off to London to stay with Ian and Elizabeth Mills for a month, so we had the house to ourselves.

We set off a few days later, towing the caravan behind us. We stopped on the second night at a small private site near Preston. I was woken early in the morning by David's groans of agony.

"Whatever is the matter?" I asked, appalled at the look of him. His face was as white as a sheet, beads of perspiration pouring off his face, and he was clutching his stomach.

"I don't know. I've had a terrible night and the pain is just increasing. It's now unbearable."

"I think I had better run over to the house and get a doctor." I looked at him again, knowing in my heart that this was some kind of an emergency.

I pulled back the curtain dividing our half of the caravan off from the children. "Quick, wake up and get dressed, as fast as you can. I may have to take Dad to a doctor in about ten minutes." The three children emerged from their sleeping bags and I made sure they were properly awake.

I threw on my favourite grey cord trousers and sweater, and ran across the damp dew-laden grass towards the large house. I rang the door bell. Shortly afterwards the door opened. "Sorry to disturb you! We are the people camping in your field. My husband has been taken ill and is in terrible pain. Can you phone for a doctor please?" I said hurriedly.

The woman who opened the door called to her husband. He came to the door and said, "What's the problem?" I repeated what I had just said. "He's in terrible pain," I repeated again, to make sure he realised it was serious.

"I will get onto this straight away. I will come across to your caravan and tell you what is happening." The man was already walking away to the phone in his hallway.

I ran back to the caravan hoping David would be sitting up and feeling better. He was still curled up in a ball in agony. The children were almost dressed.

There was a bang on the caravan door. "An ambulance is on its way to take your husband to hospital. Let me know how it goes, please." The owner of the house and field waited for me to assure him I would, and then he walked away.

About five minutes later a large heavy ambulance ploughed onto the field and stopped right outside our caravan. They pulled out a stretcher and David was quickly despatched inside. "You can come as well!" the ambulance driver said.

"Is there room for me and three children?" I asked.

"Oh, I think you had better follow us in your car, if you can drive?"

By the time Tessa, Nigel, Abigail and I were in our car, the ambulance was already disappearing across the damp field, making great tyre marks as it went. I turned our car round and followed as fast as I could. It was 8.30am and rush hour. The ambulance had its blue light flashing and the siren ringing. I caught up with it and followed as closely as I could. It was overtaking streams of traffic, and drivers were pulling into the side of the road to let us pass. I put my headlights on and kept as close to the ambulance as possible. I had no idea if Preston had more than one hospital – either way I didn't have a map and could get completely lost. It was a nightmare journey at huge speeds, breaking many highway code rules, I am sure.

We arrived at the hospital, and David was taken out of the ambulance and taken into a waiting room with a few other people waiting. We waited a couple of hours and apart from a few questions being asked no one took any action. "This is going to be a long wait," I said to David. "I think I had better go back to the caravan and give the children their breakfast, then come back here again."

David nodded. I felt terrible leaving him, but he was in the best place, so I thought. I'm not sure how I found the way back to the camp site, but we arrived back within about twenty minutes. I laid the table and the children sat down and started to eat. I was about to walk over to the house when the owner came across and knocked on the door.

"What's happening with your husband? Have they found out what is wrong with him?" he asked.

"No one has attended to him yet, so I brought the children back so they could have their breakfast." I answered.

"WHAT!" he shouted. "Your husband still hasn't been treated? Right leave this with me."

He strode angrily back across the grass to the big house.

Five minutes later he was back.

"Okay! I phoned the hospital. They admitted your husband was still waiting to be seen. I ordered them to get onto treating him immediately. They assured me they would."

"Well, that's extremely kind of you! I'm sorry to have had to bother you."

"You came to the right camp field last night. I happen to be the Chief Coroner for Preston. In the last few weeks I have had cause to rebuke the hospital on three separate occasions. When they heard my name this morning they knew they would be in trouble if they left your husband waiting any longer. I have no doubt he will be having the best of investigations by the medical staff by now."

"Thank you so much! We will go back there shortly." I said, glancing around at the three children munching their breakfast cereals.

"Please report back to me." The Coroner said as he turned to walk away.

We drove back to the hospital, and found that David was on a ward. He had been given strong pain killers and had been x-rayed. They planned to keep him overnight for observation, but thought the diagnosis was probably a twisted bowel. I reported back to the Coroner via his wife, as he was out at work.

Tessa, Nigel and I spent a quiet night in our caravan, the only one parked on the field that night. In the morning we quickly got dressed. I donned my favourite grey cord trousers again. Why were they my favourite? Well they had been rather boring grey flared trousers but they were brand new for our first youth camp at Post Green. Unfortunately I had jumped over a barb wire fence and miscalculated the height. Consequently I ripped them, badly. I managed to find a lovely silk tartan hanky which just fitted the split. Having sewn the patch on, it turned the boring trousers into something quite stunning – a bright scarlet tartan patch seemed to accentuate the flared trousers, and they lasted me for years to come.

David was allowed out after the doctor's rounds next morning. We could continue with our holiday but for the next few days we needed to make sure we were within easy reach of a hospital in case the problem reoccurred.

The timing was perfect. We picked Patsy up from the agreed rendezvous point and drove on towards Inverness. We parked the caravan on a fairly deserted Caravan Club site at Culloden. The site office gave out pamphlets on tourist places in the nearby locality. We read up about the Battle of Culloden, and walked across to the field and woodland area nearby where the main battle had taken place. It was eerie and atmospheric in the extreme: an unforgettable place. The feeling of the massacre was everywhere. There seemed to be few birds singing – a kind of deathly hush lay over the land.

David was still swallowing pain killers but otherwise seemed none the worse for his episode. We decided to stay on this site, not far from Inverness Hospital, for a few days to make sure he was totally recovered before we set off into the remote Highland areas. There was a great deal to see in and around Inverness.

Patsy was getting on well with all three children and seemed to love being with them. I discovered she was fourteen, going on fifteen. She was good fun to have around, although at times she was possibly a bit possessive of me, which annoyed my three children. I tried to keep it all in balance, sharing out my time and attention equally!

I woke one morning with a feeling that God was trying to tell me something. And I knew that I had some thinking and praying to do following what I had seen Him doing at camp. Being an introvert I was always challenged at any and every camp. I recharge my batteries by being alone! I can last out so long in company then I feel drained and have to be on my own to recover! At times in a concentrated event like camp I feel challenged and drained. I give out as much as I can, chatting with people, and caring for them, but then I long, long, to be on my own!

David was asking everyone what they wanted to do today in Inverness. "I want to spend my pocket money!" Nigel piped up.

"Oh, yes, let's look around the shops!" said Tessa. "I've got two week's pocket money, plus some money Grandpa gave me!"

The general consensus was to take a trip into Inverness town centre.

"Would you mind terribly if I didn't come? I need to do a few chores while everyone is out, and then perhaps do some reading." I asked.

Everyone was happy to give me a couple of hours on my own, and they all drove off happily to spend their money.

I quickly cleaned and tidied up the caravan, then made myself a cup of coffee. The sun was shining through the windows, and I sat down by the window, looking out onto the forest of trees, quietly drawing strength from the silence and the warmth of the sun. I opened the chest of drawers and pulled out my Bible and notebook. I started to write down my prayer to God.

"Lord, I'm onto the same subject – Love! I saw Love in action throughout the whole time of camp. It was gentle, powerful, all encompassing. I see Jean Darnall giving out your Love as she faithfully explains the truths of the Bible, and explains how it can change people's lives. I feel your Love when Faith Lees speaks. Sometimes it's "tough love", but I know deep inside me it's your Love. I still feel as though I am missing something! As though I don't quite belong.... Help me, please Lord. Speak to me and explain it to me, please."

I sat quietly for a while, and I somehow found myself reading a passage in my Bible from Ephesians chapter five:

"Be imitators of God, as beloved children, and walk in love, as Christ loved us, and gave himself up for us, a fragrant offering and sacrifice to God." (Ephesians 5 verses one and two).

All the words popped out of the pages of my Bible, as though in technicolour!

"Imitate God!" however does one do that? God is huge, the Great Creator of the Universe! He is Eternal and all Powerful. How can I imitate that? A clue comes in the next phrase, "as beloved children". If we are His children, then He is our Father – a father/daughter relationship! Or a father/son relationship. In other words a family relationship. Okay....

"Walk in love...." I'm trying to do that, Lord, but actually I'm still finding it hard to trust Love, and so it's hard to walk in love without trust.

". . . as Christ loved us...." Oh, I see! To imitate God we look at Jesus and imitate Him! He was God on earth! He showed us the living God by the way He lived His life on earth. Yes, He was very loving, caring, forgiving, understanding: all of those things.

"(Christ) gave Himself up for us, a fragrant offering and sacrifice to God." That is the height of love, to give yourself up to death on behalf of those who don't even care or know about you!

Having seen films depicting the crucifixion, I couldn't think there was anything fragrant about it! It was just appalling torture and murder. Horrid. And yet, Jesus did it voluntarily as a sacrifice to save and heal us. What Love! It's all too big for me! I don't know where to start on this love journey.

Yet as I thought about it, I knew I was well on this "love journey". God had called David and me to Post Green – we were seeing God's love in action time and time again. We were living in an environment of love. It wasn't always perfect, but when things went wrong there was always forgiveness, and people saying, "I'm sorry!" and offering a hug.

I felt God wanted to say more to me. I looked at my watch. I hoped the pocket money was lasting out and that no one would be back too soon!

Then the Lord started to speak: precious, loving words of instruction and understanding.

"You must be capable of that kind of love on each occasion it's needed. To be given as I show the need: to show that love with action. Not to hold back because of self-consciousness. Your loving capacity is being stretched. You need to see the deficiency in your loving capacity so that you can let Me repair the breaches. I want you to be affectionate: that is, I want you not only to love, but to show your love. For some people this comes easily, for others it is much harder. For you at the moment it is hard. But it is important that you learn to show love, not only in acts of kindness but in deeper ways.

"You can be kind and thoughtful yet not love. I loved when sometimes I could do no act of kindness because they would not receive it. My Heart yearned to give but they would not receive. When you love like that you can pray when you can do nothing else.

"Loving is praying for a person; loving is creating a new person out of an imperfect broken person. Loving is believing great things will be done in that person. Loving is yielding yourself to a person, even if you know you'll get hurt.

"Loving is making yourself available, when you want to do something else. Loving is being good tempered when you are being irritated.

"Loving is laughing when you feel sad. Loving is rejoicing when others rejoice. Loving is weeping when others weep. Loving is responding. Loving is sharing.

Loving is obeying. Loving is yielding. Loving is keeping the confidence placed in you. Loving is seeing people whole and free and praying them into it. Loving is looking at Me, Jesus, constantly, and sharing that look with others.

"Loving is above all, beyond all, beneath all, around all. Love is never ceasing, all powerful, all creative, all healing, all delivering, all freeing. Love is the most gentle, most powerful force in all the world. My Love cannot end."

Overwhelming silence! How wonderfully God had answered all my questions. It put it all into context for me. But it seemed that I had an enormous amount of work to do, and an impossible mountain to climb. I had a long way to go, but at least I knew in which direction I was meant to travel.

A car was driving slowly up the road, and turned into the camp site. The family had returned. Thank you, Lord – brilliant timing!

The rest of the holiday tour of Scotland was marvellous! We returned Patsy to an airport on a given day, and drove on up to Scourie where Tom, Faith and family were holidaying. We spent a few days with them, marvelling at the most wonderful scenery on the tip of the north west coast of Scotland. To experience the Lees' family on holiday was very different from life at Post Green in some ways as the pressure of other people's demands was off the family, and they were free to enjoy themselves. They were very adventurous, and we joined in where we could – climbing, walking, and sailing.

We returned to Post Green at the end of August ready for whatever lay ahead for us all.

I have recently re-read some of Patsy's letters that she wrote after her holiday with us in Scotland – it was certainly a special experience for her to be part of a family with other children. From then on she began to fly down from the Isle of Man to Heathrow, and stay with us for all her school holidays, unless she was flying out to Oman to see her father. She fitted in well with our family and was fun to have around, although one felt there were under-lying problems in her life that would have to be dealt with at some point in the future. She could be quite demanding, particularly of my time, and I would be totally exhausted by the time she went back to school.

On one occasion when we drove her back from Dorset to Heathrow, we stopped off for a lovely picnic en route on the edge of farmland. It was warm and sunny and we all relaxed and laughed together. We then continued on our way and arrived in good time at the airport. Before we had a chance to book Patsy through security she somehow managed to disappear. The flight was announced and she did not appear. We went to the airport enquiry desk and explained the situation. As she was a minor she had to be accompanied by designated airport staff through to Birmingham or Manchester and then on to the flight for the Isle of Man. The airport put out a loudspeaker call for Patricia MacArthur to come to the enquiry desk – but she did not appear! In the end the airport police got involved and said they would find her and get her back to school and advised us to leave! So we left and drove back to Dorset. We had a phone call from the airport staff shortly after we arrived home to say she was safely en route for the Isle of Man.

Patsy was an amazingly gifted young lady and a brilliant pianist and singer – but she mostly kept her talents to herself and I was always amazed when I had evidence of yet another of her skills. When she finished school she opted to go to King Alfred's College in Winchester to train as a teacher. She had often helped my children with their homework and was a born teacher, so I thought she would do well in her chosen career.

She was only at King Alfred's College about two weeks when Post Green was due to send a music/drama team to the college for a Sunday evening worship concert. I was part of the team, and had written to Patsy to say we were coming and hoped to see her.

When we arrived at the College, we rang the door bell, and it was promptly opened. Before we could be ushered in, the girl on the door said, "Which one of you is Daphne Mills?" I stepped forward and introduced myself, puzzled!

"Well, Matron would like to see you immediately. She said you were to come and see her as soon as your team arrived!" I was told.

The girl quickly told the team which room to enter, and then led me down a dark passageway and knocked on a door labelled "Matron".

Matron called "Come in!" and I walked in and said, "I'm Daphne Mills. You wanted to see me?"

"I believe you know Patricia MacArthur?" she said, quickly and firmly.

"Yes." I replied, wondering what on earth was coming next.

"Well, she cannot stay here! Night after night we have to put up with her screaming and sleep walking, and all the other girls are frightened, and they can't sleep properly themselves. We just can't have this type of behaviour. I've spoken to Patricia several times on the matter but it still goes on. She can't sleep here another night. I'm afraid you will have to take her away – tonight." Matron said.

"Well, I can't just take her home with me. I have to phone and check with my household that it is convenient to have her and make sure we have a spare bed for her." I tried to stand my ground.

"I'm sorry – you have no choice. Patricia has been told to pack her bags and they are standing in the hallway by the back exit. Patricia has been told to attend your concert tonight and that she has to leave with you at the end of the evening."

"Well, please at least let me use the phone to warn the household what's happening." I asked.

Matron slid her phone across to me, and watched as I dialled the Panorama phone number. I was able to warn whoever answered the phone that Patsy would be with me on my return late that night and could they get a bed ready. I knew there would be grumbles in the household that I had made a decision on my own to bring Patsy back, but I had no choice.

Once Matron was satisfied that Patsy wouldn't be with her one more night, she relaxed a bit and told me in which room I would find everyone. I found the hall, and immediately saw Patsy, sat away from the rest of the college audience. She had perched herself on a table at the back of the hall, dressed like a princess, including a beautiful fur muff into which her hands were placed. She was clearly making a statement, but I am not sure what it was! I felt annoyed with her, maybe unreasonably, but I was mystified to see her dolled up to the nines when such a crisis had arisen and she was being expelled from college. I walked over to her and said she was coming back with us, and then I concentrated on the evening ahead.

Patsy had been suffering from anorexia for two or three years by now, but very little was known about the syndrome in those days. It soon became apparent, once she was back at Panorama, that she was eating almost nothing. My life became a nightmare as I felt responsible for her and did everything I could to get her to eat, even a lettuce leaf, or drink a cup of tea! The days went by and Patsy's lack of eating or drinking became a huge worry to me. I phoned Faith and consulted her, and she suggested I brought Patsy down to Post Green for the morning. It seemed another battle of wills, and neither loving persuasion, encouragement or threats would make Patsy put her hand to her mouth with either food or drink.

I felt I was betraying her, but we called in the doctor and he insisted she went into hospital. The nightmare of watching someone you love refuse to eat is quite terrible.

More about Patsy later!

CHAPTER NINETEEN

As well as a large area team helping us at Post Green with the conferences and camps, we also had over one hundred Bible College students assisting us. Although it was optional for them to help, the students were glad to get hands-on experience. They helped to prepare the big dome marquee ready for all the people who were coming. We always supplied tea and coffee, and squash for the children. We also bought a smaller marquee, and this was available for counselling and smaller meetings.

There was initially a lively debate as to which of the students could help with counselling. Some were very new Christians. We had older students, in their forties, fifties and sixties, who had well established careers. Others had only just left school or university and were new to the problems of adult life. When discussing who or which of the students were mature enough to counsel we came across problems. Firstly Elmer Darnall was emphatic that all his students should be allowed and capable of counselling. Secondly if there was a sort of two-tier system of those who could counsel and those who were too immature, this did not always work out. Often the person that needed counselling was sat right next to you! And although we were able to say, "Just a minute, I will go and get someone who can chat to you!" it wasn't always that easy. They had opened their heart up to you before you could say that! So in the end it was agreed we would trust God! That the right person would be counselling the right person! The system worked well.

One Saturday, during a conference weekend, we were just clearing away the lunchtime cups and saucers at Post Green in the house. Frances, one of the Bible College students had walked in through the side entrance bringing an elderly lady with her. She sat the lady down at the kitchen table and proceeded to make her a cup of tea, explaining as she was putting the kettle on that she had found Dorrie walking up the road towards Post Green.

Faith and I happened to be in the kitchen. I sat and chatted to Dorrie while she sipped her tea, while Frances took Faith on one side and explained further. Frances had also been walking up the lane and had caught up with this lady, walking very slowly. She had an overcoat on and a headscarf that covered all her hair and part of her face. Frances presumed she was coming to the meeting in the marquee. Apparently not! The lady confessed that she had left her home in Bournemouth about seven that morning. She had been walking ever since – probably about five or six miles. She admitted that her handbag was full of pills and that she planned to swallow them all, once she was out of sight of the road and any possible passer-by.

Frances had said to her: "Look I have some friends who live in this house you can see from the road here. They will give you a cup of tea and let you sit down for a while."

Dorrie had agreed. She was tired and weak – actually exhausted. I worked out her age to be around seventy years.

Faith came and sat down at the kitchen table with Dorrie and myself. "Would you like to come and sit in the other room? It's more comfortable! And we could have a chat if you like?"

Dorrie nodded, looking at Faith. "Daph, would you like to join us?" Faith continued.

I could tell by her voice that to reply "No!" wasn't an option!

We walked into the drawing room, and Dorrie sat down on the ancient settee. Jean Darnall called that particular settee The Predicament, as it was so hard to get out of it, once seated.

"Dorrie, do you want to tell us how you come to be here? I believe you live in Bournemouth." Faith said gently to her.

Dorrie sat hunched up on the low settee, and I sat next to her. Faith had brought up a chair and sat close to her. Dorrie admitted that her handbag was full of pills. Life wasn't worth living anymore. She just wanted to die.

"When did you start feeling like this?" Faith asked her.

"When my sister died." She replied.

I immediately jumped to the obvious conclusion: she was grieving for her beloved sister.

Fortunately Faith wasn't so easily satisfied, and definitely had the gift of discernment on such occasions.

"What actually happened that started you feeling like this?" Faith gently persisted.

"I don't know. Well, at the time of her death someone gave me a necklace. I was told never to take it off, or something nasty would happen to me." She replied.

Faith knew that God was already showing us the root of the problem. "Do you believe that if you take it off you will suffer in some way?"

"Yes. I'm too scared to take it off." Dorrie bowed her head further.

"Daph and I have seen God do marvellous things, and we have great faith that God will do what we ask Him to do. We don't believe God wants you to suffer like this. Will you trust us to pray for you? We will ask God about this necklace and see what He says."

Dorrie nodded.

Faith began to pray, a most wonderful prayer. I held Dorrie's hand. She began to weep. I felt a bit out of my depth, and I knew God was showing Faith what to do next, so I sat quietly, waiting.

"Dorrie, do you think the person who gave this necklace to you could have put a curse on you?" Faith asked her.

Dorrie looked up at Faith, startled. "The person who gave it to me doesn't like me at all. I was very surprised to be given the necklace. And the way she gave it to me did seem like a threat. I was too scared not to wear it, and far too frightened to then take it off."

" Don't worry, Dorrie!" Faith reached over and held her hand as she began to cry again. "Daph and I will pray, and ask God to deal with this matter. We will ask him to lift the curse from you."

Faith proceeded to pray quite a long prayer, covering every possible angle from which Satan had attacked Dorrie, or could try and attack her again. Faith prayed quietly and firmly, asking Jesus Christ to remove the curse by the power He gained by His sacrifice and death on the cross. It was a sacred, holy moment.

I added my prayer that all would be well when Dorrie got back home, and that her husband wouldn't be too upset or angry!

We finished praying, and Dorrie looked up. Her face had completely changed. She shook her head and took off her scarf. Faith and I were both amazed. She looked about fifty years of age at the most. The old lady, bowed under a curse, had gone. She was back to her youthful self. Dorrie began to talk about work, and how she used to be the life and soul of the factory where she worked. She had been off sick with depression for several months. "I'm going back to work on Monday! I feel absolutely fine again. Thank you. I don't know what you've done, but I feel well again!"

We encouraged her to thank God, and continue to thank God for His deliverance and healing from the terrible curse put on her.

"Dorrie, you can take off the necklace now!" Faith smiled at her encouragingly.

Dorrie reached behind her neck and proceeded to unclip it. She handed it to Faith. "I don't ever want to see it again." She said.

Faith put it in her pocket and said she would get rid of it for her. I went out into the kitchen and made more tea. The afternoon's conference was well underway, but neither Faith nor myself had special duties for the day. I asked Dorrie if I could phone her husband, and tell him she was with us, and we would drop her home shortly. She nodded, pleased. I took down the number and went into the kitchen to phone him.

The husband seemed fairly unperturbed. Maybe he didn't show his emotions, or maybe she had disappeared before?

Dorrie chatted happily all the way back home. I thought of her trudging all that way all morning, and we were able to do the journey in about twenty minutes. Faith and I took her to her front door and met her husband. We gave her a hug and said we would keep in touch. She smiled back radiantly.

Faith made sure that Frances heard the end of the story of the "old" woman she had rescued. She was most interested and was so glad she hadn't overtaken her but had got into conversation with her. Faith and I visited regularly for a few months but Dorrie had no setbacks.

One evening about six months later, I felt strongly that we should go and visit Dorrie. I phoned Faith and asked her if she was free. Unfortunately she had other commitments. "If you have a feeling you should visit, please go, Daphne. You don't need me along with you."

I drove over to her house around seven that evening. Her husband opened the door. He was pleased to see me, but said Dorrie had gone out, and he wasn't sure what time she would be back. "Please come in, I was just about to make a cup of tea."

I would have refused. But I was so sure that God had told me to go round that evening.

The television was on, as always. Faith and I had learnt to talk over it on our visits! Shortly after the husband handed me my cup of tea, the television started a documentary on the 1939-1945 war, with black and white footage of appalling suffering of the British soldiers fighting in France and Germany. He sat with his back to the television, slightly blocking my view, thank goodness!

I sat there puzzling why I was there! It was a good halfway through the programme I remembered something Dorrie had said. Her husband had fought in that war, and suffered terrible injuries and nightmares; she thought he would never get over the damage it had done. He was prone to depression at times because of his experiences.

The husband continued to talk to me for the whole length of the war programme. His back was still turned towards the television. He was happily telling me all about Dorrie, and the huge change in her life since her visit to us six months ago.

Then he went on to talk about his work, and how he enjoyed it and what he did. I could hardly concentrate, listening to him, and trying not to look at the documentary going on behind him. I kept praying, "Please God, don't let him turn round! Keep him talking!" The programme went on for about an hour. Just as the programme finished, and a nice cheery lady announced the up-coming sit-com, he turned round and looked at the television.

"I think I'd better be going. Thanks for the tea and chat! Please give Dorrie our love!" I said, getting up from my chair, and slipping my coat back on again.

"I really enjoyed my evening, thank you! And of course I will tell Dorrie you came. And give our love to Faith when you see her, please!"

I walked back to the car and drove slowly home.

When I saw Faith the next morning she said, "How was Dorrie? What was the problem? Why did God want you to go there?"

I laughed. "You'll never guess! Dorrie was out. But her husband missed a very nasty war programme he was planning to watch. It would have really upset him if he'd seen it! He sent his and Dorrie's love to you."

"I'm so glad you went!" Faith said, as she handed me a pile of letters to type. "Oh and can you phone Jean and Elmer and see if they can come to supper on Saturday, please?"

A new day had begun.

CHAPTER TWENTY

The drive down from Panorama in Lytchett Matravers to Post Green in Lytchett Minster was a great joy every day. I loved the countryside, the green fields, the woodlands and the farm yard smells; I didn't mind at all slowing up and going two miles an hour behind a herd of cows, walking slowly along the road in front of me, tails swishing. Sometimes if I was a bit late, I would try overtaking the herd, very, very slowly. Then the cows would hurry up and start overtaking me, blocking my progress. They would bang their bodies against the car door and the car mirror. I would give up and stop and let them all go past.

I never wasted my journey down the hill. David and I both had separate cars, and if I wasn't dropping Tessa or Abigail off to school, together with neighbour's children, I would do my singing practice. It was almost my only chance on my own.

I remember one particular morning singing "One Fine Day" from the opera "Madam Butterfly". It has a couple of very high notes in a very dramatic part of the song. I was driving down towards the junction at the bottom of the hill, just reaching my important crescendo, when Elmer Darnall appeared driving his little car on the other road towards the same junction. It was my right of way, so I took a snap decision to trust him to stop and I launched into my high note, top A. Elmer didn't give way. He didn't even slow up. I saw him take avoiding action into a farm gateway. I was well on my way on up the hill by this time. I glanced in the car mirror and saw his car reversing out of the field. If I hadn't seen him coming out of the field, of course, I would have stopped and checked him over. Elmer was renowned for being a bad driver!

I arrived at Post Green office a trifle late and morning prayers were just beginning. Elmer walked in about five minutes later, huffing and puffing. "Sorry, I'm late! I had a very near scrape on the way down the hill: gave me a fright!" Elmer said as he sat down. I think he was oblivious that it was me he had nearly hit! From then on I always called the junction "Elmer's End". A few years later the road priority was changed, by which time Elmer had long since left and moved to London with Jean.

Singing was my great joy. Back when Dad, Mum, Valerie and I lived at the White House I used to go up into the attics and sing. I didn't know many songs at all, so I would yodel and exercise my voice with trills. Once we got to Post Green it was a different kind of singing. There were new worship songs coming out all the time. Jean Darnall picked up new ones as she preached all over the country and in the United States. She would teach them from the platform, usually unaccompanied by the pianist or organist. The Bible college students added to our repertoire as well.

We had a rather temperamental pianist/organist who was booked to play for all our conferences in the Dome. But he often would turn up very late. Faith would come running into the house, looking for me. "He's not turned up yet so can you lead the singing till he comes, please?"

I dreaded it! I might be a trained singer, but to choose the right note to start each song or hymn for a large congregation to sing was a nightmare! Somehow I managed. Sometimes the pianist would arrive just as the first song was announced. In the early days we did a mixture of well-known hymns and new songs. I think even at the last camp we still had one or two traditional hymns as well as modern songs. I firmly believe this is the way the church should be today, with a mixture of old and new, to suit all tastes.

All of my singing training came in handy at one time or another. Jean Darnall sent a message to me via Faith one day. "Jean's just off to America. She wants you to put all the Post Green songs onto a tape for her so she can teach them in the States." At least I had fore-warning! Help! I went and consulted Faith who said, "Look Louise Jolly is back from playing with an orchestra on the Continent. I'm sure she would help you."

"But she doesn't know many of the songs! How can she accompany me?" I said, helplessly to Faith.

"Louise is a brilliant musician. I've known her for years. Just sing the songs to her, and she will learn them in no time, and then play them for you on the piano or organ." Faith smiled, encouragingly. "I'll phone and ask her. Are you free this afternoon?"

It was all arranged. Louise and I walked over to the Dome, and Louise sat down at the piano. I had all the songs typed up on a Post Green Song Sheet. "Jean wants them all. Let's just go straight through the sheet, rather than bob around, shall we?" We worked well together; I sang each song, and Louise worked out the key in which each song should be sung and transcribed them onto manuscript paper.

Someone in the house was in the recording studio, so when we were ready we liaised from the Dome via microphones and recorded each song. It took all afternoon. One of the songs was an anthem that I had turned into a song. It was one of my favourite anthems by Mendelssohn that I learnt at Avenue Church. "As the deer pants after the waterbrooks, so panteth my soul for thee, O God." It became quite popular, so we included that one too.

A few copies were run off on tape copiers and given to Jean, who reported back weeks later that they had worked perfectly for her.

In the early days in Dorset I would probably be invited to sing and speak at various churches or women's meetings about four or five times a year. This increased considerably once the work of Post Green enlarged and we went all over the country sending out teaching teams each weekend. Then I probably went at least once a month on an away trip usually speaking rather than singing, but continuing to sing locally.

Meantime the work was expanding hugely and there were various demands being made on the ministry of Post Green which made us have to consider putting the work on a more formal basis.

We were working in all the mainline denominations of the Church: Church of England (Anglican), Methodist, Baptist, Congregational/United Reformed, and Free Church; occasionally Pentecostal and Catholic churches.

After lots of late night meetings we came to an agreement. The meetings had to be late because Tom Lees, Denis Ball, and David Mills were all teaching at Christian Life College each evening. Later Dr Jim Bigelow and his wife Debbie joined us, and Jim also was teaching at the college. The meetings would start about 9.45pm and go on until after 11pm. By 11pm my brain had shut shop and it became a nightmare to stay awake and concentrate. Eventually I was allowed to go home at 11pm regardless of where the meeting had got to! The others all seemed to be night owls and were happy to chat till the early hours of the morning.

The agreement we reached was that Post Green needed to become an officially recognised religious community. This would mean having the backing of all the mainline churches, and particularly the blessing of the local Bishop of Sherborne and the Bishop of Salisbury, under whose authority we would then be.

All the local church leaders were contacted and a big day was planned during the summer of 1975. The service was held in the parish church of Lytchett Minster, and presided over by the Bishop of Sherborne. Leaders of other local churches took part, and we were then officially recognised as a religious community. As well as this being an advantage because we could be seen to have "recognised credentials", it also meant that those in full time ministry would be excused from national insurance contributions for the duration of their ministry. Later with over one hundred people living in the community this was a huge financial help. Nevertheless the main reason for the official ceremony was to give us acceptable status in the Church rather than that we were a group of people who had gathered together ad hoc.

The pattern of our ministry was approximately the same for many years: two Spring Holiday Family Camps, two Youth camps in July, and one or two family camps at the end of August. In the early days we had more camp applications than places and sadly had to turn people away. We had to decide who could come and who couldn't, which was awful! We would allow newcomers a place, and turn down applications from people who had been to several camps. We had to limit the number of children people could bring, as quite a few people started bringing neighbours' children as well as their own, and we didn't have enough resources for the huge number of children who were coming.

We had fifty or more helpers at most camps. The camps were divided into units – say seven to ten units – in different areas of the camp field. Each unit would have two Unit Leaders, and several helpers. At the start of every day at camp all the leaders and helpers would meet "in the barn" to share, talk, pray, and encourage one another. If there was a specific problem this would be shared and prayed over. Any good news and answers to prayer were rejoiced over! Team helpers' children were welcome to come, from crawling or toddling babes to more mature youngsters longing to be involved in helping at camp. Straight from this meeting was the Unit Meeting! If we hadn't had breakfast we would run back to our caravan and grab something to eat during the Unit Meeting. This gathering was often much more personal; we shared in depth any problems that had come up the day before on the unit. We had many people come who had quite deep personal problems, family problems, health problems, and we would share these needs together and we would pray for each person on our unit and particularly any who obviously needed help. We saw miracles at every camp. I think in the early days with Jean Darnall leading all the camps we saw more dramatic miracles, and I don't think anyone left camp without having been touched by God.

I think in the latter camps in the 1980s and 1990s there was a different kind of work going on amongst the campers. Nevertheless many people drove out of the gate on the last day of camp having had their lives changed, and were returning home with renewed vision and energy for what lay ahead.

For the first few years camps were held in the paddock adjoining Post Green house, and then when they became larger and more frequent, they were moved to East Holton, on the road from Lytchett Minster to Wareham. The atmosphere of the camps changed because they were no longer an extension of Post Green house, Tom and Faith's family home, with their children running in and out. But East Holton had its own charm: the ancient, nearly falling down, barn for team meetings in the early morning, and for the teenagers the rest of the day. The grounds surrounding the camp field gave scope to huge games for the children, trees to climb, ropes swinging in trees, secret camps built in the forest, and children's play equipment that gave the kids hours of fun.

There were dangers though: poisonous snakes in the woodlands, though Tom Lees would assure all the campers that if you made a lot of noise and stamped your feet they would slither away without biting you. Also a busy railway line adjoined the grounds, and could be crossed by walking over a bridge en route to the inlet beach of Poole harbour. Children were warned never to go on the line.

May Bank holiday camps were often an amazing mixture of hot sun, bitterly cold nights, and torrential rain. The two units that were assigned the land at the bottom of the field were prone to flooding. At the end of one camp we had huge hail stones that descended as everyone was packing up to go home. Tents were being dismantled, awnings attached to caravans were being packed away inside the vans: personal belongings were being stowed away in boots of cars and on roof racks. The hail stones were so huge everyone ran for shelter. I was visiting Viv Crouch, the camp nurse and member of Post Green Community. She had the misfortune to be at the bottom of the field. We were sharing our stories of camp. Wherever Viv was there always seemed to be drama: if an accident happened Viv was never far away, and we always had a great laugh hearing her stories. The hail stopped and the rain came down in torrents. I felt safe and secure in Viv's huge caravan: one of the several huge mobile homes that Post Green had got years beforehand. They were shabby but very useful! When I said reluctantly, "I'd better go now!" and opened the caravan door, I wasn't sure how I was going to go! The water lapped around the van and the caravan steps were under water. Some gallant young male campers in shorts and bare feet were doing their Sir Walter Raleigh bit – well not exactly. If they had put their coats down on the ground they would have floated away. No, they were lifting all the marooned girls and women to places of safety! So I was rescued and carried to dryer ground.

One thing I will say about Post Green: you could never get into a cosy rut! As soon as you got used to one system, one pattern, one way of doing anything, it would change. This was true of all structures, whether it was the Leadership, the way things were co-ordinated, the way camps were run, and so on. I was fortunate on several fronts, as I don't much like change if something is working well for me!

Because we had Grandpa Mills living with us as well as our own three children we only had two household moves: moving from Panorama back to Post Green house, and finally to Hillwood Cottage. I was either Faith or Tom's personal secretary the whole time I was working at Post Green and was never moved from that position. Once I was asked to be secretary to another high powered gent in the community but the amount of work landing on my desk became impossible and I was asked to choose between the two men – I chose Sir Tom! I was also fortunate to be the outreach administrator for many years, although I had a break for a while and became administrator for the graphics and printing business we ran. As I loved art I enjoyed watching book covers and record covers being designed – but it was a nightmare at times getting the graphic designers and the printer to come up with the goods on the deadlines set out by Celebration Services (Post Green) Limited, or worse still Celebration Services International!

For many years I was asked to lead Morning Chapel at the youth camps: starting at the second youth camp I attended. While the rest of the camp team met "in the barn", I led the young campers in their early morning worship. This part of the camp was totally optional for them and they could choose whether to come or not. But it was usually fully attended, and as always I felt out of my depth and would pray, "God, please help me!" I was usually assigned a musician, often a guitarist, to help lead the singing. Morning Chapel would last for about half an hour, and then the campers would have about half an hour free to wash up their breakfast things, or even to have their breakfast, before going into the main tent for the morning talks and activities. While camps were held at Post Green the Morning Chapel took place in the gardens on the other side of the house, near the pond. When camps moved out to East Holton, Morning Chapel was held in the main marquee.

For the adult camps there were usually optional seminars in the afternoons, which I couldn't often take part in as I was usually running something myself, but would join in an arts and crafts seminar if I had any free time.

Faith and I ran family seminars for several years at camps, giving a short talk to get people thinking and then answering questions on family issues, and getting people to share their experiences. One year when camps were still held at Post Green Faith and I held a family seminar in the drawing room. The numbers were way down on normal attendance, and I felt a bit disappointed. When we closed the drawing room door and started our seminar there were only nine campers there, a mixture of mums and dads and a grandmother. How we started off the seminar I don't remember, but I trust God guided us to say the right thing, as this particular afternoon proved to be somewhat harrowing. I was so glad Faith was there: a wonderful woman of strong faith, courage, and spiritual wisdom.

We sat round the drawing room on the Lees' antique arm chairs and sofas, facing each other in a semi circle, with the fireplace filling the gap. Where I sat, I could look out of the big windows onto the lawns and shrubs, and the village church in the distance. The sun was shining, and it seemed altogether a glorious day.

Faith made everyone welcome and started the seminar off. Because the seminar had so few people attending we shared a little of what God wants in our family lives, and Faith then asked each person why they had come to the seminar and what they were wanting from it. As we went round the room we discovered that every parent had lost a child that year, and the grandmother had lost a grandchild. We were appalled and humbled. Mostly we just let them all share their grief and their stories, and they ministered to one another in their sorrows, and in their faith in God to take care of their lost child.

As with most bereavement, there is unbelief and shock, then anger and possibly accusing someone; then depression sets in, sometimes numbness. We had all those emotions expressed that afternoon. One of the hardest stories was from a young mother who had had three children. Her house caught fire, her husband grabbed one child, and the mother another, and they ran out of the house to safety. One of them then ran back towards the house to get the other child, a nine year old mentally handicapped boy in a cot; but it was too late. The house was engulfed in flames. The mother confessed her terrible remorse in not choosing the handicapped child first. She thought that in that split second that she had she had favoured the normal child to snatch to safety first. What could we say? All the parents ministered to each other that afternoon, talking and sharing about forgiving oneself where they felt they had failed their child. It was a very sacred afternoon and Faith and I watched as Jesus honoured his words: "Blessed are they that mourn for they shall be comforted."

As my children grew up into little adults, I didn't feel quite so qualified to lead family seminars, and was asked to lead the Holy Spirit seminars instead. I quite often did these with Tom Lees, and we would "Blib and blob", taking it in turns to say something in the seminars! We usually had three afternoons, so would give talks on the baptism in the Holy Spirit, the fruits and gifts of the Holy Spirit, and receiving the Holy Spirit. There was an assortment of other seminars I took, sharing the responsibility with other members of the community. The subjects chosen were perceived to be what people or the Church were requiring that particular year.

If one of the team wanted to get anything from home, then we would dash away at the end of the seminar and escape from the demands of the campers for an hour or so, trying to remember to take off our camp badges before we bumped into any village people, who actually were not interested in reading our names on our sweaters!

Tessa, Nigel and Abigail had their own group of friends at the camps that they met up with each year. They made particular friends with helpers children, whom they saw more often. The teenagers had their own meetings, and were quite often taken off camp to the cinema, or swimming, to the beach or whatever. The young teens had slightly different activities, but the leaders of each group had a real heart and love for their charges and found activities that that particular age group would enjoy. I usually managed to take a group of teenage boys, plus a couple of fathers, to Poole Speedway! It was always a thoroughly enjoyable evening, but only for those twelve years and over. The younger ones got bored or too adventurous while the racing was in progress!It was amazing the number of fathers who would be rather pleased to be asked to help accompany us! Some had never been to speedway before and others confessed to having been a keen supporter of Belle Vue, Manchester, Wolverhampton or some other far away town.

Nevertheless I loved being in the evening meetings, and the Holy Spirit was always at work touching people, changing lives, and bringing a deep sense of holiness, joy and peace on the gathering. The worship group usually consisted of about six guitarists, singers and a keyboard player. The music was always of a very high standard and was the foundation of every service in the tent. The morning sessions at the Family Camps started with children's worship and there were always fun action songs, dramas, play acting, characters dressed up, and audience participation. After about forty minutes the children would all pile out of the marquee and run across the field to their various designated smaller marquees for their particular age group.

The crèche for the babies and toddlers was usually fairly full each camp. I quite enjoyed helping in this area when asked. I met young parents who were thrilled to be able to leave their babies safely while they listened to the talks in the main marquee in peace. We had forms the parents had to fill in to give us instructions about their child's particular needs, familiar words used, favourite toy, feeding needs and so on.

All the hundreds of people who helped at Post Green camps over the years have their own precious stories to tell. It was very special to witness what God can do when given the chance in people's lives!

After the evening meetings most people ambled thoughtfully back to their units for a warm drink that was provided in a tent or awning, lit up with lanterns, as the rest of the field was plunged into darkness, with just the twinkling stars and the moon to give a small amount of light. One had to be very careful not to take short cuts across other units as it was all too easy to trip over a guy rope attached to someone's tent or awning. Each unit assigned two child-walkers to take care of all the children while their parents were in the main tent for the evening meeting. Most of us took it in turns to child walk! This would mean putting the seven year olds and upwards to bed or supervising teeth cleaning, washing, and making sure all of the youngsters were where they were meant to be at a certain time. Bed times were written out in the camp books and parents urged to adhere to these times otherwise it would have been chaos!

One camp Peter Lusby Taylor and I were assigned the child walking in our unit at the top of the field, nearest to the loo block and nearest to the main marquee. There were some particularly difficult brothers, who egged each other on, and really played us up. As they were boys Peter supervised them in and out of the loo block, making sure they didn't make a dash for the woodland as they came back out. We eventually had all our children in bed except for these three boys who would appear to be safely in their tent, and then re-emerge with a complaint or a request! When all was peaceful, we breathed a sigh of relief and Peter started pointing out the names of stars and constellations, and I remember feeling like a very tiny insignificant spot on the universe – and yet! And yet! I knew God loved me personally and had done wonderful things for me. He can make the stars but he can also have a special relationship with each individual human being he has made, if they choose to ask him for that.

Before long two of the small boys were back out of their tent asking for something else! Peter went off to settle them down yet again, and then we heard the music group start up the final song of the evening! The parents came across the field. "Have our boys been all right? Have they been good? I hope they haven't been a nuisance."

"No," we replied. "They've been great!"

The following year the parents came again, bringing two of the three boys with them. Sadly the oldest one had died in a cycle accident. Post Green camps had a privileged responsibility to show the love of Christ to everyone, to the youngest and to the oldest, and to make their holiday in Dorset an opportunity to experience precious holy things in a loving environment. I was so glad we had treated the boys with love, laughter and gentle discipline at that particular camp.

When the Falkland war ended one of the men who had been on HMS Sheffield (which had been bombed during the conflict) arrived back in Portsmouth, and his first question on greeting his wife was, "Are we booked into Post Green camp?" They weren't and the camp was full. But the camp administrators quickly made space for them and phoned them back and said, "Come, you're welcome!" The sailor was in some trauma, particularly as he had had to leave his unconscious friend on board, as he was too heavy to lift up the ladder to the deck. He received a lot of prayerful help and love during the camp and felt strong enough to go back on duty when he left the camp four days later.

CHAPTER TWENTY-ONE

Our life at Post Green was constantly changing, both for the adults and for the children. When we first came to Post Green Community we were a nuclear family (i.e. just parents and children) and moved into Panorama, with my father-in-law

George Mills, and his small black poodle. We squeezed into the three bedroom bungalow, which had a spacious lounge, and large kitchen with dining area. A few months later "Grandpa" had his own two rooms, newly built over the double garage, and we were able to spread out a bit. This was in 1970.

Although Grandpa Mills brought his own car down when he moved into Panorama, we would take him on as many family outings as we could. One Sunday afternoon in the summer I invited Grandpa to join Tessa, Nigel, Abigail and myself on a nice drive though the New Forest to visit my mother. We set off in my Peugeot car, driving slowly through the forest and arriving at Rownhams House just in time for tea. We had a lovely walk around the lake in the grounds before climbing back into the car and waving farewell to my mother who was standing on the doorstep.

I decided to drive back through Romsey and head back to Dorset via the Cadnam roundabout. The roundabout was renowned for its traffic jam at the height of summer on a Sunday, but I thought we would risk it anyway. I could see the roundabout ahead and although it was busy there was no traffic jam. I put my foot on the brake, ready to slow up and negotiate the roundabout. Nothing happened – we continued at full speed ahead. In the few seconds I had I kept pressing the brake but we continue to gather speed. Poor Grandpa, sat in the passenger seat never uttered a sound. I shouted, "Oh Jesus!" – no time for more prayer! The car shot across the road, hit the grassy roundabout, and headed towards a huge tree – just as we were about to hit it the car sank into a hidden hole, and stopped. There were no cars going round the roundabout – it was like angels had stopped all the traffic – and dug a hole in the roundabout as well!

Once we realised we weren't dead, we climbed cautiously out of the car, and climbed up on to the grass. We all were quite shocked, and didn't know what to do! We had just driven past a pub, so we decided to make out way back to it and ask to use their phone. We walked across the road and into the pub. They would not allow the three children inside, but brought out a chair for Grandpa to sit on. I phoned David and explained we had crashed into Cadnam roundabout and could he come and get us. He was always brilliant in times of crisis so he asked few questions and promised he would be with us within the hour.

In the meantime I walked back to the roundabout to suss out the situation. Two policemen were standing on the pavement, pointing at the submerged car – with just the roof showing. "What stupid idiot parked his car in the middle of the roundabout?" one policeman said to the other. Well, I wasn't going to own up that

I was the stupid idiot – so I turned and walked back to the pub. David can deal with the police, I thought to myself. He arrived in record time, together with a doctor who happened to be staying at Post Green. He quickly checked us over while David went over to speak to the policemen who were inspecting my car from all angles. A garage was duly contacted and they came and towed it out of the hole and took it away for repairs.

We drove back to Dorset none the worse for our fright.

A year later, Post Green put on a huge Christian arts festival (mostly music) and drew around 3000 people over a weekend. I volunteered to fetch one of the singers from the railway station in Poole in the early afternoon. Unfortunately the bridge was up between me and the railway station. This meant I was delayed about fifteen minutes, and consequently we got back to Post Green later than the timetable had allowed. The singer I had fetched had missed her slot! This caused a fifteen minute gap in the printed programme. Two of the Christian Life College students quickly took to the stage and did some impromptu singing. Abigail, who was four years old, was called up onto the platform by Bob. He put a chair by the microphone, lifted Abigail up and asked her what she would like to sing. She then proceeded to entertain the crowds. When I drove in through the gates of Post Green, Faith was standing close by, frantically waving to me. I wound down the car window. "Hurry up! Abigail is on stage." I jumped out of the car and ran over towards the platform, just in time to see a crowd of children around Abigail. She had finished her "Act" and was signing autographs! As she had yet to learn to write her name, I think she just put crosses on their programmes! When the group around her had dispersed I had already had several people come up to me and tell me how wonderfully Abigail had entertained them. So I said to her, "I'm so sorry I missed your singing. What did you sing?"

"Oh, I sang a song I learned at playgroup: Stand up, Clap hands, Sing thank you, Lord; Thank you for the world so sweet!" I didn't know the song, but I heard it many times after that, with all the actions as well.

The whole day was a huge success, and for many years to come I would meet people who would say, "Oh, yes, I've been to Post Green; we came to a music festival there, held in a field in front of the house!"

While mixing with the crowds during that day, and making sure everyone had a programme and a song sheet, I met a couple who lived in Dorchester. They were friends of Tom and Faith. They came up to speak to me. "Are you Daphne Mills? Have we got the right person?"

"Yes!" I responded.

"Well, Faith suggested we came and spoke to you. I am Rachel and this is my husband, Sergei Tarrasenko. We used to run a youth group in France."

I could tell by Rachel's accent that she was most definitely French! She had a most appealing face, I realised, as I continued to listen to her.

"The thing is, one of our young people desperately wants to come to England to live with an English family. Her English is quite good – she's a nice girl; and we wondered if you could have her in your family as an au pair?" Rachel smiled, appealing to me earnestly! Sergei stood nearby, nodding his head.

My first thought was that we were on quite a tight budget financially and I wasn't sure I could afford to pay anybody anything! And secondly it was rather nice being just the six of us at Panorama. Before I could answer them I was interrupted by someone needing my attention. I quickly said to the Tarrasenko's, "I don't think we could manage an au pair just at the moment, but thank you for asking us." Then I smiled at them and moved away to deal with the other interruption.

The au pair idea was definitely in my too difficult tray. Later on in the afternoon I bumped into the Tarrasenko's again. "Please, please give a thought to the idea of Beatrice coming to your family!" I said again, that I really didn't think I could manage to help, but I would enquire around and see if anyone else could have her. They wrote their phone number down on a piece of paper and asked me to keep in touch.

I can't quite remember what happened over the coming days, but I do remember that Beatrice arrived from Paris, and moved in with our family! She lived with us for about a year and became indispensible. It soon became obvious that she was much calmer than me when it came to getting the three children ready for school and playgroup. Beatrice managed to get the three children dressed in their right clothes, washed, teeth cleaned, hair done, satchels ready, and sitting quietly at the breakfast table munching their cereals – with no shouting. Grandpa had long since decided it was safer to stay in his bedroom until the front door slammed around 8.30 a.m. and the banging of the car doors had been completed. As the car backed out of the drive, Grandpa would creep out of his room and pad along to the bathroom.

Beatrice remained cheerful and in control of the early morning drill every day – and we learnt to appreciate her hugely. The only reason she left was that her father was tragically killed cycling to work one day, and she packed and left the next day to help her mother. She came back for a visit three or four times, and once brought her husband and two small children.

My special friend Karen, who had been Jean Darnall's secretary for several years, and had attended the bible college with her husband Brian, had left and returned to Canada. At one point when things were a bit difficult for me at Post Green I decided to visit them in Canada. I felt a bit guilty about going as it was fairly close to Christmas and I couldn't get a return ticket. Faith's comment to me was: "It's fine for you to go to Canada, as long as you have faith that God will help you get a return ticket before Christmas!"

I flew out from Heathrow, and at the point when I thought that surely we must be nearly in Canada, an announcement came over the loudspeaker on the plane. "We regret to inform you we have dropped an engine and are having to return to London."

Dropping an engine sounded very serious indeed. I was still feeling guilty and remembered the story of Jonah who ran away from the task God had given him and caught a ship to foreign parts. The Bible says the ship got caught in a terrible storm and was sinking. Then Jonah stood up and confessed he was running away from what God had asked him to do. Jonah told the crew to throw him overboard or they would all drown. As you know, Jonah landed in the sea and was swallowed by a huge fish. He escaped and the ship didn't sink!

All this was going through my mind as the plane slowly (seemingly) returned to London! But I stayed silent and remained in my seat. At Heathrow we hung around the terminal for several hours and were put on another plane bound for Canada!

I thought by taking a trip to Canada I could break free from things that were troubling me back at Post Green. While talking with Karen and spending hours walking on the beach in Victoria together, I realised that I was my own problem!

I did all my Christmas shopping in Victoria, Vancouver Island, and returned home just before Christmas. On my first morning back I sat at the piano and composed a song, which became popular at Post Green for many years and was sung on the Fisherfolk record "Be Like Your Father". The words of the song I wrote were:

"Love, love and more love, Jesus is loving me.

Love, love and more love, how can it be?

What shall I do with the love that o'erwhelms me?

Jesus, speak to me.

'Pour out my love that others may see,

Pour out my love that they may go free!

That is my will for thee, That is my will for thee!' (see manuscript for music).

The work and ministry was mushrooming almost out of control and we were constantly taking stock. We would curtail certain activities but it seemed in no time at all that someone's bright idea, or vision from the Lord, would make us very busy again!

Following the huge success of the Arts Festival, Faith thought it would be a good idea to have an Arts Symposium. This would run for several days, and we would use Lytchett Manor rather than Post Green house, as it was larger. Lytchett Manor, being used as a secondary school, was happy to accommodate us in the school holidays. We set about organising the Symposium. First we had to find experts to lead each activity: art, pottery, writing, poetry, music, dancing – were some of the categories. It was well subscribed, and all of us on the Post Green team who weren't leading a group were encouraged to take part. I chose Poetry and Dance, and had a thoroughly enjoyable and beneficial time. The children had their own workshops and composed some music and did a wonderful dance to it. The final day was held at the Priory church in Christchurch, Bournemouth. The children were all in brightly dressed costumes and danced in at the commencement of the afternoon, making a very dramatic start to the final celebration of the Arts Symposium.

Today, in the Church, it is not uncommon to use modern music, dance, drama, poetry, and even crafts and pottery. But when we put on the Arts Symposium it was a very new concept for many churches. Edith Shaeffer had written a book called "Hidden Art" – and she was also a visionary for what the church should be doing. The understanding behind this is: God is the Creator, and He has created us in His image. Therefore if we are created in His image, we too have the ability to create. Many people don't realise they have a gift or talent because they never get the chance to do anything. Hence the Symposium – and I learnt new ways to express myself, in art, poetry and music, which have been invaluable to me over the years.

A great deal of support came from The Fisherfolk during the symposium. The group of about six or seven musicians had been down to visit us from Coventry for a couple of camps and we were fast becoming friends with them. Most of them were American, and were originally from The Church of the Redeemer in Houston, Texas. The Bishop of Coventry had invited a group from the church in Houston to come and move over to Coventry, and set up "community" in his area. The Rev Graham Pulkingham, Rector of The Church of the Redeemer in Houston, had agreed to this idea.

I had an opportunity to visit them in Coventry – there were twelve of them, living in a three bedroom bungalow, and somewhat squashed! But they were amazingly gracious, welcoming and loving. They began to have a huge impact wherever they went in England, and overseas.

Our work and ministry overlapped from time to time, and Tom and Faith went to Houston to visit the church there and see what was going on.

If by any chance you have read "The Cross and the Switchblade" by David Wilkerson, you will be able to understand better the next part of this story.

Graham Pulkingham had been called to be Rector of the Church of the Redeemer in down town Houston. Those who attended the church came from nice homes, and the music in the church was excellent, aided by a paid choir. Graham said that at the end of each service, he would walk out of his church to make his way back to the Rectory, and pass little children playing in the gutter on his way. There were prostitutes working in the area, and he found it difficult to relate what was going on in the church to what was going on in the streets around the church building. After much agonising he went to visit David Wilkerson, a Pentecostal minister in New York.

David Wilkerson talked and prayed with Graham, and Graham found himself filled with the Holy Spirit by the time he journeyed back to Houston. Over the coming months and years God led Graham to open up his home to many people, showing them the love of Jesus in a practical way. "Gathered for Power" by Graham Pulkingham tells the story of how it all happened.

The Church of the Redeemer became world famous, and a group of musicians and singers evolved from the church to become a household name – The Fisherfolk. They set a pattern for living that influenced the churches in America, England, Sweden, Australia, New Zealand, South Africa, and so on.

One of the key moves in Graham's ministry in Houston, was to encourage the Christians in his church to offer to open up their homes to people who were disadvantaged, or lonely, or needing help in some way. Also by economising and sharing finances in each household it could set free some other adults to be able to work full time in the church as the ministry grew. As this began to happen in a far larger way than one might expect, news of what was happening reached across the Atlantic Ocean, and began to make an impact in England. Graham Pulkingham was invited to speak at a Fountain Trust conference held at Guildford Cathedral and the University nearby.

Tom, Faith and I were able to attend this, and we began to hear the word "community" a great deal during this conference. I had no idea how much that word would influence my life, and the life of our family for years to come!

Graham Pulkingham and one of his key co-workers, Bill Farra, quite often visited Post Green. They weren't always impressed with some things they saw! On the other hand they were very impressed with some of our ministry and felt that the two "communities" would do well to work closer together. Our ministries began to overlap a bit, and we used the Fisherfolk worship team to lead music at our camps whenever they were free. They would come a day or two before camp started and involve in helping to set the camp up, which included collating the camp books: these books held the names and addresses of all expected campers, the units they were assigned to, and a map of the camp field. This map would show whereabouts on the field each unit was, where the loos were, water taps, manholes for emptying waste water, nearby walks, and areas closed to the public! The Fisherfolk threw themselves heartily into each job assigned to them and were very enjoyable company. I was always impressed with their gentle graciousness and their loving consideration of each other, and us too.

After two or three years of a fairly loose relationship between the two communities, things came to a head.

Faith and Tom, together with their family had gone as usual for their month's holiday in August, to Scourie in Scotland.

During this particular holiday Faith had been taken severely and seriously ill, and was fighting for her life in Inverness Hospital with cancer in the kidney area of her body. When she eventually began to recover it was felt she was too weak to be able to come back to Post Green to convalesce. She was such a "hands on" person, she would never be able to, or be allowed to take a back seat while her body recovered. Graham Pulkingham invited Faith to stay in the Fisherfolk community, now called the Community of Celebration. They were all living at the Cathedral of the Isles on the island of Cumbrae. Faith was there for many weeks recovering her strength.

In the meantime back at Post Green, although it seemed all was well, and the work was running smoothly, there were certain areas that needed some strong leadership. Tom asked Graham for advice, and after much talking it was felt that it would be an excellent idea for a group from the community living in Cumbrae to move down and share their life at Post Green. Tom returned from Scotland and began to talk to the other leaders of the possible plan and way ahead. I wasn't sure I liked the idea! This projected plan became known as "Tom's unilateral decision"!

Because I was one of the leaders it was obviously important that I was in agreement with the next step, so it was organised that I would fly up to Cumbrae and spend a week with the community there.

You might well ask who would look after the three children while I went off to Scotland! By this time we had several people living with us at Panorama. The Christian Life College ran a two year course for the students. At the end of the second year, if there were any students who showed considerable maturity and wanted to deepen their Christian faith and involve more with the ministry of Post Green, then they were invited to stay on for a third year. Consequently we had Richard Talbot, Geoff Bland, Ellie Green and Jenny Littleford living with us. With the use of bunk beds for all these young people, mostly in their twenties, we managed to squeeze them in and most of the time life was enjoyable and life-giving all round. Grandpa loved all the company!

So I flew up to the Isle of Cumbrae, and Faith had organised for me to involve in several areas around the community to get a feel for their community, and communal life. The highlight for me was the choir practice! Having been part of many choirs, and attended hundreds of choir practices I considered myself fairly experienced in choral singing. The Community choir practice was an amazing experience. The sound was awesome; the blend of voices exquisite! Heavenly! I was mystified! I learnt later, or understood later, that it was the love of the Lord that bound everyone together. Everyone listened to their neighbour, there was no voice out of sync with anyone else, and the choir sang as one voice, even though much of the singing was in four part harmony. Wow! I thought, wow! If this is what can happen at Post Green, we need it! I talked with Faith and spent time with Graham as well. As I flew back to Dorset I was able to say “yes”!

The Community of Celebration sent a group of about twelve people, including a Fisherfolk worship/music team to Post Green. We all squeezed up and made room in our houses! It was all change! Of course some of it was very hard work! And we had to make sacrifices that we never would have chosen to make in the flesh! The household money pot changed! We all handed in the money we earned to a “common pot” and then it was divided out equally to each household. We learnt ways to economise, like doing a huge vegetable shop at Wimborne market – buying in bulk for the whole Post Green community saved a lot of money – and for a small amount of household money we were given a large box of vegetables and fruit to last us the week. We had two or three very skilled “shoppers” who would do “the veg run”. They soon found a bin that contained “unsellable” perishable food! With permission given they would raid the bin each week and we might be given twenty extra bananas that needed to be made into banana bread that night! Or we might be given an extra box of rather soft tomatoes, so we would set to and make enough soup for the week - and to freeze as well!

We shared our cars and the car maintenance. We shared school runs, and out of school activities. The youngsters and teens had their own circle of friends and ways to occupy themselves. Mostly it ran well.

Whenever we meet together, which sadly isn’t often these days, there is lots of laughter and good memories of our life together. Of course in the day to day living at such close quarters with each other there were issues that came up that had to be talked through and resolved. Sometimes no resolution could be easily found, and then the people involved were encouraged to “give each other space”, and back off for a while: think about it, pray about it, and then come together in a few weeks and try and come to an agreement.

With over one hundred people and about ten households we were fairly well packed in and full most of the time. We had a very large guest ministry, with a huge number of requests to come and stay. Some people wanted to visit because they had heard about our life together and wanted to experience it for themselves. Some people had problems they couldn't resolve and wanted to come and talk things through while in residence with us. Many ministers and clergymen and their wives wanted to be part of what was going on at Post Green so that they could learn something new and take it back to their churches.

Single people, married couples, families, wrote in asking to live with us for a year or more. Consequently because of this last group we would only be able to fit them in if we organised a household move. Sometimes this only involved two households, but often it meant seven or more households changing occupants and houses. This could be a very stressful time – one always hoped to land up with people one already had a friendship or rapport with: sometimes this could not be the case. Because we were living with people that we wouldn't normally choose to live with, we learnt people skills and a depth of pastoral care and love which could only be achieved with an enormous amount of divine love and talking and praying.

Many people who came to camps, conferences and Clergy Symposiums, saw the dynamic amongst us and would ask us to come to their churches to teach what we knew about loving and caring for one another. We had teams out at various churches all over England almost every weekend of the year, except when we were running camps, when it was all hands on deck.

Before the Fisherfolk involved in the music and worship at Post Green we had our own music group. We had some immensely gifted musicians who had come to us via the Christian Life College: particularly Lindsay Treen from the Guildhall School of Music, and Celia Harrison from the Royal College of Music. Dave Porter and Richard Paine were also gifted in music. Rev Dr Denis Ball, part of the leadership of Post Green, was always willing to work with the music group. For a while I was the pastoral leader of the team. Later Betty Pulkingham and Susan Abbott, together with the leadership, asked if I would form a choir for the whole community, and conduct a choir practice each week.

I tried to get out of it as I had no experience of conducting and beating time. I have always said, while training as a singer, "I don't count, I just feel the music!" But if one is conducting every note has to be counted, and every pause in the music counted as well – not my best thing! And having been in Gilbert and Sullivan operas, I would rather use my arms to express the words of the music, than religiously beat time to each bar!

I explained all this to Betty Pulkingham! She is a famous writer and composer, and has written several hymn books, books of church anthems, and helped with the recordings of all the Fisherfolk records.

Betty arranged a time and a place and a tambourine! We met up and she taught me how to conduct. She marked some easy songs in the Fisherfolk music book to start me off, and did diagrams of how to beat in two-two time, two-three time and four-four time. Susan helped me advertise the new choir, and we were off to a good start with about 25 or 30 people. The choir practice was organised to be held at Panorama, using my beloved old piano that Grandma Lomax had given me!

I stood on a huge old family Bible (sorry, Lord) so that the choir could all see me, and we started off with some vocal exercises. Then we launched into some new songs, and some old familiar ones. At the end of each choir practice we had a fun song, and I encouraged everyone to find an instrument: car keys, wooden spoons, saucepans, etc, to beat time and finish off the evening on a high note!

I had to move the tenors to the front row in the end, to keep an eye on them – they were the best for cracking jokes and messing about (just a bit!). If we were due to sing at the Parish Church a guitarist assigned for the Sunday would help us practice our music. Either Howard Page Clark or Celia Harrrison played the piano, and eventually Celia took over the choir from me when we had got ourselves established and were beginning to make Fisherfolk recordings at Post Green. The choir were invited to take charge of the music at the local parish church on the fifth Sunday of any month! This continued until eventually we were doing the music for every church service. The music was spectacular, and we used Betty Pulkingham's King of Glory Mass for the communion services. I think this is the best and most musical mass setting ever written and I am sad I rarely hear it today.

CHAPTER TWENTY TWO

Up until the time Faith was ill I had continued to be her secretary, typing all her letters and keeping an eye on her various appointments. But while she was away convalescing in Scotland I got busy on other jobs and most of Faith's mail got dealt with at Cumbrae. When Faith returned home, Carolyn Reinhart accompanied her from Cumbrae. Faith's lifestyle changed and I wasn't needed in the same capacity, and eventually became secretary to Tom instead. Faith used to tell me that Tom said I was the best secretary he had ever had; but I think he was just being nice, as he wasn't keen on my filing system and the way I tidied the muddle on his desk at times!

One day he asked if I would go into Keith Jones Bookshop in Bournemouth and get him a Church Lectionary which he urgently needed. That little jaunt suited me fine! I checked the notice board for a free car, grabbed the keys of the Triumph Herald and I drove happily into Bournemouth town centre, parked the car and walked down the hill to the bookshop. While I was in the shop, having found Tom's required Lectionary, I browsed around the other books. Then I suddenly remembered I had a meeting at 10.30am. It was now 10.15 – and I had a journey of about 25 minutes! I quickly paid for the book, and ran up the hill to the car park. I jumped in the car, and quickly assessed the quickest route back to Lytchett Minister – the back way – longer route but less traffic and I could speed up a bit. Of course I forgot it was all 30mph between Bournemouth, Poole and Lytchett.

It wasn't long before I was flagged down by a police car! Bother!

There were two policemen in the car which had stopped me. They both got out, and one walked over to me in a slow leisurely Mr Plod fashion.

"Did you know you were exceeding the speed limit?" he asked me courteously.

"Er, oh dear, was I?" I replied, having wound down the driver's window.

"Yes, you were. You were in fact going at 57 miles an hour." He replied.

"Oh dear, was I? Oh dear, I'm so sorry." I answered, very contritely.

"Well, I'll have to take some details from you." The policeman proceeded to get out a large pad with an ominous looking form printed on it.

"Your name, please."

"Daphne Mills – Mrs." I replied, obediently.

"Your address?"

"Er, Post Green, Lytchett Minster." I said, glancing at my watch despairingly.

"Are you the registered owner of this car".

"No, I don't think so." I replied hesitatingly. (Well we owned everything in common in the community, who on earth did own it, I thought!)

The policeman sighed. "Well, is it your husband's car?" anticipating the answer would be "yes", he then asked, "Does your husband live at the same address as yourself?"

"Yes – Rev David Mills. But he's probably not the registered owner of this car."

"Well, who do you think owns it then?" the policeman asked me with exaggerated patience.

I was beginning to get a bit nervous by this time, and my meeting had now started without me.

"Well," I said helpfully. "It could be Mr Robert King."

He wrote down "Robert King" as owner. "Is that definite, that he is the registered owner? What's his address, please?"

"Well, Robert King lives at Post Green, Lytchett Minster." I said.

"Same address as yours?" the policeman seemed a bit surprised.

"Well, can you say he is definitely the owner of this car?" the policeman asked again.

I thought a bit. Robert King was in charge of the household cars at Post Green house. I had no idea where the Triumph Herald had originally come from.

"Well, it could be the Reverend Rodney Dunlop – same address." I added hastily.

I could tell the policeman was severely mystified, and I was getting more confused with this question and answer session.

"You seem very unsure who owns the car you are driving. Any other names you want to give me?" the policeman asked with greatly overdone patience.

"Well, it could be Richard Hunt. Same address as mine!" This also was written down.

I was frantically trying to think who else might own the car. Well Tom was officially head of the Post Green Community – maybe he owned the car?

I quickly volunteered: "Actually it could be owned by Sir Thomas Lees."

"Oh, and where does he live?" the policeman wasn't impressed with my name dropping at all.

"Same address as me!" I said.

By this time I was hugely embarrassed with the whole situation –the policeman probably thought I was either a very loose woman or lived in a hippy commune. Either way he gave me a verbal warning about my speed and briskly walked back to his colleague, probably for a good laugh and to try and figure out the strange conversation he had just had.

Three weeks later I had a letter to say I was being fined £60, which I couldn't pay, as I only had 50p a week pocket money. So at the next household meeting I put my hand up to say I needed money – no, not for new undies, not for new shoes – just a wretched speeding fine. £60 was an awful lot to give away in one week from the household allowance but it got paid – I think Robert King sent it off for me in his position as household treasurer!

We had had our own household up at Panorama in the village of Lytchett Matravers for about six years. As mentioned previously Beatrice, our French au pair, moved in and lived with us until she had to return to France on the death of her father. Jenny Littleford, a Bible college student, asked if she could take Beatrice's place. She was working as a children's nurse at a local hospital. So Jenny moved in. Following other Bible College students we had the Kelting family living with us. Then Dave and Val Holland moved in, with their baby Richard.

And Diane Zeisman, a lovely single American, who was excellent with our children.

Against my wishes, David, my husband, got an architect to draw up plans to put in three extra rooms and a bathroom over the kitchen. I adored the Purbeck stone wall in our hallway, and desperately wanted to keep it; and I didn't feel we needed more bedrooms for more people. But somehow it was all set up and the builders were due to start work. Grandpa Mills needed to move out for the duration of the building work, so David telephoned his brother and organised at very short notice for me to deliver Grandpa up to Ian and Elizabeth's home in London.

Grandpa never liked being moved out of his nest; but I encouraged him on our car journey up to London. We drove around the south circular, in and out of the heavy London traffic, and arrived In Lewisham around noon. I was tired from the travelling and trying to cheer Grandpa up. I also had to explain why he was suddenly being sent off to his other son's house for a month. Grandpa couldn't understand why we wanted more bedrooms; didn't we have enough bedrooms already?

I rang the doorbell, and my sister-in-law opened the front door. We trooped inside, taking my father-in-law's small suitcase with us. Elizabeth showed Grandpa to his bedroom, and encouraged me to come into the kitchen with her while she put the kettle on. She turned to face me as I was leaning against the sink. She proceeded to vent her anger on me for asking them to take father-in-law at such short notice. The arrangement normally was that they would have Grandpa for a month each summer. This was springtime, and was most unexpected, and quite unreasonable of us to ask them to have him. Elizabeth was rather ferocious in her anger and I felt totally overwhelmed with the injustice of it all.

Grandpa was not my father! I kindly looked after him because he needed a home and someone to care for him. He had been hustled up to the Mills family in London because David had planned an extension against my will. My money was paying for the extension! I tried to defend myself against the verbal onslaught, but when it continued I burst into tears! I was overwhelmed with grief.

Once I started to cry I couldn't stop. All the build up of extending Panorama had taken its toll and I was crying, not just about Grandpa, but about the way the extension had been planned. Elizabeth thought that by shouting at me and telling me to pull myself together and not be a cry-baby it would stop me in my tracks. But it only made it worse, and I cried more –and felt desperately sorry for myself.

Grandpa must have heard something of what was going on, but he was always great on discretion!

Elizabeth, in despair, raided the drinks cupboard, got out some brandy and poured it into a glass tumbler; to this she added a good swig of Coca Cola, and thrust it at me. "Drink this!" she commanded me. I didn't think I could swallow anything in between gulps of tears. But I put it to my lips and managed to swallow some of the amber brown liquid. Amazingly it stopped my sobs in its tracks! It was like a miracle drug! I then managed to verbalise why I had cried so much, and Elizabeth apologised and said, "There, there, I didn't mean to sound so cross! Friends again?" I nodded.

We made polite conversation for a short while with poor Grandpa in the lounge, and then I quickly said my goodbyes and commenced the long drive home.

Soon after this our lovely Purbeck stone in the hallway was smashed and removed, a hole cut in the ceiling, and a new open wooden staircase in situ.

Soon after the extension was built we had a New Zealand family move in with us. Ric and Penny had heard about the Community of Celebration and Ric had written to Graham Pulkingham to ask if they could come and live in the community for a while. They were assigned to Post Green. They brought with them their two daughters, both slightly younger than Abigail. The two young girls, Rachel and Joanna, shared a bedroom with Abigail. It wasn't always an easy time as Penny and the girls preferred New Zealand to England! Ric adored jumping down the last five or six stairs from their bedroom, and would land with a loud thud every time. I pleaded with him to walk down the stairs quietly but he never did remember!

Richard Talbot, the Christian Life College student, who had lived with us for two years, had moved to Post Green household and then left the community and got a job with Glaxo in London. He had spent his childhood and teens in New Zealand. It wasn't long before I realised that Richard Talbot and Ric Foxley had a unique way of asking for something they wanted, when they thought you might say no to the request!

The request was made in such a way, signed, sealed and settled, that really one couldn't say "no"!

I perceived they had both been educated the same way, and probably at the same school. When Richard came down to visit us one weekend from London, I got the two chaps together and asked about their schooling. Sure enough, they had both gone to the same strict public school in New Zealand! Having ascertained that, I tried to encourage Ric to make a request for borrowing my car, or whatever, without making the request so tight that I had no choice but to give him what he wanted! Ric and Penny were an extremely nice couple and we are still good friends. They learned a huge amount during their years in the community, as did most of us!

Of course as in all family life there are joys and sorrows, and life at Panorama was no exception. Sometimes it is easier to remember the sagas than the joys. But as I recall the past I realise there were not many sagas worth losing sleep over. One springs to mind in the early days of sharing our life in Panorama. A nice couple, Roger and Katy Kelting, moved into Panorama together with their baby. David did quite a lot of ministry (preaching and teaching) with Roger who was a most gifted teacher with a charming personality. He was very good looking – and would have made an excellent James Bond!

Because my father was always on a short fuse, and could get angry over the most seemingly innocent event, I was pretty alert to what I call "hidden anger".

Roger Kelting fitted into this category. He was the nicest, most charming, caring person. But I felt that behind all that there was a tightly coiled temper which could be unleashed with little warning. In other words, I guess he reminded me of my father!

Around this time Nigel had taken some exams at his junior school, and the teacher had phoned and asked to see me. I thought to myself: ah well, I'm sure Nigel tried his best! I arrived at the school, and walked into the classroom as all the pupils were packing up their satchels and putting on their coats. "Ah! Mrs Mills! Thank you for coming! Look, I'm a bit worried about Nigel, so I thought we had better have a chat. Do sit down."

I looked round for a chair, and grabbed one from behind a desk and drew it up towards the teacher's table. "The thing is, we are a bit mystified. These tests Nigel's done...." The teacher paused and looked at me.

I had time to think: don't say they've discovered he's dyslexic or some other complicated problem!

"Well, all we can think is that Nigel is totally bored. He's too bored to do the work – it's as though it's all beneath him and he can't be bothered."

I wondered what on earth she was going to say next! Were they going to expel him, or something? I remained silent, and continued to look at the teacher.

"The thing is, Nigel has come out top in absolutely everything! It doesn't make sense."

No, it certainly didn't! My mind was doing mental gymnastics. I wasn't sure whether to say, "Oh, dear!" and apologise on Nigel's behalf – or to say: "Well bravo, three cheers for my lovely son! I knew he could do it!"

"Between you and me, Mrs Mills – this kind of school obviously doesn't challenge your son at all. I think you should think seriously about where he goes next. He's due to leave here in July and I wonder whether you would consider sending him to a school in the private sector – he is more likely to be challenged and have to compete with boys more clever than himself."

"Do you really think that is best? If so what do you suggest?" I asked, trying to come to terms with this huge swing from despair to joy on behalf of Nigel.

"Well, put him in for the common entrance at that big public school near Wimborne, Canford - I'm sure he'd pass it easily."

I met Nigel, hovering outside the classroom, and we walked home together. He basically confirmed what the teacher said – the school work was boring. But he thought the exams were a bit of a challenge so he'd done his best on each test paper.

Tessa was already at a private school, St Monica's, and was due to take the common entrance for Wentworth Milton Mount. This was a school supported by the Congregational/United Reformed Church and as she was the daughter of a minister, her school fees would be paid for her.

After much discussion with Tessa and Nigel, it was agreed they would both go to boarding school. Nigel would go to Queens College, Taunton, with his cousins.

Tessa would board at Wentworth Milton Mount in Bournemouth. A daily school run from Lytchett was out of the question, the head mistress said. "Tessa will have a lot of homework to do each evening, and a long journey to and from school each day will just add to the pressure she will be under. I strongly recommend you let her board with us. She will enjoy it!"

I knew the headmistress very well. She had taught me at the Atherley School. I did not remind Miss Hibbert that I was one of her former pupils. After all many years had elapsed since she had last taught me! Half way through the initial interview Miss Hibbert frowned and looked at me more closely. "Don't I know you?" she asked. "No, don't say anything! Just a minute – yes I know who you are! You had a sister called Valerie. . . You're Daphne, aren't you?"

I was completely astounded at her memory. But then she let herself down! She told Tessa what a brilliant pupil I had been, and that I had never caused her any trouble!

As Miss Hibbert took Tessa for a tour of the school, and I meekly followed behind her, I reminisced about one of many instances while in her class. She had been my form mistress for two years running, and had been very strict and tiger-ish at times.

For our mock O level exams in Geography we had been studying the Americas. During the exam we were handed out a poorly duplicated sheet with a feint copy of South America. We had to fill in the principal towns, mountain ranges, rivers, marking them in different coloured pencils.

A week later, Miss Hibbert came storming into our classroom, her black university gown and hood flowing behind her. She was carrying a bunch of exam papers. The door monitor closed the door, and Miss Hibbert banged the exam papers down on the desk.

"I have never in all my life had such a disgraceful set of exam papers handed in!" she said, angrily. "You will none of you pass Geography if you can't work harder than this."

The class was shocked into total silence. All twenty-five of us sat bolt upright at our individual desks, all eyes fixed on her, wondering what was going to happen next.

"And," she went on, "one stupid girl filled in the map of South America upside down!" Miss Hibbert glared at us all. There were a few stifled giggles, that anyone could be stupid enough to put South America upside down. I probably giggled as well.

"Judith and Shirley – pass these exam papers out please and we will go through some of the corrections." The papers were duly given back to us. I was keen to see what mark I had and what I might have done wrong. I was always optimistic expecting a good high mark, which very rarely happened. My familiar handwriting landed on my desk. I flipped through the neatly filled in exam paper. It had bright red biro scribbles all over it. And my beautiful coloured-in map of South America was crossed right out. "RUBBISH" was written on it. "UPSIDE DOWN". I got 36 marks out of a hundred – not bad!

But nevertheless I left Tessa in Miss Hibbert's tender care and she lasted out the full four years at the school.

But it was hard for Tessa and she got very homesick. She wrote some sad letters home in her early days of boarding.

One Monday morning the post arrived as we sat down to breakfast at Panorama. Roger, Katy, baby, Jenny, Diane, David and Abigail were all at the table. I was impatient to open Tessa's latest letter and check whether she was settling down a bit better. I slit open the letter at the table and started to skim through it. Roger Kelting reacted very strongly and angrily. I was shocked. I knew that it wasn't really very polite to read one's letters at the meal table, but I thought with "family" it would be acceptable in the circumstances. I tried to explain to Roger that I was anxious about Tessa, but he just wouldn't calm down. I was very upset.

What I hadn't really understood was that Roger was having some problems of his own, and was getting upset about other things, nothing to do with me. But home is often where things bubble up to the surface. And Roger was bubbling. Later on in the week there was another upset between Roger and me. At some point on the Sunday Roger had phoned Susan, one of our very skilled pastoral leaders, and talked to her. I didn't know what the conversation was about but Roger came into the lounge and said Susan was coming up to Panorama for a meeting that evening to try and resolve some issues he was dealing with in regard to me!

Mid evening Tom Lees and Susan Abbott arrived. I don't any longer remember all the details, but I do know that Roger wanted a more open confrontation with me when he was angry about something, and he was annoyed because I always backed off. Susan quickly got to the nub of the problem. (I thought it was Roger's problem not mine!) But Susan turned to me and very gently said, "Daphne, why can't you face Roger's anger?"

I was fairly calm for a while, and said something like, "Well, I don't like anger – it's unnecessary. Why can't Roger keep calm about things?"

"Why don't you like anger, Daphne?" persisted Susan.

Roger, David Mills and Tom Lees all looked at me.

Help! I thought this meeting was about Roger and his anger – why pick on me? I thought!

I remained silent, my mind in a fog. Susan then said, "Who has been angry with you before?"

I immediately thought about my father, and the times Valerie and I had locked ourselves in the airing cupboard in Abbotts Way!

"Well, my father – definitely!" I said.

Susan asked a few more questions. The men in the room stayed silent.

Having found out a bit more about my father's anger while I was growing up, Susan said, "Well, you see, Daphne, the problem is Roger can't stand it when you go all silent on him when he is venting his feelings. He doesn't know where he stands with you, and it unnerves him when you walk out rather than stand and face his anger."

I still felt it was Roger's problem, not mine. I firmly said again, "I don't like anger!"

If you are really afraid of something, in fact not just afraid of it but petrified, it is very difficult to face it. I was like that with anger. So I could always sense "hidden anger" long before it showed its ugly head. And I would back off in the hope that the anger wouldn't come bubbling up to the surface and attack me.

My sister Valerie was much more courageous than me when my father was angry. I often hid behind her and felt her protection. I could never face my father myself when he was angry.

Susan and Tom spoke a great deal to me about my problem. I remember little of it now, and mostly I was sitting there trying not to cry in front of Roger in particular. The meeting seemed to go on for hours, and Katy had put her head round the door at some point and reminded Roger he still had homework to correct before school the next day.

"You go off and do your work, Roger." There were gracious hugs all round and goodnights said. Roger left the room.

That still left me! Susan tried to explain that things would never work out in our household if I couldn't stand steady and confront the anger, Roger's or anyone else's. "Are you willing to face Roger's anger?" Susan said again.

I thought if I said "no", that Roger, Katy and baby would be moved into a different household and I would no longer have the problem! So I said, "No."

I would not say I am a stubborn person. But faced with something really terrifying to me, I was not going to say "yes" to something that I knew I could not do, would not do, and did not want to do!

I stubbornly kept to my "no", and Tom and Susan persistently tried to persuade me to at least be willing to try to face anger, Roger's in particular!

The time went by, and I am sure we had a break for tea and coffee, but I do know that Tom and Susan were still talking to me at 2.30am! I was dead tired, as they must have been as well. I said, "Yes, okay, I am willing to try and face Roger's anger – and anyone else who comes to live with us." The evening, or early morning, finished off with a brief prayer and we were all able to go to bed.

Next morning my face ached I had cried so much last evening. I had been confronted with my worst fears. Looking back now I would say that the fear of anger has spoilt a lot of my progress in life. I hate conflict and would still rather back off than deal with it, unless I am very secure with the person. When we were children, I hid behind Valerie, and Mum – and they faced many of my battles for me.

As a minister's wife in charge of a church, I could have done so much more if I could have confronted people when things were going wrong.

I watched Faith and Susan in particular over many years lovingly, gently, firmly, confronting people and I saw the fruits of their labours. I envied them; I saw what a gift it was – loving confrontation – but I'm not sure I ever really got through it myself.

One day a man telephoned and asked to speak to Faith. I had answered the phone and I could tell he was furiously angry. I went and fetched Faith, and said: "Marty (not his real name) is on the phone and I think he is really angry about something!" Faith followed me back to the phone lying on the desk. "Hello, Marty! What's the problem?" she enquired confidently.

For an hour I could hear this man shouting down the phone, accusations in almost every sentence. I stood near Faith, horrified. She sat down on the office chair, and let him continue venting his feelings. Faith never once tried to defend herself. She let him get it all out of his system. I continued to stand next to Faith, praying she would have wisdom and strength to cope – I certainly couldn't have done so! Marty eventually calmed down. And I heard Faith inviting him and his wife down to Post Green for lunch on Sunday. Gracious calm words terminated the conversation, and Faith replaced the phone with a quiet sigh.

"Well done Faith!" I exclaimed and gave her a warm hug. "How could you cope with all that shouting at you? He was beside himself with anger, I could just hear it!"

"You can't reason with Marty when he's like that. He just wants to be listened to then he calms down." Faith replied, wisely and philosophically. I watched her walk out of the office and return to making the soup in the kitchen.

I would be in floods of tears if anyone had yelled at me like that, I thought.

I wrote in my prayer journal the night after my meeting about Roger's anger:

"Lord, last night was very, very, very hard. But I know I must let Roger be angry and say what he thinks. And I must not mind if I cry! And I must say what I think when I think it, not bottle it up inside. Lord, please help me. I have said "yes, I will go forward" but please help me to do that, and that it won't be half as bad as I think! Please help us to be knit together in love and care for one another in this house."

Four weeks later I wrote some scriptures down in my journal:

Luke chapter 1 v 37: With God nothing is impossible!

Genesis 18 v 14: Is anything too hard for the Lord?

Philippians 4 v 13: I can do all things through Christ who strengthens me.

Roger Kelting was going through a crisis both within the household and in the community. He was a strong person and a competent, gifted leader. He had led the Christian Union at Leicester University and the numbers had grown hugely under his leadership. He was a caring, pastoral person. But he was "small fry" within the community. We had a large number of leaders in the community at Post Green, and quite a number were ordained to the priesthood and had led their own churches. While Katy and Richard were living with us the Community of Celebration together with a Fisherfolk music/worship team moved into Post Green community and were dispersed into several households. There were many gifted leaders amongst them also. Roger was a good singer/guitarist with skills at leading worship as well. Maybe he saw his ministry disappearing – I don't know. But I certainly did not have the pastoral skills or the courage to meet Roger head on when he became angry. Six weeks later Roger, Katy and baby moved into a house on their own.

While this turmoil in my life was going on at Panorama, and the building work was continuing above the kitchen, my mother managed to come and stay with us and we had fun outings to Lulworth Cove, Corfe Castle and other beauty sites around the Purbeck Hills. Mum and I talked about the past and shared our excitement at the Saints, the Southampton Football Club, who were having a particularly good season.

A week or two later, on May 1st 1976 we had a special day. The extension was finished, and a most lovely family moved in. At 10am Dave and Val Holland arrived, together with their young son Richard, and their belongings. They had been in the community for a short while living in a house on their own, but were keen to be a part of a larger household. They were friends of Roger Kelting from Leicester and Coventry, and had moved down to Post Green after attending Post Green camps.

They quickly made themselves at home in the newly carpeted and decorated extension. I explained to them apologetically that I wanted us to have lunch early because I wanted to watch television. It seemed a poor start to their enthusiastic arrival at Panorama. I explained that my late father had been chairman of the Southampton Football Club, and Saints were in the F.A. Cup Final that afternoon. Dave immediately got excited on my behalf, and they all helped to get lunch ready. Then we rushed upstairs (the other end of the house from the new extension) and climbed the six steps up into Grandpa Mills' lounge. He was the only one with a television.

Grandpa was a keen Southampton football supporter so we all clustered around his television to watch the proceedings from start to finish. Saints were playing Manchester United and they won, one goal to nil.

This was too exciting for words! I was so thrilled! Next day, early in the afternoon, Val and Dave with baby Richard, Grandpa, Abigail, David and me, drove in our Peugeot to Southampton. We fetched Mum from Rownhams House, and drove into the centre of Southampton to watch the Saints return home, doing a lap of honour around the streets of Southampton. The media reckoned about two hundred thousand people turned out to welcome them back, with car hooters blasting away, headlights flashing, balloons flying, Saints' red and white scarves being flown out of nearly every car and house for miles around. A great day! We returned Mum to Rownhams House, and she fed us tea before we returned, happy and satisfied, to Panorama.

It was a brilliant start to the Hollands arrival as part of our household. A week later Ann Jonker, a young Canadian, moved in with us. Tessa and Ann became great friends..

An hour or two after Ann arrived, Ric, Penny, Rachel and Joanna Foxley moved in, (as mentioned previously) and we had lamb chops for supper, sitting round the extra long table in the dining area of Panorama kitchen. I see from my journal: "Abi too wild, so I shut her in my study for a while!" – poor Abi! Diane Zeisman had been part of our household for several months while the Keltings were with us, and she was an excellent friend to Abi, and used to manage to channel Abi's ingenious energies in a most creative fashion. On this particular day of great excitement Diane was the one to help Abi calm down and be sensible again! Rachel and Joanna were near to Abi's age so she suddenly had new playmates in the house. Of course it wasn't long before a few arguments cropped up and either Penny or I had to calm things down again.

The household gelled well together and there was much laughter and creativity. We had outings to the beach, or Purbeck Hills, went to the cinema occasionally if there was anything good on and we had money to spare. David or myself drove down to Taunton to visit Nigel and bring him home for exacts and end of term time – and mostly someone would offer to come and accompany us or help drive. The same went for fetching Tessa from Wentworth – but usually she much preferred us on our own.

On one occasion I was driving back from Queens College Taunton, having fetched Nigel, his school trunk and his huge double bass, when we had a puncture. I swiftly pulled the car over to the side of the road and turned off the engine. "Now what are we going to do?" I moaned gloomily.

"Well have you got your spare wheel, Mum?" said Nigel.

"Yes, but what good is that? I can't change a tyre!"

"I can!" replied Nigel.

"You can? How do you know you can?" I said stupidly.

"I've watched it done lots of times." replied my eleven year old son, already climbing out of the car. We off loaded the boot of school paraphernalia and got out the spare tyre and tools. I watched in amazement as Nigel took off the punctured tyre, replaced it with the spare, screwed all the nuts back on firmly, and replaced the tools and damaged tyre in its rightful place. We were on our way in less than twenty minutes. I was so proud of my son!

When Dave and Val Holland staggered downstairs one day, saying they were both really sick with 'flu, we sent them back to bed, having promised we would look after baby Richard. It was nine years since I had fed and changed a baby and I wondered how we were going to manage. "Don't worry, Mum. I'll look after Richard. I know what to do!" said Abigail.

There was no need to worry from then on: I could see Abigail knew just what to do, and she ran up and downstairs getting things she needed for baby Richard. She fed and changed him till his parents were well enough to take charge again! Abigail was nine years old. I was most impressed!

CHAPTER TWENTY THREE

Whenever Graham Pulkingham "came by" Post Green there always seemed to be changes following his visit. The month of July 1976 was no exception. The Community of Celebration had been invited to produce a film for the Minneapolis Book Fair. This would involve the whole of Post Green, all the households, and it would centre round a pastoral problem that had occurred within the locality.

It was a hot dry summer, and most of us were filmed either at work or at home. The situation chosen for the film was a previously dealt with marriage problem. Two Christian Life College students had got married a few years before. Janet was from the East end of London, with a glorious Eastenders accent! Tony was an orphan – a product of an unknown American serviceman and an English girl. Although Tony and Janet obviously loved each other very much they couldn't always get on very well together. They had a young son, and then a baby daughter; but the marriage was creaking at the seams and about to sink. Tony or Janet would phone Panorama at all hours of the day and night to ask David for help. David drew Susan in to try and help sort out the conflict. Despite all their pastoral skills the warring in the marriage continued and the phone calls were getting more frequent.

Then we got wind of some violence in the marriage. The pastoral leaders met together and it was decided to split them up temporarily. Janet and the children would move to Rest Harrow. Tony would move into Post Green. Richard Paine and Dave Porter would be alongside Tony, day and night. It was felt that the situation was so severe that the whole community should commit themselves to pray for the couple, and particularly Tony during the following week. All those who felt able put their name on a rota so that there were people praying for Tony around the clock, and other people to be free to chat with Tony whenever he wanted to talk things over.

We had a week of concentrated prayer. I remember doing 4am to 6am – not my favourite time for being awake. But I got up and got dressed, and drove down to Post Green, and spent the next two hours praying with one of the other community members, somewhere near Tony's suite of rooms that he had been given. If we thought we had a word from the Lord then we would have a chance to share it with Tony later on in the day.

That week was a turning point in Tony's life. It was also a turning point in their marriage. A few weeks later Janet and Tony were reunited and lived together in Rest Harrow household until they were ready to go back and live alone as a family in the next village.

This was the story chosen for the filming of "For Our Life Together". Janet, Tony and their young son, all played themselves in the film. We re-enacted some of our prayer times and meal times with Tony. Tony and Janet had to re-enact some of their rows and telephone calls to David or Susan. The film not only went to the Book Fair in the United States but was used as a teaching tool on many of our outreaches for years to come!

Several years before this Faith and Jeanne had instigated the Leadership Training Course. Large numbers of clergy, ministers and pastors, had been filled with the Holy Spirit in a powerful way and this made a huge impact on their churches. But many of them lacked the teaching necessary to lead their churches in this new wave of the Holy Spirit. Consequently Faith Lees had a vision for training these leaders right across England. People like Rev David Mills, Rev Dr Denis Ball, Tony Hyland (a local dentist, very well versed in the Bible, and part of Post Green team), and others were asked to write the course. Each person took a section. Subjects like:

Regeneration – a Biblical study on how to change one's life around, including assurance of salvation (where you go when you die...) How to lead someone to find Jesus Christ for themselves; how this can change your life; how to help a new Christian.

Baptism in the Holy Spirit: a Biblical and practical study on how to be filled with the Holy Spirit and how to pray for others to be filled with the Spirit.

The Gifts of the Holy Spirit: both for individuals and for the Church.

Living in Victory: victory is getting back to a place of utter dependence on God; including teaching on overcoming temptation, evil, evil forces, wrong things of the flesh.

Divine Healing (1) – praying for the sick; and Divine Healing (2) Deliverance from evil influences.

Prayer and worship.

The Body of Christ: sharing a common life; what it means to be "a chosen race, a royal priesthood, a holy nation". How to love our neighbours as ourselves.

Pastoral Care and oversight within the church.

This was a nine month course. Initially a team went from Post Green to which ever town was doing the Leadership Training Course. This involved nine visits including two residential weekends. The only people on the course were Clergy, Ministers, Pastors, and people acting in a leadership capacity within their own church.

Training church leaders became vital after the outpouring of the Holy Spirit in the 1960s and 1970s – because the Holy Spirit gives power for ministry. And God's power must never be misused, especially through over enthusiasm and ignorance. The Church has a great responsibility to train its leaders in the use of the gifts of the Holy Spirit. Together with this must come a very good knowledge of the scriptures and a determination to lead worship in the power of the Holy Spirit in such a way that all people can be blessed and not put off by excesses of behaviour, which sadly happens at times. Paul said in his letter to the Corinthians, "Let everything be done decently and in order."

In recent years I have witnessed church leaders who lack the knowledge and wisdom needed to guide their people in more recent outpourings of the Holy Spirit. I have witnessed church leaders condoning behaviour in worship which is not of the Lord, and it shocks me. People in leadership positions need discernment, and discernment only comes after hours of prayer and Bible study – and by listening to the still small voice of God.

Some worship leaders are leading "in the flesh" instead of "in the Spirit" and consequently there is no real lasting fruit coming, and at worst it is bringing some churches into disrepute.

Tom Lees could often be heard to say, "It is better to be loving than to be right!" and therein lies another clue to the fruit which should come from the work of the Holy Spirit: LOVE! If there is a lack of love, and if the church people criticize others for having a lesser faith or no faith at all – then where is the love? 1 Corinthians chapter 13 is often read at weddings. But it also needs to be read very slowly and thoughtfully in all churches at regular intervals. "If I don't have love, I am nothing!" says St Paul!

After we had held the Leadership Training Course once or twice in a particular area (the first being Portsmouth) then the leaders on the course were encouraged to teach the next course in their area, with leaders from Post Green coming just to the two residential weekends. All leaders on the courses had a fair amount of homework they had to commit themselves to, and this often included a book to be read or a teaching tape to be listened to.

We had about five teams committed to leading these courses, and they ran for several years. I was involved on the London, Norfolk/Suffolk, and Yorkshire courses. And for several years I led the Norfolk/Suffolk ones together with a team from Post Green. It was a huge privilege to teach and lead some very wonderful Christian leaders, and I immensely enjoyed working with other members of the community. We would meet together several times before a weekend away and got to know each other's skills and weaknesses.

One residential weekend in the Norfolk area was held in a convent or monastery. We planned to go to their morning service and then I would do my talk to the leaders after a coffee break. The morning service proceeded in a very dark but huge chapel. A priest and his acolytes swung bells and incense around several times during the service. There were a few elderly nuns in the choir stalls, and some elderly monks sat in the congregation. The incense was so heavy in the air that it was like being in a sweet smelling fog.

I turned to Rev Rodney Dunlop, part of our team, and whispered: "Help, Rodney, I don't think I can follow this!"

He looked at me and smiled and raised his eyebrows. The service continued.

I was beginning to panic. No way would my talk, due just after 11am fit into the atmosphere created by this orthodox and solemn service!

"Rodney!" I whispered again, poking him in the ribs. "Truly, I can't follow this! It won't work!"

Rodney, a delightful Anglican vicar from New Zealand with a great sense of humour, whispered back: “Don’t worry, I’ll swop with you! You do the afternoon slot!”

The service continued. It was so unfamiliar to me who had spent years in a Free Church, and I watched, fascinated, and tried not to take deep breaths. It certainly had an air of reverence, awe and beauty about it, though a lot of it was strangely new to me. With Rodney happy to do his talk next instead of me my mind was at rest.

During the many years we were running the Leadership Training Courses we were also doing weekends at many churches up and down England. I was the Outreach Co-ordinator in the community, so all the requests for a visit from the community would arrive on my desk. Having worked as a minister’s wife, I was in a good place to understand the workings of a church, and leadership structures, be it deacons, elders, “P.C.C.s” (i.e. Parish Church Councils) and so on. We had an agreed structure of what we would and would not do, or what we could and could not do. This cut down the pile of letters, and I would send a letter of apology promptly. Others needed to be brought to the Outreach Group, which included Susan Abbott and John Wilkes representing the Community of Celebration (in my mind). Carol Welsh, who had been to Christian Life College and was currently singing and doing drama with the Fisherfolk team. Tom Lees and I represented the original Post Green ethos.

Having agreed an “outreach” with a certain church, this would only go ahead with at least a couple of meetings with the vicar or minister – getting a vision for what was expected of the weekend and what was hoped to be achieved. If a vicar wanted to delegate his responsibilities to a lay leader and not visit with us himself, we usually would not continue negotiations for the weekend. Our weekends were often life-changing for the churches and if the minister or vicar wasn’t in at the planning then there could be confusion and muddle later after the weekend.

Mostly these weekends went without a hitch, having been very carefully planned. The Outreach Group would usually assess the type of outreach required and choose a person from the community to head up the weekend. That person would then choose a team around them.

I usually had the same team both for Leadership Training Courses and outreaches: chosen from the Rev Rodney Dunlop, Rev Ken Ramsey, Val Ramsey, Peter Lusby

Taylor, Val Holland, Ruth Vincent. Usually a team consisted of three or maybe four people – and had to contain a guitarist to lead worship. It helped to keep to the same teams as this saved a lot of planning time, and we knew which drama or activity we could include as well as the talks needing to be given. The weekends started on a Friday evening, and if at all possible finished by Sunday lunch time.

My husband David led a lot of Leadership Training Courses initially and I stayed at home with the children. But I asked if I could go on a residential weekend with David and his team to the Norfolk course he was running. David said, "Yes." I made arrangements for the children to be looked after and planned to come on the weekend – not to take part but just to observe. On the Friday of departure, David suddenly announced he wasn't going! He said the team could manage without him. I couldn't get a clear reason for this decision from him. So I travelled up in the car with the rest of the team – several people who I myself had never either lived with or worked with. We arrived in Norfolk – and the team seemed uncoordinated. It seemed that they expected me to lead it instead of David – and I had never led a LTC weekend before. After a somewhat hesitant start we all settled down and I enjoyed the weekend. David opted out of the rest of the Leadership Training courses run in Norfolk and Suffolk and I was asked to take over responsibility for that area.I had never felt capable of leading anything as big or as important as the church leaders' training course but having landed in the deep end I found I could swim – because I had to, or drown! It made me the stronger! Tom Lees always believed in my capabilities and was always suggesting I lead an outreach which I often felt was too big for me. But God was always faithful – if I was willing then He was able!

Gradually the subjects that I was usually asked to teach on were: The Baptism in the Holy Spirit; Healing and Deliverance; and Building an Environment of Love. Although I taught on a huge range of subjects later on, those were the main ones during Leadership Training Courses.We had some very strange accommodation at times – from being put into an empty house with no one around, or extremely poor council houses, or huge castle-like vicarages where it was nigh impossible to find your way to and from your bedroom, and every other possible home in between. One of the most memorable was in a town north of London, and our team were working in a very well known large church – Friday till Sunday. On arrival at the church we had a brief meeting with the vicar and other church leaders, and then I was driven to my accommodation by the vicar. He told me en route: "Daphne, make sure you memorise your way back to the church! The people you are staying with don't come to church, and I don't think they will turn up to any of our activities this weekend. One of their children occasionally comes to the church." I frantically tried to memorise names of roads as we whizzed past. The car drew up outside a group of fairly smart newly built semi-detached houses. "This is all right!" I said to myself.

The vicar climbed out of his car and ushered me up the little path way, and rang the door bell.

Eventually the door was cautiously opened. "This is Daphne. She's come to stay with you for the weekend, remember?" said the vicar.

"Oh, yes," said the lady, rather uncertainly. "Er, come in."

The door opened a bit wider and I picked up my bag and walked in.

"Cherrio, Daphne – see you later, meeting at 7.30 this evening." The vicar ambled back to his car, started up the engine and drove off.

If I can't find my way back, I'm sure these people will show me the way. The lady showed me into a small single bedroom. "Have you had a meal this evening?" she asked me timidly.

"No, sorry! We've just driven up from Dorset – got caught in all the rush hour traffic." I was tired and hungry!

"Oh, well, I've got to feed the children in a minute I'll get you something and bring it in to you!" I had noticed a high chair in the dining area as we had walked through to my bedroom. And she obviously had a child old enough to go to the Sunday School or something.

"Oh, thanks! I don't want to be any bother; I'll come in and eat it with you all if you like!" I said to her.

"No, I'll bring it in to you." She said firmly.

I unpacked my small weekend bag, got out my Bible, notes about the weekend, and some light reading matter. And waited!

Half an hour later there was a knock at the door. The young mother said, "I've put your tea on the table in the dining room."

"Oh, thank you very much!" I said. By the time I had stood up from the bed I had been sitting on, she had gone. I opened the bedroom door, and made my way into the dining room opposite. One place set neatly at the table: three fish fingers and some peas, a small potato, and a drink of water. I ate hungrily, feeling somewhat embarrassed sitting alone at their dining room table. It wasn't ultra smart, and had all the marks of being used regularly by the family! They were obviously eating in the kitchen on their own!

No one appeared, so when I finished eating I took my plate and knocked on the kitchen door. The woman came to the door, and took my plate and my thanks. "I'm not sure what time I will be back tonight – we've got a meeting at the church! Is it possible to have a front door key?" I asked a bit apprehensively. I didn't fancy being locked out in a strange town.

The woman walked out of the kitchen and into the hallway and hooked off a key and gave it to me. "Thanks so much for tea. I'll see you later!" I smiled at her. She looked at me blankly and turned back to the kitchen and closed the door.

It was still only about half past six. No point in hanging around, and I was anxious to make sure I could find the church again. I grabbed my bag and the key and walked out of the house, closing the front door firmly so they would know I had gone!

Luckily the church had quite a tall spire, so I aimed for that, weaving in and out of various roads en route. There were one or two of our team already back at the church setting up the amplifiers and setting out chairs.

"How's your digs, Daph? Okay?" called out one of the team.

"Fine thanks! Yours okay?" I replied.

"Yep, great thanks. Fantastic meal – they pulled out all the stops! I said "no" to the pudding and jogged all the way back to the church to run off some of the food," one team member said.

Just the thought of an abundance of food made my stomach rumble.

We were hugely busy all over the weekend, and we had a lovely team from Post Green. I wasn't one of the leaders, and was able to relax and just chat with the people and take part in a question and answer session at some point.

My hosts were not about when I found my way back to the house – my digs!

I got up Saturday morning. Not a sound anywhere. Our hosts had been instructed (so I was assured) to give us breakfast and give us a pack of sandwiches for lunch time.

No breakfast, and no pack of sandwiches. Maybe I've misunderstood and they are feeding us at the church. With this in mind I grabbed my bag and hurried off back to the church. There was a newsagent on the corner, and I ran in and bought a Mars Bar, just in case!

Most of the team were at the church early, busy setting up and getting things organised for the morning session. No food spread out anywhere. I quietly munched on my Mars Bar.

The day passed creatively and successfully, and at lunch time someone had the bright idea that they all put all the food from their picnics on plates in the middle of the table and people could help themselves! Great! What a brilliant God-given idea! I managed to top up on food and there were some sandwiches left over, enough for tea at 3.30pm. Cups of tea were provided, and I made the most of the liquid available! I helped myself to a sandwich and biscuit at the afternoon break, and at 5 o'clock we all packed up to go back to where we were staying for supper. One of the team offered to drop me back at my place, realising he was just staying around the corner. "I will pick you up at 7pm, if you like, Daph?" Dave Porter said.

"Thanks, great! See you later!" Dave drove off and I got my key out and opened the front door, ringing the door bell as well.

The husband emerged. "Oh, hello! All okay?" he said.

"Yes, fine. Have you had a nice day? " I smiled at him, but he was already turning awayl

"Yeh, took the kids to the park," he replied as he hurried back to the kitchen and shut the door.

I rested on my bed and reflected on the day we had had. Lively church, excellent teaching, especially from Dr Jim Bigelow, who was part of our team. Dave Porter had led the music with his guitar and taught a few new songs. Tom was staying at the vicarage and was obviously working very hard at some problems that had sprung up in the vicar's marriage, with a key church worker adding to the muddle.

I bet Tom invites the vicar and his wife down to Post Green! I wonder if he will check first with the household, or just invite them regardless! I thought to myself.

I looked at my watch. Help! No supper. I walked out of my room, the kitchen door was still closed, and I could hear low voices and the occasional squeal of a baby.

Do I knock on the door and say, "Where's my supper?" what if they haven't got any? Could I ask for a slice of bread? I was just about to try my luck, when voices were raised and the husband and wife started an argument - most inappropriate moment for a stranger to walk in. I went back to my room, and waited hopefully. Time ticked by.

The doorbell rang. I guessed it was Dave and got up and grabbed my bag. No one had opened the front door, and Dave was hovering by the car. I made my way down the pathway, closing the front door firmly again.

I remember the evening was super and the worship and music was very uplifting. It gave me strength to be joyful and not grumble about my digs.

The next morning the house was deadly quiet and of course there was no breakfast. "Well we are nearly done here, and then I can go back home and raid the larder to my heart's content!" I consoled myself.

The Sunday morning service held at the church was magnificent! Post Green at its best. At the end Dave asked me if I wanted a lift back to my digs again, and he would pick me up after lunch so we could assemble back at the church and sort out who was travelling in which car back to Dorset. He let slip how terribly well he was being fed at his digs, and started listing all the yummy food he had eaten.

"You lucky beggar! I haven't eaten since the sandwiches yesterday in the church!" the words fell enviously out of my mouth before I could stop myself! I wasn't one to make a fuss!

Dave looked at me, appalled. "Right! You're coming back with me! I know my hosts will be only too glad to feed you. Go on! Pick your bag up from the place you're staying at and come back with me!"

We drove back to my digs, and I quickly packed my things, called "Goodbye, thank you!" cheerfully into a seemingly empty house, and gladly climbed into the car and Dave drove on to his host's house around the corner.

We had a marvellous roast lunch and there was more than enough for us all!

Some of the community had an "Emergency Kit" which they always took on outreach: kettle, cups, tea, coffee, sugar and milk powder – and probably a packet of biscuits. I happened to mention to a lovely lady called Sue Cole, (who though she had some personal problems which she shared with me, was always keen to find out how I was doing), that the worst thing for me was being freezing cold on outreach with not enough blankets! Within the week a brown paper parcel arrived addressed to me. I untied all the string, and slowly opened the package. I recognised Sue's handwriting, but I knew she was fairly short of money a lot of the time – so what was in this large parcel? Inside the brown paper was a plastic store bag, also tied with string. I just couldn't imagine what was inside, but remembering my last conversation with Sue I thought she might have miraculously knitted up for me a thick woollen sweater, in all bright colours, like she used to wear! I untied the string, and my three children were hovering around making suggestions about what was inside. Low and behold it was a neatly shaped, dark green sleeping bag! It was tightly rolled up into its own hood, and the label assured me it would keep me warm in all weather conditions! The sleeping bag fitted into a new larger weekend bag that I bought myself and I was never cold again in anyone's house! It turned out to be a most wonderful and well used gift.

Keeping warm and fed were not the only problems to be encountered while away "doing an outreach". I remember one outreach held in the Wycliffe Bible Translators College. Some group had borrowed the college and a team from Post Green did the teaching and led the worship for the weekend. David and myself, together with Richard Talbot from our household travelled in one car. Rev. Dr. Denis Ball, together with one or two others travelled in another car. Denis was known to be a bad sleeper, and would often pace the floor at night.

On this particular occasion Denis had given up trying to sleep and was wandering around the college, mostly in darkness except for the odd corridor light. Finally he felt tired enough to go back to bed. He wandered back along the corridor, and slipped in through the open bedroom door and got into bed and fell asleep. He was woken up in minutes by a lady's scream. He had got into the wrong bed in the wrong bedroom – the door had been ajar as the occupant, a lady guest, had got out of bed to go to the loo down the corridor.

Maybe we would have heard nothing about it – but at breakfast the next morning there were some odd smiles on the faces of the people we were yet to get to know. When Denis arrived, late to breakfast, the story was allowed to be told in public and we all had a good laugh, and Denis laughed loudest of all.

I remember one night Carol Welsh and I were staying at the vicarage of a future bishop and his wife. It was a huge rambling vicarage. By now I had learnt to take a torch with me on all outreach and to ask where the loo was if I needed it in the night! This particular night Carol and I were sharing a room, which I remember was the night before Mothering Sunday – I was without my children and feeling a bit sad. Then I thought how lucky I was to have children, even if they were not with me for the weekend.

I woke up in the middle of the night, desperate to visit the loo. I got out of bed and walked towards the bedroom door. I was about to open it when I heard snoring and snuffling – it wasn't Carol. Oh, help! Are the vicar and his wife sleeping in the next door bedroom with the door wide open? I hesitated and listened. More snoring and snuffling and a chain rattled.

I knew what problem I now had – their large dog, with unpredictable behaviour, was lying against our bedroom door. I gave up and went back to bed. I lay there trying not to think about the loo, which was unreachable! In the end I knew I had to get up and find the loo whatever happened! "Please God, send that dog sound asleep. Don't let it wake up and bark the place down. Please don't let it bite me! Thank you, Lord – I trust you!"

I got out of bed and, using my torch, crept back to the door. I remembered my prayer – and trusted God. Opening the door slowly and cautiously I found the large dog fast asleep lying right across our doorway. I stepped over it, and walked quietly along the passageway to the loo and back again. The dog was still fast asleep. I stepped over him again, closed our bedroom door and went back to sleep.

Next time I go on an outreach, I thought to myself, I will take emergency dog rations as well.

David and I always liked our first cup of tea in the morning – preferably while still sitting up in bed. Every time we went on an outreach we would check where the cup of tea was coming from and what time! If it was a college, convent, conference centre or hotel, they usually had a tea station somewhere near the bedroom. Whoever woke up first would do the honours and go off and make two cups of tea. There was usually someone else at the tea station and we would have a polite chat while wiping the sleepy dust from our eyes.

One particular occasion I woke first. We were in a huge conference centre. David was still fast asleep, but I was thirsty. By the time I've made the tea, David will be awake, I thought to myself. I climbed out of bed, slipped my dressing gown on and walked out of the bedroom. I turned and checked the room number and walked to the end of the corridor. No tea station! Where's it gone? I saw it here last night! – in that little cubbyhole of a cupboard. Mystified, I decided to walk down the staircase nearby. Hurrah – there's the tea station! One floor down! I made two cups of tea and had a most delightful chat with another guest. Putting the two cups and saucers on a tray I made my way back to our bedroom – opening the door I walked in carrying the tray. Nothing had stirred – on David's side of the bed, brown wavy hair was all I could see. I approached further into the room, and time stood still. There was a woman lying in my place in bed, sound asleep! I was outraged! But luckily my brain clicked into gear rapidly – wrong husband – wrong bed – wrong room!

I backed out of the room rapidly but puzzled. "You stupid girl!" I said to myself. I hesitated – how do I find my room again? Oh – the staircase! I rapidly re-traced my steps and climbing the stairs to the correct corridor I arrived safely in the right bedroom – David was still asleep but my side of the bed was, happily, vacated.

In the early years at Post Green we had a weekly news sheet we wrote and distributed to all those living in households, working in the offices, or helping in other ways around the community. I was responsible for giving news of all outreach. This included a Diary of Forthcoming Outreaches, and a Report of Outreaches completed. One particular occasion Denis had gone off to do two outreaches in Devon and Cornwall. I couldn't contact him to get his report. But Denis was a most marvellous positive minister. He always came back from any outreach, radiant, and telling us "The Lord blessed! The Lord blessed everyone. It was a marvellous weekend. God is faithful!"

So when I couldn't get hold of Denis I took a chance and wrote the report on his behalf anyway. Using Denis's usual words I wrote briefly that the Lord had wonderfully blessed everyone on both outreaches in Devon and Cornwall. The News Sheet was printed and distributed as we all gathered together, as was our custom, on Friday lunch time. We nibbled our apples, yoghurts and sandwiches, sharing news with each other and reading the newly printed news sheet. Most people went for the cartoon first, cleverly written and drawn by Sam Simons, a Bible College student. Denis walked in late and sat down to eat his packed lunch. "How did you get on in Cornwall, Denis?" someone called out. Cornwall was a bit off the beaten track for Post Green and unknown territory for our outreach in the early 70s.

"I can't tell you how terrible it was!" said Denis gloomily. "No one was interested in what I said; they hardly listened at all – quite honestly it seemed like a waste of time!"

Some had already read my report of Denis in Cornwall and it drastically differed! "Daphne?" someone called out to me. "Sorry!" I apologised, and explained to Denis I had anticipated his Cornwall report and got it wrong. Most people were amused. Geoff Bland, who lived with us at Panorama, was not impressed - though he laughed he said, "How can we trust your reports again?"

I assured him I would check my facts more accurately in future. As he was the editor at the time he always doubled checked my outreach reports after that!

CHAPTER TWENTY FOUR

Life at Post Green was never static, and as I mentioned, whenever Graham Pulkingham came by things changed following his visits. Rev Jean Darnall lived at Post Green for about ten years, during which time she also made a huge impact on our lives and the way the ministry at Post Green was shaped. She was a powerful Holy Spirit-filled woman but she had a different ministry from Graham Pulkingham. She had a prophetic ministry and was brilliant on and off the platform. She had huge compassion for crowds and individuals. She would lay her hands on the sick and they recovered. She would pray against evil which had taken control of someone's life and they would be set free. She could launch into a worship song, not always in tune, and the Holy Spirit would fall on many in the auditorium. People at death's door were raised up as she prayed for them.

Sadly, when the Fisherfolk and the Community of Celebration moved into Post Green, Jean and Elmer Darnall left.

Basically it was all to do with "vision". If you have a vision for what needs to happen next, and the person you are living or working with has a different vision, then you have a big problem.

Graham Pulkingham saw the way forward for Post Green: and it was in a loving, caring, community of people, sharing their homes with both mature and needy people. In fact it seemed sometimes Graham was saying that we are all needy and we all need each other. No one is better than anyone else. From that "vision" came about a very different way of living, a different way of loving and sharing, and an ability to reach out to people that most of the world shunned. Through living in this deeply sharing way on a daily basis we were able to teach more effectively in the churches.

Jean was very much an evangelist – and her ministry stemmed from her profound teaching from the platforms and pulpits in Britain and in the States. Elmer felt his "vision" or "calling" was to train up young people through his Bible College. His college worked very well: it was the only college where students could go out to work during the day and study every evening – and he was always inundated with applicants.

On the last day before Jean and Elmer left, I ran upstairs in Post Green house to say goodbye to Jean. We had a short but deep conversation about the way forward for

Post Green. As I turned to leave, Jean gripped my hand and whispered: "Daphne, if I had the courage I'd stay!"

I knew what she meant! But I also knew God was not calling her to sink her ministry into the common pot at Post Green – she had a far larger ministry than could be contained in a community type situation, where we all agreed to share everything in common including our individual outreach requests.

Jean once had a prophetic word for me during a ministers' seminar being held at Post Green. She got up out of her chair and came over to me and laid her hands on me and said, "God is calling you to be a teacher. You have the gift of teaching from Him." She admitted afterwards that she had struggled to give me that word from the Lord for some time before she got up out of her chair. I didn't have the courage to ask her why so I never found out what the struggle was! I think I was rather immature at the time, except for writing "The Road to Emmaus" there wasn't much evidence that I would become a teacher! I don't know! But I do know as the years went by I did do more and more teaching on many different subjects to do with Christianity and the Bible.

Jean was one of the most gifted women ministers of the twentieth century and I still hear her quoted today, even in the Channel Islands where I am now living! It was through Jean that Post Green hosted Merv and Merla Watson, Maranatha, and the Sacred Dance group – coming from Canada and California. Jean also came back from the States hugely excited about a new musical written by Jimmie Owen called "Come Together". Somehow she brought the whole musical and ethos over to Britain, together with Pat Boone for the opening events.

When I first heard Merv and Merla I discovered a depth of music worship that resounded wholeheartedly for me. I have always loved singing, and Merla's voice to me was out of this world. She also played the viola, and Merv the guitar. Their variety of sacred music and testimonies gave us all a huge leap forward in our understanding of what the Holy Spirit wanted in the churches.

Merv and Merla stayed in Post Green house for several weeks. Abigail would visit their daughter Elana any chance she had when either David or I were visiting from Panorama. Abi and Elana had quite a power struggle, both being strong willed little girls. Abi called Elana "Banana". I see from the internet that Elana now has a huge ministry as a worship singer in her own right.

When Merv and Merla brought their large group of musicians, "Maranatha", we housed them all in our homes and any local accommodation we could find. I have an idea that there were about sixty of them. I loved driving down to Post Green in the early morning, where we met together for prayer at the start of the day: I could hear a trumpeter practicing in the orchard, and a soprano warming up her voice in the field next door. Other voices and instruments could be heard around the surrounding countryside, much to the amusement of the farm workers living in the immediate vicinity of Post Green house.

At around this time the Sacred Dance Group visited from California and were breaking new ground in churches in Britain. They had a unique ministry in dance in churches and cathedrals – expressing some Biblical theme to music and movement. Our vicar at the local parish church was not terribly enthusiastic about anything stemming from Post Green, though he tolerated our choir on the fifth Sunday of the month, when it occurred.

But when the Sacred Dance group put on an evening at Lytchett Minster School the vicar arrived and sat down near the back of the school hall. Woops, I thought – I don't think he will like this evening. The girls danced bare footed, with long flowing gowns, and mostly had long hair. They were elegant and gracious and it was an attractive form of worship to God. At the end of the evening I saw the vicar chatting with some of the girls and inviting them to take part in the next Sunday worship! They gladly accepted. From then on the vicar seemed to be much more interested in our work at Post Green and was more cooperative when we needed his help.

Denis Ball's wife Pinky was particularly attracted to the ministry of dance, and took leave from the community and spent time with the group in California. She had been gone about three weeks and although she was a member of the leadership we continued meeting without her each week. During one of the meetings the telephone rang and someone knocked on the door and asked Faith to come to the phone. Faith slipped out of the room, and came back about fifteen minutes later. "That was Pinky! I said we would ring her back later."

She walked back to her chair, deep in thought. We finished the item on the agenda we were discussing. "How's Pinky doing? When's she coming home?" Jeanne Hinton asked Faith.

"Well, she will be back in two weeks – flying into Heathrow. She is bringing Paula and the Sacred Dance Group with her. She's invited them to join Post Green and live here with us." Faith dropped the bombshell.

Denis Ball, Pinky's husband was away on an outreach so he couldn't contribute to the conversation.

The Leadership were quickly unanimous in their response. "We can't just take in the whole Sacred Dance Group – we neither have a household or any space anywhere."

"I don't think the Sacred Dance Group has the same vision as us!"

"How can we combine our vision with theirs – we appeal to completely different areas of the church. We don't feel called to use dance in the way they do."

And we all knew that you cannot have two differing visions in one community.

Tom stood up. "Are you all agreed that I phone Pinky back and say, come back without them, and we will discuss it?" Everyone nodded.

Tom left the room and went to phone Pinky. He was gone a long time and eventually returned to the drawing room. We stopped what we were talking about and looked at him.

"Pinky is adamant that she is now part of the Sacred Dance Group and that they should be part of Post Green's ministry. I tried to explain to her that it wasn't that easy. We need to talk about it first. Pinky won't change her mind. The air tickets have already been bought for the whole group. And the Sacred Dance Group's bus is already being shipped over to England on some boat." Tom said as he walked back to his chair.

You will have picked up from what I have already said about myself that I did have a bit of a problem with authority figures. And no one, but no one, would organise such a big move without consulting Tom and Faith. Yet Pinky had done so! Heavens above! She must be one very determined lady to do what she had done: that was my first thought about the whole saga.

"Well, we will house them in Hillwood Cottage and a mobile home in the farmyard next door. But we will have to have meetings with Pinky and Denis. If Pinky has already chosen the Sacred Dance Group, and we are sure that it is not part of our vision, then poor Denis will have to make a choice. He is part of the leadership of Post Green, but I am not sure he can help lead two visions either." Tom said.

Tom and Faith organised for Hillwood Cottage to be vacant, and organised the accommodation in the mobile home which was re-sited next door to the cottage. Tom and Faith were gracious and loving, but adamant that the two visions could not be combined into one. Bill and Paula who led the Sacred Dance Group in no way felt called to what Post Green was doing, and we knew it wouldn't work out.

They all arrived from California – and they were great fun to have around and we met together whenever we could. They came to our evening chapel times and we often ate our lunch together sitting outside on the lawn.

Tom and Faith met with Pinky and Denis Ball to discuss the problem that had now arisen – it was not possible to have two very different visions working alongside each other in the same community. Pinky was adamant that she felt called to work with the Sacred Dance Group, and that Paula and Bill had moved over to England permanently with their dancers. It was accepted that there would have to be a parting of the ways.

Denis had no real choice but to leave Post Green Community as well. He left the leadership of Post Green and became involved with the Sacred Dance Group and became their pastor and speaker. We were desperately sad about these events, and missed Denis and his positive and helpful input. But we invited Denis as often as we could to be a speaker at camps, conferences and the occasional outreach, when he was available.

There is one well-documented story about Denis. There was a healing conference at Post Green to be held in the house over a weekend. A vicar from the Chinnocks, Rev Percy Nichols, phoned up the day before the start. "If I bring a lady along in a wheelchair, is there a downstairs loo and is there another female who could take her to the loo?"

Tom had answered the phone and said, yes to both questions. Percy duly arrived with a woman who had been in a wheelchair with very severe arthritis for many years. She said she wanted to come to the conference as she helped at a disabled group in her village and wanted to learn how she could best help these people.

Margery sat through the morning session, firstly enjoying it all, and then finding she was getting a bit stiff and tired. Faith helped her during the lunch break to go to the loo. The afternoon session started, and after a while it was announced that anyone who needed prayer for healing should make their way from the drawing room and into the dining room. There were experienced people ready to pray for each person. Tom Lees is best telling this story: he says that he saw Margery in the wheelchair heading for the dining room but wasn't sure his faith was up to praying for a miracle! So he sat down and prayed for someone else nearby. While his back was turned and he was praying for this other person, Denis had come into the room, and seeing that no one was praying for Margery he sat down beside her. He talked with her and then he prayed for her. Tom happened to turn around moments later to see an empty wheelchair! Margery had got up and walked out of the room! Her vicar Percy Nichols was very excited and pleased for her!

Percy and Margery left for home late on Saturday afternoon, with quite a drive in front of them. As they neared their church, Margery asked Percy to stop the car outside the church. She stepped out of the car, walked up all the steps to the church, walked down the aisle, and knelt by the altar to pray and thank God. She was totally jubilant! Percy resisted the temptation to help her back into his car! She hopped in and they set off for the final leg of their journey back to her house. They drew up outside in the darkness.

Her husband had heard the car, and had quickly come out to greet them and help his crippled wife out of the car. The problem was she was no longer crippled and leapt out of the car and ran up the path. "Steady on, old girl, steady on!" he shouted. Margery continued into her house. Her mother was waiting to greet her daughter and help her into bed. She was so amazed as she saw Margery walk in, she sat on the stairs and cried.

Margery continued her work with the disabled but found she was being asked all over Dorset and further afield to give her story, her testimony, of the miracle that she experienced.

Denis just laughed delightedly whenever the story was told – usually by Tom. Tom said his back was turned when the miracle happened in his own house!

The Sacred Dance Group went on to have a large effective ministry of their own, and eventually moved away to a large property at Milbornc St Andrew near Blandford, Dorset. We remained friends and kept in touch as best we could over the coming years. Pinky and Denis's oldest son Stephen Ball already married to Lorna Friend stayed within the community of Post Green and became one of the key Fisherfolk team.

The Bible says, "Without a vision the people perish." It is a fact that we need to know what our vision is in life – sometimes we reach our goal, achieve our vision, and sometimes it changes while we are still a way off. Whether this refers to our job, our home life, our church, or the whole of our life: we need to know what we are aiming at. The wonderful thing about having a relationship with God, is that you can ask Him to give you a vision.

The Bible also says, "Can two walk together unless they are agreed?" The answer is no, or not for long! We took our vision seriously at Post Green, worked on it, checked it out frequently, made sure all we did kept us working towards our vision – and the vision, we felt, was God-given. We each had a personal vision for our lives. This incorporated the Post Green vision, but we each had to know what we were doing in the community, why we were in the community, what our calling from God was within the community.

I suppose what I am saying is that one always needs to be able to answer the question: "What is God doing in your life? And what is God saying to you?" This was especially essential when one was living in a hot house atmosphere – a kind of greenhouse – like Post Green!

For a year or so we were all divided up into small groups and met at an appropriate time to suit each other. The pastoral leader of each group would ask one question: "What has God said to you this week?" I avoided going for the first three weeks of my group. Faith was the leader, and next time I saw her she would remind me I had missed the meeting! One Wednesday morning my phone went. "Hi, Daph! Just to remind you we are meeting now." I tried to make excuses but Faith just said, "We will wait. Don't worry we won't start without you. Come as soon as you can." And the phone went dead. Clever Faith! So I rather nervously got in the car and drove down to Hillwood Cottage where the meeting was being held. Some of my favourite people were there. Faith pointed out an empty chair, handed me a cup of coffee, and the proceedings got under way. No one was pressured at any point. No one was allowed to interrupt anyone else. No one could remark on what was said. The person sharing what they thought God had said during the week could say what they liked and it would be received and understood by all. If a big problem came up then the pastoral leader would follow it up afterwards.

I went every week from then on and found it hugely helpful. Many times as I drove down the hill to Hillwood Cottage my mind would be a blank – I couldn't think of one thing I had heard God say. But as the meeting started things would come to mind – and I would have to choose which thing out of many that I would share that morning. If someone consistently didn't share anything it usually meant they were in the doldrums and Faith would get alongside them afterwards and try and help them. Obviously the easiest way to hear God daily is to read one's Bible each day. It's quite hard to hear God consistently any other way. But I found it amazing how a verse, sentence or passage of scripture could almost hop out of the page as I opened my Bible, praying God would say something to me to meet my need of the moment.

Throughout our time at Post Green there was a regular cycle of daily worship. Usually each household had morning prayers and a brief reading of scripture at the breakfast table. Most offices and the maintenance team had a prayer before the start of the day's work. At 5.30pm every weekday evening we held a chapel service, which would last for half an hour. It would include the whole community and all the children – for the teenagers it was optional. The chapel times had to be interesting to every age group and be inclusive of community members and the many visitors who were present. Consequently there was usually a drama, a mime, a story, a folk dance to one of the Fisherfolk songs, worship with simple songs that everyone could sing.

Sometimes it was an effort to get to chapel but it was always worthwhile. And with all the community there it was an opportunity to catch up with anyone you wished to talk to afterwards. Because of household moves and office job moves you were sometimes separated from people you really wanted to spend time with. Chapel time was an excellent time to see them and find out how their day had gone. The children were considered to be very important, and were included as much as possible. Small toddlers who would normally wriggle and squeal if they were sat with their parents were usually assigned to a special friend. This special friend would look after them during chapel time, and they would sit there as good as gold. It was a system that worked very well and made the whole chapel time peaceful even though there could be as many as twelve little ones present.

Post Green Community was also known as the Community of Celebration. Our worship always had a feel of celebration, and one of our most popular songs was "Ah, There's a Celebration!"

A group of us met every Tuesday and Thursday for several months learning how to lead worship. The days were creative and fun. We learnt to lead in dance and drama, mime and song. We were given a theme and had to work up a mime or drama on that theme in twenty minutes and then perform it. We learnt how to start off any worship song with no help from piano or guitar. We learnt to keep eye contact with the rest of the worship group as we were leading worship. It was a great privilege to have such training.

CHAPTER TWENTY FIVE

With Jean and Elmer gone, the community took on a completely different feel. And where as previously the Bible College students would help do the counselling at all conferences and camps, we now had to make sure the area team could fully support us when required. We had learnt to rely on the hundred or more Bible College students to help us, now they were gone. We needed a definite commitment from the old area team for every weekend conference we put on. They were a most marvellous group of people from all over the Purbecks, Dorset, Poole and Bournemouth.

We greatly missed all the students we were used to seeing around. Many of the old students who had graduated stayed in the area of Poole and Bournemouth and continued to support us with much practical help. They had settled in the area and got good jobs and housing and were happy to continue to be a part of the Post Green ministry. We could not have managed without them. Some moved into the community and stayed for many years, and were in some ways the backbone of much of our ministry.

Elmer Darnall wanted the college to be all inclusive with his students, and if they lived some distance away then they managed to enrol at the college without an interview. We found we had a few people who were at times a little unusual! But the common denominator was that they all loved the Lord Jesus, whatever their previous background.

One older student, probably in his mid thirties arrived from Scotland. He found a job with a coach company, as a mechanic I think. I will call him Jock for the sake of his privacy, though sadly he has since died. Elmer was initially very happy to have him attend college.

He seemed to settle in well, then began to cause disturbances having imbibed too much alcohol – and this began to happen with increasing frequency. One evening during a camp being held in the field in front of Post Green house, Jock drew up outside the house in his Mini. He got out of the car and engaged me in conversation while I was standing outside the front door. He was obviously in a black mood. But we got into conversation. I then said, “Look Jock, I need to go over to the tent now, as I’m due to sing a song in a minute. Why don’t you come in and listen? You might even feel like staying! I will sing the song especially for you!” He grunted and made some ambiguous reply. I slipped into the tent and was shortly called up onto the platform.

The song I had chosen to sing was, “I’d rather have Jesus than silver or gold, I’d rather have Him than have riches untold. I’d rather have Jesus than anything, this world affords today!” It was a song that had been popular at the Billy Graham crusades sung by George Beverley Shea.

While I was singing I saw Jock standing at the entrance to the tent. As I finished the song I noticed him turn round quickly and walk back out. A few seconds later I heard the roar of the Mini’s engine and it was obvious that Jock had driven out of the drive.

The evening camp meeting proceeded as usual, and Jean Darnall spoke for about three quarters of an hour. She then invited anyone who wanted to sort out their relationship with God, or who wanted prayer for anything to come and stand or kneel in front of the platform. I was standing at the back of the tent by the doorway.

The camp field was in darkness, well populated with little tents, big tents, family tents and caravans of every shape and size. All the little ones were in bed, the teens were finishing their meeting and ambling back to their beds, and the child walkers on each unit were keeping a watchful eye on their area of the field.

Suddenly there was a huge roar of a car – Jock was returning to Post Green in his Mini. Unknown to us he had spent the rest of the evening down at St Peter’s Finger, our local pub, and was very drunk. He drove twice round the circular driveway at great speed then drove into the tent, through the tent doorway. Faith Lees jumped out as Jock drove down the aisle. She jumped in front of the speeding car and shouted, “In the name of Jesus, stop!” The car stalled instantly. If it hadn’t it would have knocked Faith down. What courage! What faith in the name of Jesus!

Jock jumped out of the car and stood on the bonnet shouting abuse at everyone and especially Faith.

Tony Churchill, meanwhile, reached into the car and took out the ignition keys. (Good thinking, Tony).

Faith saw Tony's action.

"Please put the keys back in the car, Tony. Jock, get down off the car and reverse your car out of the tent immediately."

Tony obviously wanted to argue with Faith, but as he hesitated Faith repeated her request. Jock carried on hurling abuse. But Faith repeated her command to Jock, and he climbed angrily off the car, opened the car door and started the engine. I am sure everyone in the tent was praying. I had moved slightly away from the tent doorway, but was holding my breath to see if he would reverse back out again. The car started reversing at huge speed, out of the tent. Jock drove twice around the circular driveway – in any normal event one would be terrified that he would just drive crazily amongst the vulnerable tents crowded in and around the campers' field. But Jock then drove furiously towards the house, slammed on the brakes and got out.

Tom and Faith ushered him into Post Green house, and gave him a bed for the night in the small dressing room adjoining their bedroom.

Their courage surpassed anything I had ever witnessed. But when Jock had sobered up the next morning Tom and Faith, particularly at Jean Darnall's request, told Jock to leave Post Green. He had already been involved in another incident where he had chased Sister Mary Magdalene, a nun living with us, around the kitchen with a carving knife, and then had tried to set fire to the tent. I missed some of the action as a Bible college student, named Timotheus, sat in the kitchen making remarks that were inflaming the situation. As I walked into the kitchen, Faith asked me very firmly to take Timotheus down to her office for the duration and she would come and fetch us later. This I did. Timotheus was a nice lad, but he was oblivious to the danger that he and anyone else in the kitchen was in.

Jock returned occasionally, having spent a spell in prison after his long time girl friend and he had got into a drunken fight one breakfast time and she died in a stabbing incident. Years later he happened to call in on the evening of Elizabeth Lees' birthday celebration. We all did some dancing during the evening and for a while Jock was my partner. I thought, "This is amazing, Dancing with Jock, after all the dangerous sagas I've witnessed."

Tom and Faith were the most brave, faith-filled, loving people I had ever had the privilege to live with. Jean Darnall felt Jock had had enough chances and was too much of a danger to be allowed to continue at the Bible College. He admitted that when he drove the car into the tent he was aiming to kill Jean and anyone else in his way.

Whether Jock stopped the car so suddenly or the Holy Spirit did it, I don't know. But I will never forget Faith Lees jumping out in front of the car as it sped down the aisle.

Jock was actually a nice person – but once he had too much alcohol he was extremely dangerous. He put his problems down to an incident in his childhood. His best friend and he were playing with a rain filled large water butt. Jock's friend fell in, and Jock was unable to rescue him before he drowned. Jock said he was blamed for the incident, and he never recovered from the terrible accusation. He later took to drink to drown his miseries.

As well as immense faith and courage Faith was great fun to have around. She had excellent leadership skills and people enjoyed being around her. I remember one incident when we were having a meeting in Post Green garden. It was summer time, the sun was shining, and we were sat on chairs under the veranda. The roses were out in full bloom and we could see the village church and Poole harbour in the distance. In the middle of the discussion Faith did a somersault, on the lawn, and continued doing somersaults till she reached the fence at the bottom of the lawn some considerable distance away. Sister Mary Magdalene stopped mid sentence and watched in astonishment as Faith rolled further and further away. It was very amusing, as the nun had yet to unbend in the community. Faith, having reached the boundary fence, walked slowly back up the lawn, sat back down in her chair and continued the conversation as though she had been sat there all the time.

Over the years we had many people come who had huge problems and were potentially dangerous to themselves and sometimes a danger to others.

The Community expanded and went from strength to strength. We had a good leadership structure that changed as and when it was felt necessary. We had a group of coordinators, people who headed up each area of our life and work – this became necessary as muddles occurred and we sometimes double booked dates or rooms or people! So the coordinators met once a week and it was considered vital for everyone to turn up. I usually took the Minutes of the meeting (it helped me to concentrate, and left me free to doodle on my writing pad). I got quite good at summing up a long, lively or boring discussion that went on for half an hour – sometimes someone threw a wobbly and emotions were flying about. I gave up trying to take notes of who said what, and wrote: "A lively discussion ensued and it was agreed to delay a decision until next week!" (or whatever the decision was, if any!).

Meanwhile Tessa was settling in at Wentworth Milton Mount, and sometimes brought a friend back for the Sunday exeat. Some of her friends were struck dumb with shock at the number of people sat at the dining room table, and were not always keen on the (rather international) food we ate. Tessa made friends with the assistant matron and discovered she had a bit of a sad story, so could she bring her home for a weekend? We were happy to invite her. It turned out she had been a nun – she was still very young but had taken her life vows, and then had second thoughts. I think her doubts were to do with the average age of the other nuns, most in the eighties. She asked if she could leave, and a year elapsed and no decision was made, although she kept asking. In the end in desperation, she told me, she put a spare pair of convent knickers into a brown paper bag, and escaped over the wall.

As she had nowhere to live and no job, she took a job at Wentworth Milton Mount, with accommodation, food, and a salary! I kept in touch with her for several years and last time I visited her in Wales she was married and had two lovely children.

Tessa was always on the alert for people needing help, and she is a very pastoral caring person today. She speaks affectionately of life at Post Green and how much she learnt in the process. As she is now in charge of a large number of staff in her current job I am sure she is able to put all her pastoral skills into action as well as the disciplines she learnt at her school.

Nigel settled in well at Queens College in Taunton and on exeat weekends usually stayed with my sister and her boys if we were unable to make it down to Somerset to fetch him home. In the junior school he soon became head of dormitory. He was so tall and mature for his age that the school had mistaken his age and added a year. Nigel was very cross when we corrected the error!

While he was in the junior school of Queens he was consistently top or second in his class. But when he moved up into the senior school everything became much harder and more competitive and, unknown to David and me, Nigel was struggling to enjoy life at the school anymore.

This all came to our attention one morning when the telephone rang, and the headmaster of Queens College was on the line. “I’m sorry to report that your son disappeared from the school dormitory around one or two o’clock this morning.”

“What?” said David to the headmaster, in complete shock. “Can you tell us anything more?”

“Well it seems that another boy is with Nigel, much less mature than your son. We aren’t really concerned for their safety – Nigel is very capable. I think there was some kind of an upset yesterday, and Nigel linked up with another boy who was homesick and wanted to go home. We’ve called the police and asked them to look out for two school boys. We guess they are making for Yeovil as that is where the other lad’s family live.”

“Okay! Would you please keep us informed of developments, Headmaster?” David said, and the telephone conversation terminated.

“Whatever is going on?” I asked David when he came back into the room.

“Nigel’s gone missing – run away from school.”

“Well, if he was unhappy why on earth didn’t he go to Valerie and Basil’s house? They are only two miles away at most.” I frowned, trying not to panic.

David and I discussed the matter and felt somewhat helpless. We phoned the school at hourly intervals. Around three in the afternoon we had a phone call from Nigel. He was phoning from a telephone box in Yeovil. He was desperate to come home.

“Nigel, the headmaster said that when you turned up you had to be brought straight back to school. He was very firm about that.” We told him. Nigel was equally adamant that he wanted to come home and said if we took him back to school he would walk out again at the first opportunity. We gave in and telephoned the school. The headmaster was very angry that we were not returning Nigel immediately, and I pleaded with him that Nigel be allowed to stay home with us for the weekend so we could talk things through with him and would return him on Sunday evening. Finally this was agreed.

We drove up to Yeovil where we found Nigel waiting at the agreed rendezvous. Nigel looked tired and pale but otherwise fine. We asked him what happened and he admitted there had been an upset at school and a prank that had misfired. He and the other lad had got emergency supplies (bread, torch, gloves, map) and had left school in the middle of the night. They had walked from Taunton to Yeovil, often via fields so as not to be picked up by passing motorists.

"The funny thing was," said Nigel, "We got to the outskirts of Yeovil and a police patrol car stopped and asked us if we wanted a lift. We were so tired, and we had almost arrived at our destination, so we said yes. They gave us a lift into the town centre and asked us where we wanted to be dropped. We told them to drop us outside Tesco's. We guessed the police were out looking for us – the school would have raised the alarm. And these two policemen never realised that we were the boys they were looking for!"

We would have been amused, but were too stressed about it all to see the humour in it then.

Nigel reluctantly returned to school on Sunday night. We went into see the headmaster, who seemed somewhat defensive about the whole episode.

A few weeks later Nigel was back at Post Green for the holidays. He had a few moans about school but we thought it was just typical school boy complaints. But towards the end of the holiday I happened to notice a list beside Nigel's bed. There were several items written down that looked a bit ominous to me: Torch, woolly hat, gloves, scarf, bread, map ....

"Nigel, are you okay about going back to school?"

"No, Mum – I hate it! I don't want to go back."

I looked at him, thoughtfully. I didn't tell him I had seen the list by his bedside. Had he left it there deliberately for me to see so that I would draw my own conclusions? Or was it a secret list and another planned escape from school?

"Well, if you don't go back to Queens where will you go to school? There's only Lytchett Minster Secondary School, or that school in Wimborne."

"Let's try both, shall we, Mum? Will Dad mind?"

David and I telephoned the Wimborne school and went along for an interview. The headmaster phoned Queens school and reported back to us that he wouldn't take Nigel! We were indignant and surprised. We had heard of a brand new school just opened in Corfe Mullen, so we phoned the headmaster and asked if we could come and see him.

We explained that Queen Elizabeth School had turned Nigel down because of a report from Nigel's headmaster at Queens. "We are not interested in the past of any pupil who comes here. Each pupil starts afresh when he arrives on day one here. We would be glad to take Nigel, but you realise he will be the oldest boy in the school?"

We really liked the look of the school and the teachers we met. Nigel started right away and did very well at the school, and never gave us any cause for concern.

By the time Tessa left Wentworth Milton Mount, Abigail was due to start there. For a while she did well, and wrote lively letters home about her daring escapades. She always headed the address as "Colditz", but we presumed she was only copying the other pupils. We felt Abi needed the strict discipline at the school as she was very outgoing and always vied with authority figures. In fact, I felt, she needed taming. She was the only child who stood up to Faith, and won! And it wasn't good for her.

CHAPTER TWENTY SIX

Because of the heavy schedule of outreach engagements, with teams from Post Green out most weekends, it was decided that for a little while all the leaders and teachers should live in the same household and catch up with each other. The teaching needed to be coordinated and a schedule drawn up for the future. Faith Lees and Jeanne Hinton were keen that we learnt new ways of teaching, and used new media techniques to reach more people.

Consequently it was all change again. New household lists were drawn up and everyone interviewed about their new home and household. It was a stressful time for many of us. We had formed good household units and made good friendships with many living in our homes. I particularly liked being with Dave and Val Holland and baby Richard, and I know my three children enjoyed their presence at Panorama too.

Nevertheless for me I was at times feeling a bit rebellious and unhappy. I couldn't put my finger on the problem. Susan and Tom were coming up to Panorama quite often to chat with me but nothing was resolved as I didn't know what the problem was.

During some of this time I was off the leadership group, which had been made smaller – just seven "governors" – another change brought about after one of Graham Pulkingham's visits. I was very happy to be off the leadership and was in bed by 10pm instead of midnight or after on a Monday evening! But on Tuesday mornings David would let slip some of the things talked about or agreed upon at the last evening's meeting. I found myself getting more and more negative about everything at Post Green. The joy had gone and I began to feel afraid – and wondering whether to pack my bags and go. Though I loved Dave and Val I didn't want to dump my negative feelings onto them.

Then David came back after a governors' meeting and said we would probably be moving back into Post Green house.

"What, all of us? Grandpa as well?" I was astounded.

"Yes! Grandpa can have two rooms where Granny Jessiman, Faith's mother, used to live in the west wing. Our three will probably have to share bedrooms with others of their age. All those teaching on outreach will be living in Post Green house for a few months."

Well, I thought to myself – I've nothing to lose – I feel like leaving anyway so why not give this new idea a chance?

Within two weeks we had packed and moved. Dave and Val were desperately sad to leave us and they moved into a different household as well. Dave had a full time teaching job at a local school and was not so free to go on outreaches, so they were not assigned to Post Green house. I was conscious that half the community were thrilled to bits with the new arrangements and half the community were struggling to come to terms with the changes in their lives.

We moved in the day before my birthday in April. Tom and Faith gave up their large sunny bedroom to David and me. We brought down our own bed and my favourite rocking chair which I had had since before Tessa was born! We took our clothes, our favourite books, records and games. And we left a lot behind at Panorama. We took our best family silver to Rownhams House for Mum to look after and warned the new household they would have to purchase new cutlery. Otherwise everything stayed as was. I left my pots, pans, crockery, most of our linen and most of our furniture. Grandpa took all his furniture and his television and all his belongings. No sacrifice was demanded of him, except to move location. His two new rooms had a balcony and looked out over the Post Green lawns and fields and onto the village beyond. He stayed there for seven or eight years!

On the first evening at Post Green after everyone had moved in and we had had supper all together we met in the drawing room for our first household meeting. There were twenty-seven of us including the children. The atmosphere felt good and creative, and everyone seemed excited at what lay ahead. One of the first items to be discussed was who would be household head, and I automatically thought that either Tom or Faith would be voted in for this job. But in fact there was no voting, just an open discussion and then a final show of hands in agreement with the decision. Viv Crouch and myself were chosen as household heads. So far from being able to take a back seat and observe how things would pan out in the new household I had to take a lead, together with Viv. Viv was great fun to work with, a bit of a dare devil, and happy to flaunt rules and regulations when it suited her. I was somewhat like her but without her courage! We worked well together.

Next day dawned, and when I came down to breakfast I found myself loaded with gifts and birthday cards to open. I had never had a birthday like it: such very thoughtful presents from everyone. I was truly touched and amazed. It was an excellent start after several weeks of depression!

Living together with mostly very mature Christians was like a taste of heaven to me. Consistent love shared among us all, respect for what each person said, and an agreed system of only one conversation at once at the meal table. We lived there for six or seven years as a family, though many of the other people moved out and others moved in.

We had a choice of after-breakfast-jobs to volunteer for. Breakfast was at 7.15am and we waited until everyone had appeared before we said Grace and commenced the meal! This soon sorted out those who thought they could have a lie-in and was a bit embarrassing in the early days, but soon everyone made an effort to come down to breakfast on time. The choice of jobs was house cleaning, cooking, car maintenance and laundry. I volunteered to do the laundry, which I did for about six years, and loved it! I would fetch people's laundry baskets from their room each evening, sort it into lights and darks and throw it into three big washing machines. Put the laundry baskets back. And in the morning hang it all out in the garden, or down in the cellars if it was raining. There was always another helper with me and we never had a cross word or misunderstanding.

We put shelves up in the laundry room and when everything was dry we sorted it out into neat piles on the shelves. The household members were meant to come and fetch their own clothes and take them back to their rooms. Gradually as the months went by the shelves became fuller and fuller – pants, socks, shirts, sweaters, jeans – all uncollected! About once a month someone, during a household meeting, would walk into the drawing room and dump a whole pile of uncollected clothes in the middle of the floor. There would be delighted cries, "Oh, there's my jeans!" "Oh look, my favourite socks – where've they been?" and so on. This would last about fifteen minutes by which time there was only a small pile of neglected unrecognised clothes left. After a year of this I had the bright idea of everyone marking their own clothes. Everyone was given a colour and a symbol and some embroidery thread. After about a month most of the clothes were marked. Clothes still remained on the shelves uncollected for weeks at a time, but I could always find out who the owner was and deliver it to their rooms.

For years we had people living with us for long or short stays who were, what I would describe as, "disturbed" in one way or another. Some would behave normally for even up to about three months and then their behaviour would change and they would exhibit immature or even bizarre behaviour. I could tell you so many stories as it seemed to happen on a daily basis at times – if it wasn't one person behaving oddly, it was another! I was very shocked at times when the switch came; someone who had seemed not only normal but quite mature would suddenly behave irrationally or unpredictably.

Faith, in particular, was superb at dealing with these situations and had great God-given skills to accept people as they were and bring them through to a better and more secure place in their lives. Quite honestly, most of the time, when the change in personality was exhibited it somewhat freaked me out. I would never deal with the situation on my own and usually consulted Faith as soon as I could.

There were a few exceptions, and I know as I look back that God gave me the love and the ability to get alongside these people and have the utmost patience, and no fear in what I was dealing with. I am not saying it was easy, it was exceedingly hard and costly at times.

David was working with one of the young men in the community. I will call him Jack – not his real name. David and Jack worked well together for several months and Jack moved into household at Panorama. He was a joy to have around and loved my three children. He often insisted we played a board game in the evenings so that the children could all join in. At weekends if we were all free he would organise a romp on the beach at Sandbanks or a trip onto the Purbeck Hills.

He was away on outreach with David quite a lot, and was also out with his friends quite often in the evenings. During the day he worked in the offices at Post Green. Suddenly there was a distinct change in behaviour and I noticed that the cheerful rapport between David and Jack seemed to have broken down. I also noticed that Jack was out a great deal and often didn't turn up for household meals. He often did not come home until we had all gone to bed. Then around 11.30pm I would hear his car arrive in the driveway.

I tried to encourage David to get alongside Jack again. David tried half-heartedly, and had given up because he felt he wasn't getting through to Jack. This really concerned me, especially as Jack had been the life and soul of our household – now he seemed very depressed. Tom Lees had said of Jack, "Don't say that at last we have someone move into the community who isn't going to fall apart!" Jack was a success at everything he did. It was a sort of joke that anyone could keep up an act for three months once they moved into the community – but then their true selves would emerge and they would allow themselves to lose their temper, or moan about something in the household, and generally throw a wobbly. It was all part of learning to be mature in amongst other people you were living with. We don't mind being real with our families but we like to keep up a front when others are around!

Anyway poor Jack was suffering, and the household were reacting to his behaviour. When I realised that communications had broken down between David and Jack I felt I had to get involved. He was much younger than me and I viewed him as I would my brother Roger. I started to try and get Jack to talk, and I went out of my way to show we cared about him. His behaviour got worse. Any conversation I had with Jack I would convey to David, so that he was included in what was going on. When Jack's behaviour had become almost intolerable I insisted that David, Jack and I have a chat and try and clear the air. I was pretty certain I knew what some of the problem was. He was living in a loving family environment and it was bringing up sad memories from his past.

After a somewhat difficult chat in the lounge at Panorama – Jack being very sullen and rebellious, I found myself saying, "Jack, we love you! And you are trying to reject our love. You think by your behaviour that you can stop us loving you. But I can assure you our love for you, which is God's love for you, will never snap – it won't break – I promise you."

Over the next twelve months Jack had his highs and his lows, and it sometimes seemed like a game he was playing, but deep down I could see the agony in his eyes. He was hitting out at the love that he wanted and felt. I know David loved him, but was totally infuriated with Jack's behaviour, and David could not manage having his overtures of friendship thrown back in his face.

I kept praying throughout this time and God kept reassuring me that the love was reaching Jack and that it would ultimately bring about healing in his life. After about a year Tom took over from me and Jack moved to Post Green. It was felt that our marriage needed a break from Jack's possible divisive presence in our home.

He ultimately left and held down a well paid job, got married and kept in touch.

But the cost of loving at such a depth was great. I can only speak for myself and not for David at this point, although David said later that he did not mind my friendship with Jack but he did mind the fact that I was able to get alongside him where he couldn't – it made him feel a failure.

I vowed I would never do that kind of ministry again!

We were at church one Sunday morning. Jack was also at church, sitting in the row behind me. He was visiting for the weekend as he planned to be a helper at our next Post Green camp, and had arrived down in Dorset together with some friends of his. I glanced round and saw him sitting on the end of the pew, and I couldn't help reminiscing. "That was too costly, Lord. I will never do that again, whatever you say!"

I had spent so much time, through my own personal prayers, and by talking to Jack, to get him into a good secure place in his life. But I wanted my freedom – I wanted to be able to flit in and out of people's lives and help where I could – but no long term counselling, thank you Lord.

As the Holy Communion service proceeded I was conscious that I was sat next to one of the Fisherfolk people who had recently moved into Post Green community – and had in fact moved into our household in Post Green house. I had never spoken to him and he seemed rather aloof and austere. I perceived him to be one of the leaders who had moved in from the Isle of Cumbrae.

The service culminated in everyone getting out of their seats and going up to the altar rail for Holy Communion, in front of the beautiful stained glass windows. The sun was shining through and leaving patterns of colour on the red carpet. I knelt at the rail – still conscious of Jack's arrival back at Post Green for the weekend, and as I knelt at the communion rail I said again to God: "I will never do that again – it was too costly! I can't love to that depth again in a counselling situation!" The tears came in my eyes as I felt I was giving God an ultimatum and being rebellious – but I stood by what I said.

The young man from the Fisherfolk community was kneeling beside me, and I glanced at him as I stood up to leave the altar rail – he looked like he was arguing with God too. I walked back to my pew and the young Fisherfolk chap slid in beside me. He was staring straight ahead. I wanted to lighten the situation of the solemnity of my prayer at the altar rail, so I poked Billy (not his real name) in the ribs. "What are you thinking?" I whispered. He looked at me, with his aloof look and without smiling. "I can't tell you now, but I will tell you later," he whispered back.

I promptly forgot the incident. We all piled back to Post Green in various cars for lunch, did various things in the afternoon, and around 5pm I slipped upstairs to Grandpa's flat and sat and chatted to him. He turned the television news on and I sat down on a chair near the door to watch. There were several other community members in the tiny room – it was the only television in the house! Grandpa loved this as he always had plenty of company!

By the time Billy walked in there were no free chairs and he squeezed into the crowded room and sat on the arm of my chair. We all continued to watch the news.

Then Billy leaned towards me and said quietly, "You asked me what I was thinking at Communion."

I had already forgotten, and in any case I didn't want to intrude on what had obviously been his own personal thoughts in church. I looked at him and didn't reply. But he said, "If you really want to know what I was thinking – I was saying to God: God I don't want Daphne to love me!"

His statement was too astounding for words. At the point when I was telling God I would never get alongside anyone like I had with Jack – God seemed to have already put something in place to make me change my mind.

Now, of course, I am talking about "agapao" which is God's kind of love. There is only one word for love in the English language – Love. But in the original New Testament, what we translate as love, is actually either "philio" (brotherly love) "agapao" (God's deep, unfailing love) or "eros" (the kind of love between lovers).

All through our lives at Post Green we were committed to loving one another – and by that I mean a "brotherly love" and a Godly love. We were not, obviously, allowed to go into the "eros" type of love unless it happened that two young single people fell in love. Even at that stage they would be carefully monitored – often much to their annoyance! "Eros" love was well supervised too!

Billy, having told me what his thoughts had been during the church service, continued to sit watching the news. And for once I was totally speechless and my mind went blank. The gong sounded down in the hallway, sounding the Cambridge melodic chimes. Then the large cow bell David and I had given to Post Green house, rang stridently at the bottom of the back staircase. We all stood up, and someone helped Grandpa out of his chair. Someone else pressed the button on the back stairs and Grandpa's chair trundled up to fetch him. The rest of us ran down the front stair case and took our places at the large dining table. Tom loved serving high tea on a Sunday and was organising people to carry the food in and place it on the table.

Some years before this weekend, in the early days of Post Green, Faith Lees gave an excellent talk on God's love and how to love one another. I remember her saying: "The first commandment is that we should love God, and the second commandment is that we should love our neighbours as ourselves." She had looked round at her audience, waiting for that to sink in. Then she smiled and said, "So how can we love our neighbours if we don't love ourselves? How can we love someone more than we love ourselves? It's not possible!" She continued to speak and encourage us, her listeners, to learn to love more deeply, both ourselves and our neighbours.

Jean Darnall then took over the meeting and we sang "O Love that will not let me go, I rest my weary soul in Thee, I give Thee back the life I owe, that in Thine ocean depths its flow, may richer, fuller be."

This wonderful hymn had been written by George Matheson in the late 1800s. He was in love and was engaged to be married. But then he discovered he was going blind. He told his fiancée and gave her the choice of breaking off their engagement. She chose to break it off. And George wrote the hymn – turning to the unfailing love of God as his consolation: the love that will never let go. That was the kind of love we were learning about at Post Green and experiencing in our day to day lives – the love that won't let go – the love that won't let people down – the love that persists and loves consistently. I had witnessed that kind of love with Tom and Faith for several years.

Jean Darnall asked anyone who wanted to come forward and kneel at the altar rail if they wanted prayer. Some weeks before the meeting had started I had said something defensive and unloving to Faith, and I was feeling very bad about it. I somehow thought that the prayer would be for forgiveness, if I went forward. So I took my courage in both hands, and walked forward and knelt at the rail. Jean prayed for me, while I was busy saying sorry to God, and telling him I would go and say I was sorry to Faith straight afterwards. But Jean Darnall prayed a different prayer than what I thought I had gone forward for! "O God, thank you that Daphne is committing herself to love to the same depth of love that you have for your people! . . . . . ."

The rest of the prayer went unheard! That was not why I had gone forward, I had only wanted to say sorry!

But God had a plan and I got involved in helping to love broken people when I neither felt I had the ability, and wasn't sure I wanted to do that kind of work anyway!

What Billy had said to me was a mystery. I had already told God I would not do any kind of repeat of what had happened with Jack. Consequently I avoided Billy most of the time. As far as I was concerned Billy was a mature young man and had leadership skills, and no immaturities.

God was doing something in Billy's life and he began to seek me out to chat. Fairly soon after this his anger (which I hadn't noticed) came up to the surface and he went to talk to Tom. Tom agreed to meet regularly with Billy together with another younger man in the community. I was told not to get into anything but very light conversation with Billy.

We became fairly good friends, after a fashion, and I knew that God was doing some deep healing things in Billy's life, that had remained hidden for years. Most of the time I was able to stand up to his anger when it surfaced and try and reason with him. Looking back I think I should have backed off more often. As I read my journals again written during that period, I realise now that I was at times being hooked into Billy's need for reassurance, rather than leaving him to become more mature without my encouragement.

During this time I was in constant conversation, initially with David, and later with Faith – keeping them in touch with any significant conversation I had had with Billy that might need monitoring. We always respected people's privacy in the community when they had a need to share something personal – but we always had someone who would be our advisor.

Sometimes someone would say:"Can I tell you a secret? You promise not to tell anyone?" and we would always point out that we had to be free to consult one of the other pastoral people if we felt it was necessary. Therefore we refused to make promises of total secrecy. We weren't priests in a confessional box!

God called me to get alongside many young women as well, and a few older ones, who needed a close friend while they were working through things and maturing in their Christian lives. These were often costly for me too, in time and emotional energy – and in my private prayers for them. For all these people I would pray constantly that the Lord would help me say the right things to them, or invite them on an outing or holiday if need be. Before I came to Post Green I did not have the skills I later learnt would help me so much in these relationships for the Lord.

Sometimes one had to build up a loving and caring relationship over quite a period of time before the other person could trust enough to share their deepest fears and get free of them. Sometimes it was a habit pattern learnt in childhood that needed to be broken. Sometimes the person felt they had never actually been loved – and therefore couldn't show love to others.

The Holy Spirit's guidance was always vital, every step of the way. Many times without His wisdom I would have been completely stuck and would have let the person down. Without His help sometimes someone's shocking secret would have stunned me into silence; but God always gave the love and grace necessary for that moment.

Once when I was helping out on an early outreach with Tom and Faith in Yorkshire, on the Friday evening a young couple came up to me and asked for prayer and help. Tom and Faith were busy with other people. So we sat in the choir pews, and I asked them what the problem was. They had not long been married and there were tensions showing already. I listened as they both contributed to their list of woes and problems with each other. Then I said, "Look Jesus knows what the true problem is here. Shall we pray and ask him to help you over this difficult time in your marriage?" They both nodded their heads and we all three of us closed our eyes. I started to pray and ask the Lord to help this couple, whom Jesus loved so much, to get to the root cause of the problem in their marriage and bring about healing and forgiveness.

As I was praying, the Lord said very clearly to me. "The husband is having an affair!" There was no way that I would have known from what either of them said, and I never would have guessed, that this was the source of the problem. And I could tell that the wife didn't know.

But the love of Jesus came so strongly on me and there was no possibility of my confronting the husband and spilling the beans. The Lord is gentle and compassionate and he changes lives through his great love, not by condemning people who go to him for help.

I continued to pray with the couple, but was able to add an all encompassing bit about righting any wrongs that were going on in the marriage that might hurt the other one, and so on. When we opened our eyes and looked at each other, the husband knew that I knew that he was having an affair – and the wife remained oblivious – as long as the husband terminated his affair the marriage could hopefully remain intact. If it had all been exposed I think the marriage would have collapsed immediately. Sometimes to confess infidelity makes the confessor feel good, having a clear conscience, and leaves the partner devastated and unable to love or trust again.

Of course, I am telling my story – but I know almost identical examples could be told by many of the people who lived and worked at Post Green – every time we met together to share our stories we would marvel at how great the Lord is as we listened to what people had witnessed and experienced as they had got alongside other people. Post Green was very much a praying and worshipping community and everything we did was saturated in prayer, whether it was an outreach or talking to a large group or an individual in our own community.

One guest staying at Post Green for a month or so to try and get his life sorted out was proving to be quite a problem. He was very frustrated and angry about so many things. Faith Lees encouraged him to write it all down. He wrote a huge document. He didn't want Faith to read it till it was nicely typed. Faith asked if I would mind typing up this document for this guest. He came over to the house where I was living and handed me the huge hand-written screed. I glanced at it, and said, "Don't worry, I can read your writing. I will phone you when it's done – it may take a few days as its quite long!" I could tell he wanted to stay and keep an eye on his precious document, but I felt uncomfortable in his company and ushered him promptly out of the house.

The document was full of anger, threats and violence. He had threatened his vicar at knife point! He had gone round to the vicarage in the middle of the night, shouting abuse up at his bedroom window and commanding he come down and sort things out! He was very angry at the way the vicar and everyone else was letting him down. In fact – he was dangerous!

At the point I typed the document I had a young nurse living in my house and she had just done her mental health nursing training. Initially I thought Claire could help me proof read it. When she came into the room and said, "When do you want me to help you proof read that thing you were typing?" I told her it didn't need proof reading – what I actually meant was it was so lethal it wasn't fit for anyone's eyes except a very experienced psychiatrist.

As we had, over the years, hundreds of people who came to Post Green for help, I can't tell you all the stories. There was laughter and tears – daily!

The longer we were in the job the more careful we became about who we would accept to come and stay when they needed help. Later on we would insist on a letter from the doctor involved, if it was something like recovery from a mental breakdown at University, and we always insisted that the person needing help wrote in themselves to ask for help. We would not accept a request from a friend, parent or their vicar. The person themselves had to ask for the help they needed, otherwise they often rebelled and it did no one any good.

In the early years we were not so careful. We had a lovely girl called Rosemary who came to Post Green for help. I wasn't involved in counselling her and although I could see she had problems I didn't know what they were. If there was a lot of typing to be done, Faith would ask if I would give Rosemary a job in the office. She was fast and accurate, and very quiet and competent. She was extremely thin, and probably had anorexia. She also had tried frequently to kill herself. So she was on suicide watch all the time she was at Post Green. All her pills had been taken off her and she was given the correct dose when required. Faith and Sister Mary Magdalene were in charge.

I arrived down at Post Green house at nine o'clock one morning. As long as I managed to type up all the teaching notes from a recent conference, I would be able to travel with Faith the next day to a women's meeting she was speaking at in Portsmouth. I always loved hearing Faith speak and everything she spoke about taught me more about the love of God. I worked out that I had about five hours typing and the job would be complete. There was a deadline on printing the document and it had to be printed in two days time.

I climbed out of my car and walked in the front door of Post Green house, planning to walk quickly through the kitchen and get straight on with my typing – not get caught up with chatting to whoever was in the kitchen, however interesting it might be. The larder door was wide open and before I closed it to squeeze past en route to my office I couldn't help re-reading the Snoopy poster stuck on the inside of the door.

The poster was of Linus, sucking his thumb, and holding his blanket. He was saying gloomily, "Somehow I think a crisis has arisen!"

It was so appropriate to life at Post Green that it was an in-joke.

As I was closing the larder door, I heard a loud thump on the landing, and distant other noises. I hesitated on my journey to Faith's office beyond the kitchen. Another loud thump.

Tom's voice called, "Can anyone help me?"

For once there was no one else in the kitchen. I ran to the bottom of the stairs, but couldn't see anything, so I ran further up the staircase. There was Tom, with a female body lying at his feet on the staircase leading to the bathroom.

"Rosemary's gone and taken an overdose! And she said she wanted to go to the loo."

"Oh, heavens!" I said, helplessly.

"Look, I can get her to the loo, and lift her on, but could you stay with her and sort everything out? I'll stand just outside the door. Don't lock it! Call when she's finished and I will carry her back to her bed!"

If it wasn't so deadly serious it would have been very funny. Bother it! This is eating out valuable time from my typing project, I thought. Let's get this loo trip over and done with quickly!

Tom proceeded to lift Rosemary, with difficulty as she was extremely floppy, and although underweight she was a tall girl. He plonked her down on the loo, and retreated, closing the bathroom door. Rosemary groaned. "You're on the loo? Can you go?" I said firmly to the sleeping body, holding on to her firmly to keep her in place. Another groan. I continued to hold her so she wouldn't fall. After quite a while I said, "Do you want to go back to bed now?" No answer, just another groan. I waited a bit longer then called out to Tom: "I think she's finished, can you come and get her?"

Tom came back into the bathroom, and we lifted her off the loo seat, and with difficulty carried her up the stairs. I wasn't sure how awake or asleep she was and knew she was capable of playing games with us. We tucked her up into bed.

"Thanks, Daph – glad you came! The thing is I've got a meeting with Philip James, and I'm already late. Could you sit with Rosemary this morning? Sister Mary Magdalene is out till lunch time and no one else is around."

My outing to Portsmouth with Faith was rapidly going down the drain.

"Yes, of course I will sit with Rosemary. Do you mind if I run down to Faith's office and collect my notebook and my typewriter, then I can work up here. It looks like Rosemary will sleep for hours."

Tom waited, and I ran down stairs and got my stuff. In moments I was sat alone, guarding Rosemary.

I watched her for a while and asked if she wanted anything. "No!" Rosemary muttered and dozed off again. I had a good clear three hours of typing. Only slipping out of the room a couple of times to get a drink and use the bathroom. Rosemary slept on. Around 12.30 Sister Mary Magdalene put her head around the door.

"I met Tom, he said Rosemary took an overdose and you were keeping an eye on her! Shall I sit with her so you can have your lunch? I'm free till around two."

Bother! I hoped I would be free not to come back for the afternoon!

"Thanks, Sister. That would be great and I will be back before two. The main thing is to make sure she doesn't swallow any more pills – she must have hidden some somewhere – so if she gets out of bed, watch her!" I said. As I left the room, I turned back to see Sister Mary Magdalene kneeling at the bedside with her Rosary in her hands. I ran down the stairs, slipped out of the house and commenced my drive back up to Panorama.

I had a nice lunch break, and enjoyed the sunshine, and the drive up and back through the countryside of Lytchett Minster and Lytchett Matravers.

When I drove back after lunch to Post Green there was a great fuss going on. It seemed that Rosemary had been pretending to be more asleep than she was, and somehow during the lunch break had swallowed some more pills that she had hidden in the bedclothes somewhere. The doctor had been called, and Rosemary was being admitted to hospital to have her stomach pumped.

As Rosemary departed in the ambulance, I collected my typewriter and notes, and finished it all off in the quietness of Faith's office.

Rosemary was re-admitted to a mental hospital a few weeks later, from where she had spent many months previous to her visit to Post Green. Sadly she did manage to kill herself by escaping from the mental hospital in Sussex and throwing herself off a cliff.

Another young man, in a similar situation, came to stay at Post Green in the early days, before we got much more strict about the way we admitted people with problems. His parents said he was suffering from stress and would we look after him and chat with him? They denied he was in any way under the medical profession, and never told us they had fetched him out of mental hospital and left him in our care instead. The moment his parents drove out of the drive he began to show bizarre behaviour. He was probably about twenty three years old. He ran out onto Post Green lawn and ran round and round in huge circles. Richard and Dave were immediately assigned to keep an eye on him. The young man then ran off and down into the village. Richard and Dave followed him and were gone a long time, till the man ran out of energy and was happy to walk back to Post Green.

That night he jumped out of his bedroom window, and although three floors up, he didn't even get a scratch or bruise – very mysterious!

So he also was on suicide watch until his parents could come down and fetch him. There was some delay as his parents refused to acknowledge that there was anything wrong with their son, and they wanted us to keep him a bit longer. Tom and Faith were adamant he needed to go into mental hospital for skilled help and medication.

Richard and Dave watched him avidly, day and night. I came out of Faith's office mid morning to make myself a coffee. There was a worried conversation going on in the kitchen. The young man was having a bath, insisted he could manage by himself, and had locked the bathroom door. He had been in there a long time. Richard and Dave had supervised his safety and checked that there was nothing unsafe in the bathroom. They kept checking him by calling through the bathroom door, and he would reply he was all right. Then he stopped answering. So Richard or Dave decided to get a ladder and climb up and check through the bathroom window.

I waited in the kitchen while they fetched a ladder. Within moments there was a shout, "Quick, call an ambulance – someone break down the bathroom door."

The young man had hidden a carving knife in his dressing gown and slashed his wrists, very badly. I watched as the ambulance men carried him down the staircase. He was extremely white and unconscious.

Elizabeth Hyland and I offered to clean the bathroom – the bath water was deep red, and the ceiling and walls were also covered in blood. I felt very angry and very sad. Elizabeth was stalwart and we managed to talk about other things as we washed down the walls and ceiling, and left the bathroom spotless once more.

If someone is really absolutely determined to kill themselves they frequently manage it in the end. There was no happy end to this story and he went over the same cliff as Rosemary when he managed to escape from the mental hospital.

After these two episodes all guidelines for future guests were tightened and we turned away many people who thought their healing lay at Post Green. We would no longer take people who may turn out to be suicidal. It wasn't either our calling or our skill.

Of course there was a long gap between these really difficult people staying with us, and most of the time there were wonderful stories of God's healing touch on people's lives at Post Green. We could not help everyone. Jean Darnall had the most powerful ministry when it came to really deep healing, but sometimes the needs were so great and the person so damaged that they needed more help than we had to offer. Faith was excellent at long term counselling and had an enormous amount of love and patience with people who needed to form a new pattern for living their life.

Once the Community of Celebration moved in with us, that side of our life changed. Graham Pulkingham had been doing similar work in the Church of the Redeemer, Houston. They had a different way of going about things and when we combined communities we shared our knowledge and skills, and it seemed we learnt a wiser way of who we allowed and received at Post Green. One's heart goes out to people in deep need, but we are not called to answer every need we see, it proved impossible!

CHAPTER TWENTY SEVEN

Each person or family who moved into Post Green had their own life to lead within the community structure. Each person's individuality was respected and everyone was encouraged to find out where their gifts, and God's calling on their life, lay. Many people settled into the community, and although at times it was tough going they absolutely loved the life.

There were frequent birthday parties and celebrations, and alcohol was on the table at these events and no one got drunk! We very rarely had a visit from the police – in fact I only remember one occasion, and I was sick in bed and missed the excitement.

People's perception of their own life in the community was definitely greatly influenced by the household they happened to be in. If the household was fun and everything working properly then all was well. If you were put in a household where one or more of the inmates was being insensitive then it could make your life rather difficult. There was a strong pastoral structure, and when problems arose there was always someone to talk to. That did not necessarily mean the household would change, but rather that there would be some pastoral input which could help right what was wrong.

We only had about seven or so people who actually went out to work outside of the community. This could be quite hard for them. They missed a lot of what happened during the day, and some were hardly home in time to go to the chapel worship time. Consequently they felt they were missing out. They were not always free to go on outreaches because often we had to set off on Friday morning to cover the distance necessary for the start of the weekend.

Because of the way the community finances were structured after the Community of Celebration and Fisherfolk group joined us, all income was put into the "common pot". This was the only way in which we could support so much ministry and so many guests who needed help.

Sometimes someone who had an "outside" job, gave it up and was able to work within the community, and others went out to work instead. At times the finances were pretty tight. We were committed to get out a new recording of the Fisherfolk four times a year. At one time we had Post Green Community, a Fisherfolk community in Colorado, a community at the Cathedral of the Isles in the Isle of Cumbrae, and the Church of the Redeemer in Houston, Texas, all sharing the responsibility for the music and producing Fisherfolk recordings.

Each music recording demanded about two hundred hours of preparation and rehearsal, and the children of the community were often contributors to the music as well – either their composition or their singing.

We were also publishing and selling all kinds of church teaching materials, and occasionally did graphic and printing jobs for outside companies.

For years we only had fifty pence a week pocket money, but the teenagers had their own allowance so that they could learn to use money wisely and make choices as to whether to buy a new pair of jeans or a favourite CD.

During the winter months, when there were no camps and often no conferences, we started doing theological studies. Lecturers would come from outside the community and we would do a study on a specific subject, from October to March.

I don't remember all the studies, but I do remember studying Church History (most useful and enlightening!), famous Christian people – I chose Martin Luther and Martin Luther King. We studied Liberal Theology, stemming from the South American countries who were trying to bring about Peace and Justice. We had a doctor of psychiatry talk to us about helping people with psychological problems.

And we did a Biblical study on the poor. I was amazed just how much the Bible says about helping the poor, both in the Old and the New Testaments.

During this latter study, in the middle of winter, the community ran out of money! A practical way of discovering what it is like to be truly poor? Or just a strange coincidence?

Either way, everything changed overnight. I think it coincided with a national recession. We had to halve everything – i.e. cut down use of cars by half, cut down usage of electricity and gas by half, cut down each household's allowance by half. This had to be done overnight. An American was in charge of the finances at this stage and he very efficiently gave us sheets of graph paper to fill in meter readings for gas and electricity to make sure we were keeping to the half mark! It was a very tough time. Even our dog suffered. Tessa bought him cheap tripe that was kept in the freezer. She would get it out before she went to work, so it would be unfrozen when she got back home. Then she fed Laddie.

As the winter got colder, and we lacked sufficient heat in the cottage, Tessa would return from work and find the tripe still frozen, and Laddie would have to sit and wait while she unfroze it over a small pan of boiling water!

One thing I learnt during these rather tough times: some people in the community were immensely resourceful and could still do very well. I found I wasn't resourceful and was no good at asking for things we desperately needed! We had lots of friends all over the country who soon heard about our plight and bags of clothes and even carpets and curtains arrived. We had taken over Diffy's Cottage in Lytchett Minster village – and turned it into a Swop Shop. All spare or unwanted clothes and shoes arrived at Diffy's. Two people were in charge of sorting and hanging things on rails. Sometimes a community member would walk into chapel or a birthday party and people would exclaim, "Wow, you look smart! Where did you get that from?"

"Diffy's!" was the usual reply!

One hilarious evening we had a let your hair down celebration, and some of the community did a fashion show, together with slinky music, using the clothes from Diffy's. There was a lot of laughter at the crazy mix of colours and styles appearing from behind the curtains.

It seemed that there was quite a move, which I think started in the United States, to give women more of their rightful place! Especially in the Church.

Susan Abbott gave a talk at one of our camps on Womanhood – and asked me in the loo queue afterwards what I thought it meant. Well her talk had rather gone over my head, and I didn't know how to answer her, so I just said, "Femininity"! This was probably the worst response possible, but I was out of my depth on this new subject being bandied around.

Nine months later Susan was invited to fly to the Church of the Redeemer in Texas and give some talks on the place of women today and what the Bible says about women. To this day I am still amazed that she asked me to accompany her and help with the talks! I said I'd love to go. Help!

Susan gave me what looked like a lot of books to study and take notes, and generally read up on our subject. A Danish lady in the community, who was brilliant at English, asked if she could read the books after me. She was itching to get her hands on them. I told her I was dreading trying to read them all. She bargained with me.

"Look, let me have all the books – it won't take me long to read them. I will give you a précis of each book – to save you reading them!" she offered me enthusiastically.

"Okay – but don't tell Susan! Or I will never get to Houston!" I replied.

Venka disappeared with the pile of books, and gave me a running commentary over the next couple of weeks as to how far she had got in her reading. A few days before we were due to leave she handed me a well-written and typed précis of the subject matter. Susan met with me and we discussed our subjects for this women's conference at the Church of the Redeemer. Finally it was agreed that I would speak on the Biblical attitude to women and Susan would speak on what happened in the church particularly after Christianity began to spread across the world.

It was a fascinating subject. When we had given our talks and Susan had summed up the teaching, a very beautiful American girl (originally from Russia) wept as she stood at the microphone to thank us. I realised that a lot of women felt unable truly to be themselves and many of them were kept down and treated unfairly both at work and in the church, and often by their husbands as well.

Since then there has been a huge move for justice and equality for women both in England and the States. Susan and I took a few other meetings and chatted in depth to the women in the church. We were over there for three weeks. Susan's family lived near San Antonio, so in the final week Susan and I, and her daughter Michal Ann, drove towards the Mexican border, and I had a chance to see wonderful historic places that I had only seen in Westerns at the cinema!

Just before we travelled back home I began to realise I had some problems to deal with. Abigail wrote from "Colditz" – that is Wentworth Milton Mount and warned me that if I didn't let her leave the school she would run away. The school had become increasingly strict, and also cut down the number of exeats per term. On top of that it was not unusual for a girl to be expelled and this was happening with more frequency. I wasn't sure I blamed her for wanting to leave! I wrote back that

I would talk to her at half-term and we would see what needed to be done. I finished writing the letter and put it into the Rectory post box to be collected the next day.

I then heard that Tessa had lost her job, or been made redundant and was rather upset. She was asking if she could come up to Heathrow Airport to meet us off the plane on our return from Texas: I said "yes" as long as David agreed, and also Gordon, Susan's husband, who was also coming to meet us. We had a couple of Peugeot cars with seven seats so there should be space.

There seemed to be phone calls going on between Gordon and Susan, and a bit of a fuss about who was going to go to Heathrow the following week to meet us. What's all the fuss, I thought? This is ridiculous!

Susan explained that Gordon was upset as David wanted to bring Jane (not her name) and Gordon didn't think this was right.

Then I had a telephone call from Tessa to say that her dad, David, had told her there wasn't room in the car for her, as Jane wanted, and needed, to go instead! I told Tessa I hoped she would be able to come, but if not we would have a good chat as soon as I returned.

Having done our trip to San Antonio, and Susan had visited her family, we returned to the Rectory, and took part in one final amazing service at the Church of the Redeemer in Houston: the music was beautiful beyond words. It was Palm Sunday, and the whole church processed around the district, taking their music with them. It was a joyous occasion. The weather was very hot and sunny, even though it was only March.

We said our farewells and were driven to the airport for our flight home. I had given up trying to fathom who would be at the airport to meet us, and just hoped for the best. Gordon was a very strong character and I guessed that he would have sorted out who would come up to meet Susan, Michal Ann, and me.

We landed at Heathrow early in the morning, very tired but glad to be back on English soil. We walked out of customs, and searched for familiar faces in the arrivals area as we walked out with our luggage trolleys.

There was Gordon, smiling and waving. Next to him, a few feet away, was David standing with Jane. There was something about the familiar way they were standing together that hit me in the stomach – they looked like a husband and wife team! I was tired and very shocked, and found it difficult to chat in the car on the way home. I had a feeling that my marriage was over and someone else was ready to step into my shoes. I didn't know what to do or how to find out what was going on – but knew things had to change between David and me: and I strongly doubted that they could.

I met with Tessa as soon as I could and found out what had been happening on the job front – she had other possible job applications and didn't seem too depressed. So I slipped upstairs, unpacked, and sorted out the presents I had bought at the market in San Antonio. Though I was tired and jet-lagged I knew I wouldn't sleep, so walked down to the office, which was now in the village, above the post office. It was early afternoon: a beautiful early spring day. There were lots of outreach requests and other letters to be dealt with. Having sorted everything into piles, I set to and answered the most urgent, and ran over to Kitty's Cottage next door for them to be processed and stamped. It was now nearly half past five. Kitty's Cottage kitchen held a small library of novels and biographical books, and I glanced at them absent-mindedly. I stood alone in the kitchen, studying the pattern on the kitchen carpet.

"God, I've had it! I know my marriage is over – and I don't want to go home – and I don't want to see David. He's got a strange expression on his face – and I've had it! – I can't manage anymore!"

I wasn't messing about – I knew I had come to the end of my marriage. I knew in my heart there was nothing left. As I reflected back I had begun to see that David had hurt me very deeply, in his determination to spend time with Jane and sit next to her at chapel or any other get together whenever he could. Sometimes I would see a chair free next to David and think he had saved it for me. Having reached the free chair and about to sit down, David would say that he had saved it for Jane. Humiliated I would scan the room and look for another vacant chair somewhere else.

During the previous few months I had continued my busy work load, gone on outreaches, supported my three children, and other people's children when needed. I had socialised, laughing and joining in. But I had a very heavy heart which I think I hid a lot of the time, though people who lived with me may well have thought I was a bit moody or stressed about something. I didn't know how to fight for my marriage – I couldn't think how to save it. I was in totally unchartered waters.

David was still one of the main leaders in the Community, and had had a very successful ministry throughout England.

I didn't want to rock the boat and tell anyone what I thought was going on in David's life. It was easier for me to blame myself – to tell myself I was imagining things. If I saw David with Jane, then I told myself they had only just met up and had coincidentally bumped into each other. I told myself that they hadn't spent the whole afternoon or evening together – it was easier that way.

But to try and make yourself believe something that isn't true doesn't solve anything. In my heart of hearts I was very frightened, very lonely, and very angry. As anger is a secondary emotion then I have to admit the primary cause was FEAR. Fear that my marriage was over, fear that my way of life was over, fear about the future for Tessa, Nigel and Abigail – and fear that I would have to leave Post Green. I always thought it would have to be me that left Post Green, probably leaving my children behind – never that David would leave.

One evening, just before we had gone to the States, I had popped in to see Tessa and say goodnight to her. I had been at choir practice, and David had mentioned to me that he had spent the evening with Tessa and Jane. So I said to Tessa, "I hear you had a nice evening with Dad and Jane." Tessa quickly responded, "No! I didn't! Dad popped his head round the door and said he was going out for the evening. I saw him get into a car and drive off with Jane."

I queried with David why he had told me he had spent the evening with Tessa when he hadn't, and he just said it had slipped his mind.

There had been other episodes that had made me uneasy, but I didn't know what to do about it. And rightly or wrongly as a wife I thought my first responsibility was to be loyal to David. I could have gone to Tom, Faith or Susan, and admitted that I thought there was a problem. I later found out that all three of them knew, and had forbidden David to spend time with Jane, who he had counselled for some time previously. They had tried to deal with the problem without rocking the boat. They felt if I found out what was going on I might leave! But I knew none of this as I stood in Kitty's Cottage kitchen on my return from Houston.

I walked slowly home up the hill from the village. Abigail was still at boarding school, and Nigel was upstairs doing his homework. Deep in thought, I dreaded the way ahead – but I felt I was crumbling inside, just like my marriage.

Fortunately, perhaps, it was choir that evening. Supper was particularly lively with the whole household at Post Green house asking us how we had got on in the States, and how Susan found her family, and so on. David was at the far end of the table, sitting next to his father. We ran a bit late, so there was no time to chat between supper and choir. I ran upstairs to the bedroom and got my music books and folder. David was nowhere about and I had said nothing to anybody about my "end of the road" speech to God at Kitty's Cottage that afternoon.

Choir was a light relief even though I was jet lagging. We finished our practice and shared cars to get ourselves back from choir to our various households. I thought to myself: I've got a terrible problem, but I will sleep on it. God knows I have truly got to the end of coping with David – he's been so strange recently, and when I try and talk to him he is either evasive or he doesn't tell me the truth.

I got ready for bed, and apart from saying goodnight to Tessa and Nigel, I spoke to no one. I climbed into bed and decided to read for a short while.

There was a knock at the door. It was 9.30pm. "Hi, come in!" I called. Susan popped her head round the door. "Oh, sorry, I didn't realise you were already in bed. I'm looking for David – do you know where he is?"

"No, I haven't seen him since supper time – maybe he is with Grandpa watching television." I said.

Even then I had a chance to say something to Susan about my problem. She had been a super friend to me while we were away and we had drawn closer to each other and learnt to trust each other.

"Well, I will go and look for him. Gordon and I told David we wanted a meeting with him after choir, I thought he would be around waiting for us somewhere. I think you had better be in on the meeting, Daphne, if you don't mind – it's very important!" Susan sounded "imperative" .

"Oh, okay, I'll get up and get dressed again." And I started getting out of bed.

"No, don't worry. If you don't mind having the meeting in your room, stay as you are."

The bedroom, previously Tom and Faith's, was huge, and there was a large seating area by the window overlooking the gardens. I told Susan that would be all right, and as she left to go in search of David, I got out of bed and slipped my dressing gown on. In a few minutes the bedroom door knocked again, and Susan and Gordon walked in, followed by David.

Going back to my thoughts as I had walked home from Kitty's Cottage earlier that evening, I remembered thinking: well my marriage seems to be over, and I can't manage the way things are, I guess I will have to leave – there's no room for David and me in the same community!

Over the next hour I saw the hand of God take care of the future. It was terribly hard and it still hurts, and it will always hurt. But I never had to walk away from Post Green on my own and leave my three children and David there.

We all four sat down on the chairs by the window. David sat next to me, and I could feel his discomfort. I could also feel there was something about to be said which I didn't want to hear!

Susan immediately confronted David. "I've been reading the Minutes of the Leadership meetings that took place while Daphne and I were in Houston. There are some discrepancies that involve you, David. I would like you to explain them."

I began to relax a tiny bit. At least it wasn't our marriage under discussion; I was far too fragile for that tonight. It can't be too serious. I settled more comfortably into my soft chair, watchful and curious.

Susan then began to list the discrepancies, and things David had said about Susan in the meetings. Gordon had been writing the Minutes and had noted down these remarks – Susan was really annoyed. I was astonished, because David was usually very efficient and capable – he didn't lightly mess things up and not do his job properly. The meeting continued and as it didn't involve me I let a lot of it go over my head. I did understand that for once David had severely goofed and somehow things had to be sorted. One of the issues was the Ministers and Clergy Symposium due to start next week. There was a discrepancy about who should have organised the programme and speakers (David) and that it wasn't done.

Having laid all the cards on the table, and David basically not replying, but just picking up non-existent pieces of fluff off his trousers (a sign of his great discomfort), Susan then abruptly changed the subject.

I sat bolt upright in horror. She confronted David with the devious way he had refused to take Tessa up to the airport and had taken Jane instead. He was reminded that he had been told not to spend time with Jane, and yet everyone knew (except me!) that Wednesday nights while most of the community were at choir, David went out for the evening with Jane. I was amazed at how much had been going on without my knowledge.

David had nothing to say, and no defence. I desperately wanted to protect him, defend him, cover up for him. But I remembered my decision in Kitty's Cottage kitchen, and remained silent. This problem is far too big for me, I guess it's the end of the road for all our family at Post Green, I thought, as Susan and Gordon waited for David to speak.

He still said nothing. I was wide awake, and all jetlag gone. It seemed we were on a knife edge. Tom and Faith were living up in Cumbrae, working with the Fisherfolk, Community of Celebration, for a year. But I had a feeling that Susan would have already spoken to Tom and Faith before the meeting. I knew our family were precious to them and that they loved each of us dearly.

"David, you need to make a decision about your life. You have been in leadership here ever since you came, and you have done well. But there are problems in your life which you can no longer hide. Some of the community feel they cannot trust you at the moment. From today onwards you are relieved of all your leadership duties, to give yourself time to work on your personal life. We will give you any support you want."

David nodded at what Susan had just said, hiding his feelings and his response.

"We suggest you spend time either up at Cumbrae with Tom and Faith and the community there, or if you prefer you can go to Colorado or Houston. Graham Pulkingham will be only too glad to give you whatever time you want to chat things over. Things cannot go on any longer the way they have been recently, you do understand that – don't you?"

My heart was pounding – poor David. But I had to agree things were desperate for me in the marriage. I also, deep inside me had to admit it wasn't the first time there had been another young woman that David had secretly been spending long periods of time with, excluding me in the process, and denying the whole thing. I didn't know at this stage that others on the pastoral leadership had been talking to

David about what they had noticed, and had tried to protect me from finding out how bad things were, in the hope of saving our marriage.

"You need to make a decision about where you want to be. As you cannot stay at Post Green, we think you need to decide promptly where you are going to go and get the help you need. Who do you want to talk this decision over with?"

David remained silent: then said quietly, "Richard Paine and Graham Cyster."

David had been meeting regularly to talk to these two gifted pastoral men for several weeks. I did not know what about. But I did know that David Mills and David Holland had been counselling one of the men in the community for a few weeks, and suddenly it had all collapsed because my David had admitted he had the same problem and could no longer help this man. I think the pastoral leaders got involved at this point and David began his talks with these two wise and caring men in the community.

Susan and Gordon suggested that David meet with Graham and Richard first thing in the morning and let the leadership know by lunch time where he was planning to go.

They left the room. "Oh, David!" I said.

Next morning, before I went down to the office in the village, I said to David, "I will be in my office all day. Please let me know what your decision is as soon as you've talked to Graham Cyster and Richard Paine." I couldn't concentrate at all on my work – if I wrote any outreach letters they probably were brief and not giving the information I had been asked to send. All I could think of was poor David and the decisions he had to make. I stayed in my office all morning and didn't even leave it to buy myself a treat in the Post Office downstairs.

At midday I saw Richard. "What did David decide?" I asked him. Richard looked startled and said, "What are you talking about?"

"But you were meant to have a meeting with him this morning together with Graham Cyster!" I said.

"Well, I saw David this morning but he never mentioned any meeting." Richard looked at me, puzzled. I quickly filled him in with the details, as we stood on the path outside the offices. “Don’t worry, I will go and find Graham, and we will chat with David.” He hugged me and walked off in the direction of Post Green house.

By three o’clock I had not heard from David, and rang around and couldn’t find him. By now I was desperate for a treat so I nipped into the Post Office shop for a Mars Bar, and joined the queue. Rodney Dunlop was in front of me. He turned to me and said, “I hear David is leaving the country!”

“What?” I said completely stunned.

Rodney saw the startled look on my face and said, “Don’t you know?” I shook my head, and changed my mind about the Mars Bar. I was so shocked that David’s decision had been made, and been made public, before I had heard anything from him direct. I was indignant, angry and very upset.

When I finally found David it was just before supper – we talked briefly in the bedroom – but I could tell he was avoiding me. “David, I waited all day for you to let me know what you planned to do, and where you planned to go!”

“I tried to find you, but I couldn’t!” David replied.

“I was all day in my office waiting for your phone call.”

“Well, I couldn’t find you.” David repeated.

“So what’s the plan?” I asked him.

“I’m going to Colorado to talk with Graham Pulkingham, and stay in the community for a week or two. Then I am going to Canada – to Vancouver Island.”

“Oh – to stay with Karen and Brian in Victoria?” I asked.

“No. I plan to be with Chris and Ina. They want me to help them start a community – you know I mentioned that ages ago. But Chris is under the North Pole at the moment on some military exercise. I managed to speak to him briefly on the phone today!”

“When are you coming back?” I queried.

“Well, Susan and the leadership felt three months is the maximum I should be away or it would be hard to integrate again. But I don’t plan to come back.”

I never told anyone that David did not plan to come back, in case he changed his mind. It wasn't up to me to tell the world that David Mills had left Post Green Community and his ministry, and gone to live abroad. Over the coming months people couldn't understand why I was so weepy at times. And other people said, "We can't understand why you haven't gone to Canada with David!"

Once I angrily replied, "Because he doesn't want me!" and walked away before I had to deal with their response.

CHAPTER TWENTY EIGHT

David left just after Easter in 1980. I walked down to Lytchett Minster Church on Easter Sunday morning with some of the household. The others were chatting away happily, oblivious to the reason why I was so quiet. They had been told that David was taking a sabbatical and would be away three months. It was a glorious sunny day, the birds were singing in the trees, as though they had not a care in the world! David and I had discussed which one of us should go to church as it would be too weird to sit together, and to sit apart would attract unwanted attention. I sat with a warm, friendly girl from Finland, who worked in the graphics office with me. On the other side was Miss Jeanes, Tessa and Abigail's previous headmistress of St Monica's school.

A group from the community were playing their guitars and leading some worship from the front. Then the vicar processed in together with the acolytes, who were carrying the Bible and the Cross. The vicar announced the first hymn, and the organ struck up the opening chords before I had had a chance to find my place in the hymn book.

We all stood up, and the hymn commenced – the congregation singing fervently: "The strife is o'er, the battle won, now is the triumph of our Son!"

I started to cry. And I said to God, loudly in my heart. "The strife isn't over! It's just beginning!" thinking of David's departure and all the unknown that lay ahead.

God replied very clearly to me: "For you the battle is over. For David it is just beginning." That made me cry all the more – I felt so sorry for my dear husband, and for whatever the future would hold for him. I still loved him, although I knew I could no longer cope with being married to him. I sat down at the end of the hymn and Sade and Miss Jeanes held my hands and were obviously praying for me. I began to relax and calm down, and let the rest of the service reach me and comfort me, as I prayed for David, and for our three children. It would be the start of many changes in our lives that would affect us forever.

The following year was exceedingly hard for me, my family, and for the community. I felt I was almost hanging over the edge of a cliff, and terrified that the next grief would make me let go and go plummeting down to the bottom of an abyss. David had been a key leader and pastor, and an ordained minister. People found their faith and trust shaken, and were asking many questions. There were no easy answers.

Over the next two or three years, letters were flying across from David in Canada , which added to my confusion. Much of what David said seemed either untrue or off balance and distorted. I knew I needed to chat with someone outside the community to keep everything in perspective and check out fact from fiction. I chose Rev Rex Meakin and his lovely wife Phyl.

Rex and Phyl had an open door for me whenever I phoned and wanted a chat. It became very important to have an outside opinion. Sometimes I read parts of David's letters to them, or even left a letter with them to peruse. They would constantly reassure me that it wasn't my fault: David was going through a huge personal crisis of his own which was not of my making at all. David was very well known throughout the country as a speaker, teacher, minister. It would be all too easy to blame the community for what had happened, leaping to judgement without knowing all the facts. To me it was a safety valve, somewhere to check things out, get other opinions and a source of prayer.

The children were devastated but had their own ways of coping. Abigail had already left Wentworth Milton Mount. She had found it very difficult to settle down because she was homesick and as I realised that David was leaving us I felt it better that she was at home. Together with several other community children she was now attending Lytchett Minster School, which had now gone comprehensive. Abi told me she had decided to move into a different household, away from me and my stress, and somewhere where she could rebuild her life with other friends in the community.

Just before she left I went up to her bedroom at the top of Post Green house to say goodnight to her one evening. She shared the bedroom with Tessa. It was much later than usual.

"Where's Tessa?" I asked Abigail.

"She doesn't live here anymore! Hadn't you noticed?" she said rather crossly.

"What? What do you mean? Of course she lives here!" I replied, puzzled. "She's always down at 7.15 for breakfast each day."

"Yes, she comes back about seven, to change her clothes and get ready for work!"

I found this just too hard to believe. But Abigail was always truthful! So what did it all mean – where was she living?

It turned out that she had moved in with a boyfriend some distance away. Tessa has always been well-disciplined at getting up in the morning so I guessed she just got up that much earlier.

Nigel spent a lot of time in his room, working hard for his A levels, and also working at Lytchett Minster garage to earn some pocket money. Nigel and I had gone up to Cambridge University for an interview and a look around the grounds. He was offered a place to study structural engineering, based on the good results of his O levels, and expected grades for his A levels. Sadly, I am sure due to the upheavals in his family life, he failed to get the expected high enough grades, and opted for a different career.

When David left, he first went to the Colorado community, an associate community. Rev Graham Cyster volunteered to go with him. Graham had first come to Post Green for a Ministers' Symposium. He was a Cape-coloured Baptist Minister from South Africa, who had lost several of his youth fellowship in the Soweto troubles. He had fled to Germany and had been encouraged to visit Post Green. He came for a week, and stayed seven years. He was very traumatised when he first arrived having witnessed the death of several of his young people in Soweto.

The Lord strengthened his faith and healed his emotional wounds and he became an invaluable member of the community at Post Green. He already had a couple of university degrees and was later working for his doctorate while with us.

After a few weeks David flew on to Canada and Graham returned to Post Green. I flew out to talk to David after six months, but realised that there was unlikely to be any permanent reconciliation. The week I spent out there, staying with my friends Karen and Brian, proved to me how very hard it would ever be to try and repair the marriage.

David asked me to tell the community he was not planning to return. I asked him to come back and make the statement himself – I felt it was not up to me, or a good idea, to close his ministry down! So David came back a couple of months later, and explained to the community that he felt he could no longer continue things the way they were, and that he was pursuing a solution to his personal problems by having counselling in Canada.

David came back for several visits and we tried to talk over the past and come to some kind of understanding and resolution. David kept saying that he had left Post Green "to find himself", and he had to make the journey and pursue it on his own. After three years separation there seemed still to be confusion and I was neither married nor single.

I decided to go and see a retired vicar – a canon! Even higher than a vicar! He was elderly and a bit frail and always had his housekeeper with him. But I prayed as I drove up to Wiltshire that if I was meant to discuss my marriage problem with him that I would have a chance to speak to him on his own. He said he would be in all afternoon when I had telephoned earlier.

After parking the car in his drive, I walked up the path and rang his doorbell. I had quite a long wait, and eventually Dr Richardson opened the door.

"Come in, Daphne. How nice to see you! We never get a chance to chat on our own. My housekeeper has gone to visit a friend, so we are on our own. Let's go into my study, shall we?" He walked slowly and a little unsteadily to his office and sat behind his desk.

I sat down opposite him. "Now last time you were here you were on your way back from some church weekend. And one of your team left your book with me."

It was lying on his desk – "The Road to Emmaus". "I've had a good look at it. Do you want it back?" I shook my head. He flipped the pages through his fingers, commenting on various sections. Then he slipped it into a drawer, and looked at me. "Tell me about yourself – and your family." He asked me, as he poured out a cup of tea from a tray nearby.

What an opening! So the opportunity presented itself for me to tell him everything. I summed it all up as succinctly as I could – perhaps taking about twenty minutes in all.

"Do you think there is any hope for my marriage?" I asked him, having finished trying to tell him everything.

He looked at me, kindly, thoughtfully, sadly.

"No, Daphne. I don't."

That was not the answer I was expecting. I thought any high-up churchman would never admit a marriage had had it. We then discussed the Bible teaching on divorce – and what the Church says about divorce.

Dr Richardson set me free by the things he said. The marriage was over. Don't cling to it. You both need to set each other free, or neither of you can move on.

An hour and a half later I said my farewells to the kind, elderly clergyman, and drove back to Post Green. I wept most of the way. Great sadness that a marriage that had started so well had seemingly ended in failure. But also tears of relief – I could be free and start re-building my life without the emotional tug-of-war I felt I had been in for several years.

David had only recently applied for a job in British Colombia and had phoned me early one morning and asked me to fly over for an interview with the Bishop. I was totally confused: the marriage was over, and I had seen a letter addressed to his "girl friend" proposing marriage! Yet I was needed to appear as Mrs David Mills to help him get a job. I found the phone number in British Colombia of the Bishop – and managed to speak to him – I told him I wasn't coming over and that wasn't where our marriage was at. The Bishop had understood otherwise, and had heard from David that there were a few minor problems with me but it could easily be sorted out! If I could have started again in the ministry with David I would have done. It wasn't because I didn't love him: but it was because I could no longer trust him in important areas of his life and of our life together.

I took steps to divorce David, using one of the ex-Bible college students who was a lawyer. Initially David used Prince Charles' lawyers in response, which unnerved my Bible College friend – it seemed a David and Goliath situation! but eventually David had to use Canadian legal people in Vancouver.

To try and get ourselves back together as a family unit I asked the pastoral leaders if we could move into a house and be on our own for a while. This was thought to be a good idea, and we moved into Hillwood Cottage, just across the road from Post Green – leaving Grandpa Mills in the main house. Christine Crompton, his carer, continued to come in during the day time to look after him and take him on outings in his car. She looked after my father-in-law in an excellent and honest, faithful way for many years.

We had a great time sorting ourselves out, choosing who would sleep in each bedroom and generally making ourselves at home. Abigail inherited a huge cat from Juanita, who was going back to the States to try and find her mother who had given her away for adoption as a baby. The cat was called Smarty Pants.

He was an amazing hunter and enjoyed bringing wildlife in through the cat flap, including a large rabbit. The rabbit was quickly rescued and released onto farm land nearby. Smarty Pants brought a lot of mice in. I would lie on the floor of Hillwood Cottage with my bright yellow kitchen gloves on, and a piece of cheese lying nearby. Frequently the hungry mouse would pop out to grab the cheese. I became super quick at pouncing, capturing, and releasing the mouse. The children were highly amused. I got so brave that in the end I didn't even use kitchen gloves but scooped the mice up with my bare hands.

They weren't all caught, and we would hear them running under the floorboards – like a large mouse army – between the downstairs bathroom and the airing cupboard opposite.

As our first Christmas at Hillwood Cottage drew near, Tom Lees gave us a real tree from the farm, and we stood it in the tiny sitting room, and as the days went by the mountain of presents grew higher and wider. There were odd rustles noticed when the room was quiet – gradually increasing to a constant rustling. We cautiously started moving the unwrapped Christmas presents to higher ground – yes, chewed up paper, cardboard and some chocolates were discovered! All Christmas gifts were kept off the ground and the mice gradually got bored and left.

The structure at Post Green changed after one of Graham Pulkingham's visits – I was away in Canada at the time. The choice was stark – make a permanent commitment to join the newly formed Chapter or leave.

It didn't seem a good time to make any new commitments, as I was still pulling myself together after the divorce, which had only recently gone through, so I agreed to leave. It hurt terribly!

In Devon there is a wonderful place called Lee Abbey. This was a Christian holiday centre run by a loose-knit community.

We had a reciprocal arrangement with them – if anyone needed a break from Lee Abbey they could come for a rest to Post Green. And if anyone from Post Green wanted a break they could go to Lee Abbey. So I booked to go, free of charge. The four days I was there proved encouraging. I prayed about the way forward and what to do next. Get an outside job, sell Panorama – or get the money for it – and buy somewhere else nearby. God assured me He would look after us and that I need not worry about money.

With this assurance I came back to Hillwood in a happier frame of mind.

Tessa, Nigel and Abigail, whilst all living at the cottage, were getting on well with their own lives. Most of the time we lived very happily together, with only the odd misunderstanding or saga to liven things up.

One day Tessa was getting ready to go out. "Mum!" I heard her shout.

I emerged from my downstairs bedroom. Tessa had just come downstairs and we met in the sitting room. "I've lost a contact lens! I can't go out till I've found it."

We tried to work out where she may have lost it so that we could start looking for it. "It could be anywhere! I've no idea where I lost it!"

We all tried to help find it, crawling all over the cottage on hands and knees. No success. "I need it desperately!" Tessa reminded us, when we had just about given up the search.

"Well, God knows where it is, let's pray." So we held hands in the sitting room and asked God to show us where it was.

Tessa went back upstairs to try and finish getting ready. Abigail ran upstairs to fetch something. I turned round and started to go back to my bedroom.

There was a loud screech and thump –and more thumps and a yell: then another shriek – from Abigail. I ran back into the sitting room. "Look what I've found!" said Abigail, sitting on the bottom stair.

We all gathered around her – "How ever did you find it? Where was it?" we asked her.

Abigail grinned, sighed and groaned at the same time. "I fell over that stupid pile of laundry at the top of the stairs. And when I landed at the bottom I found myself looking at the lens shining on the stair carpet!" We all congratulated her, and once Tessa had safely taken charge of the lens, we commiserated with Abi on her (relatively mild) injuries!

It was such a good time, having the three children living together with me in Hillwood Cottage. Of course we had our highs and lows, sagas and adventures during the time we lived there. But altogether it was a very healing time for the family and we were able to re-build our family life. Eventually they all got married, within twelve months of each other. It was a strange year: Four Weddings and a Funeral, and Two Baptisms!

Tessa married Nick Legg, a local young man living in Upton, Poole. They chose to get married in Lytchett Minster United Reformed Church, as Nick had been married before. In those days it was impossible to get re-married in an Anglican Church. The tiny chapel seated eighty people. Tessa invited eighty people, and then daily invited more until the numbers were up around one hundred and twenty people! Extra seating was used in the church hall and everyone squeezed in. David came over from Canada to give Tessa away. The wedding reception was held at the village hall in Lytchett Matravers, and all the Post Green Community was invited plus many other friends and relations.

Abigail married Gary Mears, who was a submariner based at HMS Dolphin in Gosport. They chose to marry at Corfe Mullen Baptist Church, Dorset. The tiny church was packed with Post Green Community members including many of the Fisherfolk who helped with the singing. The Wedding Reception was held in Post Green house, very kindly and generously hosted by Tom and Faith.

Shortly afterwards Nigel married Ruth Paris at a Roman Catholic Church in Bournemouth. To be able to marry in an R.C. Church meant he had to prove he had been baptised. As Tessa, Nigel, and Abigail had all been dedicated at birth, this was a problem! Nigel chatted with our vicar in Lytchett Minster and he organised a baptismal service. Abigail asked to be baptised as well, so we had two baptisms.

Sadly around this time Grandpa Mills died. It seemed a year of always walking down a church aisle for some important event or other.

David Mills also remarried in Canada to Carol, within the same twelve months, but none of us attended from England.

Abigail and Gary were first to start a family. They moved back into Hillwood for a few weeks when Jenna was born, as Gary was in the navy and Abi didn't want to be on her own with the baby. Shortly after that Nigel and Ruth were married and their son Luke was born, six months after Jenna. After Tessa married Nick they moved to Upton, a village near Lytchett Minster but they waited a few years before they had Robert.

David continued to live in Canada and come over occasionally for visits to see the children and some of his old friends. He had survived a breakdown, some mild heart attacks, and eventually had a heart transplant in Canada.

Several of us in Post Green Community were looking for outside jobs, either because we were leaving or because the Community needed more people outside earning a living to help the finances. Some were looking in the jobs section of The Times, The Guardian, The Daily Telegraph. I was hunting for a job in the local rag. This wasn't so easy. Though I had loads of experience in administration and helping churches and people sort themselves out, I couldn't prove I was good in a secular job! So I started with a secretarial agency. A new job every week – imagine the stress! New names, new office layout, different typewriter and telephone systems – different words and phrases to learn for shorthand dictation. It was a nightmare!

One job I quite enjoyed, several years later, still temping, was with McCarthy and Stone who build homes for the elderly. And I worked in the travel section, typing brochures for holidays for their residents. I was asked to stay on another few weeks and work for one of the directors, but as it was in the finance sector I didn't really fancy that job. I really had no choice but to agree to turn up on Monday morning in the new department.

But in the meantime I had gone to visit Abigail, who was living with her husband Gary, in naval quarters in Gosport. We were having a lovely day together, and after a little outing to the shops and children's play area we had arrived home for a cup of tea.

As Abigail was making the tea I took baby Jenna on my lap – she had already kicked off her shoes and socks. I noticed some blistery spots on her feet. I searched more carefully and found some more on her hands. "Hey, Abigail! Come and have a look! What's Jenna got?"

Abi came rushing in – I held Jenna's feet up for inspection. We lifted up her vest and peered at her chest: nothing. "Well it's not chicken pox," I said.

"We'd better take her up to the doctor and get him to check her over."

After drinking our tea as quickly as we could, we drove up to the surgery and the doctor inspected Jenna. "Hand, Foot and Mouth!" he pronounced.

He gave Abigail some instructions on how to care for Jenna – and added that it was an infectious disease.

Low and behold, the day before I was due to start working for the Finance Director, I found blistery spots on my hands – and on my feet, and a few blisters in my mouth. First thing Monday morning I telephoned the secretarial agency, and said I wasn't well and wouldn't be going into work at McCarthy and Stone. "Oh, well I'm sorry, Daphne, but we are desperately short of staff. You will have to come in even if you feel sick."

"Okay," I said, "but you need to know I am infectious. I've got Hand, Foot and Mouth disease!"

I played my trump card – and got two weeks off work. But then when I was better (I hadn't been very ill anyway) I got sent to an Arabian shipping company. I walked out after a week, refusing to go back. The secretarial agency pleaded with me. There was an exceedingly unpleasant man running the office (English, not Arab). I refused to go, even when they offered me more pay and a permanent job with the shipping company! When I finally managed to convince them I would absolutely not go back again to be bullied and yelled at, the agency admitted that no one would work there and they had no more staff to send there!

Amazingly I found another temporary job after a short while with a local large comprehensive school. At the interview I was asked what my spelling was like: "Pretty good!" I volunteered.

"Well, it won't be when you've worked here a while!" said Elizabeth, the senior school secretary who was interviewing me.

The job was mine. I turned up, in all innocence, with my lunch box and my dictionary for my first day at my new job. I was handed a huge list of names. "These are all the staff. If I or Mairie are busy, you answer the phone. They may ask for a member of staff by Christian name, surname or nickname – learn them all." There seemed to be about one hundred names, many with nicknames.

"You may also be asked by the caller to be put through to the Geography Master, or the Science Master, or the Head of one of the Houses," she said, and added: "You need to learn them too, as quickly as possible."

The desk and typewriter assigned to me was near the door, but facing the hatch that the pupils came to if they needed anything.

"Oh, and Daphne, if a parent needs to be called, you must check the pupil's card file carefully. Parents have to be called in an emergency. Quite a few of the parents are separated, so make sure you call the right one – it's written on the card. Don't get it wrong, or there will be trouble."

My dictionary was placed beside my typewriter and I was given three letters to type. I was given three pieces of headed notepaper, one piece of carbon paper, and three pieces of flimsy paper. I obviously wasn't meant to make a mistake - and if I did I would have to ask for another sheet of paper – how awful. It felt like being back at school. Ha, Ha!

At one o'clock I stopped typing some Geography test paper, and got out my sandwich box – not sure if I was meant to eat it at my desk, or go outside somewhere. As I hesitated, Elizabeth said, very firmly: "We don't stop for lunch. We don't have time. We eat as we work!"

"Ah!" I responded, and thought what a ghastly job this is. I've been spoilt in the loving environment of Post Green, and reflected longingly of the bench in the sunshine outside Kitty's Cottage where we often sat altogether, laughing and talking as we ate our sandwiches, and often shared out food with each other.

The highlight of any day at the school was to be sent along to someone's classroom with a message. The building was huge, and I loved knocking on the classroom door, and seeing the children being taught at their desks. Once I had to interrupt a drama class in the main hall – chaotic and noisy. The teacher was smaller than the pupils and it took me sometime to find her and deliver the message.

The headmaster was quite a handsome chap - and I discovered he had a short temper at times. I'd only been at the job two weeks and Elizabeth kept a tight control over the office and what she considered were her unique duties, which included ringing the complicated system of bells.

I arrived at my usual time – 8.45am. Elizabeth was not in the office – unusual. Maire wasn't in the office either: just me. The headmaster rushed in: "Why haven't you rung the school bell? It's time for the second bell, and the first bell hasn't been rung yet!" He stood hovering just inside the school office.

"Go on, ring it right away – the first bell, and wait two minutes then ring the second bell!" he emphasised, really agitated.

"Sorry, but I don't know how to ring the bell; Elizabeth always does it!"

He stomped across the office, fiddled around with the switchboard, and I heard a bell ringing in the distance.

He strode out of the room and disappeared. I pulled a nervous face, which only the ceiling would have seen!

I took the cover off my typewriter, and had almost sat down, when the headmaster reappeared. "Come over here. Look this is what you do – and then this, then this, then you do that – got it?" Another bell rang, sounding a bit different to the first.

He hurried out of the room again, just as Mairie walked in and was almost knocked over as he swung round the corner.

"I see the Head is upset! What's up?"

"Well, the bells didn't get rung and Elizabeth isn't in yet. You'd better show me how to do the bells and I will write down how to do it."

After about six weeks I got my first pay check from Dorset County Council – every half hour I worked was carefully calculated and I insisted that my non-existent lunch hour be included in my working day, so I got paid for that as well.

One of the senior masters came into the office, wanting a letter done in a hurry – it was only two paragraphs – a doddle for me! He left the room to go and take his class. I skimmed through the letter. There were several words misspelt. That was obvious. Another word looked plausible but I was sure if it was the correct spelling. I got out my small dictionary, and holding his letter aloft, I searched for the word in question.

The master walked back into the office. He saw me checking his spelling with my dictionary! "Nothing wrong, is there, Daphne?" he demanded rather imperiously.

"No, nothing!" I hastily answered.

I fiddled around till he left, checked the spelling in my dictionary, and never told him his spelling was pathetic!

In the meantime I asked the community if they would give me the money at the going rate for Panorama, or sell it. David wanted a share of it, whatever the decision. The present household moved out and dispersed into other houses, and I put Panorama up for sale. This proved to be extremely hard, as word had got round the village that it was liable to subsidence because of the two extensions. I eventually sold it for far less than the value put on it, and David had a proportion of the sale money as well.

Initially, when David left, I felt unable to do any more outreach or speaking engagements, but as time went on I was gradually encouraged to get involved again. Tom encouraged me to lead a team that was requested for a large successful Baptist church. They planned to have a residential weekend in a conference centre in Hampshire. They were at a crossroads and it would be an important weekend for them.

I nervously agreed to lead it. On the first evening I was very cautious and gave a rather bland talk on Jesus saying we are the salt of the earth. Included in the talk were some boring, scientific details of what salt does! Afterwards one of the leaders came up to me and asked me to counsel one of the women on the weekend. "I believe you have been through what she is going through. She is a pastor's wife – and they are having problems! God told me you've been through something similar recently."

I spent some considerable time talking with the woman. For me that proved to be quite an important part of the weekend, as I realised I had worked through a lot of my anger and pain, and was beginning to feel like a normal capable human being again! I was shocked that someone else had gone though something similar and realised the huge pressures that are on clergy marriages. Because we are in the Church it doesn't protect us from human frailties.

There were two men helping me on the team from Post Green, and one woman. I asked if our team could meet with all their elders and deacons first thing Saturday morning. This was arranged. By the time we walked into the room where we had arranged to meet, all the elders were already there. (Maybe they'd had a meeting together earlier?)

I looked around in surprise. There were no women amongst them. After we dealt with the plan for the weekend, and what our aim was, and what we expected to achieve, I asked them a question.

"Where are the women? Don't you have any women in leadership?"

The assistant minister, who I knew well from our days of living in Brighton, admitted that they had no women elders, or in leadership at all, except for the Sunday school.

"Well, how do the women make their views known? How do they have input into the running of the church?" I asked.

"We are all married. Our wives tell us what is going on amongst the other women and we bring it to the elders meeting when necessary."

The Post Green team tried to encourage them to broaden their vision and allow women to be in more obvious leadership instead of prodding their husbands at home.

It was one of the most important church conferences I have ever been involved in, and we remained in contact with them over the following few months while they worked on a large crisis that had occurred just before we met.

Tom, Faith and Susan encouraged me to attend and sometimes speak at the clergy and ministers symposiums that we ran. Although reluctant to do so, I eventually agreed. And I found myself appealing to the clergy that if they had any personal problems, whatever they were, please find someone to confide in and start getting it sorted out. I felt very strongly about this as I had begun to realise that David's problems which had begun to surface and had caused him to leave me, the children, his ministry, his job, were the result of a personal problem he had felt unable to deal with. His main problem stemmed from early childhood and he had tried valiantly to overcome it without confiding in anyone, but in the end it was all too much for him when he had to counsel someone else with the same problem.

A year or two later I began to discover some of the truth of David's dilemma and his personal problem. I felt so sad that he never found anyone he could trust to share his problem. And that is the position many clergy find themselves in. They are expected to have got their lives sorted out and be whole, healed people before they take over a church. And sadly this is far from the truth. They should never be expected to be perfect – even though God has called them, they are still human!

You have only to read the story of Moses: he stuttered so much, that when God called him to lead the Israelites out of Egypt, Moses asked if his brother Aaron could do the talking for him! Moses went on to do a marvellous job. But he made mistakes and in the end God forbade him to take the Israelites over the borders into Palestine, because he had disobeyed God by hitting a rock, instead of speaking to the rock, to get water out of it for the thirsty people.

And Abraham – world renowned for his call from God that he would be the father of many nations: He was aged about one hundred, and his wife Sarah was about ninety years old – and they had no children. After a while Abraham got fed up with waiting for God and had a child via one of his slaves. God forgave him, and eventually he and Sarah had a son of their own – Isaac. But the slave's son and Sarah's son were always at enmity with one another – hence we have the Arabs and the Jews – all descended from their father Abraham, and still enemies.

King David – he wrote many of the Psalms, and God deeply loved him: But David was far from perfect. He committed adultery, organised the murder of the woman's husband, and eventually married her. God was greatly displeased. But King David sorted out his life and in spite of mistakes became a world famous leader, and mightily used by God.

God calls men and women of faith to work for him. They may well have many personal problems to overcome. We all have – and we are all on a journey in our lives: just like John Bunyan's wonderful book Pilgrim's Progress.

While I was living at Hillwood Cottage I was asked by the pastoral team to talk with two ministers whose ministries were in jeopardy because of their personal lives.

One minister who came to Post Green Community for help was very well known and had a huge ministry. He was in danger of losing it all because of muddles in his personal life. Dave Holland and I were assigned to meet with him and he felt free to confess what was going on. We gently got alongside him and helped him sort it all out and gave him guidelines so that it couldn't ruin his ministry in the future. He took notice of what we advised, and set up a support structure, and I still see his name in the Christian press today –and he's holding his ministry together and is being used to help many people.

Another minister came for help, together with his wife, and Rev Graham Cyster and I were asked to spend time with them both, listening to them and again setting out guidelines for the way forward. This particular minister heard what we said but refused to take our advice. Later the marriage collapsed and because of unwise things he did I think he had to leave his church.

Choices! We all have choices in life! Sometimes to go the way we know our conscience tells us, is the harder way to go. And we hope that we can continue on the other route and it won't matter. But to go the "narrow way" as Jesus called it, is by far the better route to take and in the end the joy and satisfaction comes in the knowledge we have done what is right.

But some people feel they have no choice. They find themselves compelled to act in a certain way even though they want to behave better. Because we lived with so many people we soon found out who we enjoyed living with, who was fun to be with, and who was very hard work to be with.

Despite a huge amount of counselling some people seemed totally stuck in a habit pattern or a mode of behaviour which spoilt their lives and prevented them from living life to the full, especially within their household or job.

After David had been gone a few months I became very concerned for him and his welfare, and telephoned Dr Frank Lake, a well-known doctor of psychiatry as well as a medical doctor and a missionary. I explained who I was and that I was part of Post Green Community, and that I needed some advice regarding my husband, the Rev David Mills. He immediately seemed most interested.

"Look, Daphne, as it happens I will be down in Dorset next week. I will phone you when I am there and see if I can come across to see you all. I have always wanted to visit Post Green!" Frank Lake said.

True to his word he telephoned the following week and came over to chat with me and to talk to the leadership of the community and the pastoral leaders in particular.

He gave me names of helpful people David could talk to in British Columbia, Canada, which I passed onto David. David pursued this and made a couple of visits to see a psychologist over near Vancouver, which was quite a distance away from where he was living in Victoria. He found it wasn't practical because of long distances involved for a regular appointment. A year or so later, while David was in England, he visited Frank Lake and spent a weekend with him. Obviously the meetings were confidential, but when I saw Frank Lake afterwards, he was utterly compassionate towards David. I understood from Frank that David had huge problems stemming from very early on in his life. David continued to work hard on sorting himself out over the following years.

Frank began to come to Post Green on a regular basis for several years after that. He helped the community solve the mystery of why some people seemed totally stuck and unable to move on from some habit pattern that was spoiling their lives.

Frank Lake explained his own personal journey in his professional career, especially when he got into psychiatry. Through various drugs and techniques he had helped people to remember episodes in their very early childhood – with some success. But some people found they still hadn't got to the root of their problems. Then Frank had managed to help people get back to the point of their birth. If the birth had been traumatic – such as the umbilical cord around their neck, forceps delivery, Caesarean birth, premature birth – this could have a detrimental effect on the person's life through a well-hidden, sub-conscious feeling they couldn't get a handle on and therefore couldn't deal with.

Once these memories surfaced they could be talked through and prayed about and the person found themselves free of something that had bothered them all their lives.

Frank then told us stories of episodes that had happened in a mother's life while she was pregnant. On counselling that person years later it was discovered that there was a link between the episode that happened to the mother and the effect it had on the unborn child much later in their life. This is understood more today than it was in the 1980s when it was rather disbelieved: that anything could affect a baby in the womb and all outside influences began after the birth.

Frank discovered a way of deep breathing, prayer, and speaking to a person, while lying in a foetal position, that released the memories from the womb. Almost all the community eventually opted to go through this experience. I think most of us were greatly helped and discovered why we felt the way we did about certain things that defied logic.

For me, although I thought I would discover no interesting issues at all, I found that I had a battle to survive in the womb and was immensely lonely. In fact I felt abandoned. This continued in early birth and influenced the way I shut out a lot of my emotions until I was about twelve. It was only after doing this primal work that I found I was free of this horrid feeling of being abandoned.

I could tell many wonderful stories of how people were helped when they did their "primal" work, but they are not my stories to tell in this book. Many people in the community found their lives changed for the better – and I wish that it was more available today for anyone who finds themselves stuck in a habit pattern or negative memory that seems to have no logical source to it.

Primal therapy, as we all called it, became a vital tool within the community; it was always done lovingly, caringly and with much prayer. The week before we discovered about primal therapy the community was meeting for its weekly get-together. Susan read out a scripture from the book of Isaiah. She said she thought God was about to reveal treasures to us, though she didn't know how or what they were! This is what Susan read out:

"I will give you the treasures in darkness and the hoards in secret places."

Isaiah says, in the same passage: "I will go before you and level the mountains. I will break in pieces the doors of bronze and cut asunder the bars of iron.... that you may know that it is I, the Lord, the God of Israel, who call you by your name." Isaiah chapter 45, verses 2,3.

That prophecy came true for most of us in the community who had the opportunity to pursue our pre-birth experiences and receive healing from areas that had remained hidden behind locked doors, as it were.

To get rid of this horrid feeling of being abandoned, was such a release for me, and I gladly worked with others to help them on their journey of healing and restoration too.

CHAPTER TWENTY NINE

Secretarial temping continued to be very interesting but also scary and eventually I settled into a permanent full time job with Sovereign Kitchens. I did book keeping (my mother quickly taught me over a weekend after I had been given the job!) and typed quotes for new kitchens and did the wages. Initially all the wages were paid in cash on a Friday lunch time. This was quite thrilling for me! Jenny Cobb and I would work out what every person had earned – totting up timesheets and sorting out how many hours they worked. Then having worked out the total sum, Jenny would go off to the Bank. On returning back within the hour, we spread out all the money on the desks, spread out all the wage packets, and proceeded to fill each little brown bag with the right money. We never sealed the packets until we made sure everything balanced.

Sometimes the men would argue about the money – it might have been an overtime disagreement or occasionally it was a nasty lump sum taken off for tax – either way we couldn't give them more money and so we learnt to placate, calm them down and bring peace.

One Friday Jenny and I worked together as usual. Jenny left me to stuff the wage packets while she got on and sorted out the petty cash. "Hey, Jenny – look at all this money we've got left over!" There was a wad of notes still sitting on the desk. Jenny reached over, and swiftly counted the notes.

"Two thousand pounds!" Jenny exclaimed. "Are you sure you've put the wages in all the envelopes? Oh, that's ridiculous! You could never have £2000 left over anyway!"

We looked at one another wondering what to do. "I'll phone the bank clerk who always serves me. I'll see if she's missing any money!" Jenny said, and proceeded to dial the bank. She asked for the clerk by name. She said she would check and phone back. Ten minutes later the clerk phoned. "I've made a terrible mistake! I'm two thousand pounds short! Look could you bring it back right away. I will be in terrible trouble if it's found out. I'll meet you in the bank car park, say in twenty minutes."

Jenny agreed, and stuffing the two thousand pounds in her handbag, walked out of the office, jumped in her car, and roared off down the street. I was left with all the unstuck wage envelopes!

In about forty minutes Jenny returned. "She was waiting in the car park, looking really uptight. I gave her the two thousand pounds and she stuffed it up her jumper, thanked me very profusely and slipped in through their back door!"

Jenny and I were the only women to work at Sovereign Kitchens. It was a bit daunting having to walk through the factory looking for someone needed on the telephone, but I got used to it in the end. It was a very different environment from working at a Christian establishment – no Morning Prayers for starters. To walk through the factory your eyes would be inundated with girlie calendars and pin-ups on all the walls.

One year when Bryan Cobb was particularly busy and had forgotten that the Calendar man was coming, he asked if I would choose the two calendars needed for next year: one girlie calendar and one with local views.

The Calendar man duly arrived and it took no time at all to pick out a nice calendar with local scenes. Half the job done! "Now, we've got some really good classy pictures for the blokes for this year!" says the Calendar man. He proceeded to rummage in his large briefcase and fish out about six girlie calendars. He then proceeded to show me each picture – January to December – with various girls in bikinis, half topless, all topless and nude. "So which do you think?" he says after showing them all to me. I had tried to memorise the least revealing of all the half dressed and topless girls, and picked that calendar.

"That one seems nice!" I murmured.

"Okay! Same heading as last year?" the salesman said, happily.

"Yes, same wording as last year, thanks." I replied.

He happily packed up his calendars and popped them into his brief case and waved goodbye.

That evening I was due to go to supper at Post Green. I arrived at six o'clock, as the gong was just sounding. There were about twelve of us sat around the dining table: I just happened to be sitting next to Gershom, an Arch Deacon from the Anglican Church in Tanzania. We hardly had time for our first mouthful of food when Gershom chattily went around the table asking everyone what they had done that day. I was horrified! One or two had met with some clergy to arrange a visit to a parish church weekend, a couple more had been counselling someone. Someone else was busy writing a book, and someone else writing Bible study notes. I was very aware that if I told Gershom exactly what I had been doing he would have been a bit surprised.

When Gershom turned to me to ask what I had done, I tamely said, "Just ordinary office work, oh and choosing next year's company calendar!" I could see all the partially nude girls in my memory but luckily the subject wasn't pursued. How life had changed for me!

Even though I was no longer a member of the community, I was still asked to do quite a lot of outreach, and also take seminars at the camps. It was good still to be involved and I felt the hand of God on my life. For the first time ever I had to stand totally on my own feet, earning enough money to support myself and pay all household bills. I had to buy myself a car and make sure it was maintained properly. I had to learn how to check oil, water and tyres. Here, Abigail's husband Gary was hugely helpful, either checking things when they came to visit or showing me how to do it for myself.

When I moved out of Hillwood Cottage I was giving accommodation to a student who was working on the Lytchett Minster Caravan Site that we ran as a community. Mary Ann was a student at a teacher training college, but had fallen apart during her teaching practice. Devastated, she had taken time off and was doing voluntary work at Post Green. She was a simply lovely person and we got on well together. Her visit coincided with my move to Vetlanda, a bungalow in Upton, two miles away. She helped pack things up and we moved together.

Smarty Pants, the cat, moved with us. I felt sorry for Smarty Pants being on his own while we were out at work, so I bought a lovely Siamese Colour Point kitten. But Smarty Pants was very cross, and walked up and down the piano keys making a huge noise to express his annoyance. Abigail came to the rescue and took Smarty Pants off to Gosport. And Sheri stayed with me.

Faith Lees phoned and asked to chat with me about a girl needing a home. So I drove up to Post Green and listened to what she said. "Okay, I hear you! Nancy (not her real name) has had problems but is mostly over them, and needs a loving stable place to stay?"

"Yes. She will pay her way and we will give her some voluntary work up at Post Green, to occupy her," said Faith.

So the deal was struck and Nancy moved in with Mary Ann and me.

Within three days I felt I had to bring the subject up with Mary Ann, who was only about twenty years old, but I was beginning to think I might be going mad!

"Is it my imagination, Mary Ann, or is the bathroom light going on and off all night? And I keep thinking I can hear the cistern hissing in the loft above my bed, hour after hour at night!"

"Well, I didn't like to say anything to you, but I think Nancy is up most of the night – just going to the bathroom!" she offered in reply.

"Well what could she be doing?"

Mary Ann shrugged her shoulders at my question. "I don't know but it does disturb me at night!"

We both agreed to keep an eye on the situation. Nancy loved cooking cakes for other people, and would wash up but never dry up and put things away. So I would come back from work to find the draining board stacked high with clean drip-drying baking pans and utensils.

“Nancy, be a dear, and put the things away when you have finished, please!” I requested several times with no result.

Nancy was reluctant to pull her weight around the house when it came to housework and cleaning. But on Sunday evenings, while we were watching television, Nancy would get up and furtively put out the garbage in black bin liners on the front lawn ready for collection the next day. I was always mystified as to why she chose to do that job!

One day Nancy left for Post Green earlier than usual. I was about to get into my car to drive off to work, when I realised the dustmen hadn’t collected the bags yet. I counted five large bin bags on the lawn. The maximum we ever put out was two! So out of curiosity I checked the bags. They were all tightly tied up. But I quickly untied them – three bags contained wads of Kleenex tissues.

“Ah!” I thought to myself. “Poor Nancy really does have a severe problem!”

That night I managed to raise the subject with her. Nancy totally denied any problem at all – I didn’t let her know I knew about the vast number of tissues she was using. I persisted, very gently, in enquiring about the water running most of the night. By this time the bathroom light was left on all night so we didn’t hear it click on and off all the time!

Eventually Nancy confessed that she couldn’t get her hands clean. “As soon as I’ve washed my hands, and turned off the tap, they are dirty again. So I have to wash the taps and start again. Then if I touch the door handle, my hands get dirty again, so I have to re-wash them. I dry my hands on tissues as that’s cleaner than a towel which has already been used.”

“Look, Nancy. It’s okay! I’m sorry! I don’t mind you washing your hands all the time, but please don’t be furtive about it. Don’t creep around the house as that doesn’t give a good atmosphere. Try and be open with yourself and with Mary Ann and me!”

“Oh, I will. I will. I’ve only had the problem since I got back from the East. I wore sandals and the streets were filthy. And we went into temples and took our shoes off. I’ve felt unclean ever since.”

Nancy tried. I talked to Faith and other pastoral people for support, but Nancy’s problem increased to such an extent it was taking our house over. Nancy became more furtive in her behaviour and when she began to cause misunderstandings between me and pastoral people at Post Green, I felt it was time to ask her to go. It was a painful decision, but she needed expert help, and as Mary Ann had left to go back home, I was on my own with a very disturbed woman.

She moved away but had long term counselling at Post Green for many years to come, especially after she married and had children. The only way to keep the marriage together was constant chats with Faith, Carolyn and Gerry.

I wasn't on my own long! I was again asked if I would have someone who had had a breakdown and needed somewhere to stay. I was assured she was all sorted out and steady again. I later found out she had been suicidal, and wouldn't speak!

That was a bad button to press for me. I am not good if someone ignores me, especially for days at a time! In the end I said to Jennifer (not her real name), "Look, I understand you don't want to speak to me; but I'm going to ask you to do something very simple. Please say "Hello" at the start of the day, "Goodbye" when you are going out. Oh, and "Goodnight" when you retire for the night. I also need to know if you are in or out for meals. So could you just say I'm in for supper tonight, or not?"

Jennifer nodded. "I will try."

We managed to have some really nice conversations but they were few and far between. Jennifer still seemed to find it impossible to speak most days even to offer a greeting or farewell. After living like that for several months I was nearly in despair. I decided to put a bit of pressure on her one day – not a gentle, please speak to me talk, but a demand that if she wants to carry on living with me she must speak! Just the basic courtesy of hello and goodbye! She got very angry and swept all the things off my desk and having gone a bit wild, began to run out of the front door. I managed to grab her jumper and held on – after it had stretched about twice its length, she gave in and ran into the lounge and sat down. I telephoned Post Green and Tom came immediately.

Tom was totally brilliant with Jennifer, and knew more of her past history than I did. But he did tell her it was unfair and not liveable with, if she wouldn't speak to me.

Eventually it was agreed that she would catch a train the next day and return home for a while. She left her belongings behind, and after a few weeks asked me to put them on the train for her, packed into her trunk. Although we left on good terms, she refused to pay the carriage price for her trunk!

It's one thing to help people with personal problems in a community type situation, but it is not easy when one is living on one's own. There is power in God's people gathered together in a worshipping praying environment. People with special problems need a group around them, all telling them the same thing in a loving way. Because I was on my own it was all too easy for them to attack me verbally, rather than face into their problems and be healed.

Vetlanda became more of a home again, even though it was just the cat, Sheri and me. Vetlanda was a lovely three bed bungalow, with huge great windows facing south west. The French windows opened up onto a sheltered garden, with a gate at the bottom. The gate led through woodland and down onto a beach, part of Poole harbour. It was very peaceful and beautiful all the year round. I thought I would be there till I retired and beyond!

But you never know what is round the corner!

After a few months I saw an advert in a shop window in the village, a young girl wanting accommodation. I wasn't so keen on living on my own, so I phoned her up and she came to see me the following day after work. She was an orphan, and had been brought up in a children's home. I really enjoyed her company and we got on excellently. Her name was Ellen Maxwell.

Her brother lived nearby with his wife and family, so Ellen used to visit them quite often. Ellen lived with me for a year or more, and we never had any problems – though I did need to rescue her a few times when she was stuck somewhere with no buses or trains. She loved the Fun Fair, and always dreamed of joining it one day. I've lost touch with her now but would love to know how she is doing.

By now I had trained as a Fashion Colour analyst. This suited my creative nature and I loved helping people find the best colours. Having found the colours that best suited them I would put the right coloured make-up on their faces, and send them home looking beautiful! I had hundreds of clients over several years, including working with some quite large groups that would come to my studio at Vetlanda.

Various clubs, churches, groups would also book me and I would do demonstrations, using one or two people picked out of the audience usually by the chair person. I was also asked to do a consultation with a Reverend Mother and sort out her best colours for new clothes, as the Convent was choosing to come out of their habits. Then she invited me to come up to the convent in north Dorset to sort out the best colours for her nuns to wear. They had given up their black robes, and had gone down to the market and come back with an assortment of new gaily coloured clothes. But they had no idea of colours or matching outfits, and the first experience of clothes buying proved disastrous! Once I had sorted out their colours and given them colour swatches they went shopping again with confidence, and much laughter.

One of the most difficult demonstrations I did was a Clergy Wives Day! I got severely barracked by two or three of the wives, who thought that make-up was sinful and had no place in the church. I firmly defended the use of make-up and said that Christians should look as lovely as they possibly could. Certain scriptures sprung to mind that I managed to quote in the rather emotionally charged atmosphere. I spoke more calmly than I felt. The Bishop's wife who had invited me to do the demonstration, laughed afterwards when I asked why she didn't rescue me from these female dragons. "I thought you were handling them perfectly well without my interference!" she said.

Two friends, Gerry and Carolyn, in the Community had suggested the change of career to me. They thought it would suit my artistic personality and love of colour. Most of my colour analysis skills were learnt in Canada, although Abigail taught me the cosmetic side.

Tessa, Nick and I had flown out to Canada together. Tessa and Nick were going to visit David who lived somewhere north of Victoria on Vancouver Island.

I was going to visit my friend Karen and her husband Brian in Victoria. We parted at the airport on Vancouver Island. David was there to meet Tessa and Nick. And Karen had come to fetch me. We had been travelling for nearly twenty-four hours and were quite tired.

Karen explained to me that her mother was very ill in hospital and had just come out of theatre. Would I mind diverting via the hospital? Of course I said that was fine. We drove to the hospital and Karen's mother Violet was out of theatre and the doctor was waiting to talk to Karen. He told her that her mother was very ill with cancer. It was inoperable.

The following day we discovered that overnight they had had to resuscitate Violet and had broken some of her ribs, so she was alive but in a lot of pain.

I had booked to stay two or three weeks, and planned to travel back to England with Tessa and Nick on our pre-booked return flight. But Karen was very upset about her mother, and begged me not to go back until after her mother had died. Her mother rallied, though remained in hospital and did not die for another three months. Karen and I visited almost every day until she died. I stayed with Karen for the funeral and the sorting out of her mother's belongings and furniture ready for the house sale.

It was a challenging time in one way but I did enjoy being with the family and spending time with Lisa and Christie, the two daughters, whom I had known since their births. They were brilliant musicians and life was full of music practices at all hours.

I flew back just before Christmas, having been in Canada since August. But during that time I had asked Karen about "Colour Me Beautiful" and what it was all about, and she took me to a nearby shopping mall. We both got our wardrobe colours sorted out and were told what make-up would suit us. I was so impressed, having worn the wrong colours for most of my life, I decided to pursue it and set up my own business in England. As it happened the people supplying the colour wallets in Canada were trying to get into the English market and made me their main agent.

There was only one downside to the job – you only see the client once! Then they are sorted out for life! So I constantly had to find new clients, advertising and by recommendation. And I missed getting to know people, like one would if one was seeing the same people regularly. So I also did some more secretarial temping and twice worked at Tessa's office, where she worked for a local newspaper.

CHAPTER THIRTY

It was the day of my fiftieth birthday and it was also speedway night. April 1988! As often as I could, for many years, I had gone to Poole Speedway on a Wednesday evening.

I thought speedway was left behind in my childhood, but when we lived at Panorama, Lytchett Matravers, one of our household Ric Foxley had got chatting with our neighbour over the front hedge. I had seen him at a distance but never chatted with him. Ric discovered that he, Jack Knott, came from Southampton and that his father Charlie Knott used to run Southampton Speedway, as well as the Southampton ice rink, and greyhound racing. He also discovered that our neighbour's father had known my father very well.

So I went next door to introduce myself – and he said I could go for free any week I wanted, and have a seat in the Directors' Box. David and I took him up on his offer the following week. To my great surprise a close friend of my father's, whom we called Uncle Charles was also in the Directors' Box. I was so excited.

The first race started: four riders revving up at the start gate – the tapes go up and they are off! Sixty miles an hour around an oval track and no gears or brakes! The sound and the smell took me right back to some wonderful times as a child! I was hooked once more.

Then gradually my children got keen on speedway, especially the two girls! Years later Tessa managed to get a press pass from her newspaper as long as we did a report. So we took it in turns to stand on the green in the centre of the track, and then wrote a report afterwards.

Later Abigail became hooked and through a girl friend at speedway met her future husband Gary Mears, a sub-mariner in the Navy. Gary got involved in helping as a mechanic in the pits in his spare time, and we began to get to know the riders a bit.

Abigail phoned me: "Happy Birthday Mum! We will be down in time for supper before speedway as usual. What are you wearing tonight? Make sure you've got your jeans on!"

I was suspicious, as Abigail wasn't usually interested in what I wore to speedway. They duly arrived, with baby Jenna, now three years old. After a quick supper we drove off to the stadium. At half time, during the interval, an announcement came over the loudspeakers: "Congratulations to Daphne Mills on her fiftieth birthday. If she would like to make her way to the pits she will be given a lap of honour by one of the riders!"

Abi was laughing - as she had organised it all. I ran round to the pits, and was introduced to Gary Allan, the New Zealand Speedway Champion. I hopped on the back of his bike, and he rode out of the pits and onto the track. "You'd better wave to the crowd as we go round!" he said in his southern accent! So I clung on with one hand around his waist, and wave rather sheepishly to the huge crowd at the stadium. I think we went around twice, and then drove into the pits again, and my moment of glory was over!

As well as a surprise ride on a speedway bike, Tessa, Nigel and Abigail organised a surprise birthday party. I was sent off to Tessa's house to pick up something for her baby Robert. Young Jenna came with me. We had about ten miles to travel, so I sang some Fisherfolk children's songs for Jenna. This led into quite a deep conversation with her on our way back in the car, and I then asked Jenna: "Do you know who Jesus is?"

"Yes, Jesus is God!" was her very firm reply. That was an amazingly perceptive answer for a three year old! Sometimes I think children are able to accept the truth simply and straightforwardly, with no hang-ups. Some adults find it much harder!

When we got back to the house, it was full of people, food and drink! We all had a wonderful time and it was a lovely memorable birthday for me.

That was in April. A month later Gary Allan, the New Zealand speedway rider, had a terrible crash, hitting the safety fence at the stadium at full speed. The accident looked very bad, and it was a long time before he was picked up off the track and stretchered into a waiting ambulance and taken to Poole Hospital. His father, a retired speedway rider, was in England, though the family now lived in Australia.

A few days later I was due to go away on holiday, and Abigail phoned me from Gosport and asked if I would mind lending my bungalow, Vetlanda, to Gordon Allan, while his son was in hospital. Of course I said yes. I drove into Poole and visited Gary in the hospital. He had a broken leg. I left a front door key with Gary and told him I'd made a bed up for Gordon in the spare room.

Then I went off on a two week holiday. When I got back home, I went into visit Gary and see if I could meet up with Gordon, who was obviously still in residence at Vetlanda. Gary's bed was not just empty – it was gone! A nurse saw me hesitate in the doorway. "Have you come to visit Gary Allan? Are you a relative?"

"Yes, where's Gary gone?" my heart was in my mouth! "I'm not a relative, but his father is living at my house!"

The nurse said: "Unfortunately Gary has had an episode and we are trying to locate his father."

I had no idea what an episode was but it sounded serious. I offered to wait by the hospital entrance and try and intercept Gordon before he got a shock and found Gary and bed gone.

On walking to the hospital entrance I saw Gordon making his way up the hill from the town. I waited until he was closer then went to meet him. I explained the situation, and Gordon instantly looked very worried. We both hastened to intensive care.

"The problem is that Gary is allergic to iodine, which is the substance we use to try and trace whatever is causing the problem. We think it is possibly a bone fragment that is loose in his blood stream." The nurse said.

Over the following crucial hours Gary had to be resuscitated four times. I decided to go and find the hospital chapel and pray in the quietness and away from the stress of the emergency on the ward. As I walked along the corridor outside intensive care, I bumped into a friend who worked in the hospital theatre.

"Hello, Daphne! Whatever are you doing here?" Peter said.

"I'm here with Gary Allan." I told him.

Peter stood and stared at me for a moment, hesitating. Then he said: "You know he's not expected to last the night, don't you?"

"I know things are very serious. Please pray! I don't think he's meant to die yet!" I smiled at him. Peter was obviously busy, but he promised to pray and he would get his wife, Sue to pray as well. I had known Sue since Fountain Trust days when I had met her at Ashburnham Place at one of the conferences there. It was wonderful still to be in touch after all these years.

I found the chapel, and prayed for a while. I was sure that Gary's life hung by a thread; but it wasn't time for him to die yet – but a battle had to be won, and the only way to win it was by prayer.

I walked slowly back to the ward. The atmosphere was tense. I was told the doctor in charge was talking to a hospital in London about a possible chemical, other than iodine, that would show up where the problem lay. Gordon said he would stay till late evening and get something to eat in the canteen. It was May, and the evenings were getting lighter – summer was upon us and the warm fresh air greeted me as I walked out of the hospital.

What a home-coming from my lovely holiday. I had some telephoning to do when I reached home: I needed to get as many people praying as possible – day and night for the next few days, but crucially for this very night. I telephoned Post Green and asked if everyone could pray for Gary Allan, an injured speedway rider, aged twenty, not expected to live the night. I telephoned a few other friends who I knew were faithful prayer warriors. Then I phoned my friends Brian and Karen in Canada. While we sleep they are awake – they are eight hours behind us on the clock! That would mean we could still have people praying while we were asleep.

Prayers were answered. The crisis passed. When Gary saw me next he said, "I know I've been very ill – I saw a man in a black cloak, and a black hood, standing at the bottom of my bed!"

I thought to myself, "That wasn't Jesus!" – it confirmed to me that there had been a real battle with "death" – and Gary had survived, thanks to God answering many people's prayers. Months later I told Gary what had happened – he was very moved and amazed.

As Gary began to recover he made friends with many nurses, and while he was asleep they painted his toe nails. So Gary, feeling powerless, asked me to bring in a child's water pistol; this I did and Gary had great fun using it on the nurses who were playing jokes on him.

Gary fell deeply in love with one of the nurses. I didn't know this until the day I went to fetch him from the hospital – the day before being "let out", Gary was absolutely jubilant. But as I went up to the ward, Gary was definitely in an unhappy mood. He asked me to take his bag, but he wasn't ready to come home yet. He wouldn't say much else, but I gathered later that the nurse he had fallen in love with was off duty that day. He was hoping she would come back later in the day.

Gary was on medication and needed to be near the hospital. Gordon planned to stay around for awhile before returning to Australia. Luckily I had two spare bedrooms, and re-organised my studio so they could use both spare bedrooms.

As soon as Gary arrived at Vetlanda, hobbling in on his crutches, he took out a video of the speedway meeting when he had crashed. He spun through the video till he found his crash – then he watched it and watched it – yelling out the first few times he saw it, re-living it all!

The following day, with permission from me to move into Vetlanda for the rest of the season, Gary and Gordon went back to Weymouth and got their stuff. I think they were up two floors so it took quite a while to load the van. They brought back Gary's two speedway bikes, then asked if they could tidy up and clear out my garage for the bikes and all the tools they needed, plus a work bench.

It took no time at all for them to turn the garage into a workshop, and despite his leg being in plaster, Gary worked hard tuning his bikes, cleaning his bikes, and eventually starting them up.

"Hey, Daphne, I'm gonna start the bike up again in a minute! Want a ride?" I stood on the front door step watching Gary kick the bike into action. "Go on, get on it! That's the throttle – don't forget there's no brake!"

Probably one of my great ambitions in life had been to ride a speedway bike – here I was at fifty years of age – just about to have a second ride on a speedway bike – but this time it was solo, not pillion!

I sat astride it. Gary stepped aside. The throb of the engine underneath me reminded me how very powerful the engine was! I opened the throttle, slowly, gently, and coasted down the driveway, turning right onto the road. I opened the throttle up some more and roared off down the road – the sound of a speedway engine is unique and easily recognisable. I'm sure the neighbours were staring out of their windows! When I could see the end of the road I put my feet down on the tarmac, closing the throttle and slowing the bike up. I turned it round at the end of the road, doing a u-turn, and rode back. I thought Gary would be anxiously waiting on the pavement, but he was back in the garage tinkering with his other bike, totally trusting me to take care of his precious machine!

Gordon felt it safe to leave Gary and return to Australia. Gary had been trying to persuade the managers of Poole Speedway to let him ride as soon as his plaster was off, but they were not happy for this to happen. Gary spent hours on the phone arguing with them. In the meantime his romance was blossoming. Claire was a frequent visitor to our house and we quickly became the best of friends.

At the end of the speedway season in October, Gary left to return to Australia. Before leaving, he asked if he could continue to stay at Vetlanda when the new speedway season started up again in March the following year. The five months sped by and in no time at all Gary was back again, re-tuning his speedway bike engines, and gearing up for the new season.

Claire was living at the nurses' home attached to Poole hospital, but continued to visit when off duty.

For several years I had been going to the Early Bird swimming session at Queen Elizabeth School in Wimborne. Stephen Budd, who was helping out at Post Green, often came with me – I would pick him up on my way. He was living with Tom Lees' sister Jane in her house opposite Post Green. When Gary found out where I was going at seven in the morning he decided to come too. We had great fun, but sadly all this was about to end.

CHAPTER THIRTY ONE

Even though I was no longer a member of The Community of Celebration at Post Green, I still continued to keep in close contact with everyone and to go to chapel each evening. But one night I had a dream: in the dream I saw Faith Lees crying, and when I asked her what was the matter she said, "Graham Pulkingham thinks he's right but I think I'm right. I'm sure I'm right!" The dream was very vivid. As it happened I found myself sitting next to Tom Lees that evening at Chapel time. Afterwards I rather light-heartedly told Tom about my dream. He didn't laugh at all, but took my dream seriously and asked if I had told Faith. No, I hadn't! Tom said I should tell her the dream. But I didn't, as I presumed Tom would tell her if he thought it was important.

Not long after this, I happened to call into Post Green one evening, and the community were coming out of the drawing room, and several people were in tears, and others looked very glum. Some were talking and some were silently sombre.

I realised I had walked in on something, so quickly slipped off home.

Later I found out that the Community had split in two. The Community of Celebration were going to leave Post Green and find other accommodation elsewhere in the country. As I wasn't involved in the talks I don't know exactly what happened. I'm not sure what I should have done about my dream – probably gone and spoken to Faith, and certainly I should have prayed about the looming crisis.

I know Tom and Faith agonised over what was happening in the Community - it all came to a head, and the split happened. It then became like a divorce – dividing up the ministry, the property, the businesses, publications, files and photographic records. Even I got caught up in that, and agonised when I saw a friend, who was moving away with the Community of Celebration, burning historic photos and records that had been held in my graphics office. I was handed back the last of "The Road To Emmaus" and "Come Walk with Jesus" books that had not been sold. Later I was able to get back the copyright too.

In my heart I had known for years that there were two visions, overlapping, within the community.

Looking back at our outreach meetings to plan which invitations to accept and which to reject, I had known that we actually felt called, at times, to different ministries to the churches. Much of our ministry was one and the same – but some areas were different and always remained separate, though this seemed mostly unnoticed.

After many months the Community of Celebration left the area and moved to Surrey: some original Post Green people left with them. Some left the community and stayed in the area and got jobs.

Tom and Faith came to see me fairly soon after the split. They told me they were planning to re-start Post Green Community, and asked if I would like to rejoin! I was very glad and said "yes" immediately. It was only then, during the conversation, that they realised I had not left the Community of Celebration (Post Green) voluntarily, but had been asked to leave. They were very surprised and shocked. The two communities had almost equal numbers. Several original Fisherfolk/Community of Celebration people stayed at Post Green and joined the newly formed community.

Camps were planned for the coming summer, and even there the pain of the "divorce" was evident. People, being human, wanted to know what had happened and some took sides and a further "split" seemed to occur. When this happens there has to be much talking through, listening to each other, and most of all forgiveness and love.

I continued to do some teaching at camps and helped to run seminars.

At the end of May 1989 I was running the Holy Spirit seminars at camp. Fortunately I had asked Tom to help me run them, each afternoon, during the camp. The first afternoon went fairly well. The second afternoon for some reason I felt rather tired and wasn't so chatty. As Tom and I had worked together a lot, "blibbing and blobbing" – that is, taking it in turns to speak, Tom quickly filled in the gaps and the seminar went well. The last afternoon, the third in the session was very important. It was at this point that final questions were asked and answered and everyone was given the opportunity to be prayed for to receive the Holy Spirit for themselves – a precious and holy time. But on the last afternoon I was so unbelievably sleepy, I could hardly function. Tom did brilliantly and the seminar didn't suffer at all from my sleepy silence.

The following day I was still feeling very sleepy, but managed to say goodbye to campers and then we had a fun Goldie Hawn film that evening as a team so we could relax. I was very irritable and didn't enjoy it at all.

We had a couple of day's gap before the next camp. I thought I would have time to rest and recover before involving in the next camp. Leaving the film before it finished, I walked across the darkened camp field to my tiny little caravan. I was now the proud owner of a Thompson Mini Glen – a very tiny van with a double bunk, which in the day time became two double seats either side of a dining table. I was sharing the caravan with Carys, a lovely Welsh girl, who was doing children's work at the camp.

I made the bed in the caravan, by lowering the dining table onto its ledge and sliding the cushions down flat. I climbed into my sleeping bag, leaving a light on at the far end for Carys.

Next morning I joined in team prayers, and did one or two chores around the camp field, but I felt odd and tired, and my skin hurt. "I wonder if I have a temperature!"

I asked myself. I grabbed my car keys and walked over to the car park and drove back to Vetlanda, my lovely bungalow about four miles away.

Gary Allan was out, and the garage door firmly locked. I walked into the house, and found the thermometer in the bathroom cupboard. Sitting on the side of the bath I proceeded to take my temperature. 102.5 degrees – no wonder I felt ill. I wandered into the kitchen and made myself some coffee, and flopped down on the settee, gazing out of the patio doors onto the lawn and woodland beyond. I could just catch a sight of the sea shimmering in the sunlight through the trees. I was so relieved to lie down. In the Thompson Mini Glen I could only sit upright once the bed had been folded back. With Carys coming in and out, and other visitors to the caravan it had been impossible to lie down during the daytime.

I fell sound asleep. Gary returned home and walked into the lounge.

"Hi, Daphne, how you doing?" he said. I sat up and smiled, "Well to tell the truth, I'm not sure! I've got a temperature and feel sleepy!"

"Do you want a sandwich?" was Gary's response.

"No thanks, I think I might go to bed for a while. I just want to sleep!" I slid off the settee and decided to take my temperature again. It had gone even higher.

I climbed into bed and slept for an hour or two. On waking I came to the conclusion I was actually ill, but I didn't know what was wrong. Then I remembered camp – the caravan – my handbag and belongings still there – help!

I phoned East Holton farmhouse, near where the camp was being held. It was a community household. Howard answered the phone. "Hi, Howard it's Daphne here. Look, I've picked up some bug and have a very high temperature. I'm sure I won't be back for the next camp, so sorry. Can you tell Tom? Perhaps he could get someone else to help run the seminars with him? And sorry, I've left my handbag in the caravan and I might need it!"

Howard listened quietly. "Oh and could you please let Carys know that she's got the caravan to herself!"

"Oh, Daphne, I'm sorry. So sorry! I'll rescue your handbag and get someone to drop it into you – is there anything else you want?"

"No thanks! I will collect the rest when I fetch the caravan at the end of camp. But if you can drop my handbag back to me, could you also bring my Bible – it's in the caravan somewhere – it's got a blue denim cover with a picture embroidered on it, thanks!"

An hour later the door bell rang. There was Howard with the handbag and Bible. I apologised again for letting everyone down, and Howard left quickly to return to the camp field.

The days passed in a fog. My temperature remained high and I had a scratchy throat. No other symptoms and I didn't feel well enough to go up to the doctor. I slept and slept. I decided I had "sleeping sickness" whatever that was!

Gary continued working on his bikes, visiting Claire at the hospital, and riding speedway a couple of times a week – one home meeting and one away meeting.

I stayed in bed a lot of the time, sipping orange squash, and not much else.

Camp came to an end, in my absence.

The door bell rang. I slipped on my dressing gown and went to open it. It was Howard. I could see in the driveway behind him that my caravan was neatly parked, back home again!

"Oh thanks so much, Howard. That's very kind of you!"

"Are you feeling any better? You don't look too good!"

"Well I've got a bit of a sore throat, so I guess it's some flu thing! I'll be better soon!"

Howard handed me the keys to the caravan and waving goodbye walked back down the drive.

After another few days of high temperature and sore throat and supreme sleepiness I was beginning to get fed up.

I decided to take a leisurely bath and try to pull myself together. After ten minutes in the bath I realised that I had gone "blue". My inner arms, wrists, palms of my hands – blue. My first thought was "I've got leukaemia!"

I made an appointment to see the doctor, as at last I had proper symptoms! He did a blood test. I waited a week then phoned up for the result. “Yes, the results are in. But the doctor wants to see you!”

Later on that day I drove up to the surgery, and was told I had “Glandular Fever”.

“I’ll sign you off for a couple of weeks.” The doctor said, and handed me a sick certificate.

Two more weeks of illness, then I will be better! Great!

The sore throat got worse. By now June was nearly over. I was no better in July either. I kept telephoning Post Green and apologising for not turning up at the usual Monday Community evening.

I was still very sleepy, but the worst was the terrible sore throat, and a general feeling of being unwell. Gary still needed feeding, and handed me his monthly cheque for food and accommodation. On a good day, relatively speaking, I would go up to the supermarket, load the trolley up and push it to the counter. I was so weak! But would stagger back to the car and dump the bags in the boot and drive home. If Gary was around he would help off load the car. Once the food was stowed in the cupboards I would go back to bed, feeling terrible.

Halfway through August, the door bell rang.

I glanced out of the window and saw Tom’s car with a boat trailer behind it. I got out of bed and put on my dressing gown!

Tom was obviously surprised that I wasn’t up and dressed as it was late afternoon. “Are you not well?” he asked.

Then I was amazed! Did everyone at Post Green think I had been pretending to be ill, or what?

I explained I still had glandular fever. Tom could see I was really unwell, and said immediately, “You need looking after properly. You must move into Post Green. Come now and we will get a bed made up for you and you must come and stay till you’re better.”

This was too overwhelming! I was too weak to pack and sort myself out! And organise Gary! And who would look after the cat? But Tom was persuasive and insistent. He apologised and said he had no idea I was so ill. I agreed to come – tomorrow.

My dear friend, Stephen Budd, arrived just after Tom had gone. I explained my dilemma.

"Look, tell Gary tonight he will have to look after himself. Maybe Claire will come and look after him! He can feed the cat everyday and do the shopping. He's twenty-one now, he's a grown up! I will come back tomorrow at 10.30 in the morning and give you a lift up there. If you want your car later we can fetch it together."

"You're an angel, Stephen. Thanks so much!" I said.

Stephen used to come to speedway with me most weeks and we had a lovely platonic, brother/sister friendship that was a great blessing to me, and hopefully to him too.

The next morning Stephen arrived in his Citroen Deux Chevoux, and I squeezed in with my overnight bag and my lovely crochet blanket that went everywhere with me. I'd got some odd balls of wool, and decided that if I had energy while at Post Green I would enlarge it.

Once we arrived at Post Green I was greeted warmly, and told which bedroom I was assigned. It was in Grandpa Mills' previous lounge – now a very nice single bedroom. I had a balcony with a view of the garden and Poole Harbour in the distance. The whole move had exhausted me and I flopped onto the bed. My throat was still so sore I could hardly swallow. Faith usually brought my meals up to me, well-liquidised for the first couple of weeks, and then gradually I could swallow normal food. Eventually I got dressed and came downstairs for meals, which was wonderful.

There were some lovely guests staying at Post Green for a few months, so I had good company, when everyone else was out at work.

My mother telephoned one morning and said she was free to drive down from Rownhams House to see me, if I was up to it! I was very pleased. She phoned me at 9 a.m. At 9.50 a.m. there was a knock at the bedroom door. Faith put her head around the door. "Your mother's here!" she said. I couldn't help glancing at my watch again! How on earth did Mum get down all those stairs at Rownhams House (she now lived upstairs in her own flat since my father had died), walk all the way out to the garage, and drive through the New Forest in fifty minutes?

Mum walked in and sat down in the chair by the window and we had a good visit together.

Once I got to Post Green I was able to relax a bit. I was fed and watered and had no chores to do. I could rest completely.

A phrase kept buzzing around my head: "To thine ownself be true!"

The words were familiar, but I had no idea where they came from. Was it the Bible? I got out my concordance and hunted through – no – I don't think so.

Stephen Budd knocked on my bedroom door. "Hi, Daphne, I thought I would pop in and see if you need anything."

"Well, yes, actually, I need your brains!" I replied.

Stephen laughed. He had a degree in classics, and although very humble, he was a delight to be with, if you wanted intelligent conversation!

"Ah!" said Stephen, "What's up?"

"Well, I've got the phrase buzzing around my head, and I feel God is trying to say something to me. But I can't find where it's written or what the context is. It's "To thine own self be true." And I wondered if you knew where the phrase comes from."

"Yes, it's Shakespeare, so you won't find it in the Bible." Stephen then explained the phrase and context and added, "It's funny you should pick that phrase. I've got something for you – I won't be a moment."

Stephen walked out of the room, and clattered down the back staircase. I heard the outer door open and shut. Less than five minutes later Stephen was back, climbing the stairs two at a time.

"Look! I got given this the other day. It's a leaflet written by a nun, entitled "To Thine Own Self Be True". You can borrow it for a while." Stephen handed me the leaflet.

"Well, that's amazing! Thanks, Stevie. How brilliant! I will read it carefully. What's God trying to say, do you think?"

"Let me know when you find out, it might be useful for me too. I'm off home for my tea now. Jane was just cooking it when I ran back just now."

"Thanks again, Stevie, you're a wonder!" I laughed and he waved and ran back down the staircase. He was living at Jarvis – Tom sister Jane's house opposite Post Green. Jane had her own ministry in the area and especially at the prison at Portland. She came to all the meetings at Post Green that she could over the years, and at times put us to shame with her love and care for the "unloveable".

After Stephen had left I thought again about the phrase "to thine own self be true." It was good to have something to chew on – I needed something to think about, rather than the mess I was in! Mostly I was living day to day and not thinking about the future. I was mystified as to why I wasn't getting better, though some of the symptoms were easing. I still was very weak and I would only have a few days free of a sore throat before it would flare up again.

The nun's leaflet was helpful and encouraging. It was a reminder about how important it is not to compromise one's beliefs to please other people or to do anything that in your heart you know is not right. Only now as I write this am I beginning to see what God might have been saying to me. I half heard Him, while I was ill. But now looking back I think there was a relationship in my life that I should have walked away from and firmly shut the door.

As I mentioned earlier, there are different kinds of love: in the English language we mostly use the word "love" to cover a huge number of things – but in the Greek language there were different words to describe different "loves". Agapao, or agapao : God's love, and all encompassing love with no hidden agenda, a high, devoted love ; a true deep love that is given freely at all times. Phileo: brotherly love, or love for a friend – which is a more humble type of love. Eros: erotic love, a physical attraction between men and women. The perfect marriage would have all three types of loves.

I remember saying to Faith once: "Love is love!" if you love someone, you love them! To counsel someone over many months or even years demands love. To keep up a friendship over many years demands love. To be married to someone demands love, through thick and thin!

But I gradually learnt over the coming years that some friendships or relationships can be "toxic" relationships. In other words, whether there is love or not, that relationship is doing you no good, and probably isn't doing the other person any good either. Sometimes it is appropriate to walk away and move on.

When one has lived in a loving community for many years it is hard to walk away from a relationship. It makes you feel "selfish" and "unloving". This is where one needs to analyse very carefully where the friendship is going and if it still needs to continue – and if it is causing one or both people a lot of hurt. Sometimes it is a worthy thing to hang in there, constantly forgive, and keep working at it. But sometimes a wise friend and counsellor would say:"Enough is enough – it's time to move on."

Just because there are some good times, friendly times, creative times, in a relationship, doesn't mean it must continue. If there is an area where one could call it "toxic" – even if it rears its head only occasionally, it is time to have a very good look at it.

I admit now that I was in such a situation while I was ill. It had a sufficient comfort zone in the midst of the toxins for me to allow it to continue. Every time I felt it was time to let go I would tell myself that I would give the relationship one more chance! After a hundred chances and eleven years, I let go, with great relief, mingled with a little sadness. This had been a relationship with someone outside the Community but a friendship that had started in my teens. I wrote the following poem about this time:

Lord, your waves and billows have gone over me.

The rock on the shore is you – is me

Cemented together:

You protecting me

From your holy judgement

And awesome Majesty.

Alone, I would be

Scrunched into sand,

And scattered on the shore,

And lost to the waves.

But Your Love surrounds me,

In the presence of your Son.

The clouds are heavy with storm and rain,

And darken the tumbling, tumultuous waves.

Yet your Light shines through,

As the sun dispels the darkness

And my Rock begins

To feel its warmth, its presence, its healing.

Stay with me, Lord,

Till I am clean and whole once more.

(December 2nd 1990) Daphne Mills.

Eventually while convalescing at Post Green I began to go home for a while each day and come back for meals. Then I felt well enough to manage on my own. The doctors had long since given up on me and refused to give me sick certificates. The exhaustion I felt was ghastly. The doctor insisted I went back to work.

I didn't have the energy to run my business of fashion colour analysis so found a job working for a travel agent – just sitting at a desk all day typing – at least it would be money coming in, and surely I could sit and type? I typed holidaymakers' tickets all morning including eleven carbon copies, so no room for mistakes. I typed slowly and carefully. At lunch time I staggered back to my car in the car park in Bournemouth, ate my sandwiches and tipped the seat back and tried to rest. At 2 o'clock I was back at my desk – more tickets to type. At the end of the afternoon I handed in all the tickets and walked very slowly back to the car. The telephone was ringing as I got indoors.

"Daphne Mills?"

"Yes," I said tiredly.

"This is Baxton Travel (not it's real name). I've spoken to Mr Baxton. He's seen your work today, and I'm afraid he doesn't want you to work for him: your work isn't up to standard. So don't come back tomorrow. I will make sure you get paid for today – a cheque for seventeen pounds will be in the post at the end of the week."

I was utterly shocked. One of my friends, Margaret Mather from Post Green, came down immediately I phoned her. She knew what an excellent typist I was, and how many books and teaching leaflets I had typed over the years. But she was also a pastorally caring person. After I told her of the day's events and had cried a bit, she consoled me and said she didn't think I was well enough to work anyway.

In my heart of hearts I knew this to be true. I had had a huge struggle to walk from the car park to the travel agent and back again, and working in the office had felt unreal. I also knew that my brain was half asleep, not ever having recovered from glandular fever. I relaxed for a few days and eagerly awaited my precious cheque for seventeen pounds!

An old friend from Post Green, working now as a vicar in London, telephoned me and said he was taking a day off to visit Dorset.

"I can't wait to get out onto the Purbeck Hills. Do you want a day out, Daphne? I'll be down by ten o'clock if you can meet the train. I will treat you to a meal out, if you use your car!"

Next day I met Andy off the train. He was bright eyed and bushy tailed and ready for his trip into the hills. "I thought we could park the car at Corfe Castle, wander around there, and then walk along the footpath towards Swanage, or something?" he said enthusiastically.

"Andy, I can't manage that! I told you I hadn't been well."

"That was ages ago. What's the matter now?" he asked as we crossed over the road to the car.

"I'm still ghastly tired, and my limbs ache, and my mind is a fog! I never got better from glandular fever, though I have longer gaps between sore throats." I explained.

"Well, I know what's wrong with you! You've got M.E. My girlfriend in London has it, and I would recognise the symptoms anywhere."

"What's M.E.?" I had heard of it several months before from my lovely friend Chrissie. She told me she had gone down with M.E. and was terribly fatigued. She said she had tried all sorts of doctors and treatments and so far she was as ill as ever. I couldn't believe the weird coincidence that I also might have gone down with the same illness, so soon afterwards.

Andy continued to explain: "Myalgic Encepholomitis. It's also called chronic fatigue syndrome, and it's caused by a virus. The virus, it could be any virus, does some damage somewhere, the medical profession don't know where exactly, and people don't often fully recover from the illness."

This sounded a bit dubious to me. "Come on, let's cross over the road and go to Smith's. They are bound to have a book on M.E." Andy said, pulling me along towards the shops.

Sure enough Smith's had a book on M.E. Andy flipped open the book to the first chapter. "Look there is a list of all the symptoms! Familiar to you, are they?"

My eyes skimmed the list. I'd got all the symptoms, undoubtedly. I felt like crying, both with great sadness at the sentence that warned it was difficult to get rid of the illness and there was no treatment, and sheer relief than there was a name to my illness and that I was not going mad. I bought the book, which I could hardly afford, but felt it necessary to read.

I started reading the book as soon as we got back to the station car park. Glandular Fever was a well-known trigger for M.E., I discovered. It confirmed why I felt extremely fatigued sometimes after the slightest exertion and would take days to recover. Other times I could exert myself and could recover in a few hours. As I skimmed through the book it confirmed to me how vicious M.E. is. Why? Because it is so unpredictable. Someone can see you out shopping, or at a party and think: "Oh she's obviously better!" But they aren't there when you get back home, desperate for a cup of coffee but you are too weak to make it. You want to go to bed – but the staircase looks like Mount Everest in the worst of weathers. I had already experienced a fair amount of isolation because so many of my friends just couldn't see the "illness" I was experiencing, often suffering behind closed doors. Had I realised this was going to be my way of life for over ten years I think I would have sunk into deep depression. But despite what I read about there being no known cure, I was optimistic that God was in control of my life and He would sort it out. I never realised how long it would take!

I have since met, and counselled, many people with M.E. including children and teenagers, and it is heart-breaking. Apart from believing in the Lord for a miracle it is hard to offer any other hope in most cases. Some recover sufficiently to return to work or college, but often have to be very careful what they eat, and they have to rest, rest, and rest.

Andy and I had a lovely day in the Purbecks, and I rested in the car quite a bit while Andy went exploring. We even got onto Portland where there are two huge prisons I had heard about and never seen. They seemed to be hidden under huge grass mounds!

At the end of the day Andy caught the train home, and I fell onto my bed and hardly surfaced for the next couple of days, I was so exhausted after my outing in the Purbecks.

As there were no sick certificates forthcoming from the surgery, however hard I tried to explain my illness, things became difficult financially. At this point my mother insisted on giving me the same amount as her pension every week – that was a most marvellous gift and I was very grateful to her for her great generosity.

The days were made up of highs and lows. Low days usually followed after a good day when I had been able to do something enjoyable! I soon realised there was a pattern to M.E. It was exactly like a flat elderly battery. Re-charge it and it gives a bit of life – then it goes flat and has to be re-charged again. Sometimes the re-charging takes days, sometimes only hours! If I wanted to go to a wedding or special "do", then I had to rest carefully for a few days before and a few days afterwards. If I miscalculated and got overtired while I was still out somewhere then it was often difficult to get back home.

I began to visit my mother much more often. She was energetic, but also at times not well, so we supported each other and understood what it was like to be unfit.

One day Mum asked if I would like to go with her to Romsey, four miles away from Rownhams House. As I was spending the day with her, I was happy to go. We set off for Romsey and looked in two or three shops, browsing around. Then Mum and I returned to a lovely china shop, and Mum started to make her purchase.

I felt as weak as a kitten. I looked round for somewhere to sit – nothing and nowhere – only boxes of unopened expensive china – too risky to sit on. By the time we were stepping out of the shop, I reluctantly had to admit to Mum that I couldn't walk back to the car. Messages from my brain to my legs to move one foot in front of the other were non-existent. We stood outside the shop and I leaned against the door frame. I felt very sorry for Mum as she wasn't well that day either, and that was why I had gone up to Rownhams. She thought with my help, driving to Romsey and so on, that she would manage to buy the much needed Christening gift.

After a while we walked very slowly back to the car, and got ourselves home. Fortunately Mum had a chair lift up the two staircases, so we took it in turns to ride up to her flat. This was one of very many occasions when Mum saw me at my worst. Mostly on bad days I wouldn't go out and no one saw me when I could hardly walk. Mum was incredibly supportive of me and I didn't mind her seeing me so weak and pathetic, as long as she didn't worry too much. We had lots of laughs, and really it was no big deal: I always knew that after a long or short rest I'd be okay again – and Mum got used to the pattern and understood.

Although my illness was unrecognised and unaccepted by any of the doctors at the surgery, I decided to join the M.E. Association, and get their magazine and updates on possible treatments. The organisation was very helpful – but there was no sign of a cure. Statistics showed that it was very rare to recover completely, although with lots of rest some people were able to return to work, but only on condition that they rested a large amount before and after. There were lots of articles and letters about how unhelpful the medical profession were with regard to recognising, let along trying to treat, M.E.

I tried to get another job – painting little cottages – models already made up and ready to paint. I passed the interview and said I would take the job on condition I could rest when I needed to. That was fine! I then was shown around the factory – and as we passed by a trolley – huge and full of cottages all lying haphazardly, I stopped. "What are all these cottages doing in here?"

"Oh they are all destined to be steamrollered under the roads!" the lady replied.

"What do you mean?"

"Well, they aren't good enough. Some have the wrong mix of paint, some have the wrong colour on the roof, or the side of the house..."

She went on to explain all the (petty) faults. I knew everyone was paid only for each cottage they had successfully painted. I also knew you had to mix your own colours, according to some huge loose leaf binder file. You also had to buy your own paints!

No! No! No! Thanks – I don't want the job.

I gave up and drove home!

Sometimes I did voluntary work at Post Green, a fair amount of copy typing, and no time pressure - fine – that was okay.

One day Howard telephoned me.

"Are you busy today, Daph?" he asked.

"No. Why, do you need some help?"

"Well, we need to get out a pile of letters – it's only a case of stuffing envelopes and putting stamps on. We are a bit short staffed." Howard told me.

"Okay, I will be up shortly." I replied.

It was just after nine in the morning and I hadn't found out whether today was a good day or a bad day! On driving up to the office, two miles away, I wasn't sure it was my best day. I parked the car and climbed the stairs, slowly!

Howard happily laid everything out on the desk. "Look here's the pile of envelopes, just a few hundred. Now these two leaflets need to be folded and then this piece of paper needs to be added to them. And all three pieces of paper go in each envelope."

Easy!

Within ten minutes at most I was finding it almost impossible to fold and stuff. Howard was sitting in the office with his back to me. I gradually ground to a halt.

“Howard!” I said, timidly. “I’m not managing this! Can I stick stamps on the envelopes instead?”

Howard had a habit of responding with silence. Today was no different. He seemed to slowly assimilate what I had just said. “Oh – er – yes. Just wait a minute and I will run downstairs to the post office and get the stamps – I won’t be long. Help yourself to a cup of tea or coffee if you like.”

Howard nipped smartly out of the door and ran down the stairs.

I would love a cup of tea, but I can’t move – it’s along a short passage and down three steps.

Howard came back a few minutes later, and gave me a few pages of stamps. “Here’s the sponge if you want to use it – there are too many stamps to lick them all!” Howard smiled at me, and turned and sat down at his desk.

“Um, Howard, - sorry – but could you just wet the sponge for me?”

Howard spun his swivel chair round and looked at me, completely startled.

Was he thinking “You lazy so and so!” or “Indeed I am not your servant!”

He reached over and picked up the sponge and ran down the three stairs to the kitchen alcove and brought back a dampened sponge.

“Thanks so much, Howard.” I said, and happily began to tear the stamps in strips to put on the envelopes. I stamped about twenty, my hands moving slower and slower till I ground to a halt.

“Howard?” I said.

Howard swivelled round again, and looked at me. I shrugged my shoulders and said, “I’m really sorry, I’m not managing to stick the stamps on. I think I’d better go home. I will try and come back later.”

Howard regarded me silently - probably totally mystified. He scratched his head. I was slowly standing up and reaching for my handbag. “I will see myself out.” I said firmly, as I wasn’t sure how I was going to get downstairs and I certainly didn’t want him watching me.

"The side door is locked. The Post Office is too vulnerable to leave the door open. I will have to come down and let you out!" Howard stood up and reached for the keys on the window sill. On checking I was ready Howard ran down the stairs.

With huge difficulty I got myself down the first three stairs, and turned the corner to deal with the main staircase. I saw Howard standing on the mat at the bottom of the stairs, holding the side door open for me. He had obviously thought I would be right behind him.

The only way I could get down was to hold the banister with both hands and go down exceedingly slowly, sideways! Howard waited at the bottom.

I hated it - I hated anyone to see me this bad, but Howard had to lock the door behind me as it was the Post Office building. I reached the bottom of the stairs. Howard then said, "Are you sure you can get to the car? Do you want me to help you? Do you need someone to drive you home?"

To be on my own was all I wanted! I said, "No thank you." Howard asked me again, and I thanked him again and said I could manage. It took an age to walk to the car. I got in and sat down, sheer relief!

I soon discovered I couldn't change gear, too weak and my brain wasn't telling my muscles what to do – so I drove home in first gear, very slowly and the car didn't like it and made a lot of noise!

On returning home I parked right outside the front door. I rang Abigail. I just wanted a friendly chat, but I found myself crying and telling her I didn't feel very well.

"Oh, Mum! Look I will come straight down. I will bring Gavin with me, and Gary will fetch Jenna from school." Abigail responded immediately.

Two hours later Abi arrived and insisted we phone the surgery and make an appointment. She would come with me. We got an appointment for mid-afternoon and made our way to the surgery. My name was called on time. "Mrs Mills, please, Room Two". I was able to walk a bit better and made my way very slowly to Room Two. Abi was right behind me. I walked in the door and greeted the doctor and said my daughter wants to be with me. The doctor was very annoyed and was just saying No, when Abi walked in and confronted her.

"My mother brought us three children up on her own and now look at her! What have you got to say about her now?"

The doctor slid her chair back from her desk, obviously startled. The daughter was one strong lady!

She immediately, defensively, replied to Abi: "Well the trouble with M.E. is it's difficult to diagnose." She went on into some medical discussion with Abi as though I wasn't there. As the consultation continued it was then suggested that we get a second opinion. The doctor agreed to this.

I already knew the name of the doctor in Bournemouth who specialised in M.E. I mentioned his name. "Oh, yes, I know him well. Yes, by all means go and see him. I'll make an appointment for you!" The doctor was calming down again and being more affable. Abigail was firmly in control and was obviously not going to be fobbed off like I had been for nearly two years.

The appointment was made. The diagnosis was Post Viral Fatigue Syndrome, i.e. M.E. and the long term prognosis was that I was not ever expected to make a full recovery.

As a result of Abi coming to the doctor with me, and the second opinion, I got sick certificates back dated as far as legally allowed. And a long term sick certificate for life, in other words permanently disabled.

It was a huge relief to be properly diagnosed medically, and have the support of the medics at long last. The surgery sent me to their M.E. group that met every Friday morning, supported by the health visitor. We all started off laughing and chatting, sipping our drinks and sitting upright. Before an hour was up the room became quieter and quieter. Almost everyone was slumped in their chairs, drained of energy. There were about twelve of us – many young mums and one young dad – a kitchen fitter who had three small children and no wages coming in.

The health visitor put me on an anti-candida diet – which improved my immune system and got rid of my constant sore throats and laryngitis.

My early morning swimming in Wimborne with Stephen Budd and Gary Allen were a thing of the past.

But a new way of life was just beginning!

CHAPTER THIRTY TWO

Once I had a confirmed diagnosis it made a huge difference to me. I knew I couldn't "strive" to get better. All the books and advice on M.E. said that rest was the only way forward. Have lots of rest, and you will be able to manage to get on with life. Obviously if you can only do a small amount each day, you do what is absolutely essential in the way of looking after yourself, and in any spare time you have left you make sure you creatively enjoy yourself.

I sold the little caravan with its horrid upright seats, and went looking for something more suitable, as I still wanted to go to camps. Exactly a year after I had gone down with glandular fever at camp, my lovely friend Carys got glandular fever. We still shared a caravan, and rested together, but she still insisted on helping out with the young people, though she admitted she had a terrible sore throat.

After one false start I managed to find the perfect caravan. It was an old classic Cheltenham Fawn, ten feet long, two settee type berths, and a small kitchen and loo. Perfect. I joined the Baptist Caravan Fellowship and made friends with Julie, another single lady. She had her own caravan and we often met up together with or without our caravans.

In the meantime Gary and Claire had got engaged and were busy planning their wedding.

"Daphi, I've got a great favour to ask of you," said Claire one day. "Could you possibly sing Ave Maria at our wedding?"

"Oh, I'd love to! But I hardly ever sing now!" I said, lamely.

"We hear you singing around the house – go on – you can do it!" said Gary.

"Well, all right. What date is the wedding again?" I asked.

It was eight months away – fine! Time to get rid of yet another sore throat and start practising! A couple of months after that I saw an advert in the paper. A local singing teacher was advertising for pupils. I telephoned her, and she asked me to come for an audition. I explained that I had previously had lessons, but needed to learn to sing Ave Maria for a wedding in September.

A time was arranged and I duly went along with a couple of songs, plus a copy of Gounod's Ave Maria.

I sang two songs. "Is that all the volume you can manage?" the teacher, Penny Landi asked me.

"Yes."

"Well by the time I've worked on your voice you will be able to sing at Covent Garden on the opera house stage!"

She was as good as her word, and although I never sang at Covent Garden she taught me to sing operatic arias and I only needed to use a microphone once or twice when I sang at an open air occasion. We worked well together and she was a joy to be with at every lesson. Sometimes I had to cancel because of extremely sore throats, but I tried to warn Penny ahead of time and not let her down at the last minute. It was extremely good discipline for me, and it was the one appointment in the week which I aimed to keep if at all possible.

It was a long time since I had sung on my own but on the day of Gary and Claire's wedding I walked to the front of the Lytchett Minster Parish Church when the song Ave Maria was announced. Claire had warned me that she had chosen the song as a surprise for her father, John Fenton, who was sat in the front row. I was conscious of his emotions as I sang. Later when I read his incredible book "Please Don't Make Me Go!" I was so very glad I had sung it for him. The Ave Maria was very significant to him in his unbelievably terrible childhood.

Since learning to sing the song for him, I have sung it at many weddings!

Penny was keen to put me in for the Bournemouth Music Festival to which I reluctantly agreed.

There was a Baptist Caravan rally immediately before the week of the Festival, so I asked if I could use the local church hall to practice. Once the Baptists knew I could sing I was booked to sing at almost every rally from then on. Consequently I sang at churches all over the country for the next ten years! On social evenings I sang opera or songs from the shows. On Sundays I sang one or two songs from the Fisherfolk, or oratorio, or famous sacred songs I had learnt from the radio. Penny always encouraged me in my choice of songs.

Because of Claire's request that I sing Ave Maria for her father I had re-started singing training again. I remained studying with Penny Landi for many years. Later when I moved back to Rownhams I trained with another very good singing teacher, Carol Bishop, and enjoyed doing concerts and shows with her other pupils.

The Baptist Caravan Fellowship became a lifeline. With lots of rest before, during and after rallies I managed very well and had loads of fun and made many new friends. After a few years I was asked to be the Rally organiser for the Southern Region. I asked my friend Dorothy Hawkins, and John Cox, to help. The three of us met regularly during the winter months to plan the rallies for the year after next! We went to sites all over the south to check them out, and booked local churches who wanted us to come and take the Sunday services while we were camping nearby. They usually were only too glad for us to organise a social evening on the Saturday, often with a strong musical element to it. John Cox played the piano to accompany me for eight years or more.

As I was doing less at Post Green, I had lots of opportunity for ministry at the Baptist Caravan rallies: preaching, teaching and praying for people were often part of a weekend – and with my caravan nearby I could always go and have lots of rest.

Dorothy used to arrive on site at the beginning of a rally weekend in her small camper van and two or three dogs. We used to go on doggy walks, and chat while the dogs ran off their energy. Dorothy wasn't terribly fit so gentle dog walks worked well for me. When I went home I used to miss the dogs a great deal.

I was on my own at Vetlanda again, as Gary and Claire moved into a mobile home after they were married. But I began to feel it was time for me to move back to Rownhams. Mum wasn't well and on several occasions I had had to drive at speed through the New Forest to take her to hospital as she had turned down the offer of an ambulance. When I first tried to put Vetlanda on the market the estate agent warned me against moving while I was ill. So I waited another year. By this time Gary and Claire had moved back into Vetlanda but were planning to go to Australia at the end of the speedway season and not return to Britain.

Of course I kept praying about what was the right thing to do, and suddenly I knew it was time to "return home". I put the house on the market, and that same day I phoned Mum and asked if I could call in and see her.

"Yes, I'm free all day. Don't worry, I'll have the chair lift at the bottom of the stairs ready for you!" she said. "In fact I've got something to tell you!"

"And I've got something to tell you, Mum, as well. What fun! Secrets" I laughed.

I drove through the New Forest; it was early autumn and the trees were just turning golden and yellow, and it felt great to be alive!

Parking the car at the front of the house, I rang the door bell and Mum and I exchanged a brief word on the outer door phone system. The front door buzzed and I pushed it open.

I walked across the entrance hall. How many hours I had spent here, in that corner by the window, answering calls on the switchboard. I stood and stared at the now empty corner. We had had a huge switchboard in days long past. Ten outside lines and one hundred extension lines. I loved being on the switchboard most of the time. I knew so many telephone numbers off by heart, and I was super quick at connecting people up via all the extension wires.

For a time my future mother-in-law played tricks on me and would phone while she knew I was on the switchboard at 5pm when all the rest of the office staff had gone home. I had to stay on it until the transport office closed, whenever.. but usually around 5.45 p.m. Mrs Mills would pretend to be someone else and mess me about and it made me quite jumpy at times. I asked David if he would have a word with her and tell her not to do it.

Sometimes the traffic office would get very impatient and say I had put the wrong person through to the wrong extension, and while I was trying to sort that out other extensions would be flapping up and down demanding my attention. On more than one occasion when it seemed the whole switchboard was out of control, I would grab all the extension wires (like bright red fat shoe laces) and tug them all out of their sockets.

Blissful silence, nothing moving! Then some courageous desperate person would start flapping their phone again! My father was on Extension 1 and 2. So I was always careful not to tug out his line if he was on the phone. But once I didn't notice as I pulled the lot out. He came swiftly out into the hall: "I've just been cut off. I was on an important call."

"Oh, dear. I'm not sure how that could have happened. Who were you on to? I will get them back for you!" I said.

Those were the days! So much has happened since then! I turned away from the empty corner and rang Mum's own doorbell, then using my key I unlocked the door and walked in. I sat on the chair and pressed the button and glided up the wide curved staircase. Halfway up, I slowly climbed off, and moved onto the next chair lift and continued up to the top. Mum was leaning over the banisters at the top, and the sunlight from the huge glass dome above shone down on us both.

"What's your news then, Mum?" I asked, smiling at her.

"No, you tell me yours first!" she said. I gave her a little kiss and we walked into her kitchen and she switched on the kettle. I sat down on a chair by the table.

"I've decided to move back here, Mum. The house is already on the market!" I told her excitedly. "The estate agent doesn't think it will take long to sell, so I want to start house-hunting soon, up in this area. I thought we might try and visit some agents in Romsey and get some idea of house prices in various areas." I told her.

"Oh, that's marvellous!" Mum responded as she filled the silver teapot with boiling water. She laid two Wedgewood cups and saucers on the table, put the milk jug and sugar bowl on the table and sat down.

"What's your news then?" I asked her.

"Well I am just in the process of passing some money on to you. I know you've been very short recently and I thought it would be helpful at this time."

"Oh Mum!" I said, as she told me how much. "That will help with moving house, thank you so much."

As I reflected on it, I thought God's timing is perfect. If Mum had told me about the money before I had decided to move back to Rownhams she might have thought I was moving back out of gratitude to her. As it was the decision was already made and the house was already on the market!

That afternoon we drove into Romsey and got some house details. "Don't send me any details of houses with a long straight staircase! It has to have a landing so I can stop halfway for a rest!" were my main instructions.

Over the coming months Mum and I had fun looking at places. I got stuck again with a bad M.E. type attack – and as we were a couple of miles from Rownhams I pulled onto a garage forecourt and Mum got out and fetched some chocolate for me. After a rest and a bar of chocolate I managed to drive us back home again.

I was negotiating to buy a house in Chandlers Ford, when my house sale fell through and I lost the property I was trying to purchase. I was disappointed but thought, oh well, God must have something better for me!

Tessa heard about my disappointment and she decided to go house hunting for me! She came up with three house details. The third house was perfect and I bought it.

It was the hand of God! Because I moved to that particular house, I met my future husband, John Hope! But I am leaping ahead too fast.

There was a time gap between selling and buying, so I put my furniture in store, and my beautiful Persian kitten into a cattery nearby in Lytchett Minster and moved back into Post Green house for a month. With much regret I resigned as a trustee of Post Green Community Trust, and also as a member of the Post Green Community; but it was time to move on. And I was permanently sick and not much good to anyone!

Post Green held a farewell service for me. I had found it impossible to continue to be a member of the Community as I was too unwell to last out for the length of the weekly meetings and not much good at doing anything else to support them. With huge sadness I left. But I knew that God had a plan and that I was moving onto the next phase in my journey. So there was joy as well as my sadness. At my farewell service at Post Green house I asked Jodi Page Clark to sing her wonderful song: "Do you know that I love you?" which I have sung myself many times as a solo in numerous churches over the years. But Jodi, as the composer of the words and the music, always touched me deeply with her singing of that song, and many other songs that she has written.

I had talked to the Bishop of Southampton Rev John Perry, who was our official Visitor to the Community. I had talked to the spiritual advisor of the community. I had gone for counselling to a lovely Reverend Mother of a convent in Shaftesbury.

But although everyone was helpful, no one could give me back the energy I needed to be able to pull my weight in the Community.

The month I stayed in the house at Post Green was excellent and a time of consolidation and moving on. Then I said farewell to everyone, and got into my car, and drove out of the now very familiar gates of Post Green. I fetched my beautiful Persian kitten, Jasper. Sadly Sheri had died recently of kidney failure and I couldn't bear the silence or her absence from my bed at night. So Jasper came to live with me! He was a real Tom Cat male: nothing feminine about him at all. So different from dainty Sheri, my Siamese colour point.

I then moved in to Rownhams House, bringing my kitten with me. Mum adored Jasper. We kept him indoors, but took him out for short walks on a harness once he had settled. He had his dirt box half way along the corridor, between Mum's bedroom and mine. He made a huge noise scratching up the Catsan each time he used the box, and always did a thorough job, scattering white granules all across the carpet.

He soon learnt that if he sat on the chair lift, someone would press a button and he could have a ride up the stairs. When my children and grandchildren visited us, the lift could be heard doing overtime up and down the stairs, with Jasper sat bolt upright like a prince.

Mum became increasingly unwell, spending a long time two or three times a day on her nebulizer to help with her asthma. She also had a spell in hospital, during which time her bedroom was redecorated, and I reorganised her wardrobe as I put her clothes back, so it was much easier for her to manage. A few weeks after she came out of hospital it was becoming obvious that she needed her own space again, and fortunately the house Tessa had found for me, was now vacant.

Jasper, the grey fluffy Persian kitten and I moved into Swans Nest in Rownhams and settled in happily.

Over the coming years I attended two churches, St John's Church in the village of Rownhams, and my old church Avenue St Andrews near the Common in Southampton. I rejoined the Avenue choir and loved being back there again. The Minister, Rev Cliff Bembridge, knew I had M.E. and promised me that God would one day heal me through prayer.

I was prayed for many times while I was ill. Almost always the person praying for me would say something like: "I feel God is saying, wait, rest. You will be healed one day! In the meantime, rest and wait. Be at peace!"

One of the worst things about M.E. is that resting, and resting and then resting again is the only way through this horrid disease. During this illness I wrote a poem about my thoughts on the problem of always having to rest.

O ELUSIVE REST!

O elusive rest, O mysterious quiet.

What are you in the busy-ness of life?

You call me. You beckon me.

You say you are my health.

I glimpse you for a moment.

I hold you fleetingly.

Then you are gone, as my mind rushes on.

Aching limbs and tired mind,

Respond to your call.

But as you refresh me, I race on into life.

Now burnt out like a heap of ashes,

Sparks falsely flicker and embers lie low.

I turn and look at you again.

"Rest" is your name.

You call me toward you. I don't want to come.

You want me to choose you, for you are my friend.

I love fast flowing streams, and moss covered rocks,

Cascading waterfalls, swift moving fish.

You are so quiet, serene and calm.

So slow moving, just glimmers of life,

Sunlight speckled rocks, safe stepping-stone paths.

And a place

To rest.

1992, Daphne Mills

CHAPTER THIRTY THREE

Fortunately Rownhams was still within easy reach of my three children and all the grandchildren I now had. The house with its conservatory and safe garden was perfect for everyone to visit me. Although I had M.E. and was at times terribly exhausted, it was always a great joy for me when the children and grandchildren came to visit; I couldn't always manage them for a long length of time, or cook great meals for them, but it was always a good time for each of us.

My children may well have a different perception of how they were brought up than the way I see it. Although my parents were very strict and we always had to say where we were going, it also seemed that we had a fair amount of freedom once we had moved to Rownhams House. For my father to trust me to ride on my motorbike from Southampton to Kent was a wonderful gift to me. And for my parents to allow me to fly to Paris on my own when I had just had my sixteenth birthday, and then to spend the day alone in Paris and later find the railway station to catch a train to Lyons was also a memorable gift to me!

Tessa and Nigel had a few years of "normal" childhood before living at Post Green. Abigail remembers nothing of her childhood before Post Green. They would all admit it was a very different childhood compared with the average person, but they developed people skills and leadership skills through their unique upbringing. Maybe they will put in writing their own experiences one day, but this book is about my life, not theirs – they have their own unique stories to tell.

They had a lot of fun and freedom at Post Green – but there were downs as well as ups, of course. We are all on a journey, and the journey is bound to have hills and valleys – and there are lessons to be learnt on the way.

Some of the hardest times in my life have become the most useful once I have got through them. But sometimes to process the "downs" of life we need help, both from the Lord, and from wise friends – otherwise we become bitter, angry and resentful.

After David left me and the children, it was the hardest time of my life so far. But I had lots of people I could talk to, and turn to for chats, advice, and prayer. During this time Abigail asked me if I would go and see a school-friend's mother, whose husband had just left her. I went round to see her. She was sat hunched up by the fire in the kitchen and for the hour I was there she hardly stopped her angry and vitriolic tirade against her ex-husband. And she certainly didn't want to listen to me. I felt so sad for her, hurting so much but unable to receive help.

I hope that the upbringing that Tessa, Nigel and Abigail had received taught them valuable lessons of life to take with them into the future. I am immensely appreciative and gratified at how well each of them has managed throughout their lives. At different times they have all gone through "the valley of shadows", but have come out the other end, stronger and gracious and forgiving. As I say, it is not for me to tell their stories, but just to say none of them have had it easy all of the time (who has?) and they have come out well at the end of it.

Over the years I tended to babysit Tessa and Abigail's children, usually at my house, so I got to know the children very well. Nigel had his wife Ruth's parents nearby and so I saw less of his four children, Luke, Ben, Joseph and Jasmin, while they were growing up.

Sometimes I child-minded Tessa's first son Robert, from early morning until early evening, and later shared the time with Tessa's mother in-law Vera Legg. Robert was always a joy to have and never caused me any worry. Gary Allan used to let him sit on his speedway bike when Robert was only a few months old! Seven years later Tessa and her second husband Stewart had a lovely young son Matthew. While Matthew was being born, Robert and I went to Hythe, about eight miles away, to sort out some furniture for Tessa and Stewart. Robert was looking forward to having a baby in the family and kept wondering what "it" would be called. Later in the day I took Robert into the hospital and he met his young brother Matthew for the first time.

Tessa and Stewart were temporarily living in a cottage in the grounds of Rownhams House, belonging to my brother at this time. As I lived only half a mile away I was able to see them quite often. As I was no longer well enough to do daily child-minding Tessa found a childminder living near my house, and I would quite often see Robert coming home from school and Matthew being pushed along beside him in his buggy. It seemed strange to see my grandchildren with someone else but as the years went by, when I was out and about in Rownhams, I would often hear: "Hello Nanny!" I would look around and in amongst a crowd of children would be either Robert, Jenna or Gavin. I loved being invited to watch their school plays or go to their sports day.

When with great sadness Abigail's marriage to Gary came to an end, she moved for a while into my brother's empty flat in Rownhams House, and then into a cottage in the grounds. Abigail and Gary had been living in North Baddesley for a while, which was about two miles from my house in Rownhams. They had a gorgeous Husky dog called Ice. Jenna and Gavin were at school, Abi and Gary were out at work. So as often as I was well enough, I would drive down to their house and take Ice out for a walk. He was a pure white, large dog. And Husky dogs are born to pull! So I would clip his lead on him, and tie some strong rope to the lead, then wrap the rope about three times around my waist and hold on tight. Ice could not be let off the lead or he would be gone in a flash, and the risk of him coming back with a neighbour's pet rabbit in his mouth was high. We would walk into a field nearby and depending on my M.E. Ice would have half a walk around the field or a complete walk around the field.

One day, just before Christmas, I nipped in to check on Ice but had decided I wasn't up to walking that day. I opened the front door, and stepped into the lounge. There on the floor lay the beautifully decorated Christmas tree. Decorations had rolled all over the floor and under the settee. Ice was sitting proudly in the middle of the chaotic scene. I tried to clear it up as best I could, but the Christmas tree was wrecked.

All this time, while the grandchildren were growing up, I was going away about five times a year with the Baptist Caravan Club. As I mentioned before, as often as I could I spent time with Dorothy and her dogs, Zen, Tomo and later Mika.

I began to get very fond of dogs, and gentle doggy walking, and began to wonder if I could possibly manage a dog myself. Two things happened during this time.

I was on my way to see a very special friend who was dying of cancer. I was only just leaving Rownhams when I witnessed a beautiful German Shepherd dog, in the care of two small boys, run out in front of the car preceding me. I slammed on my brakes, and ran to the scene. I stroked and comforted the dog until he died a few minutes later. I tried to comfort the boys who were totally distraught, and rang their step mother who was at work, to tell her what had happened. She arrived about twenty minutes later, and screamed at the two boys, and told them they would be put on the first train back to London that night to their mother's house and forfeit their holiday. They had been told not to take the dog out of the house. Then a policeman came up to me and wanted a witness statement. By then I could no longer keep my tears back, and wept for the unknown dog that had died.

When it was all over, I drove slowly back home, and left it several days before I felt strong enough to visit my friend in the hospice. I couldn't get over the death of the dog, even though I had only been with it for a few minutes.

It was a turning point for me and I resolved to get my own dog, to replace the unknown German Shepherd dog that had died!

Next time I took Ice out for a walk, with the rope firmly wrapped around my waist, we walked through the field and I got chatting to a woman with a huge white dog – twice the size of Ice. "What breed of dog is that?" I asked her.

"Oh, that's a Pyrenean Mountain Dog! They make wonderful pets. They are no trouble at all and easy to train!"

A big dog was definitely my aim, as it would make me feel safe on walks on my own.

We carried on chatting and I asked her a few more questions about doggy care. She insisted the dog had never given her a day's grief, ever.

"You can tell the dog to stay, and you could tie it to a twig and it wouldn't move – so obedient and tame! – even though they are so large, wouldn't hurt a fly," she carried on extolling the virtues of the breed. I was impressed.

"And they will eat anything you put before them – they aren't fussy eaters." The owner continued selling me the breed. I was almost persuaded.

"And do you know, one Christmas – I'd cooked the turkey, got it out of the oven and put it on the kitchen table. I carried the vegetables into the dining room and got chatting with our guests. Went back into the kitchen to fetch the turkey – it had completely disappeared! Couldn't find it anywhere! And can you believe it, the dog had got it!"

I cancelled the idea of a Pyrenean Mountain Dog.

Maybe it wasn't a good idea to get a dog after all! So I binned the idea for a few months. But then after awhile I started thinking about it again. I started buying dog magazines, and one magazine offered a facility where you describe your circumstances, lifestyle, house, garden, any financial restraints, and they will make suggestions as to the best breed for you. I filled in the questionnaire and posted it off. In great excitement I waited for a reply. About a week later I had a lovely personal letter, caringly written – because I had M.E. but had a safe enclosed garden, the recommendation was a Golden Retriever.

I went down to the shops and bought the local newspaper and local advertising rag as well. Then with a cup of coffee in one hand and a pencil in the other, I flopped down onto my chair and got myself comfortable – this was going to be one of the most important decisions of my life - outside of marriage!

Skimming the dog page in one of the papers was an advert for a Golden Retriever puppy. "Delivery possible" it read. On telephoning the advertiser I discovered they had a litter of puppies eight weeks old – and yes a female puppy was available. They lived on the Welsh border. We arranged to meet halfway, at Chieveley Service Station on the M4/A34 junction on the Newbury road.

Jenna and I had been invited to stay with my brother Roger, his wife Penny, and their children for a visit to their home in Sherborne, Dorset. Jenna had a marvellous time with her cousins, Amelia, Lucia and Isabelle. She went to some glamorous party with the two older girls and arrived home quite late. The next morning I woke up early. This was the day of the arranged pick up of the puppy!

I sat up in bed, and read the Psalm for the day, as recommended in the daily Lectionary. Then I wrote down my prayer on a piece of paper I had kept in my Bible for years. The little green book mark already had something written on it by Mother Basilea Schlink. It said: "Praising God the Father for the loveliness of His creation is a glorious task. It has a heavenly quality, for in heaven there will be ceaseless praise and worship. Join in giving praise, and heaven will enter your heart."

I kept it in my Bible as a constant reminder about how important it is to praise God - and it is in praising God that joy (or heaven) enters our hearts.

I find when I am feeling sad it is worth saying to myself: count ten things that are good in your life! Then say thank you to God! There are always more than ten things however sad I might be at the time!

Anyway, on the back of this little green piece of paper of Mother Basilea Schlink's, I wrote in pencil:

"January 4th 1997. This is the last few hours before we fetch Amber Anna – I'm very scared – adopting a new family member to live with me for may be fifteen plus years. I pray we will bond easily and with Jasper (my cat) too. Lord, I give this all into your hands and pray it will be the beginning of a new and very happy, long-lasting relationship, which will be life-giving and healing and a joy to me and others. I need your wisdom and help in training her, settling her in, and making her part of the family. Thank you, Lord. This is a BIG BOUNDARY BREAKING DAY. Amen."

Jenna had helped draw up a list of all possible names! And we had had a long discussion about them. In the end I chose two names Anna and Amber. On looking up the meaning of the name Amber I discovered it meant "healing and salvation from God". And Anna was a very old and faithful servant of God in the New Testament. I had a feeling that Amber Anna would be a very faithful dog, and would be a source of healing and love to me and many others – I believe that these names chosen were prophetic and came true as Amber Anna became a part of my life and the lives of many other people we came across in the following twelve years.

After breakfast, Jenna and I packed our bags and assembled in the front hall, where Roger, Penny, Amelia, Lucia and Isabelle all hugged and kissed us and sent us on our way. Roger held the gate open for us as we drove out, calling out reminders of how to find Chieveley Service Station as we left.

We drew up an hour later at the huge service station, and were appalled when we saw how huge the car park was! This was not going to be easy! Were we going to walk up and down, peering in each car for a golden retriever puppy? Jenna and I looked at each other, both obviously thinking the same thing. How do you find a needle in a very large haystack? Jenna was twelve years old, and full of good ideas. We had just started talking about them when there was a knock on the car passenger window. There stood a lady with a huge white ball of fluff in her arms. It was raining, so we quickly organised for her to sit in the back seat with the puppy.

We paid the money to her, and she gave instructions about food, injections, and other health issues. Then she got out of the car, and handed the puppy into Jenna's care. I got into the driver's seat and the lady disappeared into the maze of parked cars. Jenna and I made lots of fuss of Amber Anna – and I gave her a chocolate button, which I thought might be the quickest way to win a dog's heart. Luckily we didn't give her much chocolate as I learnt later it can be poisonous to dogs. Though I don't think it was poisonous to Anna. She found some chocolate a year or so later that I had hidden behind a cushion so the grandchildren wouldn't nick it. She ate it all and left the purple wrapping paper for me. And another time she stole all the chocolate decorations off my future sister-in-law, Marjorie's Christmas tree.

Amber Anna, often shortened to Anna, came with me everywhere! She was hard work to begin with and for the first three nights Jenna stayed with her and slept on the floor in the lounge, but on the third night when Anna wet Jenna's pillow, she announced that it was time for the puppy to learn to be on her own at night! I quickly discovered that Anna thoroughly disliked being on her own – and I would come back from a brief outing to find the carpet chewed, the under-felt eaten, the telephone wire chewed in half, plus messes galore on the carpet.

So I took her in the car wherever I went. She slept in a cardboard box on the back seat, and was extremely good. When I first had her, I was helping out in a choir in Hedge End, Southampton. We were rehearsing "The Crucifixion" by Stainer. I would come out in the interval and check on Anna, and take her for quick walkies. Over the following weeks the cardboard box became too small, so I got a larger, then larger one for her. Soon she learnt to climb out of it, and when I came back to the car I would find her in the driving seat – and refusing to budge. She was heavy and it was hard work persuading her that we were going nowhere unless she moved!

She attended many rehearsals with me over the years, and put up with my daily vocal warm-ups and song singing! She seemed to love all music and would lie down as close as possible to the piano whenever she had the chance.

I had only been living in Rownhams for eight months when my mother died. This was a very difficult time for my sister Valerie, my brother Roger and me. But I had had eight excellent months with Mum and we had gone on many outings together. The week before she died we had a lovely drive in the car out in the nearby countryside, and stopping off on the way back in Stockbridge so that Mum could do the last of her Christmas shopping. Sadly she never made Christmas, but I have total confidence that she had the best Christmas ever with the Lord Jesus in heaven, especially as her birthday was on Christmas Day, when she would be eighty-five!

Mum adored big fluffy Jasper, and I know she would have loved Amber Anna too, but I didn't get my dog until two years after Mum had gone. I often walked around Rownhams House gardens with Anna, but learnt quickly that if I let Anna off the lead she would be in the lake within seconds. The lake is well silted up and surrounded by deep black mud if the water level is low. Anna would come back smiling, and black rather than golden. Then I would have to hose her down at the tap to clean her up.

Mum had made friends with two foxes, who came out at dusk beneath her window – and she started throwing out scraps of food for them. Then every evening as it became dusk, you could see the two foxes waiting in the Rhododendron bushes for the squeak of the dining room window as it opened. They would cautiously come out and grab the food. Soon there were baby cubs, and they gathered, less shyly, on the lawn waiting for feeding time. Long after Mum died, when Roy the gardener/caretaker had taken on the feeding of the foxes, the numbers rose to somewhere in their twenties. By this time it was agreed that they were costing too much and there were too many foxes to be contained in the grounds – so the food allowance was cut considerably. But the office staff, in the various offices in Rownhams House, would often throw their leftovers out and the foxes continued to eat healthily.

I was always a bit nervous that Anna might catch something unhealthy from them as she loved finding the fox dens, and putting her head down the holes, wagging her tail at the sounds she could hear deep underground.

The person who would be most pleased to hear of my having a dog was my dear friend Dorothy Hawkins with her two dogs Zen and Tomo (Mika came along later). I kept a journal of the early days of Anna's arrival then sent the book off to Dorothy to read. She was on the phone in no time – very excited for me. When Anna proved rather difficult to train, Dorothy recommended her friend Hilary Jordon, who had been a trainer for Guide Dogs for the Blind. Anna went on a five day course and came back a different dog – well I should say – I came back different! I got a couple of hours training myself. When Anna and I had arrived in Berkshire to meet Hilary, she made me walk in front of her, doing a doggy walk through the park. Then she asked me what were the two main commands I used for Anna: "Quickly – and quietly." I replied.

Hilary was quite astonished – "I've never heard either of those commands for dogs!" was her response! Anna was left in her care for her five days training. When I fetched her later that week I was soon taught the proper commands and how dogs need the same clear word for everything. It was excellent training for us both and we drove home happy.

With Anna as company and security I started going further afield with my caravan – and took my first holiday with just the two of us, down to Cornwall. We had a most marvellous time, and it was great to be out and about again – just hook up the caravan and take off whenever I pleased. I still suffered a great deal with M.E. with no improvement – but I was learning a new way of living my life: it was far better than languishing at home day by day. With careful planning, conserving what little energy I had, trying to keep calm and move slowly, I managed to have some marvellous trips out with the caravan.

Before I had Anna, Abigail's daughter Jenna quite often volunteered to come away with me in the caravan. By the time I had Anna, Jenna's brother Gavin was making noises about coming away in the caravan with me. We decided to go north up to my old home in Newcastle under Lyme. I had already sold my smaller Cheltenham for a slightly larger one, because of Amber Anna. It still only had two berths but it had much more floor space, so I could step over Anna and her bedding. But Anna preferred to sleep on one of the berths and look out of the window. Besides it was more comfortable than the floor!

On Gavin's first trip with me, we towed the van up to Staffordshire, and when it was time for bed, Gavin and I sorted out our sleeping bags and got into our bunks. But Gavin was on Anna's bunk! So she hopped up and lay on top of him! She was a very heavy dog, but Gavin assured me he didn't mind, and somehow they got themselves comfortable and had a good warm night.

We called in to visit Sybil Bradley, who was now living with her daughter Elaine, and son-in-law Robert, and their family. Gavin immediately made friends with their daughter Helen, who helped him with his school holiday project. We took Anna for lots of walks up to the cricket pitch nearby.

Gavin had taken his new roller blades but because it was such a hilly area he found it hard going. Then he had the idea that Anna could tow him along with a piece of rope. Anna soon cottoned on to the scheme, and ran as fast as she could, running along the pavements and ignoring bumps and driveways. Helen Malkin and I had the most amusing time being entertained by one small boy and one very happy dog.

When we finally got back home, Gavin stayed an extra night with me in my house. I thought it was time he had a bath! While Gavin got himself undressed I filled up the bath with warm water and lots of lovely bubbles. Before Gavin had a chance to get in, Anna crept up behind me and hopped over the edge of the bath and immersed herself in the bubbles.

It would have been funny, but I was terribly tired. I had no energy to start the procedure all over again – and Gavin was definitely in need of a bath. "Go on, hop in Gavin." I said firmly.

Gavin objected because Anna was already in amongst the bubbles. "Oh don't be so fussy, Gavin. Go on, get in the bath." I tried to say it more firmly, no room for negotiation.

"Huh, I've never had to have a bath with a dog before!" Gavin grumbled and climbed into the bath (the water was already turning slightly brown!). As soon as Gavin was in the water Anna got very excited and so did Gavin. It took about half an hour for me to get them both out and I think they had the most marvellous bath ever.

Jenna called in one day to play with Anna, and she commented on the pile of things waiting at the bottom of the stairs. "Why is there always a pile of things at the bottom of your stairs, Nan?" she asked. "And there is often a pile at the top as well, I've noticed!"

"Well when I don't feel great I stay downstairs all day. I can't keep running up and downstairs with things! And sometimes I have to hold onto the banisters to get myself upstairs (or crawl up!) and I can't carry things."

Jenna thought for a bit. "I'm going to sort that problem out for you, Nan!" She knew my house quite well and in no time at all she had found a plastic basket and some rope. She organised a pulley system! Then she put everything in the basket and pulled it up over the banisters, showing me how the scheme worked. "There you are, Nan. Now there won't be a mess at the bottom of your stairs when I come to see you!"

The pulley system was in action for the next few years. We also organised a "tea station" upstairs, so that when I couldn't manage to get downstairs, I could make myself a drink upstairs!

There were days when Anna didn't get a walk, but I was assured by the dog people in the magazine I had written to, that it wouldn't matter as long as she had a garden to play in. Sometimes I didn't manage the walk till late evening. It would be dark, and we would walk along the lamp lit roads near our house. Anna loved it – except sometimes she would woof and growl suddenly and make me nervous. I gradually realised that she would see a cat hiding under a car or in a bush. I would reprimand Anna and say, "For goodness sake, Anna. Be brave – and don't frighten me either!"

Whenever we had a family gathering my grandson Benjamin Mills always volunteered to keep an eye on Anna, and take her out for a walk, which I always appreciated and Anna loved it. Benjamin seemed at times to be the most mischievous of all the grandchildren, but he was certainly a very thoughtful young man, and always considerate towards me.

My longest and best holiday in the caravan with Amber Anna was when she was two years old. I was watching television just after Christmas – it was snowing up in the Lake District, and I had a sudden longing to be there! So we loaded the caravan with warm clothes, Anna's toys and blankets, food for us both, hitched up and left. Anna and I stopped off for a few days in Newcastle, Staffordshire to visit Sybil Bradley, Elaine and her family. We stayed at Trentham Gardens – a vast empty site with woodland and a lake. The wardens on site were very casual – the water froze, the electricity died, my gas froze. We waited most of the day for the electricity to come back on, and in the meantime I drove over to a caravan sales place and explained our predicament. "Oh you need a different kind of gas, one that doesn't freeze. Don't worry, we will sort it out for you – bring your gas bottles in and we will exchange them for you and give you an adapter for the new kind. We will sell you a couple of water carriers to keep inside the caravan and hopefully they won't freeze!"

In no time at all everything was up and running again – Anna slept with one hot water bottle and I had two hot water bottles. I lay in my bunk gazing up at the snow laden trees and glorious blue sky in the early mornings. We were situated deep in woodland, and Anna chased through the snow covered brambles, leaping and rolling with joy. After a lovely visit with Sybil, Elaine and Robert and family, plus some lovely dog walks around the cricket pitch with Helen, their youngest daughter, we waved goodbye. With great difficulty we got the caravan off an awkward snow frozen pitch, and drove further north.

On arriving in the Lake District, the vista was divine – we were surrounded by snow and the white purity of the fields, hills, and mountains. My heart lifted with excitement. I managed to pitch the caravan on tarmac at the Caravan Club Site and the facilities were very user friendly for winter holidaymakers.

My friend, John Cox, drove up from Winchester in his camper van and met up with me. He stayed for a couple of days and then drove south. I was hankering to go further north! I was very vague with John about my plans as I thought he would have a fit if he knew I was thinking of towing the van further north and deeper into the snow! Half an hour after John Cox had left, I hooked up the caravan and left the site. We drove north to Edinburgh. After pitching the caravan in the Caravan Club site I explored Edinburgh Castle – Anna waited patiently in the car as she wasn't allowed in. All her life Anna adored being in the car, and never minded being left there, as long as it wasn't too hot of course. I spent longer than I intended in the Castle as I was searching for my Uncle Eric Barber's name in the memorial book: I found it in the end under the Officers page. He had been a captain in the Kings Own Scottish Borderers when he had died on exercise during the war.

I knew two couples who had been part of the Community of Celebration who now lived in Edinburgh. On investigation I found one couple were very close to my caravan site and on visiting them, they invited me to a Healing Service the following evening. Their church members were busy studying my book The Road to Emmaus. Douglas and Arabella were sad to hear I wasn't well, and we had a good chat and meal in the vicarage kitchen. Douglas was the vicar of the local church. I made sure I had enough energy to get myself to their church on the Friday evening, and after a lovely service of worship I went forward for anointing of oil and prayer for healing. Although I was not any better physically, I was immensely encouraged that my healing was not far away. In fact it was unbelievably close!

There was a brilliant doggy walk on the caravan site. For the first time I heard a bird trill a mobile phone call in a tree above my head! As I was totally alone in the dog walk, except for Anna, I was a bit spooked – until I looked up and realised where the sound was coming from!

We explored Perth and I bought a kilt and a Scottish teddy bear dressed in the same tartan "Pride of Scotland". I looked at the map and longed to go further north, but I knew the snow was thick on the roads, so sadly turned the car and caravan around and drove slowly southward. John Cox and Dorothy Hawkins both drove up in their camper vans to the Cotswolds and we spent a few pleasant days together before returning to our various homes.

I called the trip my "odyssey"!

CHAPTER THIRTY FOUR

Having moved back to Rownhams for the next seven years I sang in both St John's Church choir in Rownhams and the choir at my old church Avenue, now called Avenue St Andrews, at different times! Originally I was at St John's church while I was looking after my mother, but someone in the church was beginning to cause me a lot of grief, so one Sunday I decided to take a break and visit my old church in The Avenue. I was late arriving and slipped quietly into the back pew. I loved the organ music and the hymns were some of my old favourites. At the end of the service a woman in front of me introduced herself and said her husband was playing the organ that day. I mentioned that I used to be in the choir many years ago as a teenager. She insisted that I go with her up into the choir vestry and meet everyone.

We walked down the aisle together and I recognised quite a number of old friends. We climbed up the stairs and entered the vestry. The choir were all busy taking off their robes and white cuffs, and sliding the wardrobe doors to and fro, just like old times. I got such a shock: "Hello, Daphne!" came from all over the room! Many of the old choir members were still faithfully singing, Sunday by Sunday.

After finding that I had moved back to Southampton they insisted I sing with them in the choir for the special music they were doing for Easter Sunday in two week's time. So I couldn't resist. I went to the Friday choir practice, and another held mid-week during Holy Week. The new church magazine came out on Easter Sunday. It announced that Daphne Mills had rejoined the choir after many years away from Southampton!

Maybe fate had a hand, but I think it was God. I stayed with the choir for several years, and sang several solos and duets, as well as anthems. The Minister of Avenue St Andrews soon discovered I had M.E., but invited me to come to the worship planning group which met occasionally. After much persuasion I agreed to be music director as long as I could work with another lady, who was far better qualified musically, to help me. This was agreed and announced. But even before we had the special prayer and dedication during a morning service, I had a sinking feeling about it. Martha (not her real name) began to show signs of strange "over-the-top" behaviour, and jumping ahead of the job before we had discussed and agreed things. This got more and more out of control. As a person I liked her very much, or I would not have asked her to help me, but the way she went about the job of sharing the music leadership was, basically, to not share it. I would find that everything was all done and arranged and I was side-lined. This was a very tricky situation – not only was I struggling with M.E. with all its horrid fatigue and other symptoms, but we had some very important worship services coming up that were due to be broadcast on radio and television.

Now I have to go back in history to explain why Avenue St Andrews was having an unusual flurry of broadcasting!

The oldest Congregational church in Southampton was founded in 1662 and was built near the Bargate. It's most famous member and deacon was Isaac Watts, a preacher and writer of hymns. Isaac Watts wrote over 750 hymns, and landed up in prison twice for his beliefs! When this wonderful ancient church was bombed in 1940 the congregation moved up to St Andrews Presbyterian church, a couple of miles further north. In 1972 The Avenue Congregational Church, which stood nearby, and St Andrews Presbyterian Church merged and became Avenue St Andrews United Reformed Church. The two combined churches decided to use the Avenue Congregational Church buildings as being more suitable for the merger.

So Isaac Watts became historically part of Avenue St Andrews. Some of his most famous hymns are "Joy to the World", (often sung at Christmas), and "When I survey the wondrous Cross" (often sung over Easter).

In Southampton the Civic Centre clock regularly chimes out the hymn "Our God, our help in ages past, our hope for years to come, our shelter from the stormy blast and our eternal home." This hymn also was written by Isaac Watts. But why was he sent to prison – twice? And why did he write "Our God our help in ages past"?

Isaac Watts was born in 1674. In those days it was forbidden to sing anything in the church except Psalms from the Bible, set to music. Isaac Watts objected to this and wanted to modernise the hymns to include Jesus and the New Testament! He also had other ideas to modernise the church. He became both very popular and very unpopular – just like Jesus was! Because Isaac Watts was a "Dissenter" and didn't attend the established Church of England, but wanted to be part of the free church movement, he was in danger of being arrested at any time. On the night before Queen Anne was due to sign a new edict which would have made things even worse for the free church believers, including Isaac Watts, she fortunately died.

Isaac set to, and wrote another hymn: "Our God our help in ages past . . ." and the second verse reads: "under the shadow of thy throne, thy saints have dwelt secure; sufficient is thine arm alone, and our defence is sure." It was a hymn of praise and thanks to God for rescuing them in their hour of need.

Avenue St Andrews felt it important to mark the 250th anniversary of Isaac Watts' death. We did two radio broadcasts and a television broadcast. The choir were very involved, singing many Isaac Watts hymns and some more modern composers' hymns too. This meant a huge amount of work and a lot of rehearsals for the choir. My friend Martha's behaviour became even more difficult, and especially toward me, shutting me out of the planning and arranging.

One evening just before the television broadcast I had to go to the church to take back some choir gowns. I parked the car in the church car park. Anna was lying on the back seat as usual. “I won’t be a moment, Anna. Wait!” I said to her as I took out some of the choir gowns I had repaired and smartened up. I walked up the steps to the front door of the church and used my key to get in. I knew there was no one around as there were no cars in the church car park, and all was silent. It was pitch dark, except for one low light. I don’t really like being anywhere either in pitch darkness or semi darkness! But I bravely, and cautiously, started walking down the long main aisle of the church. But then I saw a man, standing stationary near the south side aisle. He didn’t move or look up at me, and he had a funny hat on him. I nervously moved towards him, too embarrassed to speak! I got up closer and in the gloom I realised it was a life-size model of Isaac Watts himself!

I hastily put on as many lights as I could find, and ran up the stairs to the choir vestry, put the gowns in the wardrobe and walked back into the church again. Isaac Watts was still there. “Goodnight, Isaac!” I called out, as I switched off the lights again and walked quickly up the aisle and out of the church.

After all the excitement of the broadcasts in November 1998 we were into Christmas planning. Martha and I worked together as best we could but it was a nightmare for me, as the ground kept shifting beneath my feet! Once Christmas and all the music and services were over I had a chance to relax.

That was when I took my month off and Anna and I drove off with the caravan, Augusta, into the snowbound north!

The months went by and I decided to resign from the music leadership and let Martha continue on her own. I didn’t need that stress in my life!

Spring came and went, in a bit of a fog for me. I was so lethargic and unwell. May arrived and summer was on her way. The sun was shining and everything seemed like it was bursting into life – except me. I counted up the years I had been ill. At the end of May I would have been ill for ten years! I was only 51 when I became ill, and now I had my invalidity pension and my old age pension at the age of 61. The invalidity pension hadn’t been taxable, but now I had the old age pension it was taxable, and I received less than 50 pence invalidity benefit per month!

I cried out to God again, and echoed the words of Psalm 13, which I had originally marked and dated in my Bible, after I had been ill for over two years. Now another seven or more years had passed.

"How long, O Lord? Will you forget me forever? How long will you hide your face from me? How long must I wrestle with my thoughts, and every day have sorrow in my heart? Look on me and answer me, O Lord. Give light to my eyes lest I sleep the sleep of death. . . . But I trust in your unfailing love, my heart rejoices in your salvation. I will sing to the Lord for he has been good to me."

That totally summed up my prayer and my cry to God.

The phone rang. "Mum? It's Abi here! Look I was just reading in my Bible and I came across this verse: it says, 'If any of you are sick, call for the elders of the church to pray and anoint you with oil in the name of the Lord. The prayer offered in faith will make the sick person well: the Lord will raise him up.' It's in James chapter 5. What about it, Mum?"

I was a bit startled as Abi was quite emphatic! And I had been prayed for many times, and anointed with oil – and although receiving encouragement and faith that God had it all in hand, nothing else had happened and I hadn't got better!

I know Abigail very well: she pursues you after she has given advice! The following Sunday it so happened that I bumped into my minister Cliff Bembridge just after the service, and had a chance to ask him if I could come to the next Elders' Meeting and receive prayer and anointing with oil. He seemed pleased, if a little startled. A few weeks passed and Cliff came up to me in church and said that my request had gone to the Elders Meeting and to the Church Meeting. It was agreed I could have whatever service I liked, wherever I wanted it and Cliff would organise it for me. I thought for a while and said I would like it to be a Holy Communion service, in the church, midweek and open to anyone to come, especially any who would like to be anointed with oil. This all took some arranging but eventually it was set for August 10th 1999.

I told Abi the date and invited her along; in the meantime I had run out of books to read! As Abi was just off to see her friend Janine in Gosport, I asked her to see if Janine had any books I could read.

I was an avid reader at the best of times, but with so much time spent resting, books became even more essential to me!

Abi returned that evening with three books from Janine. "When I got to Janine's, before I could ask her for any books, she gave me a bag and said 'These are for your Mum!'"

The three books turned out to be essential reading before I got prayed for in August! They were all books about how God heals, and they were all true stories of what God had done in three other people's lives, including a young teenager healed of M.E. The books were very helpful and thought provoking and helped me prepare myself for my anointing with oil and prayer for healing. The teenager's book on how she was healed particularly struck a chord. Her minister had written a chapter at the end of the book. He wrote: "The key to her healing lay in forgiveness. She had to forgive all those who had hurt her while she was ill. Only then could she be healed!"

That rang a loud bell for me. I had suffered as much from people's hurtful reactions and ignorance of my illness, as I had from the illness itself.

I sat in church the following Sunday – and during the service reflected on the forgiveness issue. There was a huge list of names of people who had hurt me, some more than others, and particularly in the Community at Post Green – accusing me of not wanting to come to meetings, when actually I was too weak or sick to manage!

There was a particularly hurtful remark made to me a few years back.

The telephone had rung while I was living at Vetlanda in Poole. "Is that Daphne? It's Mrs Smith here! It's about Patsy – she's very ill in hospital, in intensive care. I'm afraid she's dying."

"Oh dear!" I responded, my heart sinking. "Do you want me to come over?"

"Yes, please, if you could, Daphne."

"All right, I will get onto the airlines and find the best way to get to you. Should I aim for Belfast Airport?"

"Yes, get yourself to Belfast. Then you can catch a bus, via Lurgin and onto Portadown. Let me know what time you think you will arrive and I will meet you at the bus stop in Portadown." Mrs Smith banged down the receiver! She was a truly admirable elderly lady: she had owned and run her own school in Blackpool for many years. It was here that Mr MacArthur had left his daughter, Patsy, when she was so ill with anorexia . He had taken her straight from my house in Dorset, Panorama, and Mrs Smith had taken her in – seen her through teacher training college and given her a job at the end of it. Patsy was extremely gifted and talented, and a wonderful teacher. But she was also dogged by personal problems.

I needed to travel to Ireland to visit Patsy. Mrs Smith was obviously very upset. I had to go. I had kept in touch with Patsy ever since the early 1970s, and she had visited occasionally after her disastrous exit from King Alfred's College, and I had been up to visit her in Mrs Smith's school in Blackpool.

Claire and Gary had helped me book an airline ticket and we got out a map to see where I was meant to be aiming for in Northern Ireland. The six o'clock news came on. "A massive bomb has gone off in the centre of Lurgin, near Portadown in Northern Ireland. The whole of the high street is in ruins."

Claire and I looked at each other. It wasn't going to be an easy journey for me anyway – let alone a huge bomb going off just where I was aiming for. But there was nothing for it. I had to go and see Patsy.

The next day I flew to Belfast and caught a bus to Portadown. We stopped in Lurgin, avoiding the main street. I glanced to my right out of the window: the street was like a black and white photo – all of the colour had gone – no brightly coloured painted shops, and the windows were smashed and everything was black or grey. It was truly shocking – another example of the conflict that poor Ireland was suffering – both north and south.

On arriving in Portadown, Mrs Smith met me and we went straight to the hospital. I was horrified to see how old Patsy appeared, lying unconscious in her special ripple bed – still in her 30s but looking like a seventy-year old. I stayed for several days and spent almost every day at the hospital either by Patsy's bedside or in the attractive waiting room with a beautiful aquarium full of brightly coloured fish. Every time there was some procedure to do for Patsy in the intensive care ward I was ushered out into the waiting room by one of the nurses. On one occasion as we walked out of the security door the ward sister said, "The trouble is we don't know what's actually wrong with Patricia, and what's causing all these problems."

I looked at her, very surprised. "Well, you know she has anorexia, don't you?" I told her.

"No – we did not know she has anorexia: are you sure? That could be the key to the whole situation."

"I am quite sure. Patsy has been suffering with anorexia on and off since she was a teenager." I confirmed. I wondered why Mrs Smith hadn't told them – perhaps she was afraid that they wouldn't treat Patsy if they considered her illness self-inflicted. More is known and understood about anorexia now than when I was in Ireland in the early 90s.

At one point my visit coincided with a Church Army woman, and we agreed together to pray for Patsy, there and then beside her bed.

God moves in all kinds of ways – and often gently and silently. All I know is that the next morning the previously unconscious Patsy was sat upright in bed, laughing and talking – thrilled to see me – and about to be moved onto a main ward. By the time I flew home she was making a very good recovery.

But when I got home to Poole, I got accused of being well enough to go to Ireland but not well enough to go to meetings at Post Green. It was only one person that said it, but it really hurt. She didn't know how difficult it was for me to travel there, nor how many hours I rested, both at the hospital and at Mrs Smith's house.

Many years later, as my healing service at Avenue St Andrews drew nearer, I knew from the book I had recently read that I had to forgive the person who had made such hurtful and accusing remarks. I needed to forgive many other people as well, who had not accepted that I was truly ill and genuinely unable to work or hold down a job.

While I was seated in Avenue St Andrews Church shortly before my healing service I prayed: "God, I know I have to forgive – there are about twenty people on my list! I want to forgive but it still hurts and I am not sure I can forgive them." During the intercessional prayers in the church service I spent the time reflecting and trying to forgive, and asking God to help me. By the time Cliff Bembridge had finished leading the intercessional prayers I felt an unbelievable lightness of spirit – and knew God had done a miracle and enabled me to forgive those that had hurt me over the previous ten years.

Wednesday August 10th 1999 dawned, warm and sunny. In the evening Abigail and I made our way to Avenue St Andrews. Amber Anna was in her usual place in the back of the car, with the windows open. She was quite familiar with the church car park by this time! I had invited several close friends including two of my friends from the Baptist Caravan Fellowship: Dorothy Hawkins and John Cox.

I had chosen the hymns and the format of the service together with the Rev.Cliff Bembridge.

The service proceeded as planned, and we shared the bread and wine together during the Communion. There were over twenty people, all sat round in the choir pews in the sanctuary of the church. After Communion Cliff came towards me carrying the jar of oil. I found myself quickly praying, "Please God give me an outward sign of your healing touch." (Because the trouble with M.E. is that you can have several good days before you go crashing down again and I wanted to know that I was definitely healed and not just in a good patch!).

Cliff leaned forward and prayed, and anointed me with oil. I felt the oil touch my forehead as Cliff made the sign of the Cross. After he moved on to the next person who asked for anointing with oil, I began to notice that the sign of the cross made with oil on my forehead felt very heavy! I said to myself, "Oil isn't that heavy!" Within a few seconds two Elders came and laid their hands on my head and prayed for me for my healing. The sign of the Cross on my forehead still felt very heavy!

Eventually I lifted my head up and watched the others being prayed for. We had a final Bible reading and sang the last hymn. The Healing Service was over. We chatted politely to everyone and mingled for a while among the semi-circular choir pews. I thanked Cliff for the service, said goodbye to my friends and thanked them very much for making the effort to come. Both Dorothy Hawkins and John Cox said they would not have missed it for anything. And I am so glad they were witnesses.

Abi and I drove back to Rownhams. She was living in one of my brother Roger's cottages in the grounds of Rownhams House, which he had kindly lent to her after the break-up of her marriage to Gary.

When I was finally alone, exhausted but exhilarated with emotion, I was still conscious of the heavy oil on my forehead! It puzzled me until I remember my prayer, asking God for an outward sign of my healing! Then I felt totally jubilant, and exceedingly grateful and thankful and full of wonder at the greatness of God's love and mercy.

I have never had any symptoms of M.E. since then – and recovered my strength almost immediately. But what was more amazing was how my brain cleared. I had no idea how much the M.E. had affected my brain, causing it to slow right up. I suddenly could think clearly, read more quickly, and read sub-titles on the television before they disappeared!

I was healed – one hundred per cent.

When I worked out how long I had been sick – I realised it was ten years, ten weeks and ten days: and I was healed on August 10th. Coincidence? No I don't think so. It was ten long years of walking by faith believing I would be healed in the end, because God kept telling me I would. Some prayers take years to answer, but the journey taken during those years is a special time of learning and trusting God that He will answer the prayers one day!

Cliff Bembridge, and his wife Daphne, had always assured me that I would be healed by prayer, and they knew a young student in Ireland who had had M.E. and been healed through prayer. They, together with others, encouraged me as the months and years went by. The young student's story is told in her book "Held: a journey through illness to healing", by Angela Nichol, available through Amazon.

A week after my healing service Cliff asked if I could possibly sing something the following Sunday: he would be away and there was a visiting preacher, who had especially requested John Bell's setting of Psalm 13. I was very excited as it was my special Psalm when I was ill (as quoted earlier in this chapter). John Cox very kindly taught me the music during the week, and it fitted in brilliantly with the pathos of the words. I sang it the following Sunday, and many times afterwards when I was asked to say how I was healed. I usually combined it with the song from My Fair Lady: "I Could Have Danced All Night" – as that was how I felt when I was healed!

CHAPTER THIRTY FIVE

Four months before this happened I met a wonderful man! He lived in Germany, but occasionally visited my next door neighbours, Ron and Diane English. He would stay for a few days, then leave his car in our shared driveway and fly over to his original home in Jersey. I had seen him quite a few times but had never met him.

On this particular occasion, around Easter 1999, Ron and Diane were away and I was feeding their cat and their rabbit for them. They told me John might be coming by and staying for a few days, so check out with him who was going to feed the animals while he was visiting. And also, would I run him to the airport when he left as he was on his way to Jersey?

His visit coincided with a rehearsal I held in my music room. John Cox came over and we were practicing for that evening's visit to Winchester prison for the weekly service for the prisoners. I was working on the song from the "Titanic": "The Heart will Go On", and the hymn "Amazing Grace". While we were rehearsing the door bell rang.

"I could hear your singing through the wall, would you mind if I come in and listen? I love music!" said John Hope from next door. So he came in, met John Cox, and listened while we practiced. At the end of the rehearsal our visitor said, "Bravo!" and invited me out for a meal, that day. I said I couldn't manage it as I was singing in the evening. I didn't tell him I had M.E. and had to rest all the afternoon so I could manage the prison engagement. John seemed a bit disappointed but I couldn't risk running out of energy before the evening's singing engagement. Eventually it was agreed we would have a meal, a take-away, when I returned from Winchester prison.

Singing at the prison was most interesting! None of the prisoners had seen "Titanic" but loved the song, and they all knew Amazing Grace. We stayed for a chat and a drink afterwards – there were a lot of young men and some loveable rogues amongst them. One of them, who was in for some violent act, told me he was refusing to go on the anger management course – so I tried to persuade him it might turn out to be for his own benefit.

John Cox dropped me back to Rownhams and then drove off to his house in Winchester at the end of our prison visit. I looked forward to a sit down and the planned take-away with my new acquaintance John Hope. We talked a lot about music and lifestyles. John was somewhat amazed at how tired I was and that I cut the evening short rather abruptly. I didn't say I had M.E. It always seemed to need explaining and then people would say, "Oh you mean Yuppy Flu!" Or if they didn't say it, it seemed that they thought it!

We had opportunity for another chat before he left for the airport – and I remember telling him about Martha and the difficulties I had with her, while trying to run the choir. We also talked about electronic bugging! A "friend" had bugged my house, without telling me and had refused to say what the device was or where it was. I had tried to get an agency in to de-bug the house but it would be too expensive, besides the fact that they said they might not be able to find it. It sounded like a very new device to them.

I asked John, eventually, what rank he had been in the army. "Lieutenant Colonel," he answered. As I am somewhat allergic to authority figures I knew I was definitely not likely ever to be friends with a brigadier, or a general, or even a colonel. Probably not even a major! I took a deep breath and thought to myself, "He's probably one strong cookie and best to be avoided in future!"

He was very informative about bugging devices and we had an interesting chat. Then I took him to the airport. I didn't see John again until after I was healed.

My lovely Dutch friend Jacoba Maria Helena van der Stigchel, (nicknamed Co) was planning to come over to stay with me. We had been friends since we were teenagers, when the Avenue Church minister, Rev Vine Russell had introduced us at church one Sunday. Co asked me if I would sing to her while she was over. I sent her a list of songs and she ticked about eight or ten of them! John Cox was happy to play for me – and as some of the songs were better accompanied by the organ, I asked the vicar if we could borrow St John's, Rownhams, to practice in. John Cox and I did a few practices and I borrowed the key off the vicar each time, and returned it on my way home. As I returned the key one day, the vicar asked if anyone else could come. Would I allow the church people to come and listen as well. I shrugged my shoulders and said, well yes, if they would like to. We could pass the hat round afterwards and collect some money for the repairs urgently needed in the church!

We did the concert, and I sang about fourteen songs, with two or three intervals using young musicians from the Church to do instrumental items, to give me and the audience a break. The church was packed and extra chairs had to be brought in. Some people were standing at the back. I had lit some candles around the church and it was quite atmospheric. I called it a Celebration Concert as a thank offering for my healing from M.E. My daughter Abigail brought several friends who were in wheelchairs, and we had two dogs in attendance which looked after their disabled owners. Tessa and Nigel and their families were there as was the rest of my family. It was a wonderful celebration for me.

The concert was a great success, and I was asked to do two further concerts in the following two years – always by candlelight!

John Cox continued to play for me but when he made a proposal of marriage to me, and I sadly turned him down, it made things a bit awkward and the music and singing began to suffer.

My new friend, John Hope, had visited another couple of times in the following year and I found myself very attracted to him. I felt he was a man of great compassion and integrity: and my heart was drawn to him. I kept remembering the phrase coined by Rev Dr Peter Marshall (in his story "a Man Called Peter" by Catherine Marshall) "… the highest halls of human happiness…". I thought John Hope was wonderful! So after John Cox proposed yet again, I had to tell him "my heart is elsewhere".

John Hope and his wife Ingrid had been living separately for about several years, and just after I met John sadly Ingrid lost her battle with cancer.

John and I had kept in touch with occasional letters and phone calls. And at one point we met up and went to see Pete Goss's huge catamaran being built in Devon, which I had seen earlier with my sister Valerie.

While I lived at Post Green I had done a lot of sailing on Tom and Faith's yacht Cardhu – usually with a crew of about ten people! So I always did the same two jobs – helping to hoist sails, and helming. It was reminiscent of my time as a child out on Dad's boat most weekends during the summer. I loved being out on the water.

John Hope had just finished rebuilding his "first" Minerva, and had now purchased a larger sailing boat, also called Minerva. So next time he was over in England he showed me some photos of the boat, and said he would keep her at the British Kiel Yacht Club in Germany. When I got an invitation to sail on her I was glad to accept.

I think my three children would say this is when I started gallivanting around the world with John, as over the next twelve months I sailed in the Baltic Sea and up into Denmark from Germany; then I flew over to Jersey for a week; and later visited Portugal, Majorca,Thailand and Cambodia. We also had a marvellous holiday sailing around the Greek Islands with one of John's friends.

Since my mother had died I had almost lost touch with my cousin Janine and her husband Reudi. They used to come and visit Mum at Rownhams House and, if I could, I would come across and see them, either from Poole, or later my own home in Rownhams.

Now that I was "gallivanting", and free of M.E., at times I needed someone really kind to have Amber Anna for me. My son Nigel and his wife Ruth helped out, as did Abigail, but it wasn't always convenient as they were out at work all day. In desperation I contacted Janine to see if she could help by having my lovely Golden Retriever sometimes. Janine wrote back to me and said yes, on condition that she got on well with her own Golden Retriever, Sam. We arranged a visit to their house. Anna immediately made herself three new friends and made herself at home. Janine and Reudi offered to help out by having Anna any time I needed to be away. This was an enormous help and a load off my mind. Anna adored visiting them, and sometimes if I visited Janine and Reudi for an afternoon, Anna would sit on her bottom and make it quite clear she would rather stay with them for a few days!

Because of Amber Anna, John and I have become best friends with Janine and Reudi!

On one of John's visits to Rownhams, we were both invited for a meal at my daughter Tessa's house. Tessa and Stewart immediately took to John and we had a really nice evening together. As we were leaving my young grandson Matthew called out anxiously: "Look after my Nan, John!"

This was a bit embarrassing as we had no plans at that point to look after each other!

My daughter Abi and her partner Dean were house-hunting in Rownhams. Abi was expecting a baby in the summer of 2000, and it was proving difficult to find a house that would be big enough for the three of them, and Abi's two other children Jenna and Gavin. As my house was larger than I needed, I sold them my house and moved to a smaller house in the next road. This worked well, and a few months later my last grandchild was born: Jasper.

John had no children of his own but was quickly taken into the hearts of all my children and grandchildren, which was wonderful. By this time John had decided to move back to Jersey, his home island, and had been busy redecorating and sorting out the house. He had never actually lived in his house, Chalcedony, though his parents and his wife had lived there over the years since he had bought it. John was still serving in the British Army in Germany, and later took early retirement and became Liaison Officer, also in Germany.

As part of his army career in the Royal Corps of Transport, he had captained a ship called HMAV Antwerp. This ship was a 1,000 ton Army ship, with which he worked closely with the Royal Navy and did government logistic tasks, delivering awkward equipment loads, such as large generators, which could often only be delivered by beach landing. Otherwise, the main work of the Maritime Regiment was to serve the Guided Weapons Regiment in the Outer Hebrides. The most dramatic tales arose from landings on the remote Atlantic Island of St Kilda, tempered by the delight of watching the seals, puffins and gannets which abound in those waters.

John certainly had led a very interesting and varied working life. He supervised the transportation of the British Army in Germany by rail, sea, and air; and lectured at the UK National Defence College. He also commanded the British Army's winter ski training organisation (called Operation Snow Queen) in Bavaria, involving some 60,000 soldiers being trained over two winters. I eventually discovered he had been protocol officer to Princess Anne a couple of times.

It took me a very long time to discover the bare bones of John's illustrious career in the army, and I am still learning more of his army pedigree!

John qualified as a Royal Yachting Association (Ocean) Instructor in sailing and was involved in training at the Army Kiel Sail Training Centre on the Baltic Sea.

I used to remind him that while he was full time in the Queen's army I was full time in God's army – both "under orders"! It reminded me that part of my job at Post Green was to research for photos for articles in our magazine Grassroots – which tended to have a bias towards anti-nuclear warfare! I used to get photos of nuclear submarines and other helpful illustrations from the Ministry of Defence – free of charge as long as I sent them a copy of our article. So I think I was on the Ministry of Defence black list while John was doing his good works for the same department!

It wasn't long before John invited me to go sailing with him on his yacht at the British Kiel Yacht Club in northern Germany. The first evening when I arrived, John decided we would go and have a meal at the German Officers' Club, next door to where he kept his boat. I nearly freaked out: surrounded by all these Germans in army uniform! – I had spent half my childhood hiding from the German army and here I was having a meal with all these German officers! I couldn't resist getting into a discussion with one of them about the war and how they had seen it! I gradually learnt there was a big difference between the average German and a Nazi.

John speaks German fluently and excellently. He also is an excellent sailor. My first sailing trip with him was most enjoyable, and I loved visiting the little harbours and ports in Denmark. My sailing trip was quite short as I was shortly due to produce, and sing at, my second Celebration Concert: I had to rehearse daily while on the yacht – while we were out at sea I used my mini disc and sang up on deck at the bow of the boat. But when we were at the British Kiel Army Club base there was nowhere I couldn't be heard while practising, so John organised for me to go into the Germany Army base and I had a private space, singing out to sea, near the helicopter pad. Apart from the guard walking past with his German Shepherd dog I was mostly uninterrupted and could sing through my whole programme after 5 p.m. Imagine singing "The Heart will Go On" from the Titanic film gazing out to sea!

John and I were sailing back from Denmark, across the Baltic Sea. Anna was lying beside us in the cockpit. It was the middle of the day but was a bit dark and gloomy, and sea was grey and choppy. There were no other yachts in sight as far as the eye could see – we were totally alone! Suddenly out of nowhere a motorboat roared up to us, with three men in German naval uniforms, shouting in German at us. As we fly a large British flag you would think, if it was an emergency (and it sounded as though it was by the way they were shouting and gesturing) they would have tried speaking in English. I sat calmly in the cockpit as the German shouting continued. John listened and nodded and spoke quietly back to them in his perfect German. Their little motorboat swung away and disappeared at great speed. John jumped into action, started up the engine, adjusted the sails and "Minerva" swung away on a different course. John was obviously concentrating so I watched and kept quiet. When we had totally altered course, I asked: "What was all that about? Why were they shouting at us?"

"Well, we were cutting across the submarine exercise area. There was a submarine coming up just below us!"

I looked at John, appalled, and gazed back to the gloomy grey sea, where we had been a couple of minutes ago. Out of the sea emerged what looked like a black stick, then a black funnel thing, then a very large grey submarine! Woops, that was close! I wondered how long the periscope had been focused on us and if they had been able to listen to what we had been talking about. I must ask Garibaldi, my "ex-son in law" – he was a submariner in the English navy – if the Germans could have been listening to us!

When John was living back in Jersey, we spoke quite often on the telephone, and I was invited for my second visit to Chalcedony – his home on the island.

Two days before I was due to fly over something very odd happened to me.

I was sound asleep in my bed at home in Rownhams, when I suddenly woke up. It seemed the room was full of perfume. As I became aware of the fragrance around me I also felt there was "someone" standing by my bed. I was truly frightened. It was pitch dark, but "someone" was very close to me, so I couldn't get out of bed even if I had wanted to. I slid deeper under the bedclothes – but the perfume was still quite strong. Eventually after about an hour (it seemed to me) it disappeared. So I switched the light on, and crept nervously out onto the landing. I could smell the perfume in the room John used when he used to come and stay.

I switched on all the lights upstairs, and bravely went downstairs and made myself a drink. On coming back upstairs the fragrance was no longer evident anywhere. I "knew" it had something to do with John, but I didn't know what, and because I had been frightened by the episode I also felt a bit angry. "I don't need this!" I said to myself.

When daylight came, having slept quite well even after the perfume incident, I determined to try and find out what it was. The first person I telephoned was Dr Kenneth McCall, who was an experienced Christian leader, and had specialised in what one might call "odd phenomenon" - such as corn circles and the Bermuda Triangle, with most interesting results. He had written Healing the Family Tree, and other books.

He didn't say anything that really alarmed me, but questioned me on who was in my life at the moment and I mentioned John Hope. He felt the relationship was significant in what was happening to me. So then I phoned up my minister Rev Cliff Bembridge. He suggested I call in at the church and we would have a chat. I explained about the perfume and the presence of someone during the night. Although I didn't mention John, he immediately asked me about him. I explained we were just friends and that we had both agreed that neither of us was interested in getting married again. Then Cliff said, "What if John asks you to marry him?"

"He won't. We've already agreed we are happy with our single lives!" I replied firmly.

Cliff persisted: "If John asks you to marry him what would your answer be? If you don't know the answer, you need to think and pray about it. I think that was what last night's episode was all about!"

I listened to Cliff, and he is a sufficiently formidable minister that I thought I had better do what he suggested even if the question would never be put to me by John!

Two days later, as previously arranged with John, I flew over to Jersey for his birthday. On his birthday he asked me if I would marry him! I had done what Cliff had suggested, so l fortunately had my answer ready!

"Yes!"

As John had proposed to me in the middle of his birthday party, and had popped the question between his kitchen and the living room, he then burst into the room announcing our engagement, with my permission of course! John's sister Marjorie was first to offer enthusiastic congratulations, quickly followed by her husband Graeme. I already felt welcomed into the family! The lovely Portuguese family living at John's house Chalcedony were all greatly enthusiastic about our engagement and King, Ceu, and Fabio each gave me a big hug. I was exceedingly glad that I had already had time to think and pray about such a life-changing decision before I was asked. God knew! Initially when I smelt the perfume and felt someone standing by my bed I presumed it was an evil presence. I was so frightened. But actually it turned out for the good as it made me think and pray about my relationship with John, encouraged by Cliff. And when you read in the Bible about an Angel appearing to someone, the person was usually terrified at the appearance of what was obviously something, someone, unearthly!

Before our wedding in St John's Church, Rownhams, we had another sailing trip up at Kiel. Again I was practising for my third and last Celebration Concert at St John's and again I used the Germany Army Camp to do the rehearsing!

We also towed an old caravan out to Romania one weekend and helped at an orphanage, which was a most moving experience. The orphans were mostly disabled, in varying degrees, and some were very mentally and physically handicapped. The most moving experience I had was doing some gentle massage and aromatherapy, under the supervision of a trained therapist, with some of the little children strapped in their wheel chairs. Some of their muscles relaxed so much they could open their hands and wriggle their feet. How much they needed this daily – not once a year. John and I drove home, deeply moved by all our experiences there. My cousin Janine gave us a beautiful picture she had painted to take with us and that went up on the wall for the children to see. But we were sad to see that many of the soft toys sent to the orphanage were on high shelves around the rooms, where the children couldn't touch them.

As we drove away I felt very strongly that the children needed lots of music therapy and yearned to have the facility to help in that direction. I also felt that rather than so many people travelling out to Romania to "help" it would be far better to use the travelling money to bring the children's helpers over to the United Kingdom to teach the carers how to play with the children, and how to teach them whatever they were capable of learning.

Of course we had various adventures on the way to and from Romania, and especially at the border controls. Fortunately because the caravan we had been given to tow out there looked so terrible (because it had been power-washed and all the paint had come off) we were let through fairly easily as they could see that we were very poor – even though we were loaded to the gunnels with toys, baby supplies, shoes, and blankets!

Do you want to hear about the saga of my wedding dress? My grandsons can skip this bit if they want!

I was twenty one years old when I married the first time, and I was married to David Mills for twenty one years; and then I was on my own for twenty one years! Then came my second wedding – by which time I was sixty three years of age! So

I chose a nice pale blue demure suit to get married in. But John got more and more excited about the wedding, and decided to get married in a Morning Suit. And his best man, Martin White would also be in Morning Suit. Somehow I didn't feel my new pale blue suit would fit too well with that. Eventually, egged on by friends and family, I bought a beautiful pearl encrusted Cinderella type white wedding dress. I left it with my next door neighbour who said she would be only too glad to look after it while we were away in Romania (as I didn't want John to see it).

On our return from Romania I fetched my wedding dress from my neighbour, covered in the sheet I had supplied with it. It had to go back to the dress shop to have the hem taken up an inch or so. When I returned a week later to try it on, I realised it had been taken up at the waist not the hem, and was all bunched and looked awful. Abigail was with me. We complained about the way it looked but they said it wasn't their fault and nothing could be done about it. I was very disappointed, and in the end we gave up and drove home. I then went over to my neighbour and told her something awful had happened to my dress and they had ruined it. She listened to me and then said, "What would you say if I told you I have an identical dress upstairs?"

As she was very slim and very tiny, and not engaged to be married, I was speechless. She ran upstairs and came down with an identical dress in my size! "The thing is, I wasn't going to tell you! But a cat got in and pee-ed all over your dress. It smelt awful. The owners of the cat said they would pay for the cleaning of the dress and we sent it off to be dry-cleaned. But I panicked and thought it would still smell - so I decided to buy an identical dress. It is that dress you had altered. This is your dress which I still had hanging upstairs! This has been to the cleaners!"

As the altered dress was almost un-wearable, she gave me back my dress, and I was truly grateful to have a lovely unspoilt wedding dress, even if the cat had soiled it! I told John all about it after the wedding was well and truly over. I got to wear the dress a second time, when we had a Marriage Blessing service in Jersey a couple of weeks later for all John's family and friends in Jersey. Tessa as my chief bridesmaid came across for the occasion and had a chance to wear her silver bridesmaid's dress again too.

On the day of the wedding I had most of my grandsons as ushers, and also my grand-daughter Jasmin. My oldest grand-daughter Jenna was also a bridesmaid and wore a gold-coloured dress. The vicar of Rownhams, Rev Julian Williams took the service, and Rev Cliff Bembridge led the prayers.

St John's Church, Rownhams, is a wonderful setting for a wedding. I had sung in the choir there for many weddings over the years. Now it was my turn, unbelievably! My singing teacher from Bournemouth, Penny Landi, offered to sing for me. She sang "Ave Maria" and "The Lord's Prayer". It was a very special occasion. Once all the photographs had been taken, we all slipped across the road to Rownhams House. My young brother Roger had kindly lent us the house and grounds for our Wedding Reception. A friend, Colin Jones, brought a small boat round and the children had great entertainment rowing on the lake.

Amber Anna, in the meantime, was being looked after by Janine and Reudi, and greeted us afterwards with a big red bow tied onto her collar. Little did she know her life was about to change as well. I had thought that I wouldn't be able to take her to Jersey and that she would stay with Janine and Reudi, so I wrote Amber Anna a letter:

"L'Abri, Rownhams, Southampton:

"Dearest Amber Anna, I wish I could tell you what you have done for me! When I named you Anna – for faithfulness, to God and people, and Amber – for healing – I had a feeling that I would become fit, or fitter, again during our time together. Both happened.

"I am now totally fit because of a miracle of God – and I became fitter than I had been because of fresh air and exercise. You got me out of the house, introduced me to the children of the neighbourhood and found me lots of friends while doggy walking!

"You have been an amazing gentle faithful friend. Not always obedient! But you have tried! Anna – thank you so much for the joy and friendship and healthy lifestyle you have given me.

"Now a chapter is closing and you will be with Janine and Reudi. They love you very much as well. Come and visit when we are around and be happy. Anna, I love you and want the very best for you, that's why I've made this decision. Where I am going it is too far away for you to keep travelling. We will be coming and going and you wouldn't like to be crated up on the ferry. And we couldn't keep taking the car across just for you to have a better crossing. I will miss all the doggy walks

– to the football field, around Rownhams cycle paths, to Rownhams House – and Farley Mount with Judith, Hindon with Valerie, Caravan Rallies with Dorothy, Zen, Tomo and Mica.

"Dearest Anna – bring lots of happiness to Janine and Reudi and Sam – and we will come and see you whenever we can. Thank you for your love and faithfulness, your gentleness and patience – your friendliness to all the children, dogs, ducks, neighbours, and most especially me!

"I love you Anna, from Daphi.

"P.S. The squirrels around L'Abri will miss you!!"

That was my "farewell" letter I wrote in Anna's journal. But later that day when I took Amber Anna to my cousin's, I was persuaded to give it a try with Anna in Jersey – and Janine and Reudi would stand by to help look after Anna whenever it was needed.

When we loaded up Colin Jones' old ambulance to take all my clothes, books, music and other personal belongings, John made a comfortable space in the van. Anna hopped in happily and crossed with us over to Jersey. The Portuguese family living at Chalcedony were standing on the doorstep when we arrived early evening, and Fabio announced to everyone that Anna was his sister. Fabio had to go to hospital frequently because he was born with a cleft palate – if they asked him if he had brothers or sisters – he would say he had a sister called Anna!

Anna took to the beaches with a passion, and every day, even if it snowed, she would go swimming!

When I first moved into Chalcedony and took Anna for a walk before bedtime, I couldn't always remember, in the darkness, which was our house. But Anna would have no difficulty swinging into our driveway, tail wagging, even on her first evening walk. But it was a few weeks before John trusted me with the car out on my own. "Daphne, you take the car this afternoon – while I mow the lawn," he offered, very unexpectedly.

"Great!" I thought, "I know where I want to go! Come on, Anna – walkies – we go in the car!" Anna wagged her tail, and I fetched her lead and my purse.

"Don't get lost!" was John's anxious parting remark to me.

We drove off before he could change his mind. I headed west and then up the coast and around towards the north – not quite sure of my way, so I slowed up at each signpost. At last I found the right road, and we drove down a hill, and arrived at the very beach I was seeking. My great plan was to buy myself a Knickerbocker Glory – my favourite ice cream and fruit salad. I don't think I had had one since I used to come to Jersey as a teenager! It was a warm day, so I got Anna out of the car and hooked on her lead, We walked up to the cafe, and I tied Anna up to a huge wire trolley, containing beach regalia – buckets, spades, sun hats, large and small balls, and other toys.

"Stay, Anna!" I spoke to her and signalled for her to sit down. She promptly lay down, and I happily walked into the cafe. "One Knickerbocker Glory, please."

"That'll be two pounds and ten pence. You'll have to wait a moment or two!" I handed over my money and waited, and waited.

There was a loud shout at the door. "Who owns the Golden Retriever?"

I turned round, concerned. A man stood in the doorway – and I could see Anna standing with him, peering into the cafe. "I do." I called and ran towards the door, first checking that there was still no sign of my Knickerbocker Glory.

"Something spooked her!" the man said, as he handed me Anna on her lead. I looked around aghast. As far as the eye could see, were buckets, spades, balls, and other bright coloured objects. Some of the balls were rolling over the edge of the road and onto the beach below. The trolley on wheels, to which I had tied Anna, was in the middle of the road, on its side. Holding Anna with one hand I scooped up as much of the beach merchandise as I could, and the man helpfully lifted the trolley upright and wheeled it back to its original place.

"One Knickerbocker Glory ready" came a shout from inside. I ran in with Anna, fetched my much longed for feast, and sat outside amongst the chairs and tables enjoying my special treat. After a prance on the beach and a swim in the sea, Anna was ready for our homeward journey. With the map beside me we managed to find St Brelade, and Chalcedony. A few days later I told John of our adventure, worried he might not let us out alone again without him supervising us!

But Anna saved her best adventures for her sailing holidays in Germany. Most of the time she adored sailing with us, and even when the sea got very rough she would hop off the seats in the cockpit and lie on the floor, and if it was even more rough we would put her in her berth in the main cabin, which she could access easily from the cockpit. She always had her life jacket on if it looked like it was going to be a rough sea.

One day we stopped over at a harbour on the border of Germany and Denmark, moored up in the marina. There was a special festival on and the walkways were crowded. Anna found a German Shepherd dog to play with on a small beach, and when its owner whistled for it to come, Anna went chasing after them down towards where our boat was moored. As Anna was running she bumped a German woman walking in the same direction. The woman was very angry, and turned and saw me carrying a dog lead, and was obviously swearing at me – in German. I shrugged my shoulders and said, "English?", and she turned and stamped up the steps of the harbour master's office.

It was high time Anna and I disappeared, but Anna had continued to run off after the German Shepherd dog. So I ran back to the boat and hid in the cabin, explaining to John I was in trouble. Anna came running back, hopped back onto the yacht, and I pushed her quickly into her berth, out of sight. There we stayed for several hours!

About an hour later an official, in dark suit and brief case, walked up and down our pontoon, obviously looking for an English Golden Retriever – who was nowhere in sight. It was dark before Anna was allowed out for her next walk!

Most of the time Anna was very well-behaved, but she objected to being left on the boat by herself, unless she could see us. One evening, while moored up in Denmark, we went out for a meal, and left Anna on deck, telling her we won't be long. But she had seen us meet up with our friends Janet and Horst, and their Spanish Greyhound, Bella. Unknown to us, while we were having our meal, Anna jumped overboard and swam towards the shore. A fisherman saw her and helped her get ashore safely and took her up to the yacht club. Of course Anna had a disc around her neck with my telephone number. My phone rang in the restaurant. "We have a very wet dog sitting in our dining room. We've given her a meal, but we thought you might like to come and fetch her!"

I ran all the way back to the Yacht Club, and there was Anna, still dripping wet, gazing out of the window. She got what she wanted – I walked her back to the restaurant and she lay on the floor with Bella, sleeping heavily after her swim and smart yacht club meal.

Anna disgraced us threc times, while John and I were helping to co-host the Queen's Birthday Parade at British Kiel Yacht Club. We were all dressed up in our finery, specially brought from Jersey for the occasion. All the guests, probably about two hundred, were all poshed up as well in their smartest clothes. Each year, as well as a marvellous marching display, "Beating Retreat", by some army band, there was also a demonstration of sky-diving. We would all stand out on the balcony of the yacht club after we had finished eating the canapés and making polite conversation to senior army and civic officials, both German and English. We would gaze up into the sky awaiting our first glimpse of the four or five parachutists coming down, aiming to land on a large orange buoy just beneath where we stood.

We would be able to see Anna, happily sitting on the deck of our yacht, watching the crowd, though hopefully not being able to identify us at that distance. Three years running, she suddenly appeared in the crowd while we were gazing up at the sky, soaking wet, having jumped overboard and then run up the jetty to find us. Her wet tail would wag everywhere, and would wag even harder as soon as she saw us. This was a bad distraction just as the guys were landing by the orange buoy! Then I would have to grab her collar, and get her back on to our boat, in my smart clothes and tight skirt in front of two hundred people. We realised later that there was some kind of sonic boom as the plane went over, dropping the men out as it went. We couldn't hear the boom, but Anna did and she didn't like it, it frightened her!

As I write this I realise that Anna will never again be able to disrupt the Queen's Birthday Parade, as she died a month ago – and John and I are grieving her loss terribly. She was The Best!

We have travelled back to England many times with Anna on the ferry; she didn't like being in the kennel on the car deck, but she was very well behaved and never complained. But she preferred it when we took the car across and she could lie on the back seat and guard the car for us. Janine and Reudi had her for holidays many times, joining their own golden retriever, Sam and later their new dog Poppy.

Janine and Reudi searched for another Golden Retriever for many months after Sam died. They didn't want a puppy as they were getting a bit older and would prefer to have a rescue dog. They travelled all over the place and always came home disappointed. John and I called in to see them and left Anna with them while we went down to Taunton to look after my sister's dogs while her husband Basil was in hospital. We took our caravan and parked it on a site nearby.

We had prayed so much for Janine and Reudi to find another Golden Retriever, and when we had left Anna with them they told us they had given up looking, as it was too stressful. But John and I carried on praying anyway!

On our first morning on the camp site, it was a bit chilly so I switched on the fan heater, and climbed back into my sleeping bag. John got up a bit later, and switched on the kettle. Bang! All the electrics blew. It wasn't an internal fault. The electrics had blown on the camp field. John waited until 7.30am and then went over to the warden's house. They had a yard full of rescued Jack Russell dogs and Whippets. John rang the door bell and explained to the warden that we had blown the electrics. She came across and fiddled with something on the post where we had plugged in to the electrics and got it all up and working again. In the meantime John chattily asked her about her dogs and happened to mention we were looking for a rescue golden retriever. "Oh, I know of one, three years old, desperate for a good home. I will give you the phone number if I find it is still available." She turned and walked back to her house. Later she gave us the contact name and telephone number, saying the dog was still not yet re-homed.

John and I immediately telephoned Janine and Reudi, explaining our possible find. With various instructions about what to look for, we arranged to see the dog at 5pm. By 6pm we were back at the caravan having been to see the dog: an exquisitely , uniquely beautiful, golden retriever, called Poppy. We had paid the agreed amount, brought her toys and some food, and had driven back to the caravan. Next day we delivered her safely to Janine and Reudi, where she settled in immediately. She seemed like a precious answer to many prayers.

As soon as Poppy met Reudi she snuggled into his arms, bonding immediately with him, and John burst into tears of joy! Poppy always remembers us when we visit her and squeals with joy, running around the house and garden with her current favourite toy and running up to us for another hug.

When I see Poppy, it makes me think: when God gives a gift it is perfect! Janine and Reudi tell us that when they take her out somewhere everyone stops and marvels at how beautiful she is! They call her their miracle!

It was a huge wrench to leave my family and friends and move to Jersey. The plus side was that I had a wonderful new husband, kind, caring, generous, thoughtful – and clever! It was also a bonus that we had a lovely Portuguese family living in a part of Chalcedony. I got on brilliantly with all of them – and having lived in community and large households for a lot of my life – it was great to have "family" around. Ceu (pronounced Sayoo) sometimes called me "Mummy" and Fabio regarded us as his Jersey Grandparents, though he also had grandparents in Portugal. Ceu's husband was called Jaoquim (nicknamed King). We had lots of fun and laughter and it made up a bit for my missing my wonderful children and grandchildren.

I certainly didn't like a lot of the decor in Chalcedony and set about getting rid of colours I didn't like – dark browns and sludgy greens! – bringing in blues and turquoises wherever I could. One day while John was out in the garden I started to paint the kitchen tiles a fairly bright turquoise. Fabio came in from school: "Does Mr Hope know you're painting his tiles? Has he seen the colour?" he asked in panic. "No!" I said. "Well, Daphie, I don't think you better do anymore till he sees it!" That was over seven years ago and the turquoise tiles still look magnificent!

The scenery on Jersey and the rest of the Channel Islands is out of this world! Even last night, John and I drove down to the lighthouse at La Corbiere on the south west corner of the island, and marvelled at God's "painting" of the sunset over the sea, with the islands of Guernsey, Sark, and Herm visible on the horizon as purple blue haze, impossible to describe or even photograph accurately.

The tides in the Channel Islands are huge – with a rise of twelve to thirteen metres at times. When the tide is out the rocks that are uncovered by the retreating water make it look like a lunar landscape or something out of a science fiction film. My favourite place is La Corbiere – the rocks, the panoramic views of the sea, and the long causeway leading to the lighthouse, which is well covered at high tide for several hours. One day John and I were walking Anna along the causeway, but it was still covered with sea water, but I could see the causeway underneath, as a lighter colour of blue. The impulse took me, and I ran, nearly knee deep at times, through the sea across the causeway to dry land up by the lighthouse. I glanced back to see Anna following me, leaping and prancing through the water. John was still standing where I had left him. I was laughing with joy, it was such fun. Then as I stood near the lighthouse I thought: "Oh – help! Is the tide coming in or going out? If it's coming in Anna and I are stuck for several hours – marooned beside the lighthouse."

John was too far away for me to shout and ask him. I looked around helplessly, while Anna was lying down chewing some seaweed. "I think the tide is going out!" I waved to John and we happily walked the final distance up to the rocks on which the lighthouse was perched, with my wet jeans slapping round my ankles and my shoes squelching with sea-water.

If John was nervous about letting me drive round Jersey, in the early days, in his little Mazda run-about car, he certainly wasn't keen for me to drive his much larger and newer Mercedes. I didn't mind at all – it is a monster of a car and has a strange hand-brake system unfamiliar to me. But early on in our marriage John went off one evening to his old school reunion dinner at Victoria College. Anna and I were very happy to be on our own, and the Pinto family were upstairs, anyway. King came downstairs later in the evening and was washing up their dinner plates in the sink. I decided to be very helpful, and back the Mercedes into the garage so John wouldn't have to do it when he came home. Anyway, I thought, he might have had some alcohol and have a mishap while putting the car away in the darkness!

Unfortunately it was pitch dark already: but I found the car keys, started up the Mercedes and put it into reverse. I don't know how I figured out the brake system but it must have worked as the car slowly and gently went backwards. I neatly, slowly and cautiously backed the car into the garage. It was three quarters inside when there was a most horrid crunch. I had reversed into a jutting out concrete post that I hadn't noticed was there. I got out and checked where the post was and how much clearance I had the other side, re-positioned the car and backed it more carefully, hitting nothing en route. I then pressed the garage door button and the garage door closed automatically.

On re-entering the kitchen King was still laboriously washing up their dinner things.

"King?" I said, prodding him to get his attention. Although they had been in Jersey for about nine years his English was still very limited. He turned round and looked at me. With hand signals and facial expressions I said, very anxiously: "I've just bumped Mr Hope's car."

Of course, what I wanted King to say was, "Oh, don't worry, Mr Hope won't mind at all."

But King looked at me with total horror on his face. Speechless. We stared at each other in silence! Then King said: “The Mazda?”

“No, the Mercedes!” I replied, nervously.

King’s face took on a look of excruciating pain. He said nothing. Then he shrugged his shoulders and turned back to his washing up.

This made me panic more. I hadn’t known John long enough to know how mad he might get.

I stood around in the kitchen. King finished washing up. “Go – see Mr Hope’s car!” he said. So we made our way out to the garage and switched on the lights. He stroked the damaged rear wing of the car as though it was his wife. Another shrug, and he walked silently back towards the house.

John came home around midnight, very happy and full of the wonderful time he had had with all his old school chums. I listened while he waxed lyrical about the evening. Then he asked me about my evening. Oh, I just spent it quietly, reading and watching the television!

Next morning, I still hadn’t told John about his precious Mercedes. After our morning cup of tea in bed we usually have a little Quiet Time, reading a Psalm and then praying for whoever or whatever we want to pray for. On this particular morning, we closed our eyes to pray. I prayed aloud: “O God help John not to be cross that I banged his car last night!”

“WHAT!” shouted John. The prayer time aborted for the time being and explanations were given. John jumped out of bed, grabbing his dressing gown on the way out to the garage to check on his precious car. He was as bad as King, stroking the car as though it was his wife! And me – standing there watching. John cheered up later that morning after talking to his friend Uve in Germany who said he would get the dent out and re-spray the damaged area of the car on our next visit.

Since living in Jersey we have attended many of the island’s churches, some for two or more years, but we have yet to find a true spiritual home – but may be that is what God wants for us for the time being. In the mean time we attend whatever church we feel led to on any particular Sunday but find ourselves being drawn gradually into the life of the local parish church at St Brelades where we live. We are certainly meeting many people and experiencing church life throughout the island. There are some wonderful Christians around!

I have heard God say to me is: “The Church is not part of the Trinity!”

The Trinity is: God, the Father; God, the Son; and God, the Holy Spirit. Our relationship needs to be with God – Father, Son and Holy Spirit. We are not to neglect meeting regularly with other Christians. The Bible calls them the ecclesia – which means the Church. But we must always make sure our worship is directed towards God, and not that we are “worshipping the church”. This is a bit complex, but as you think and pray about it you will understand what God is saying. In other words don’t make the Church more important than God.

One Christmas John and I volunteered to go carol singing with a nearby church in Jersey. I had only just recovered from a rather tedious bout of laryngitis so decided to treat my vocal chords with care on this particular evening. It wasn’t long before the group of carol singers were in difficulties as there was no musician amongst them. John spoke to the leader of the group, and I was asked if I would take over choosing how many verses of each carol and starting everyone off on the right note. I didn’t mind doing this, but I had more and more trouble “shouting” above the babble to announce the next carol – so I asked John if he would do the announcing. Nevertheless I could feel my vocal chords were warning me I was overdoing things. I felt stressed and irritable by the time we got back to the car park in the pitch darkness at the end of the evening. I couldn’t wait to get home and have a nice warm cup of tea. John drove fairly quickly (as quick as you can in Jersey with a 40 mile per hour speed limit!).

We reached our home, Chalcedony, and I jumped out of the car with only one thing on my mind – a hot cup of tea! I reached for my bunch of keys usually kept in my pocket – they weren’t there! I knew I had them when I had left home nearly three hours ago.

“John! I’ve lost my keys!” I called out as my husband was busy getting our dog Anna out of the car, and locking the car doors. After a brief discussion we realised we had no alternative but to retrace our steps.

I groaned and grumbled. John unlocked the front door and I double-checked the hook where I always hang my keys – but of course they weren’t there. I knew I had had them when we went carol singing. All ideas of having a quick cuppa vanished and John was already revving up the engine to return to our carol singing patch. We forgot to take a torch – and the mission was impossible. We quickly gave up and drove home, resolving to search next morning in the daylight.

Next morning we searched the car park and all of the streets, closes, driveways, where we had sung carols. No keys! After a long search we drove back to Chalcedony. In the car I prayed: "Please Lord, let someone have found my keys and give them back to me at church on Sunday!" I also apologised to the Lord for being grumpy and irritable while carol singing, and getting stressed with having to shout over the babble of happy carollers as we walked around the locality.

We arrived back home and John parked the car in the drive. I waited for John to get out of the car, and together with Anna, we walked to the front door. John unlocked the front door, and let me walk in first. The very first thing I saw were my keys hanging on their usual hook! I was completely stunned! Then I looked down on the hall floor and my anorak was laid out very neatly, sleeves spread out invitingly!

"Look! Look!" I cried out to John. "Look! My keys – and whoever would have laid my anorak on the floor like that?"

We discussed every possible scenario. The keys weren't there when we went out! The anorak certainly wasn't laid out neatly on the floor when we went out! If it had fallen off its hook (impossible) it wouldn't have fallen that neatly with the sleeves neatly spread. In my heart I knew who had been in the house! An angel had called while we were out!

Only one other person had a key, Brian from next door. John went round and asked him if he had been in but his astonished eyes told us the answer – he had not called into our house while we were out – he hadn't found our keys and he certainly hadn't laid out my anorak on the floor.

I felt greatly loved and comforted by God – and humbled that He should be so kind to me after I had got so irritable while carol singing for Him.

It is only recently, since living in Jersey, I have become more familiar with the tides and the tidal currents: which has now solved a childhood mystery, which has puzzled me for years. One day, when Valerie and I were probably aged about ten and eleven, Dad picked us up from school on his way to Hythe, Southampton, to take the employees' wages. It was a Friday afternoon, and Valerie and I were quite used to having about an hour to amuse ourselves, exploring around the back of the warehouses, climbing over stacks of huge lengths of wood, awaiting warehousing or delivery, and sometimes creeping though into next door, which belonged to the Ministry of Defence.

On this particular Friday Valerie and I were on Ministry of Defence land, in forbidden territory. We found a slipway leading down to a very large "rubber" or canvas type dingy. It seemed huge to me and would probably hold about eight or more sailors, but it only had netting in the bottom so the seawater sloshed around freely on the inside of the boat. I climbed on, taking care not to slip on the green slippery surface at the edge of the slipway. I sat on the edge of the boat, keeping my best brown leather school shoes high out of the water. Valerie held the rope for me and I untied the other rope and floated freely. Somehow Valerie let go of her rope and I found myself floating out to sea. I wasn't worried about the danger I was in, floating off to America or wherever, but I was scared my father would find out and be cross, very cross!

I floated further and further out to sea, and my fear mounted. Any moment now, Dad would come looking for us, and catch me doing something wrong. While I was wondering what to do, I found myself floating back in again! A miracle? I will never know! Either way, I expect the tide turned and the current drew me back into where I needed to be. I hastily threw the rope to Valerie, who was still standing on the slipway. We had just climbed into the car, and shut the doors when Dad appeared. We grabbed books out of our school satchels, and pretended to be doing our homework. He never found out about our adventure!

CHAPTER THIRTY SIX

John and I delayed our honeymoon so that Anna and I could get settled in Jersey, but the following year we took a trip to the Holy Land with a large group gathered from many churches, plus an orchestra, professional singers, a bishop and several internationally famous Christian leaders. Although it was only May it was very hot, dry and dusty. We were taken to many holy sites: tombs of some of the ancient Old Testament prophets, the site of the Road to Emmaus, the Temple area in Jerusalem, and the Wailing Wall. We spent time in the beautiful Garden of Gethsemane, where Jesus spent his last evening with his disciples after they had had Supper together. We saw the probable place where Jesus was imprisoned overnight before the Crucifixion.

We went to Nazareth and Capernaum. And we took a boat trip across the Sea of Galilee. I was invited to sing while the boat was crossing the famous lake that Jesus spent so much of his time on. So I sang the song The Stranger of Galilee:

"In fancy I stood by the shore one day of the beautiful murmuring sea. I saw the great crowds as they thronged the way, of the Stranger of Galilee. I saw how the man who was blind from birth –in a moment was made to see. The lame were made whole by the matchless skill of the Stranger of Galilee. And I felt I could love Him forever, so gracious and tender was He. I claimed Him that day as my saviour! This Stranger of Galilee."

It is a song I have sung in public many times, but I never ever expected to have the chance to sing it on the Sea of Galilee.

Of course there is still the terrible on-going war between Israel and Palestine, and though we went at a particularly dangerous time, there were no incidents or suicide bombers while we were there. One of our leaders led us in prayer for the peace of Jerusalem, and the Holy Land, each time we stopped at a particular site.

We went to the traditional site of the resurrection of Jesus, and also the site which many modern Christians prefer – a garden tomb with a most amazing atmosphere, and it seems to me to be the most likely place of the resurrection, in sight of the probable site of the Crucifixion. But many people have different opinions, and really I don't think it matters. All the places draw one into thoughtful, prayerful worship.

On the last day the group we were with held a final Holy Communion service on the shores of Galilee. It was a huge outdoor place of worship with large stone seating built around in a semi circle, carved into the hillside. John and I sat right at the back at the very top of the auditorium, facing the sea. The service was quite long. Halfway through the service, a young woman on the side furthest away from us, started shouting out. She started by shouting the name of Jesus, but that soon deteriorated into what seemed like a demonic screaming. The service ground to a halt. I watched the leaders at the front, but none of them moved – and neither did anyone else. The next item on our printed programme was meant to be a solo, sung by a lovely young woman who had performed several times while we were in the Holy Land. But she wouldn't be heard over the loud wailing of the young woman, so she remained seated. After several minutes, the conductor stood up and raised his baton to conduct the orchestra, and the soloist moved to the microphone.

I was appalled. I put myself in her place in my imagination – I just couldn't sing over the top of that terrible noise. John had his head bent in prayer as I turned to look at him. "I'm going!" I whispered to him. I moved swiftly across the crowded rows of concrete seating, glancing down at the soloist and orchestra as I went. The baton was still raised, but the music hadn't started. I finally got to the screaming, wailing woman, and put my arms around her. I found myself saying, "Jesus! Jesus loves you. Jesus! Jesus loves you!" many times. The girl turned into my arms, the wailing stopped as she slid down onto the tiered seating, and went "unconscious". The orchestra was by now playing the opening bars of the song, and the soloist began her song. The auditorium was silent. I kept my hand on the "sleeping" girl for the rest of the service, quietly praying for her.

When the service ended, the girl woke up, and I gave her another hug and reassured her that Jesus loved her, and walked back through the crowded seating to where John was still sat. When I sat down next to John he whispered to me: "I was praying you would go!" And I replied, "And I was praying someone else would go!" I knew what to do because I had seen the power in the name of Jesus, many times during my ministry. But I had felt very conspicuous climbing over everyone to get to the interruption, which I felt was Satanic.

Later, back at the hotel, almost all the church leaders and the bishop, thanked me for dealing with the interruption. I was mostly amazed that not one of the leaders, all who were sat nearer to the young woman than I was, had moved forward themselves to deal with the problem. Months later, when I remembered the occasion, I was deeply touched that Jesus allowed me - Daphne! – to take part in such an incident beside the Sea of Galilee, where Jesus had stood and ministered many times during his life.

I have come almost to the end of writing this book, primarily for my beloved grandchildren: and I came across a scrap of paper on which I had written down several scriptures during a particularly difficult time in my life while I was struggling with M.E. and broken relationships.

I want to share these scriptures with you because they are full of hope and they all came prophetically true for me, as they can for you:

"You will go out in joy and be led forth in peace; the mountains and hills will burst into song before you, and all the trees of the field will clap their hands. Instead of the thorn bush will grow the pine tree, and instead of the briers the myrtle will grow. This will be for the Lord's honour, for an everlasting sign..." (Isaiah chapter 55 verses 12-13).

"Those who sow in tears will reap with songs of joy. He who goes out weeping, carrying seed to sow, will return with songs of joy, carrying sheaves with him." (Psalm 126 verses 5,6)

"You turned my wailing into dancing; you removed my sackcloth and clothed me with joy, that my heart may sing to you and not be silent. O Lord my God, I will give you thanks forever." (Psalm 30 verses 11,12

"See! The winter is past; the rains are over and gone. Flowers appear on the earth; the season of singing has come, the cooing of doves is heard in our land. The fig tree forms its early fruit; the blossoming vines spread their fragrance." Song of Solomon chapter 2 verses 11-13.

"For God so loved the world that he gave his one and only Son, that whoever believes in him shall not perish (be ruined or lost) but have everlasting life." St.John chapter 3 verse 16.

I remember when Faith Lees was terribly ill with cancer. She had been such a friend and mentor to me, and had taught me so much about the love of God, and how to reach out to others. As I mentioned earlier in this book, when I asked Abigail what she thought Jesus looked like she had replied, "Like Aunty Faith!"

It seemed so cruel that Faith should have cancer, in the throat, so it made it very difficult for her to talk in her last few months. But as I prayed the Lord reminded me of a verse in Psalm 33.

“The eyes of the Lord are on those who fear Him, on those who hope in his unfailing love, to deliver them from death and keep them alive in famine. We wait in hope for the Lord. He is our help and our shield. In Him our hearts rejoice, for we trust in His holy name. May your unfailing love rest upon us, O Lord, even as we put our hope in you.”

As I thought about the many times Faith had “saved the day” for me, and for many others it seemed so unjust that she should be suffering in this way, before she had even reach her “three score years and ten”, which the Bible tells us is our allotted time!

As I continued to pray God seemed to say to me: “We are part of the travail on earth. We’ve come from God, and we are going back to God – we are children of God. But we have a journey to make on earth and are therefore part of the citizenship of earth – part of the earthliness that has been separated from God, and is now caught into the fall of man, the evil seeds spread worldwide, causing havoc in what was God’s perfect creation. Now we are servants among God’s creation, spoiled by the Evil One, Satan, and those who collude with him.

“We are to stand firm against the tide of evil sweeping the earth – to fight every evil seed we can until God calls us home. We are to sow seeds of love – God’s love in us – and to spread the Word of God – Jesus made flesh in the world to show us all the way back to God – who is Love, and always was Love and always will be Love.

“Fight the good fight of faith and you will be rewarded – you will not be discouraged. Keep your eye on the crown – already laid out for you in heaven. But don’t give in to the Evil One – reclaim the territory he has snatched away from you, from God. Take your authority in Jesus and use it, and go on using it. Even if you don’t seem to see results, stand your ground and continue to make your claim, and hold your claim on your territory, staking your claim in the name of Jesus. God is sovereign in the midst of pain and suffering. He is in control, but fight the seeds of the Evil One, and strengthen your fortress.”

However young you are you will have already suffered! whether it was at home, at school, at work, amongst friends, or while out and about innocently going about your daily life. Life will never be easy! But God has given us some tools to give us the ability to stand up strong in the day of our trial.

When I was "going through it" and agonising yet again about my life, it seemed that God whispered some very good advice in my ear! I wrote it down on the 19th April 1996. I think this word might be for you too:

"Be open to Me, the Lord, and follow the Holy Spirit in your daily life, that is all I ask of you, a daily walk with Me. Worship Me in your heart. Worship Me with all your heart, and soul, and mind and strength. Bow down to Me, in your heart and in your mind. Love Me as I love you. Seek Me as I seek you. Follow Me as I seek you out. You feel weak and fragile, and in many ways you are. Rest in Me and make me your confidence and your strength. Lean on Me and don't keep trying to struggle. Only do what I ask you to do – not all the rest of what you see needs doing. I will call others to do those jobs.

"You have a vision and you have seen Me at work. You truly hunger and thirst for it all but you are overwhelmed. But remember – it's My work, My harvest, My world. Back your vision, your desires, with prayer – the many prayers of the many saints who faithfully pray My will into being.

"Prayer will strengthen you, not weaken you!

"Prayer will resolve issues that at present distress you and use up emotional energy, as you worry and squirm over them. Draw strength from Me, by praying specifically for each area that weakens or overwhelms you – pray around it, over it, under it, wrap it around with prayer and give it to Me as you would a present, a gift, that's not to be taken back – except by lovingly wrapping it around with more prayer and to be left with Me.

"Let your faith become a living faith once more. Like an active volcano! And it will be like an active volcano as you launch yourself into serious prayer about the concerns and cares that so weaken you at times. You have friends praying for you right now. Support them with prayers of your own, and don't be discouraged. Discouragement leads to lack of prayer and weakens and discourages you still further.

I am calling you to pray, not "do". You know the needs and you have felt the needs. I love the church! I walk through those buildings – it is My place, My territory – and many people love Me in that place. Pray faithfully. My Holy Spirit is hovering over that place and I will ignite the flames as the wind of prayer blows upon the church and the people. Be faithful in prayer and watch Me work! You feel weak too often because you worry and feel overwhelmed and you won't get down on your knees to pray: your prayers are what I am asking for at this time in your life. Please give Me more of your life, in words of prayers for others, and for My church, and My world. That will strengthen you and encourage you and give you joy! It won't weaken you or overwhelm you. There is power in prayer: you plug in your prayers, your power – and the light, power, current, will flow. It isn't your power in prayer – it is your act of plugging in, that facilitates the spiritual forces that are needed for answered prayer.

"Don't DO anything more until you have saturated it with prayer – make no decisions yet. But understand I call you to prayer. I call you to plug into the power with your requests. And I, the Lord, will take over from that point.

"It is not your strength, your virtue that brings about answers to prayer. I, the Lord, inspire people to plug into the only resource I have given My people to bring about My will on earth. I say again, no decisions yet– just saturated prayer!

"Don't worry anymore! It will truly be fun and inspiring and exciting – and it will be your adventure with Me. Keep with Me. Stay with Me, as on a deserted island! Walk with Me in the Holy Spirit on My island – we will walk together hand in hand along the beaches. It will be your source of inspiration and hope, and therein lies your healing and your joy.

"Note down all requests for prayer, and all your concerns and worries, and visions of what could be. Pray only for those who have asked for prayer, or who have been specifically laid before you as having special needs. Don't overwhelm yourself with all and sundry, that's My problem not yours! You feel weak because you are overwhelmed instead of praying on your knees, bowed down before Me. I require of you, your time in prayer on your knees before Me – on your knees, in your heart.

"Herein lies My call on your life! It is a turning point and will be a turning point for you and therefore for many others too. Be at peace, be calm, lean back on Me and converse with Me. Imagine we are in a boat together on the sea of Galilee – just you and Me! Now talk to Me and I will listen to you! We are miles away from land, from friends, from interruptions – just you and Me. Open up your heart to Me. If you want something to happen to someone then do it through Me – just you alone with Me – and leave it with Me to do it!"

God bless each of you as you make your way through life. I love you, and what's more, Jesus loves you too! There is so much more I would love to say to each of you, but may be that is for another time! ***Daphne***

FINALLY

"Imagine Jesus in modern life. It has been truly said that Jesus could go into any Army mess, into any factory dining-hall, into any business or professional common room, into any hotel or boarding-house, into any students' hostel or college, and His presence would not make men (or women) uncomfortable. His second visit would be eagerly looked for. Why? Rarely did condemnation pass those gentle lips (unless men were religious hypocrites or cruel to little children); but in His presence men and women felt their inner, better selves suddenly revived within them. Jesus lifted men's hearts. He saw their dormant possibilities. What is more, He made men see them and desire them with a deep passionate longing, that those possibilities should actualize, and His dreams for them come true. He made men (and women) believe that they could come true!"

~Extract from The Transforming Friendship by Leslie Weatherhead.~

Love, Love and More Love

Message from Rev Cliff Bembridge,

The Minster of
Avenue St Andrews United Reformed Church:

"It is a privilege to know Daphne and to have had a chance to read her story – a story filled with her faith and love for others.

Both as a young person and in later life Daphne has been a member of what is now Avenue St Andrews United Reformed Church, Southampton, and we are delighted she has chosen that the royalties from this book be divided between three local charities the Church hosts and supports:

The Avenue Centre**:** which for over twenty years has served families with pre-school children who are under severe pressure.

The Southampton Churches Rent Deposit Scheme: which helps individuals and families with housing problems.

The Avenue Multicultural Centre: a partnership which every Friday welcomes and offers support to around one hundred asylum seekers and refugees.

Daphne suggests that if you have been given this book, or borrowed it, you might like to donate to these charities which are working to support the vulnerable in Southampton.

Please write to me with a confirmation that you wish your donation to be shared between the three charities.

Rev Cliff Bembridge, Minister,

Avenue St Andrews United Reformed Church

The Avenue

Southampton, SO17 1XQ

United Kingdom

Cheques payable to: Avenue St Andrews United Reformed Church

Please send stamped addressed envelope if you need a response, so as to keep costs and administration down to a minimum, thank you!